SINCERITY AFTER COMMUNISM

ELLEN RUTTEN

Sincerity after Communism

A CULTURAL HISTORY

Yale UNIVERSITY PRESS

NEW HAVEN AND LONDON

Yale University Press books may be purchased in quantity for educational, business, or promotional use. For information, please e-mail sales.press@yale.edu (U.S. office) or sales@yaleup.co.uk (U.K. office).

Set in Scala and Scala Sans type by Westchester Publishing Services.
Printed in the United States of America.

Library of Congress Control Number: 2016943768
ISBN 978-0-300-21398-0 (hardcover : alk. paper)

A catalogue record for this book is available from the British Library.

This paper meets the requirements of ANSI/NISO Z39.48-1992 (Permanence of Paper).

10 9 8 7 6 5 4 3 2 1

CONTENTS

Preface   vii

Introduction: Sincerity, Memory, Marketing, Media   1

1 History: Situating Sincerity   35

2 "But I Want Sincerity So Badly!" The Perestroika
   Years and Onward   78

3 "I Cried Twice": Sincerity and Life in a
   Post-Communist World   122

4 "So New Sincerity": New Century, New Media   159

Conclusion: Sincerity Dreams   195

Notes   203
Bibliography   239
Index   273

PREFACE

There was this fashion among spin doctors: "The new sincerity." . . .
The idea is that, allegedly, attempts are constantly being made trying
to lead us Russian nationalists down a false path—either by lulling
us to sleep alongside Mongols and Jews, or luring us into the dark
webs of Byzantinism. But in truth, what Russian nationalism
constitutes is very simple: that the trains in Russia should run on
time, that civil servants stop demanding bribes, that judges stop
listening to phone calls, that crude businessmen stop exporting
money to London, that policemen can live off their wages.

—*Viktor Pelevin,* S.N.U.F.F. *(2011)*

This book explores contemporary cultural production and consumption
processes—processes in which anxieties about artistic, commercial, and
political sincerity take center stage. Writers and poets, bloggers, artists,
filmmakers, (fashion) designers, critics, political commentators, PR experts: today they rarely tire of asking whether or not such-and-such a
person or phenomenon is being genuinely honest. Is U.S. President
Obama reviving sincerity in democratic politics? Are Danish films exem-
plifying a move away from postmodern sarcasm to a "neo-sincerity"? Is
Russian opposition blogger Aleksei Navalny truly politically engaged, or
is he introducing a public "new sincerity" that is primarily career driven?

A new art-house film or collection of poems, the practice of bowling,
a new Nike design, My Little Pony merchandise: in our age, there are few
phenomena that have *not* been linked at some point or other to visions of
a newly born (and, according to most commentators, emphatically "post-
postmodern" or "post-ironic") sincerity. Symptomatic of the omnipresence
of the notion is the epigraph with which this preface begins. It comes

from a novel by Russian cult writer Viktor Pelevin, who never misses a chance to parody pop-culture hypes. Pelevin's satirical definition of "the new sincerity" boils down to a detailed social diagnosis—one that, linking transport timetables to commercial activities and legislative systems, encompasses multiple layers of post-Soviet public life.

How should we understand the current infatuation with being true to oneself? And what does today's preoccupation with reviving sincerity tell us about contemporary society? These and related questions lie at the heart of this book, which monitors the ongoing public debate on revitalizing sincerity—that hard-to-monitor virtue of "being oneself" or speaking truly of one's private feelings.

As the above set of examples illustrates, the debate in question is not limited to one particular world region. Discussions on the question "What is sincerity today?"—and, in a related query, "What follows after postmodern relativism?"—do not capture the minds only of "Western" intellectuals. They are inquiries that have stirred heated debates in myriad countries—and there is, perhaps, no better place to start a quest into the discussion's non-Western hypostases than Russia, a society whose more highly educated residents have long harbored an obsessive interest in sincerity. What does it mean to be sincere and to respect the truth? This question has haunted Russian intellectuals with particular force since Stalin's death—but it began to make its mark on public discussions on selfhood in Russia long before Stalin entered the scene.

This book tracks the Russian infatuation with sincerity, paying special attention to its more recent manifestations, in perestroika-era and post-Soviet Russia. Its first outlines date back to a hot July afternoon in 2001. That day, in the solemn aula of the Dutch University of Groningen, I heard professor of literary studies Liesbeth Korthals Altes use her inaugural speech to map new literary-cultural trends. Korthals Altes observed in recent Anglo-American and French literature "a clear bias . . . towards sincere writing, engagement, and solidarity with those whom society excludes, towards a language whose rawness is supposed to guarantee authenticity. These types of books have, of course, always been written. What is new is that they now enjoy success among renowned publishers and often attract reviews full of praise from eminent critics."[1]

Korthals Altes concluded her speech by pointing to an "ethical turn" in Anglo-American literary scholarship—one that was set in motion in the 1980s and that refuted the all-pervading irony and relativism of which critics accused postmodernism.

That same summer, I had been reading analyses of contemporary culture by the Russian cultural theorist Mikhail Epstein. He similarly spoke of a new sincerity in recent poetry. In his words, recent Russian writings displayed a tendency where "the lyrical project reemerges on the vehicle of antilyrical matter, refuse from the ideological kitchen, wandering conversational clichés, elements of foreign lexicon."[2]

As divergent as Epstein's and Korthals Altes's views on new cultural developments are, they both single out the concept of a renewed sincerity. In the months and years that followed, I started tracking usage of this phrase and thinking about sincerity today. First I did so out of plain sympathy for the notion of a new sincerity in contemporary culture and art, but gradually my gaze became that of a more critical analytical observer.

The pages that follow focus on literature and new media but also monitor developments in art, design, fashion, film, music, and architecture. They are not an attempt to prove that sincerity has actually undergone a rebirth in contemporary (Russian and global) culture. Nor do they argue that we are at the dawn of a new age, or that such-and-such an artist can unmistakably be identified with an emerging new sincerity or post-postmodernism. These categorical assertions are not the types of insights that interest me. What does interest me is the critical debate that has built up around sincerity in recent decades, and the insights that this debate offers us into the emotional and cultural preoccupations of today. I focus especially on its outlines in Russia, where the concept has in recent years attracted disproportionate attention—but the Russian story interests me emphatically as part of the larger, transnational story of a "new" or "reborn" sincerity. Within that story, I analyze three discursive threads that, during my observations, struck me with particular force: those tackling questions of cultural memory, of commodification, and of mediatization. In monitoring these strands of the debate, my analyses contribute to our understanding of more than just sincerity rhetoric as such. They challenge the traditional narrative of (Russian) postmodernism, in highlighting the considerable attention that, from the start, postmodern artists paid to concerns about honest expression and reaching readers. They redress thinking on the Russian literary field, introducing emotion as a powerful analytical tool for unraveling post-Soviet literary and artistic dynamics. Last but certainly not least, they constitute a plea to move beyond Western paradigms in theoretical reflection on post-postmodernism, authenticity, and mediatization.

By exploring the threads I have just highlighted, the ensuing pages expand and refine our understanding of post-Communist space, and also of the global discourse on moving beyond postmodernism. In doing so, they express thoughts that are my own but that have been amply nourished by the intellectual generosity—and, in some cases, practical assistance—of a range of scholars, students, writers, and artists. Among many others, they include my academic colleagues Joost van Baak, Alexander Berdichevsky, Otto Boele, Sander Brouwer, Evgeny Dobrenko, Mikhail Epstein, Raoul Eshelman, Alexander Etkind, Molly Flynn, Simon Franklin, Gasan Gusejnov, Eric de Haard, Rolf Hellebust, Jana Howlett, Dennis Ioffe, Joachim Klein, Liesbeth Korthals Altes, Adi Kuntsman, Ingunn Lunde, Birgit Menzel, Brigitte Obermayr, Martin Paulsen, Oliver Ready, Stanislav Savitskii, Henrike Schmidt, Andrei Shcherbinok, Igor Smirnov, Irina Souch, Vlad Strukov, Dirk Uffelmann, Willem Weststeijn, Emma Widdis, Alexei Yurchak, and Vera Zvereva. At lectures and in M.A. courses at the Universities of Aarhus, Cambridge, Amsterdam, Nottingham, and Oxford, at Smolny College, and at the Freie Universität Berlin I was fortunate enough to meet with sophisticated audiences, whose members provided numerous helpful suggestions. Especially helpful have been conversations with the many well-informed, engaged B.A., M.A., and Ph.D. students whom I was lucky enough to teach and meet in Amsterdam. In addition, conversations with Ilya Kukulin and Mark Lipovetsky—most notably, during a daylong train ride across Germany—resulted in a series of suggestions and ideas for which I am more grateful than this short sentence can express. Maartje Janse, Bregt Lameris, Sudha Rajagopalan, and Jenny Stelleman read and provided splendidly rich, insightful comments on individual chapters. To Olga Ryabets I am grateful for effective image hunts. Finally, I thank Kyrill Dissanayake, Lieneke Luit, and, at Yale

University Press, Otto Bohlmann and Dan Heaton for impeccable manuscript editing and—in all three cases!—for cooperation that was as professionally solid as it was smooth and congenial. Needless to say, responsibility for any remaining errors or misinterpretations is mine alone.

A short separate paragraph I owe to Kyrill Dissanayake. Kyrill, who meticulously edited and polished the full manuscript of this book, sadly passed away before the book was completed. I remember him fondly, and know that Kyrill is missed as much more than an editor alone.

While profiting from these academic and editorial counselors, this book also benefits greatly from the thoughts that (relatives of) practitioners of post-Soviet creative life have been willing to share on their work, in communications that ranged from a short Facebook note to hours-long interviews in which I was generously treated to hearty food, drinks, and even one overnight stay with the family. For their time and energy I heartily thank Nadezhda Bourova, Sasha Brodsky, Sergei Gandlevskii, Dmitrii Golynko-Vol'fson, Timur Kibirov, Oleg Kulik, Sergei Kuznetsov, Evgenii Popov, Andrei Prigov, Lev Rubinstein, Vladimir Sorokin, and Dmitrii Vodennikov.

For institutional support, I am grateful to the Netherlands Scientific Organization, whose Rubicon grant allowed me to do most of the research for this book; the University of Cambridge; Pembroke College; Cambridge's Centre for Research in the Arts, Humanities and Social Sciences; the University of Bergen; and my current academic home, the University of Amsterdam. All provided inspiring intellectual homes while I conducted my research. I thank the Boekman Bibliotheek in Amsterdam, where most of the book was written. Where else would I have found an excellent cultural-studies collection, an unusually tranquil late nineteenth-century reading room, *and* a view on the city's canals and merry tourists and students in boats? Most of all, I thank the three beings who, despite this library's captivating setting, made and make me sorely want to go home after each day of work. They are Thomas van Dalen, Ulvi van Dalen, and the late Pliushkin.

Some sections of this book have been published before, in different and, invariably, shorter versions, as journal articles and book chapters. Parts of chapter 1 were published as "Situating Sincerity: The History of a Cultural Buzzword" in *To the Point: Festschrift for Eric de Haard*, edited by

Wim Honselaar, Jenny Stelleman, and Willem G. Weststeijn (Amsterdam: Pegasus 2014,) 315–30; and (with an additional analysis of sincerity in Osip Mandel'stam's writing) as " 'No Truer Truth': Sincerity Rhetoric in Soviet Russia" in *Uslyshat' os' zemnuiu: Festschrift for Thomas Langerak*, edited by Ben Dhooge and Michel de Dobbeleer (Amsterdam: Pegasus 2016), 491–503. Parts of the analysis that I unfold in the Introduction and in chapter 2 appeared as " 'En ik huilde': Nieuwe oprechtheidsretoriek in Russische poëzie" in *Nieuwe poëzie uit Rusland* (Amsterdam: Leesmagazijn 2014), 13–27; and as "Russian Literature: Reviving Sincerity in the Post-Soviet World" in *Reconsidering the Postmodern: European Literature Beyond Relativism*, edited by Yra van Dijk and Thomas Vaessens (Chicago and Amsterdam: Chicago/Amsterdam University Press 2011), 27–41. A condensed version of chapter 3 was published as "Post-Communist Sincerity and Sorokin's *Thrilogy* [sic]" in *Die nicht mehr neuen Menschen: Russische Filme und Romane der Jahrtausendwende*, edited by Bettina Lange, Nina Weller, and Georg Witte (Munich: Otto Sagner 2012), 27–57. And expanded versions of the (here brief) arguments on Vodennikov and on imperfection that I offer in chapter 4 appeared as "Sincere e-Self-Fashioning: Dmitrii Vodennikov (1968)" in *Idolizing Authorship: Literary Celebrity and the Construction of Identity*, edited by Gaston Franssen and Rick Honings (Amsterdam: Amsterdam University Press, in press when my manuscript was being completed); and as "(Russian) Writer-Bloggers: Digital Perfection and the Aesthetics of Imperfection" in *Journal of Computer-Mediated Communication* 19 (4): 744–62. I thank these publications' editors and reviewers: this book benefited from their helpful editorial suggestions and comments.

SINCERITY AFTER COMMUNISM

Sincerity, Memory, Marketing, Media

ASh (12:46 A.M.): The new sincerity

bordzhia (12:47 A.M.): Meaning?

ASh (12:48 A.M.): It's a theory that says . . . after postmodernism a new sincerity has to set in. A fundamental rejection of all literary clichés and play in the name of adequate self-expression.

bordzhia (12:48 A.M.): and does it have rhymes?

ASh (12:49 A.M.): Well, sometimes it does. Very simple ones.

ASh (12:49 A.M.): But sometimes not.

bordzhia (12:49 A.M.): What can you do? If it has to set in.

bordzhia (12:49 A.M.): Total sincerity

ASh (12:49 A.M.): Wha'anightmare

ASh (12:50 A.M.): I'm off. My roommate is waiting.

bordzhia (12:50 A.M.): Rawk on:—)[1]

Dated December 8, 2007, the above conversation between two Russian chat users signals a persistent contemporary cultural trend. I am speaking of the tendency to define literary, artistic, and other cultural expressions as emblematic of a new zeitgeist—one encapsulated in the two-word slogan "new sincerity." This short phrase is today being embraced as a late or post-postmodern philosophy of (cultural) life for people from a variety of social and professional backgrounds, from bloggers to curators, from scholars to poets, from philosophers to PR assistants, and from literary or film reviewers to visual artists. "New sincerity to the bone," "that's so new sincerity": as we speak, these and similar definitions are thriving, both online and in print.

It is not easy to define where exactly, on a map of the world, one might locate these debates over a newly discovered sincerity. The phrase "new sincerity" has been used to denote an alleged turn away from post-modernism toward a new cultural mentality in, among other countries, the United States, Estonia, France, the United Kingdom, Germany, the Netherlands, and China.[2]

This book takes a closer look at present-day sincerity rhetoric and its global outlines. In doing so, it zooms in on one country where creative professionals are particularly keen to hail a reborn sincerity as a late or post-postmodern credo. This country is Russia—a society that has historically maintained an excessive interest in the concept of sincerity. This interest all but disappeared in post-Soviet Russia: over the past few years, whenever I have run *novaia iskrennost'*—the Russian equivalent of "new sincerity"—through a blog search, its most recent usage has never dated back more than a few days, and sometimes only hours.[3] Bloggers, politicians, and cultural critics use the phrase to explain nostalgia for the Soviet era, Putin's media policy, and the Russian interventions in Ukraine;[4] Berkeley professor Alexei Yurchak brands "sincerity" the prime aesthetic mode of "post-post-Communist" animation, arts, and music;[5] internationally renowned artist Oleg Kulik places a "new sincerity" at the heart of a new phase in contemporary Russian art and praises it in the work of Alla Esipovich, among others (figure 1);[6] and in the literary sphere, which is our focus here, a new sincerity has been singled out as a salient cultural trend by such leading commentators on perestroika-era and post-Soviet culture as the late Svetlana Boym, Mikhail Epstein, and Mark Lipovetsky.[7] Besides boasting prominent institutional affiliations in the United States and the United Kingdom, all three of these voices rank as leading literary and cultural critics within Russia.

FOCUS ON SINCERITY

What, then, is the new sincerity that occupies so many minds today? To avoid false expectations, let me point out straightaway that I am not pursuing a watertight answer to this question. On the pages that follow, I am not interested in establishing what the new sincerity that so many cultural commentators observe "really" is. Nor do I seek to demonstrate

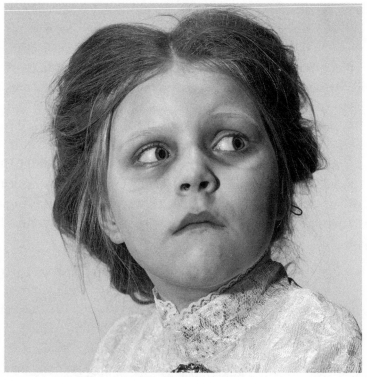

FIGURE 1   Alla Esipovich, Untitled (From the Sandbox Series), 2004–5.
Artist Oleg Kulik singles out Esipovich as one of five representatives of a
"new sincerity" in contemporary Russian art. Kulik 2007. For the full series,
see www.esipovich.com/node/30. Photograph courtesy of Alla Esipovich.

that Russian author X or musician Y "actually is" a "new sincere" artist.
I do not think that a new sincerity is *the* leading cultural trend following
postmodernism, or even that it is necessarily following postmodernism
at all. And I do not intend to prove that "sincerity"—the quality of being
sincere, not pretended, or genuine, according to the *Oxford English
Dictionary*—is the twenty-first century's new *adagium* par excellence.

   In existing explorations of a new or post-postmodern sincerity, the
argumentative mode reigns: scholars and critics eagerly demonstrate
why a particular writer, artist, or cultural trend does or does not rank as
new sincere. *Sincerity after Communism* eschews this mode. Instead, I
adopt the analytical perspective of a cultural historian—one who (while
acknowledging the fundamental impossibility of a neutral gaze) aims to

refrain from actively defending or criticizing the notion of a new sincerity but who seeks rather to observe its vital role in processes of contemporary cultural production and consumption. One, moreover, who feels that new-sincerity rhetoric provides an important starting point for public debates on mental categories as varied as identity, language, memory, commodification, and media.

My main argument in this book is that in today's Russia, debates on sincerity and its inevitable contemporary twin, postmodernism, are always and inevitably debates on sincerity *after Communism*. I chose this phrase for the title of my book as a nod toward *Romanticism after Auschwitz* (2007), Sara Guyer's study of romantic paradigms in post-Holocaust writing.[8] In a not wholly unrelated quest, the analyses that follow

1. explore visions of sincerity in a society shaped by the desire to cope with the Soviet trauma and the failed Communist experiment;
2. interrogate the status of sincerity in a post-Communist economy that recognizes honesty and authenticity as potential market devices; and
3. examine talk of an interrelationship between sincerity and the rise, after the collapse of the propaganda-ridden Soviet mediascape, of a post-Soviet, (post)digital mediascape.

In this list of aims I speak, albeit with some reservations, of a *post-Soviet* and *post-Communist* sincerity discourse. It is with good reason that I use these not unproblematic and—as colleagues rightly put it—"much bandied-about" terms.[9] If the contemporary Russian debate on sincerity naturally intertwines closely with global discourses on honest self-expression, it blends in, too, with an insistence on sincerity specifically in what has often been called "post-Soviet" or "post-Communist" space: the region of the world that shares a recent infatuation with Communist ideologies, and, partly, a historical connection with the Soviet Union. Scholars rightly debate how long it will remain appropriate to refer to this region with such temporally and socially limiting terms as "post-Communist" and "postsocialist."[10] They ask quite reasonably whether it is correct to think of "the conformity of ideology and policy under socialism . . . as relatively greater than that present in states we characterize as 'capitalist.'"[11] In many cases, the reply to this question has to be negative: contemporary life in Russia and, say, Romania is shaped only partly by their shared twentieth-century preoccupation with Communism.

For this study's object, however, the answer to the same question, I would argue, is yes. As I will demonstrate, today the Communist (or, if you like, socialist) experience remains formative to sincerity rhetoric across the cultural space we once knew as "the East." Talk of reviving sincerity is, to take two examples, thriving in the Bulgarian public sphere, with its manifold blog discussions about a post-postmodern sincerity,[12] and it strikes a chord in (strictly speaking still Communist) China, whose contemporary art scene is entangled in a persistent "search of a New Sincerity"—or so a 2007 exhibition at Tate Liverpool argued.[13] What is more, if many writers, artists, and online commentators in my book are commonly labeled as Russians, several have ancestral roots, live, or have lived in other states that used to be part of the Soviet Union—such as Ukraine and Belarus.

To the pages that follow, this larger post-Communist picture is seminal. I acknowledge its importance; but both for practical reasons (I am a Russianist) and for conceptual reasons (sincerity has a special historical status in Russian public thinking) my empirical examples draw the reader's attention to new-sincerity rhetoric specifically in Russia. More specifically, my analyses focus on one social stratum within Russian society. They zoom in on a group that is perhaps best defined by using media and culture theorist David Hesmondhalgh's term "cultural worker." Hesmondhalgh uses this term to refer to laborers in the so-called cultural industries—the social domain where "cultural goods are produced and disseminated in modern economies and societies." In this book, I call cultural workers "creative professionals." I do so to circumvent the highbrow connotations and political associations that the terms "cultural" and "worker"/"laborer," respectively, are bound to evoke in post-Soviet space—but I share others' skepticism toward the unduly cheering and corporate tone that dominates creative-industries and "creative-class" research.[14]

Within this social group, I pay special attention to professionals in the fields of Russian new media, cultural criticism, and literature. All three are prominent disciplines within global debates on reviving sincerity, but literature also serves as an ultimate locus for examining specifically post-Soviet sincerity discourse. If Russian writers and intellectuals today struggle to "remain relevant after communism," to cite literary scholar Andrew Wachtel, they have not entirely lost their traditional position of spokesmen of the nation.[15] In cultural historian Rosalind Marsh's words, "It is still important for historians of contemporary Russia to take account of cultural developments and public debates among the intelligentsia, since many Russian intellectuals . . . are prominent public figures, and their ideas have exerted considerable influence on the political leaders and the population at large."[16]

New-sincerity rhetoric is one literary-intellectual debate that has a tangible impact on the post-Soviet public sphere. In unraveling that debate, I emphatically address a large audience—one that extends beyond region specialists. Having witnessed a bias in post-postmodernism studies on the United States and on Western Europe, I feel urged to point to a larger cultural diversification within these trends than others acknowledge. As the ensuing pages attest, the cardinal question "In which cultural era do we live today (and how does it relate to postmodernism)?" is an object of fierce debate in a much broader international context than the space traditionally labeled the West. That wider transcultural context has not been left unnoted in scholarship—and it does trickle down to Western audiences to some extent (incidental translations and analyses by Epstein, Lipovetsky, and a handful of other Slavic scholars and writers have, for instance, been helpful in introducing to Anglophone audiences late and post-postmodern Russian trends).[17] To date, transculturally inclusive studies of post-postmodern discourse remain sparse, however. Now that the idea that we inhabit a transnational or postnational public sphere is becoming common coin, awareness of those discussions matters, perhaps, more than ever.[18]

NEW SINCERITY: A WORKING DEFINITION

"Moscow Conceptualism, at bottom, is nothing more than a rumor, a supposition, a suspicion." With these words, cultural theorist Boris Groys defines the artistic approach that dominated the late Soviet and perestroika era.[19] The Moscow Conceptualist scene is a critical art movement that united some of Soviet Russia's leading creative minds from roughly the 1970s to the turn of the twenty-first century. Its representatives subverted socialist-realist ideals through conceptual analysis and pop-art-esque appropriation, in artistic practices that, in retrospect, are easily recognizable as postmodern.

In the perestroika years, Moscow Conceptualism preserved its cultural supremacy, but experts more or less agree that it lost ground to new artistic developments toward the end of the 1990s. Among these developments, more than one critic singles out a new sincerity as the next cultural adagium. The defenders of this slogan dispute more than they concur, but they do agree on one point: the new sincerity is no less hard to pinpoint (and critics have failed to pinpoint it) in a language of hard facts than its conceptualist predecessor. Literary historian and critic Ilya Kukulin, when I interviewed him for this book, put it thus: "New sincerity," if worthy of scholarly attention, is strongly "underdeveloped as a theoretical problem."[20]

I have already warned that this book does not offer an exhaustive theoretical definition of the term "sincerity" or of its supposed predecessor, postmodernism—not least because I doubt that such comprehensive descriptions exist. In a study that devotes itself to the phrase "new sincerity," however, a working definition is not out of place.[21]

First of all, in this book "new sincerity" refers to the current infatuation with reviving sincerity as a *trend*—that is, to cite a (slightly hermetically formulated) scholarly definition of that term, as "an intrinsically determined monotonic function within a certain temporal span."[22] In this particular case, we look at a monotonically repeated reference to the phrase "new sincerity" within the delineated time span of the years between the mid-1980s and the early 2010s, when this book was written.

Despite its wide range of usage in Russia—how does one reconcile the first, densely theoretical reference to "a New Sincerity" with the "oh, that's *rrrreally* new sincerity!" of an excited blogger?—the phrase "new sincerity" does occur in situations that share common denominators. Most important, it is a reactive or, as some commentators put it, "dialectical" concept.[23] Just as, say, Russian Romanticism is inexplicable except as a reaction to neoclassicism, so the new sincerity cannot be comprehended without an understanding of the paradigm to which it responds and whose lessons it incorporates: postmodernism. Not fortuitously, both in and outside Russia new-sincerity advocates continuously refer—either explicitly or implicitly—to postmodernism.

In itself, that shared feature still fails to tell us much about new-sincerity rhetoric: if few experts disagree that postmodernism was launched as a skeptical artistic and intellectual lens on reality, the notion is today so widely used that it has gradually lost all definitional clarity. Sociologist Dick Hebdige famously criticized this discursive opacity as early as 1988. In his words, we are dealing with a hardcore buzzword:

> When it becomes possible for a people to describe as "post-modern" the décor of a room, the design of a building, the diegesis of a film, the construction of a record, or a "scratch" video, a television commercial, or an arts documentary, or the "intertextual" relations between them, the layout of a page in a fashion magazine or critical journal, an antiteleological tendency within epistemology, the attack on the "metaphysics of presence," a general attenuation of feeling, the collective chagrin and morbid projections of a post-War generation of baby boomers confronting disillusioned middle-age, the "predicament" of reflexivity, a group of rhetorical tropes, a proliferation of surfaces, a new phase in commodity fetishism, a fascination for images, codes and styles, a process of cultural, political, or existential fragmentation and/or crisis, the "decenter-ing" of the subject, an "incredulity toward metanarratives," the replacement of unitary power axes by a plurality of power/discourse formations, the "implosion of meaning," the collapse of cultural hierarchies, the dread engendered by the threat of nuclear self-destruction, the decline of the university, the functioning and effects of the new miniaturised technologies, broad societal and economic shifts into a "media," "consumer" or "multinational" phase, a sense (depending on who you read) of "placelessness" or the abandonment of placelessness ("critical regionalism") or (even) a generalized substitution of spatial for temporal coordinates—when it becomes possible to describe all these things as "Postmodern" (or more simply using a current abbreviation as "post" or "very post"), then it's clear we are in the presence of a buzzword.[24]

Hebdige palpably delights in lengthening his inventory to the near-endless. In doing so he follows a stylistic approach very different from that taken by adepts of a revived sincerity. They find fault with a short—and, as a rule, rather caricaturized—list of supposedly postmodern features: they berate postmodernism for excessive relativism, cynicism, mockery, an anything-goes mentality, and ethical indifference.

Instead of these "ugly postmodern" traits, new-sincerity aficionados propose an alternative cultural condition. In the formulation of Russia's best-known advocate of the trend, the cultural theorist Mikhail Epstein, they defend an aesthetics that is "defined not by the sincerity of the author or the quotedness of his style, but by the mutual interaction of the two, [whereby] the elusive border of their difference . . . allows even the most sincere utterance to be perceived as a subtly quoted imitation, while a commonplace quotation may sound like a piercingly lyrical confession."[25]

Though published in 1999, Epstein's definition evokes a rhetoric that thrived much earlier, in 1950s Russia—a time and place that I explore in detail in chapter 1—when he claims that new-sincere aesthetics revive and revalue "words such as 'soul,' 'tear,' 'beauty,' 'truth,' and 'the Kingdom of Heaven.'" Having become "stiff through centuries of traditional, official usage," today for him these words are "purified by being kept out of circulation. After going through a period of radical deadening and carnivalesque derision, they are now returning to a transcendental transparency and lightness, as if they were not of this world."[26]

That Epstein's writing is markedly mystical is hard to miss in this fragment. That it is no direct source of inspiration to every user of the term is also beyond doubt: in online writing, for instance, "new sincerity" is often proposed as a behavioral model ("by exposing my inner life online I enact a previously unheard-of sincerity") or identity marker ("I call myself a new sincerity adept and therefore I love singer X or poet Y"), rather than a carefully wrought theoretical concept.

Epstein's is not the final word on the topic either. As we shall see in the chapters that follow, theoreticians of a Russian new sincerity have repeatedly defined it as an offspring of new-media or mass-media culture and of postsocialism. But Epstein's definition does capture the crux of new-sincerity rhetoric, Russian and global alike. It points to the central status, in this rhetoric, of the discursive gesture of honest self-disclosure (whether the artist in question is indeed honest is another question; what matters is her or his insistence on the trope of emotional transparency).

Epstein's description also illustrates that "new-sincerity talk" cannot be isolated from a larger cultural debate. This debate could be summarized with the question: "Is postmodernism over, and, if so, what comes next?" It revolves around the belief—propagated by some, contested by others—that (early) postmodern devices have now exhausted themselves and that new cultural trends are taking their place. At the University of Amsterdam, we studied the comparative outlines of this "beyond-postmodernism" discourse with a team of literary scholars and historians of philosophy.[27] Featuring experts on American, British, French, Russian, Bosnian, German, Polish, Norwegian, and Dutch intellectual cultures, the group compiled a list of discussion catchwords that serves as a fruitful micro-summary of "beyond-postmodernism" thinking. The list entails the following words: irony, relativism, ethics, engagement, metafiction, authenticity, sincerity, sentimentalism, return of the self, narrativity, regionalism, and postmodernism.[28]

Analyzing exactly how these words interrelate within the transnational debate on contemporary culture is no easy task, as we discovered in Amsterdam. In most of the areas under discussion, when referring to "the contemporary condition" the different terms can acquire both negative and positive connotations, depending on the speaker. For some participants in the various local debates on postmodernism, irony and relativism are now taboo; for others, they are precisely what makes "post-postmodern sincerity," "new narrativity," or "new authenticity" valuable. Some critics argue that today's "renewed" sincerity, engagement, or any of the other terms in the list break radically with postmodern mentality and that we are witnessing a new mega-era on a par with the Renaissance or Romanticism. Others claim that contemporary trends merely correct flaws in existing (post)modern thinking, marking a new stage in the larger project of either modernity or postmodernity; yet others, that we should distrust advocates of a post-ironic age: after postmodernism, how can we return to sincerity or seriousness as if nothing had happened? To add to the confusion, participants in the discussion tend to use highly divergent buzzwords in the same breath, as different name tags for one phenomenon.

Epstein is in tune with international developments in this last respect, too: to him, new-sincere aesthetics fuse and overlap with a mishmash of self-defined (and more or less interchangeable) new trends, including "post-quotational art," "post-postmodernism," "trans-lyricism," "neo-sentimentality," "post-Conceptualism," "trans-utopianism," "trans-subjectivity," "trans-idealism," "trans-originality," "trans-sentimentality"—and, to top it all off, a series of "as if" isms, including "'as if' lyricism," "'as if' idealism," and "'as if' utopianism."[29]

Given the hodgepodge of interchangeable tags, one might wonder: why, in this study, do I single out sincerity as a central concern? Why not explore discourse on, say, a new idealism or a revival of lyricism? The answer to these questions is: public resonance. More than several other phrases mentioned—most of which died a quiet death after Epstein introduced them—"new sincerity" has become a catchphrase in post-Soviet culture. So, admittedly, have some other isms that allegedly followed postmodernism: critics, for one, enthusiastically define Russian creative professionals as devotees of a "new seriousness" (*novaia ser'eznost'*), a "new authenticity" (*novaia podlinnost'*), or a "postrealism" or "new realism" (*postrealizm, novyi realizm*).[30] But the slogan "new sincerity" strikes more of a chord among a broad (if mostly higher-educated and urban-based) audience than any of its siblings. So, at least, a search on the Web suggests.[31] In writing this book, I repeatedly searched for the phrase "new sincerity" with Google and its Russian equivalent, the search engine Yandex. During my numerous online searches for its English translation between 2005 and 2013, the search results could vary wildly from day to day—these and other online search tools easily lead us into statistical minefields—but they always suggested that the word combination "new sincerity" occupied a strong position within both post-postmodern and popular discourse. On May 31, 2013, for instance, an extensive digital search for the phrase in English produced 7,680 general hits and 1,810 blog hits (as I was finalizing this introduction, on May 25, 2016, the number of search hits for "new sincerity" had boomed to 45,700—but as by then problems had arisen with blog search tools, I chose to stick to the 2013 numbers here).[32] The top result was the concept's own Wikipedia entry, which—while working on this project—I gradually saw evolve from a brief paragraph into an extensively annotated text with nine subsections.[33] Over the course of the 2000s, internationally renowned media—the *New York Times* (which hailed, for instance, the American indie band Bright Eyes as emblematic of the new sincerity; figure 2), the *Guardian*, the *Times, TAZ, Die Zeit*—also

FIGURE 2   Conor Oberst, singer of indie band Bright
Eyes, whose folk and electronic pop-rock songs the *New
York Times* branded the ultimate "symbol of the new
sincerity" in 2005. Sanneh, "Mr. Sincerity Tries a New Trick."
Photograph courtesy of Butch Hogan.

increasingly resorted to the phrase, in reviews that discuss a "new-
sincere turn" after postmodernism as a self-evident given.[34]

Searches for the term in Russian generated similar results. What
stood out in my Russian-language searches was its popularity in weblogs and chat forums. On the same May 31, 2013, a Yandex search for
the phrase "new sincerity" in Russian-language blogs and forums generated 1,736 hits, compared with 51 for "new authenticity" and 1,094 for
"new realism" (all entered in Russian and Cyrillic).[35]

Russian bloggers and chatters, in other words, opt for the phrase "new
sincerity" substantially more often than for alternative "post-postmodern"
slogans. It is not hard to see why. First, "new sincerity" is a more accessible

slogan than the more jargonistic word "post-postmodernism," or Epstein's "post" and "trans" terms. Although (as Epstein himself pointed out) such terms as "soul," "tear," and "sincerity" were approached with caution in highbrow postmodern discourse, they have always preserved a prominent place in popular culture. Second, and perhaps yet more important, sincerity has long held a special place in Russian minds, especially so since—as I explain in chapter 1—it was a 1953 essay on artistic sincerity that paved the way for critical reflections on the Stalinist era.

NEW SINCERITY: MY APPROACH

In the chapters that follow, I unpack and historically contextualize new-sincerity rhetoric. I do so with a special interest in the concept or, put more narrowly, in the word "sincerity." To avoid stylistic monotony, in my analyses I occasionally alternate usage of that word with related terms— say, "honesty," "self-disclosure," or even "intimacy." I do so, however, in the perfect awareness that these concepts are no full-fledged synonyms for the term "sincerity." Rather than the wider thematic cluster that they together form, I offer a so-called *Begriffsgeschichte*—a semantic history— of the word "sincerity," and of recent couplings of this particular word to notions of renewal and revival.

Sincerity after Communism revisits Russian new-sincerity discourse as a transcultural and historically layered story. Chapter 1 offers a transnational historical inquiry into sincerity rhetoric—and specifically into those traditions within older debates that inform and shape today's sincerity concerns. The subsequent chapters take us through to the present, and to Russia. They offer a more or less chronological exploration of new-sincerity rhetoric in the years between the first recorded Russian use of the term, in the mid-1980s, and the early 2010s, when the bulk of this book was written.[36]

Chapters 2 to 4 trace the routes that new-sincerity rhetoric travels in this period. With time, the phrase gradually morphs from a concept used by a handful of little-read writers into a catchword of mainstream culture. In 1985, the then already well-known underground poet Dmitrii Prigov introduces it as a poetic formula. Prigov then launches—in the grassroots hand-to-hand mode that marks Soviet-Russian samizdat (clandestinely circulated publishing, that is)—a collection of poems with the title *New Sincerity* (*Novaia Iskrennost'*). In a foreword, he defines how the sincerity of his poems contrasts with traditional poetic sincerity. In the somewhat formal-jargonistic scholarly style without which Prigov would not be Prigov, he explains: "Like the reader, the poet is always sincere in himself. These poems summon up the sincerity of communication, they are signs of a situation of sincerity with a full understanding of the conditions of both the zone and the signs of its appearance."[37] The contrast between this definition and the usage of the phrase "new sincerity" today could hardly be greater. By the early 2010s, the same phrase has become the Russian social-media user's slogan for such diverse phenomena as the popular Uzbek singer Jimmy, cute girls at Starbucks, or new urban hipster hangouts.[38]

In chapters 2 to 4, I monitor new-sincerity rhetoric between these starting and end points. My analyses scrutinize its dynamics in a plethora of cultural disciplines—literature, first of all, but also film, architecture, design, art, music, fashion, television, and new media. In blending these different cultural spheres, the book inevitably ventures into fields in which its author has limited theoretical training. My reason for nevertheless embedding them in the narrative is articulated eloquently by philologist Glenn Most. Studies of "processes of cultural transmission," says Most, "necessarily transgress the boundaries that academic disciplines have, wisely or not, seen fit to draw around themselves.... The question is therefore not whether interdisciplinarity is to be accepted— no other procedure is fitted to this object—but to what extent its risks can be minimized."[39]

On the following pages, avoiding interdisciplinarity altogether would indeed feel artificial: its advocates tag the label "new sincerity" to written texts no less readily than to films or fashion labels. But while generously embracing the different fields in which the concept emerges, the following analyses do have a disciplinary focus. They concentrate in the first place on developments in literature and new media.

In examining new-sincerity rhetoric in these disciplines, I lean on existing approaches to the insolubly melded fields of literary and cultural history. I take inspiration from the historical wanderings of New Historicist scholars, with their "intensified willingness to read all of the textual traces of the past with the attention traditionally conferred only on literary texts."[40] I borrow insights, too, from discourse studies on "the use of spoken, written and signed language and multimodal/multimedia forms of communication . . . rang[ing] from silence, to a single utterance (such as 'ok'), to a novel, a set of newspaper articles or a conversation."[41] Discourse studies are one inspiration for my choice here to concentrate not on concrete literary texts but rather on talk about those texts, and on the settings in which they circulate. What this book primarily traces are metadiscursive sources, varying from self-fashioning acts by writers and social-media users—in interviews, poems, essays, conversations that I had with them, or in blog posts—to writings about their ideas by others in reviews, (more) blog posts, and scholarly analyses.

Armed with discourse experts' lessons and other academic anchorages, *Sincerity after Communism* follows sincerity talk in its travels through recent history. Tracing that journey means facing a surplus of theoretical questions. Some I have left untouched. I do not take up the intriguing challenge of defining post-Soviet sincerity from a hard-science perspective—that is, as a neurological phenomenon. Although I am enthusiastic about the future potential of neurological research for the humanities, I sympathize with colleagues who feel that, at this stage, "historians of emotion had better not unscrupulously borrow methods from the natural sciences"[42]—and I have decided not to work with cognitive methods in this particular study. Another dimension to which I devote little attention is gender. The literary authors who are central to my argument happen to be men; and the question of how sincerity rhetoric is constructed and read when used by male as opposed to female speakers—relevant as I consider it to be—remains unanswered here. Equally unanswered—to mention a last important problem that I do not actively address—I leave questions about the intersection between new-sincerity discourse and religion.

Gender and cognitive perspectives on sincerity matter—but in this book, I focus on other questions. The analyses that follow concentrate on three questions that obtruded themselves with particular force on my empirical data. They involve three dimensions of public life that are contested with a special vigor in post-Communist Russia, and that merit some attention in this introductory overview: those of collective remembrance, of commodification, and of (new) media.

CURATIVE SINCERITY: SINCERITY AND MEMORY

My first question involves the interweaving of literature with history and memory. In post-Soviet Russia, how does talk of a newly sincere condition interrelate with the ongoing debate on the recent past? *That* the two interact is beyond doubt. Russian discussions on a post- or late postmodern sincerity occur in an era of all-permeating internal unrest: that of the collapse of the Soviet Union and its aftermath. This era is not only a background against which the debates take place, it also forms one of their key preoccupations. Sincerity may traditionally be located in the sphere of intimately private emotions—but in discussing a newly born sincerity, Russian writers, critics, and scholars alike readily revert to sociopolitical or historiographical terms. They eagerly project (in)sincerity onto specific sociocultural groups, by attributing hypocrisy to the Soviet authorities, for instance, or to Russia's current rulers.

Illustrative of this habit to locate sincerity in concrete social strata and deny it to others is "the new sincerity" that Kirill Medvedev envisions in Vladimir Putin's Russia. Poet-cum-political activist Medvedev (not to be confused with his Kremlin-leader namesake) points at President Putin, Belarusian president Lukashenko, and "the Russian blogosphere" as embodiments of a cultural mentality that reigned in the Russia of the 2000s. In "the new sincerity," as Medvedev brands the new mentality, unscrupulous political PR goes hand in hand with an insistence on unmediated expression.[43] Recent history is formative to this new emotional state: Medvedev frames today's sincerity as "a tool" that can potentially "force open" existing cultural discourses, including "the rough, ideologized Soviet one."[44] He envisions, in short, "the new sincerity" as a therapeutic tool for dealing with historical trauma.

Medvedev is not unique. The conviction that sincerity can be instrumental in coping with recent history has bloomed in Russia ever since the dawn of the perestroika period—and memory-driven views on sincerity have flourished in other times and places, too. In chapter 1, we shall see that the tradition of proposing sincerity as a creative alternative to a hypocritical past was formative to Russian creative culture in the 1950s and early 1960s; and that the related trend to locate sincerity in specific sociocultural groups harks back at least as far as the early modern era. In the same chapter we shall see how, in the 2000s, cultural critics across the United States and Europe link a purported shift to a "post-ironic" sincerity with the need to overcome the traumatic attacks on the World Trade Center on September 11, 2001.

Political history looms particularly large over new-sincerity discourse in contemporary Russia, where the Soviet trauma is an open wound. "What it emulates and struggles with, is history"—thus the renowned historian Alexander Etkind summarizes post-Soviet literature's credo.[45] That *Sincerity after Communism* is sensitive to that "memory struggle" is not fortuitous. This book took shape at the University of Cambridge, where, in the 2000s and early 2010s, I joined Etkind and others in their powerful attempts to put Eastern European memory studies on the map as a recognized academic discipline.[46] Inspired by the Cambridge team's findings, I have found it hard not to notice the politico-historical bias that runs through post-Soviet sincerity discourse as a basso continuo. The memory thread is central to chapter 2 of this book, which opens with the 1980s and ends in the early 2010s. The chapter focuses on Dmitrii Prigov—the poet who coined a "New Sincerity" as his credo in 1985—as a particularly eloquent example of a writer for whom talk about sincerity is, necessarily, also talk about trauma.

Chapter 2 embeds Prigov's story in a wider narrative of sincerity and collective remembering. This wider narrative is helpful in nuancing our understanding of sincerity in more than one respect. First, it modifies existing thinking on sincerity and social or political conflict, by criticizing the view—proposed by Mieke Bal and others—that sincerity rhetoric flourishes specifically in times of intercultural conflict.[47] The story of Prigov and his contemporaries challenges this view: it implies that sincerity talk intensifies, too, at times of *intra*cultural tumult.

Second, the story told in chapter 2 refines our knowledge of late and post-Soviet creative life in a number of ways. To start with, it thickens existing thinking on post-Soviet memory. In Russia, the darker pages of the past remain unsettled to this day—and specialists have repeatedly argued that contemporary Russia does not share the recent infatuation with traumatic national memory witnessed in many Western societies. Post-Soviet Russia insists not on remembering but on a collective forgetting of the gloomier pages of Soviet history. In the words of Etkind, "The only certainty about the Soviet catastrophe, apart from its massive scale, is its very uncertainty. We do not have anything like a full list of victims; we do not have anything like a full list of executioners;

and we do not have adequate memorials, museums, and monuments, which could stabilize the understanding of these events for generations to come."[48]

For the lack of monuments, state laws, or court decisions that critically assess the recent past, Etkind uses a metaphor borrowed from computing language. Russia, he says, lacks "hard memory." He extends the metaphor by explaining that remembrances of Soviet terror which cannot crystallize into hard memory instead adopt "soft" forms—they morph into literary creations, historical studies, or other textual narratives.[49]

Etkind explores "soft memory" primarily in literary and historiographical writing. Together with other helpful analyses, my studies suggest that it makes sense to widen our definition of the soft space that he outlines. Between the early perestroika years and today, critical interrogations of the past have blossomed in Russian culture industries at large—in literature, but also in, say, film, music, and the visual arts, as well as in meta-artistic debate *about* these different disciplines.

My material, in short, helps to broaden our picture of what Etkind calls "the software of cultural memory." It also modifies our view on perestroika-era and post-Soviet culture in one last, quite fundamental way. It demonstrates that, from the mid-1980s onward, as Russian creative professionals started to view the Soviet period as a bygone era, they began to persistently frame the category of sincerity as a healing tool. In other words, they singled out sincerity as an instrument to be used to help cope with the Soviet experience. In highlighting this insistence on a *curative sincerity*—sincerity as a near-medical tool for dealing with social memory—my analyses reshape the dominant views of the postmodern experiment in Russia. This view stresses the "skeptical, ironic" (albeit "secretly sentimental") nature of Russian postmodernism;[50] its "deliberately nonserious," playful, "demythologizing" stance;[51] or its "ironic gayness" and habit of "defying random aesthetic taboos."[52] Where experts speak of more "serious" or "sincere" strands within postmodern discourse, they tend to locate these alternative paradigms in a secondary, "late postmodernist" phase—but they allocate marginal importance to the sincere vector within the postmodern experience as a whole.[53]

Without denying the validity of these and related claims, I argue that they warrant modification.[54] Throughout the period that traditional narratives of postmodernism label as playful and relativizing, Russian intellectuals insist on problematizing affective anxieties that, in these same narratives, either lack attention or are reduced to mere deconstructionist moves. These anxieties—as chapter 2 illustrates in detail—are concerns about sincere expression. To leading thinkers and makers of the time, sincerity can simultaneously act as a myth that they dismantle *and* as a potential curative force in digesting a troubled past.

SINCERITY AND STRATEGY: MARKETING THE SELF

In Russian new-sincerity talk, the question how to digest a traumatic past reverberates to this day. While a key issue in the early phases of the debate, however, memory gradually makes place for alternative—socioeconomically rather than historically—motivated conceptualizations of sincerity in the late 1990s and early 2000s. This shift raises a second question that informs my explorations: for the debate's participants, how do artistic and more pragmatic factors interact?

In post-Soviet Russia, the careers of writers who explicitly adopt a "(new) sincere" stance are frequently success stories. Topping the cultural hierarchy, they are, more often than not, best-selling authors who comfortably manage to live off their writing. Not surprisingly, discussions of writer X or Y's switch from a postmodern to a more sincere position share an ongoing concern: is that switch literarily or socioeconomically motivated?

Chapter 3 explores one particularly vehement discussion on sincerity and commodification: that around Vladimir Sorokin's "sincere turn." Having gained fame as a nonconformist writer in the late Soviet era, Sorokin had acquired the status of a postmodernist Russian classic by the turn of the twenty-first century. At this point he astounded his public with a prose trilogy that revolved wholly around the need for human sincerity and for "speaking with the heart." In interviews, he now abandoned the classically postmodern views that he had expressed in earlier public talks. From an outright dismissal of socioethical commitment,[55] he now moved to classic literary self-fashioning models to which openness and truth telling are imperative. His new writings, he claimed, formed his "first attempt at a direct utterance about our life;"[56] they were products of his "nostalgia for . . . the unmediated."[57]

Colleagues and critics have met the drastic shift in Sorokin's public presentation with surprise—and a strong dose of skepticism. Was, critics wonder, Sorokin's sudden longing for unmediated, sincere expression in the late 1990s spurred by a desire for artistic change? Or was it merely an attempt to reach a larger audience—and, by implication, to sell more books? Well-known poet Timur Kibirov expressed a widely held feeling about "the new Sorokin" when I interviewed him in 2009: "He wrote the book that people wanted. Everyone wants to win as many readers' souls as possible. But I think that it is a huge mistake to use this principle to guess what people want and then write and publish precisely that."[58]

Literary historian Susan Rosenbaum demonstrated that similar anxieties over literature and commodification follow a long-standing tradition in conceptions of lyrical sincerity. In a groundbreaking study of modern lyric poetry, she unravels how the trend toward contesting sincerity rhetoric heightens at times of radical changes in the literary field.[59] My analyses are an attempt to test Rosenbaum's insights—which build on British and American sources—against contemporary Russia. Emerging in the perestroika era and consolidating in the early post-Soviet years, the sincerity debates that I trace here overlap with the fall of the Soviet Union and the subsequent need for authors to adopt new socio-economic survival strategies. How, participants of the discussions muse, do sincere impulses relate to strategy? And how does (or how should) literature relate to the whims and fancies of the market?

Chapter 3 uses the controversy surrounding Sorokin to interrogate post-Communist thinking about artistic self-expression and commodification. It does so without seeking to answer the question whether post-Soviet writers are, in fact, sincere. I do not believe that this is a fruitful question to ask in the first place. Instead, I propose a nonessentialist approach—one that, as I explain below in more detail, is inspired by recent theorizations of sincerity by Rosenbaum and like-minded scholars.[60] These scholars advocate a reading of the concept that accepts the tension between sincerity's moral charge—the value that this concept places upon acting in accord with one's innermost feelings—and an artist's inevitable involvement in market mechanisms. I agree with them—and move away from asking how sincere Sorokin "truly" *is*, to study instead how sincerity rhetoric *works* in his public self-fashioning and reception.

Not unrelated, and an inspiration for my research, too, are the insights into literature as a field of competing forces put forward in Pierre Bourdieu's and Gisèle Sapiro's sociologically inspired explorations of French literature.[61] Such scholars of post-Soviet culture as Mikhail Berg, Birgit Menzel, and Andrew Wachtel have extended Bourdieu's blend of institutional and literary analysis to the area that interests me.[62] This book profits from their findings, by exploring sincerity not as an intra-textual motif but rather as an emotional technique—one that authors and critics can employ to position themselves and others within the intellectual arena. As I explain in chapter 3, I am not alone in doing so. In one of the strange twists that studying one's own era involves, the same Bourdieu-inspired insights that help me in reading post-Soviet sincerity discourses are, at the same time, part and parcel of those same discourses. Sorokin's critics, for one, eagerly rely on them when critically pondering the author's glorification of sincerity.

In tracking discourses on sincerity and strategy, I am not only aiming to map out a debate. Rather than a mere rough guide to turn-of-the-century sincerity talk, chapter 3 is set up as an intervention. It redresses Rosenbaum's English-only sincerity studies, but it also amends thinking on post-Soviet creative life. First, like chapter 2, chapter 3 addresses the need to allocate a more central role to sincerity concerns in post-modern theorizing. In the chapter I explain why they do—but in this introduction I want to halt at another need that they highlight.

Existing studies of the post-Soviet literary field (I am thinking, once again, of Berg and others) have done much to deepen our understanding of this field, and of the socioeconomic dynamics that inform literary and creative practices. They have contributed to important debates on artistic coping strategies and on literature and art as symbolic and economic capital. What they do not (or only marginally) bring into the discussion, however, is the category of emotion.[63] Which artistic coping strategy works? Which cultural object acquires symbolic or economic capital? These questions cannot be answered without considering how emotional norms, communities, and regimes shape a particular cultural-historical period. Chapter 3 challenges scholarship on the post-Soviet literary market by meriting these affective categories the detailed attention that most existing studies lack—and by enhancing our sensitivity to emotion as a driving force in creative production and consumption processes.

SINCERITY AND AUTHENTICITY IN A (POST)DIGITAL WORLD

In post-Soviet Russia, discussions on sincerity and commodification acquired particular vigor in the late 1990s and early 2000s—the years that saw the new capitalist economy begin to take root. From then on, commercialization concerns began to make way for a third "sincerity concern": that of mediatization. This concern is related to the third question that I pose in this book: to new-sincerity adepts, how do visions of a revived sincerity relate to the rise of digital media?

As with sincerity and memory, there is little doubt *that* sincerity and media interrelate. From early modernism onward, we find claims that new (printing, sound, and so on) technologies are either leading us away from unfiltered self-expression *or* are generating more sincere modes of communication. These old claims—whose historic persistence I discuss in detail in chapter 1—resurfaced with vigor across different world localities as soon as social media acquired wider public popularity, in the early 2000s. They are vital to debates on our age of the "postdigital"—a term that scholars and practitioners use to theorize (I am citing the description of David Berry and Michael Dieter's book-length study of the paradigm) "our newly computational everyday lives," in which offline and online inextricably interlace and the digital is norm not novelty. Reiterating the assertion that new media foster more genuine communication, for instance, is American critic Sofia Leiby's belief that "the Internet is not a place for hiding, for irony, coldness and nostalgia, but a place that makes sincere, open, warm, and human gestures in art."[64]

In Russia, from the early 2000s onward a new generation of writers and bloggers began vivid discussions on the nexus between sincerity and mediatization.[65] To these new voices, the Soviet trauma and the shock transition to a capitalist economy—the factors that shaped late perestroika-era and early post-Soviet sincerity talk—are not irrelevant, of course. But in recent decades their topicality has gradually made way for other anxieties—anxieties that are globally rather than nationally defined. In the Russia of the 2000s and early 2010s, the notion of sincerity resonates with particular force in discussions on digitization and the increasing automatization of daily life. After the collapse of the propaganda-ridden "media empire" built by the Soviet authorities (I am citing media historian Kristin Roth-Ey),[66] the 2000s saw a wholly different, partly digitized mediascape—one whose sociocultural meanings and implications have eagerly been pondered by cultural critics. In Russia as elsewhere, critical commentators have repeatedly argued that new media's bottom-up publication modes facilitate a brand-new writing culture. To some, this new written culture is substantially more conducive to sincere, unmediated expression than (propagandist as well as free) print and broadcast media have ever been. To others, new technologies lead to dehumanization—a trend that must be countered by placing a greater emphasis on sincerity within online art and writing.

What—in the mostly online discussions on these opposing views— is the precise interrelationship between sincerity and digitization? And how does sincerity relate to such central concepts in the sincerity-and-media debate as amateurism, imperfection, and craft? In exploring these questions in chapter 4, I do not focus on one specific author. Instead, I track the many online "produsers"—media expert Axel Bruns's term for denoting that, online, "distinctions between producers and users of content have faded into comparative insignificance"[67]—who use online self-publishing tools to publicly share their takes on sincerity.

Like the preceding chapters, chapter 4 is no mere descriptive survey of a debate. In juxtaposing different voices in the discussion, this chapter problematizes existing thinking on mediatization and authenticity. Current debates about our "mediated" world—to cite anthropologist Thomas de Zengotita's popular description for today's media-saturated society[68]—tend to present that world as a remarkably homogeneous entity. When speaking of *the* media, they tend to refer to Anglo-American media sources, without specifying that, say, Russia, or Iran, boast very different mediascapes. And when they criticize *our* media's preference for "truthiness"—American satirist Stephen Colbert's term for the feeling that something is true and requires no factual corroboration[69]—they rely primarily on North American examples. These and many other leading analyses of our media culture claim global significance without reckoning with the linguo-cultural demarcations of their allegations.

I use chapter 4 to plead for a move beyond Western paradigms and more transcultural sensitiveness in the academic debate on new media, reality, and honesty. Most important, I take issue with existing studies' near-exclusive emphasis on sincerity's conceptual twin, authenticity.[70] Like the interrelationship between *authenticity* and technology discourse foregrounded in "Western" scholarship, so the interrelationship between *sincerity* and technologization has a rich discursive history (one that I explore in detail in chapter 1). In chapter 4 I examine recent debates over both—but we shall see that in post-Soviet space those who reflect on the impact of new media on our lives display a special interest not in authenticity but in the related concept that, in Russia, has such a loaded history: sincerity.

STUDYING SINCERITY

Given the broad resonance of newborn sincerity across culture industries and in popular culture, it comes as little surprise that visions of it are slowly but inevitably invading academia. Ever since the early 1990s—when scholars first probed the question "What comes after postmodernism?" (or "Into which new forms does it morph?")—sincerity has been addressed as a prime paradigm by experts in fields ranging from design to theology.[71] Once theorists started pondering the features of a post-postmodern, late postmodern, or neomodern era, the notion of sincerity emerged as one among a series of semantically related, prominent contemporary cultural preoccupations—think authenticity, ethics, or (a new, post, or even "dirty") realism.[72]

Sincerity, let me hasten to add, is far from new as an object of theoretical thought. As classic explorations of the concept by Lionel Trilling and Henri Peyre demonstrate, critical thinking on sincerity goes back at least as far as Renaissance culture.[73] More recently, scholars have begun dating critical philosophical reflection on the notion—and on its Chinese sibling *ch'eng*—even earlier, to the writings of Aristotle and Confucius.[74]

Today, multiple theorists revisit these historical reflections on sincerity—and in doing so they push an agenda that looks toward the future rather than the past. Between the early 1990s and today, more than one cultural commentator has argued that in contemporary society the concept of sincerity requires a redefinition, post-postmodern or otherwise. The need for such a revised conceptualization is expressed in bewilderingly diverse academic settings—it can be heard in disciplines that range from law to film studies, and that tackle geopolitical areas that extend from China to Persia. It resounds in Ernst van Alphen,

Mieke Bal, and Carel Smith's collection *The Rhetoric of Sincerity* (2009), which covers critical theory, literature, theater, art, and law, among other fields; in a book-length essay on ritual and sincerity (2008)—one that blends anthropology, psychoanalysis, and religious studies—by Adam Seligman, Robert Weller, Michael Puett, and Bennett Simon; in Timothy Milnes and Kerry Sinanan's book *Romanticism, Sincerity, and Authenticity* (2010), which proposes reviving sincerity (and authenticity) as a critical tool for understanding Romanticism; and in Jay Magill Jr.'s *Sincerity* (2012), a book that explains (in the words of its subtitle) "how a moral ideal born five hundred years ago inspired religious wars, modern art, hipster chic, and the curious notion that we all have something to say (no matter how dull)." It resonates, too, in the work of William Beeman (who discusses sincerity from a linguistic perspective), Yanming An, Aleida Assmann, Claudia Benthien and Steffen Martus, Allard den Dulk, Adam Kelly, Liesbeth Korthals Altes, and Susan Rosenbaum (who all discuss sincerity in literature and philosophy), Efrat Tseëlon (in critical theory), John Jackson (anthropology), Jim Collins, David Foster Wallace, Patrick Garlinger, Florian Gross, Barton Palmer (film, literature, and television), Matthew Wikander (theater), Yupin Chung and Thomas Jacobi, Boris Groys (visual arts and media), Jennifer Ashton, Andrew Chen, Katy Henriksen (new media), Amanda Anderson, Elizabeth Markovits, Greg Myers (media and politics), Christy Wampole, Jonathan D. Fitzgerald (pop culture), Michael Corcoran, Chuck Klosterman (pop music), and Sandra Gountas and Felix Mavondo (marketing).[75]

I cite this long list of names for a reason. Its length illustrates perfectly just how vital sincerity is today as a topic of academic inquiry. The same list demonstrates that the concept of a new sincerity currently attracts insistent attention: of the scholars mentioned, several utilize and analyze it as a counterreaction either to postmodernism or to (new-) media culture.[76]

Not unexpectedly, given its prominent status as an object of contemporary scholarly exploration, new-sincerity scholarship is institutionalizing with considerable speed. Workshops and article-length analyses devoted to the trend have found their way into renowned academic presses and museums.[77] At each of the five universities where I have studied or worked while writing this book, visions of a new sincerity are—independently of my own activities—either taught in classes or discussed at workshops and conferences.[78] I have seen the topic gain ground in my own discipline: "New Sincerity" was singled out as a special interest at the 2001 Slavic Forum; and the 2008 and 2009 AAASS (today ASEEES) conferences—major meeting points for specialists on Russia, Eurasia, and Central/Eastern Europe—each had a panel scheduled on "Sincerity and Voice" in contemporary Russian poetry.[79]

Despite this growing academic fascination, to this day an integral and culturally inclusive analysis of new-sincerity rhetoric remains to be done. My studies of the debate cater to the need for such analysis—by juxtaposing a wide range of Western *and* non-Western voices within the discussion, for one; but also by tracking the debate's diachronic development; and, ultimately, by investigating how sincerity rhetoric feeds off and, in turn, impacts contemporary creative life.

In offering this integral perspective on the debate, I am not operating without external help—and my approach to sincerity cannot be isolated from wider developments in the humanities and social sciences. In recent years, both have witnessed a staggering growth of interest in emotions and feelings.[80] This book gratefully builds on the insights that the study or history of emotion—as the new field is commonly labeled—has generated. Admittedly, sincerity is, to cite one expert on the topic, "not itself an affective state. . . . It is rather the assessment by addressees that the expressions of addressers are true representations of their feelings and emotional state. . . . Sincerity is thus a paradoxical affective expression in that its presence or absence is ultimately ascertained not by the expressor(s), but by the persons to whom it is expressed."[81] Sincerity, in other words, is not an emotive state proper. The concept *is,* however, firmly lodged in the *sphere* of feeling and emotion.

Accordingly, the notion of sincerity has been taken on board in many recent inquiries into emotion as an object of critical or historical analysis.[82] These inquiries defy the view of emotions as psychological states located inside bodies that have to be expressed or taken out. "Emotions," to cite a groundbreaking study of emotion by Sara Ahmed, "should not be regarded as psychological states, but as social and cultural practices," which can act as "a form of politics or world making."[83] New theorizations of sincerity follow Ahmed's advice when they challenge classic views of sincerity as a "performance of an inner state on one's outer surface so that others can witness it."[84] This traditional definition relies on clear-cut binary oppositions of an inner self and an outer body—oppositions that today many scholars contest. Experts now plead for an understanding of the term in which sincerity and theatricality are intertwined rather than diametrically contrasted.[85] They strive, in the words of cultural historians Mieke Bal and Ernst Van Alphen, to protect the notion of sincerity against "a dualistic perspective of rights and wrongs" by acknowledging that "the issue of sincerity is no longer one of 'being' sincere but of 'doing' sincerity."[86] In my interrogations of the concept, I show a similar interest in what, in Russian and global public debate today, sincerity *does* and how it *works*, rather than what it *is*.

STUDYING SINCERITY: POST-SOVIET SURVEYS

Contemporary readings of sincerity have graciously refined existing thinking on the subject. They lack, however, another form of refinement. As I mentioned earlier, as a rule they suggest that debates over a newly defined sincerity are limited mainly to Western Europe and the United States. With this book I hope to boost awareness of the much broader international scope in ongoing sincerity debates. I have already mentioned China and Bulgaria. In rummaging through sincerity literature for this project, I also came upon an anthology from an Indonesian poetry festival whose 2006 edition revolved around "Poetry and Sincerity." In an introductory text that reads like a new-sincerity manifesto, the organizers plea for the "cleans[ing]," in today's globalized world, of the words that "surround us, the words that kill, and the words that have been killed," by injecting them with . . . "sincerity."[87]

Contrary to what many an existing study on new-sincerity talk suggests, the optimal place to start an inquiry into new-sincerity discourse is well away from Anglo-American spheres. I am speaking of the geopolitical space at which we are looking here: post-Soviet Russia. It was in Russia, in the 1950s, that sincerity gained a status as a buzzword that it has never lost since; it was in Russia that, in the earliest years of perestroika, literary professionals introduced the phrase "new sincerity" as it is popularly used today; and it is in Russia that bloggers eagerly appropriate it for social identity building.

With its focus on Russian examples, *Sincerity after Communism* is my contribution to the task of integrating non-Western European and non-American cultures into the scholarly discussion on post-postmodern discourse. This is no irrelevant task: although they receive scarce attention abroad, in Russia theoretical debates on a late or post-postmodern cultural turn are thriving. What is more, the question "What comes after postmodernism?" has been part of the Russian discussion on postmodernism from the start. In Russia, the term "postmodernism" began to be more or less commonly used in the early 1990s.[88] As an articulated theoretical trend, Russian postmodernism was thus flourishing relatively late, at a time when postmodern devices had long been marking Russian artistic culture (in retrospect, postmodern thinking had been percolating into Soviet-era cultural production at least since the late 1960s). Not surprisingly, once postmodernism was introduced as a theoretical model, its effects more or less instantly evoked wariness. Apart from traditionalist rejections of postmodern values, the "critical war against postmodernism"[89] included ample self-critical voices. Manifold were the Russian artists and critics who initially embraced the postmodern experience but sought to "move beyond it" (or, like Anatolii Osmolovskii, to develop scenarios for an art "after postmodernism"; figure 3) as soon as it was articulated as a full-fledged theoretical paradigm.

From roughly the mid-1990s onward, the thought that postmodernism—or its Soviet exponent, Moscow Conceptualism—was either dead or mutating into new forms thrived in Russian theoretical thinking. Its exhaustion was discussed in detail in Russian-language publications by leading cultural theoreticians and critics, such as Mark Lipovetsky, Mikhail Aizenberg, Mikhail Epstein, Natalia Ivanova, and Viacheslav Kuritsyn.[90] In 1994, the notion of the death of postmodernism was taken to its literal extreme by artist Aleksandr Brener: by way of a hunger strike he called, among other things, for the end—"it's him or me"—of postmodernism.[91]

Brener soon abolished his strike, but the notion of a late or post-postmodern cultural era—in literature, but also in film, visual arts, and new media—began to crowd the pages of scholarly publications even more heavily toward the end of the 1990s. Russian textbooks and university courses on contemporary Russian literature then also began to pay increasing attention to late or post-postmodern trends[92]—and between the late 1990s and today, the same trends have been diagnosed in several book-length Russian studies of postmodernism.[93] A prime ex-

FIGURE 3 Anatolii Osmolovskii's acoustic photo installation "After Postmodernism, All One Can Do Is Scream" (1992). Photograph courtesy of www.osmopolis.ru.

ample is *Paralogues* (*Paralogii*, 2008), a widely acclaimed study on "(post)modern discourse" in Russian art, literature, and cinema by Mark Lipovetsky. In this book Lipovetsky uses Russia as a test case for Douwe Fokkema's hypothesis of a "late postmodernism"—that is, of a "cesura" between an early, radically relativizing and a less antimodernist late postmodern phase.[94] Like Fokkema, Lipovetsky is critical of visions of postmodernism's death—but he maps late postmodernism in terms that actively engage with these visions and that turn them into one of the book's central thematic concerns.[95]

Lipovetsky's book is exemplary of a flourishing of late or post-postmodern rhetoric in post-Soviet Russia. Within this wealth of Russian-language post-postmodern scholarship, new-sincerity discourse has not suffered from a lack of attention. In the 1990s, Epstein, Nadezhda

Man'kovskaia, and Svetlana Boym all identified it as a prominent trend in theoretical analyses of contemporary culture; and Lipovetsky mentions the phrase in a 1999 study of postmodernist fiction, signaling a crisis of postmodernism and the "search for a sincere tone" in contemporary writing.[96] In *Paralogues*, Lipovetsky would adopt a more skeptical view—but he did so while, again, angling "new sincerity" out of the pick-and-mix of post-postmodern labels and endowing this particular rhetorical trend with lengthy critical assessment.[97] Lipovetsky was not alone at the time: in the 2000s, the phrase "new sincerity" became a regular feature on the pages of renowned Russian academic journals. Their contributors sometimes rejected the trend ("new sincerity was invented by inept critics and poets") and sometimes praised it ("this is *the* answer to postmodernism")—but in either case they tended to discuss it as an inevitable, if problematic, ingredient in contemporary culture.[98] By the early 2010s, the notion of a newborn post-Soviet sincerity had also made its way to foreign scholarship on Russia, and to textbooks on contemporary Russian literature; just how canonical it was now becoming in literary scholarship illustrates Sergei Chuprinin's choice, in 2007, to merit "new sincerity" its own lemma in his well-read handbook of contemporary literary concepts.[99]

The debate on a revived post-Communist sincerity boasts a remarkable disciplinary breadth. In signaling a Russian revival of sincerity, commentators focus mostly on literary developments—we shall see numerous examples in chapters 2, 3, and 4—but they take other creative disciplines on board, too. Epstein borrows as many samples from visual arts as he does from the literary sphere. Art historians and critics Vladislav Sofronov, Valerii Savchuk, Marina Koldobskaia, and Ekaterina Degot' discern a renewed Russian emphasis on sincerity specifically in contemporary art.[100] Alexei Yurchak—in an anthropological analysis of oral rather than written sincerity rhetoric—explores expressions of a "post-post-Communist sincerity" in post-Soviet cartoons and electronic music.[101] In addition, sincerity has become a cherished object of theoretical reflection in studies of new media—a field to which we return in detail in chapter 4.

In short, post-postmodern and new-sincerity rhetoric are solid components of critical and scholarly thinking on contemporary Russia. In the pages that follow, I blend the different perspectives on both into an integral analysis of contemporary Russian sincerity talk—one that explores what its travels through numerous different disciplines, perspectives, and moments in time tell us about post-Soviet life at large.

NEW SINCERITY—*NOVAIA ISKRENNOST'*:
A TRANSNATIONAL TAKE

My interest in sincerity rhetoric arose out of a social phenomenon to which I shall devote a few words before concluding this introduction: that of cultural transfer. In the early 2000s, I heard about Russian and Western visions of a post-postmodern sincerity on a number of separate occasions, but at approximately the same moment. I began to wonder: how do the Russian and other sincerity debates relate to one another? Is one local new-sincerity discourse formative to another, and if so, how do they travel across space? Or are the two discourses expressions of a broader shift of cultural paradigms, and did they materialize independently of one another?

As so often, the answer to the above inquiries is: a little bit of both. It is hard—even, or perhaps especially, in a digitized age—to pinpoint the exact "movement" of discursive trends through geographical space. But a closer investigation indicates that traditional views on cultural transfer—with megatrends traveling mostly from an intellectually superior West to a backward Russia—do not pertain here.

The theoretical vocabulary of postmodernism may have reached Russia long after it had been launched by Western thinkers; but visions of moving beyond postmodernism's purportedly all-pervading irony surfaced early in Russia. Dmitrii Prigov first calls for a post-ironic "New Sincerity" in 1985—at a time when, according to my data, outside Russia this notion only resonated among a hardcore music in crowd in Texas.[102] Although informal contacts between Prigov and Western European or American colleagues of course provided mutual inspiration, no source indicates that the two forms of new-sincerity rhetoric (which, despite local variations, share a defiance of hard-boiled irony and relativizing) did *not* evolve to a large extent independently of one another.

The same is true of later Russian discussions on a post-postmodern sincerity. These are influenced, but not initiated, by Russian translations of such American and Norwegian icons of a "new sincere condition" as the writers Dave Eggers and Erlend Loe.[103] When Eggers's and

Loe's translations appeared, Russian new-sincerity debates were already in full swing. In return, American writer-bloggers eagerly embraced the writings on post-postmodernity and a new sincerity of Epstein, who rapidly made English-language versions of these writings available online after their original publication in the late 1990s.[104] The English-language Wikipedia entry on "New Sincerity" makes avid use of Russian sources on the subject, and devotes a well-documented separate section to "New Sincerity in Russia."

In short, there is no such thing as either a purely independent or an entirely interdependent Russian or non-Russian sincerity debate. The local versions of current sincerity discussions revolve around one another in a complex choreography, in which global, national, and regional levels constantly overlap and intersect with other, economically or socially rather than spatially defined, variations within the debate. In the ensuing pages, I attempt to take these nuances into account by opting for a postnational or transnational perspective on contemporary sincerity rhetoric—one that, although focusing on Russian cases, refuses to call a halt at the borders of the Russian nation-state.[105] From this perspective, the take on sincerity of someone like Russian-speaking blogger flippi754—who posts feel-good photos of girls at Starbucks and explains, "This is the new sincerity: little drops of spring rain on your cheeks, and hot coffee in your mouth"—may be rooted in post-Stalinist rhetoric no less than in popular debates on the American cult band Bright Eyes.[106]

IN CONCLUSION

Sincerity after Communism examines global discussions on reviving sincerity, and it offers a synthetic discussion of post-Communist—especially Russian—pendants of these debates. It originates in a feeling that these debates require a reading somewhat different from the ones they have spurred so far—one that is sensitive to their diachronic development, and that exchanges involvement in the debate for a more external prism. Existing studies of Russian new-sincere thinking criticize it, they defend it, they constitute themselves as its personal agent, or they vehemently reject it—in short, they actively engage with it. This book tries walking a different path. I do not have the illusion that I can provide rigid neutrality—but I have been able to observe the genesis and diachronic transformations of the debate from the vantage point of a relative outsider. This position has its disadvantages (how, for instance, does one fully grasp the hodgepodge of perestroika-era creative initiatives without having experienced them firsthand?)—but it is ideal for obtaining a panoramic view of post-Soviet sincerity debates, a view that has so far been missing.

In this book, I meticulously explore the debates as a cultural-historical fact. I explore, too, what contemporary Russia's "sincerity haunters" tell us about postsocialist public life and the role that Soviet and personal memory, commodification, and mediatization play in that life.

Why does post-Soviet sincerity discourse warrant such meticulous cultural-historical analysis? This question is best answered, perhaps, by pointing to those who, together, create the discourse. Bloggers repeatedly complain that they are "truly tired" of hearing about the new sincerity on every street corner; journalists are certain that the new sincerity, "if not entirely waggish, is surely beyond being new, almost old";[107] and ASh and bordzhia, the chat users with whom this introduction opened, treat the concept with a somewhat dismissive irony. As we saw, ASh feels the new credo is intriguing enough to mention it in an online chat with a friend but makes sure to express tedium in doing so. After a brief and off-hand discussion of "the new theory," the two users agree that it is time to leave the "nightmare" of "total sincerity" to its own devices for now, and turn their minds elsewhere.

This reputation—of a concept which people mildly mock, which the public deems "so last year"—indicates perfectly just what a day-to-day constituent of post-Soviet culture new-sincerity rhetoric has now become. Both in Russia and elsewhere, this everyday phrase keeps surfacing with tenacious frequency—in blogs, on Twitter, and on other social media, as well as in leading intellectual publications. It keeps stirring controversies, too. In November 2012, Princeton literature professor Christy Wampole published a *New York Times* article entitled "How to Live without Irony." Wampole's call for a move away from ironic social forms and hipster culture toward a "cultivation of sincerity, humility and self-effacement"[108] struck a tender nerve: in the comments section alone, the article generated more than seven hundred responses, and in an interview Wampole explained that she had received more than four hundred e-mail reactions from all over the world.[109] The authors of those messages all felt the urge to share with Wampole their take on irony and (a new or revitalized) sincerity. The stir that Wampole caused illustrates my point in this book: visions of reviving sincerity today thrive with special force.

Contemporary sincerity adepts do not emerge like Venus from the sea, however. Harking back to ancient visions of truthfulness and self, their rhetoric is indebted to such paragons of cultural history as Confucius, Aristotle, and, to mention a Russian influence, the grumpy seventeenth-century archpriest Avvakum. The chapter to which you now turn explores these historical roots and explains how they relate to the preoccupation with sincerity of chat users ASh and bordzhia, of the poet Prigov, of literature professor Wampole, and of their myriad contemporaries.

CHAPTER ONE

History

"Rigorous minds have scoffed at it; analytical definers have tried to explode it; professors have ruthlessly underscored in their students' papers the easy explanation for the greatness of almost any work by its 'sincerity.' . . . The concept of sincerity has become the most potent idée-force in the literature and psychology of our age."

Henri Peyre, Literature and Sincerity, *14*

"At a certain point in history . . . the value that [certain men and classes of men] attached to the enterprise of sincerity became a salient, perhaps a definitive, characteristic of Western culture for some four hundred years."

Lionel Trilling, Sincerity and Authenticity, *6*

Unhampered by fears of overstating their cases, Henri Peyre and Lionel Trilling employed these characterizations to open inquiries into the history of sincerity in the 1960s. Together with other explorers of the concept's journey through time, they have done much to clarify the cultural and literary roots of the concept. This chapter does not retell their story—and such human milestones in the history of sincerity rhetoric as, say, Michel de Montaigne and François de La Rochefoucauld do not adorn its pages. Neither does it exhaustively map the history of performativity, irony, subjectivity, and the self—the semantic cluster that talk about sincerity inevitably involves. This chapter is not the place to seek for, say, Richard Rorty's name, no matter how formative Rorty's reflections on performativity and on irony are to contemporary sincerity rhetoric.

My task is narrower. On the pages that follow, I offer a diachronic overview that couples Peyre's and Trilling's classical studies to recent research into sincerity rhetoric. I do so while scrutinizing those discursive historical threads that prevail in contemporary readings of the term especially (although not only) in Russia.

Why, the non-region-expert may wonder, Russia, out of all possible world regions? This choice is no random decision: as one influential critic puts it, Russia's entire literary history "is determined [by] the dichotomy sincerity/irony."[1] I do not believe that such a hardboiled dichotomy between sincerity and irony is in itself productive, but I *am* interested in its popularity in Russia as a cultural-historical fact. That popularity is undisputed: from especially the Soviet era onward—as Birgit Beumers and Mark Lipovetsky recently put it—"the concept of 'sincerity' has been endowed with disproportionately high significance in Russian culture."[2]

Russia, then, has our special attention in the transnational history that we trace in this chapter. On the ensuing pages, I examine the historical roots of the three thematic interconnections that dominate contemporary sincerity talk: sincerity and memory, sincerity and commodification, and sincerity and media. As I explained in this book's introduction, my interest is attracted, first, to the thread of history and memory. In contemporary discourse, sincerity is firmly lodged in historico-political and commemorative spheres. When the term crops up in post-Soviet intellectual debate, notions of sociopolitical opposition (to "hypocritical" official culture) or strivings to cope with the ("insincere") recent past are rarely far away. Often speakers relate the notion to a particular nation or social group—by specifically branding Russia, or the intellectual elite, sincere, for instance.

Second, talk of sincerity today inevitably includes feelings of *doubt,* and—philosophical and more practical—suspicions. Can an artist or writer be sincere anyhow? How does sincere spontaneity rhyme with the often markedly rational, laborious task of creating art? These questions lie at the heart of current anxieties about the concept.

Finally, in the twenty-first century sincerity is often conceptualized as a notion endemic to new media. To some commentators, social media form a prime locus for writing modes that display a hitherto unthinkable, post-postmodern sincerity. Others see automatization as a threat to person-to-person contact, a threat that only authentic human sincerity can address.

In short, contemporary views of sincerity are (a) sociopolitically defined; (b) skeptical by default; and (c) media specific. Where do these takes on the notion take root? Just how idiosyncratic are they for post-Soviet Russia? And how do post-Soviet takes on sincerity use and revise historical and non-Russian readings of sincerity? These are central questions in this historical chapter. The discussion that follows naturally answers them only partially: I make giant leaps through time and space, and (although occasionally peeping into law, art, and other discursive and creative fields) I lean mostly on literary and philosophical sources—the material that has my special interest as a scholar. These inevitable limitations notwithstanding, the rough historical guide that follows will serve as an indispensable analytical peg once we reach post-Soviet territory.

ENTER SINCERITY: FROM THE ANCIENTS
TO EARLY MODERNITY

Emotional norms change over time, and even in one lifetime a person can simultaneously belong to several emotional communities with distinct emotive value sets. This view is common coin in the current theorizing of emotions.[3] The same is true for historical readings of sincerity: the question "What is sincere behavior, and what is not?" has been answered in different ways in different periods and in different locations. In the diverging responses to this question, one feature recurs with relentless persistence, however: where the word "sincerity" appears, doubts *about* sincerity surface. It is no coincidence that the noun is readily combined—both in historical and in more contemporary usage—with verbs denoting nonverifiable outward performance and suspicion: sincerity is something that an addresser "demonstrates" or "shows," or that the addressee "doubts."[4]

Long before the term entered our vocabulary, the connotations of distrust that haunt the concept today already clung to the notions that the word "sincerity" would later unite: genuineness, truthfulness, and the quality of not pretending. They do so not only in the geopolitical space now called the West—and I disagree with those scholars who insist that sincerity concerns are "a foundational act" specifically "of Western metaphysics."[5] In the fourth and third centuries B.C. in China, for instance, Confucian teachings single out *cheng* and *chengshen*— terms now commonly translated as "sincerity," which literally mean "truthfulness to oneself"—as a moral responsibility.[6] That status, of chengshen as a duty one should bear, implies that fears of *in*sincerity loomed large even in this early, Asia-based example.

In another corner of the globe, similar anxieties materialized a little earlier in what is commonly called "the Platonic distinction"—the "opening up of a rift between seeming and being" that was vital to Plato's thinking.[7] In ancient Greek philosophy, sincerity concerns resonated, too, in the figure of speech called *parrhesia*—a speaker's moral duty to speak openly and, if necessary, critically, to those in authority.[8] They also resounded in Aristotle's *Rhetorics*. In the words of cultural historian Liesbeth Korthals Altes, "In the three 'pisteis' or means of persuasion distinguished by Aristotle and Cicero, *ethos, pathos* and *logos*, attention is called to aspects of communication that come close to what speech act theory nowadays subsumes under sincerity . . . ethos encompasses for Aristotle 'three things making the orator himself trustworthy (. . .). These are good sense, goodness and goodwill [toward the audience].' Speakers are wrong [among others] if out of 'wickedness they do not say what they think.' "[9]

Being honest toward an external audience: this was a cherished personal feature in ancient cultures. It remained an esteemed emotional quality in the Middle Ages, as a prizewinning study by cultural historian Irene van Renswoude recently demonstrated. Rulers—so van Renswoude argues—then tolerated fierce criticisms out of a belief that in a healthy society the monarch's "critic needs to be sincere" (in van Renswoude's view, this ancient belief prefigures the current glorification of free speech as a hallmark for "courage, authenticity, non-conformity and sincerity" by such populist politicians as, in the Netherlands, Geert Wilders).[10] In the same cultures, the question of whether a person is honest to her or his *own* "self" rather than to external parties is less prominent.[11] That situation changed in early Christianity, when the confessional writings of Saint Paul and Saint Augustine famously introduced more problematized visions of selfhood—visions in which the inability to be "true to oneself" take center stage.

But the question of whether a speaker is honest or upright truly became a pivotal cultural concern only in early modernity, when the word "sincerity" entered the French and, later, English languages. Deriving from the Latin *sincerus*—"clean," "sound," or "pure"—it initially served as an adjective for unmixed material objects ("sincere wine") or consistently virtuous persons ("sincere behavior").[12] In the new conceptualizations of self and subjectivity that mark early modern thinking—in Stephen Greenblatt's famous words, in Renaissance thought "there were both selves and a sense that they could be fashioned"[13]—the concept of sincerity is soon presented as a problem. "What does it mean to be sincere?" So contemporary thinkers asked, as a dazzling range of cultural transitions inevitably colored existing worldviews and traditional divisions between private and public. I am thinking not only of the introduction of theater as an artistic discipline but also of the shift from handwritten text to printed book; of the intensifying assaults on the "hypocritical" Catholic religion; and of this era's increasing levels of urbanization. The advent of staged plays, of standardized rather than handcrafted media, of a Calvinist counterreligion prompting a "willing and sincere" posture, and this age's rapid rise in social mobility—all these societal factors helped to give rise to a heightened concern with questions of self, truth, and truth telling.[14] In the words of sincerity expert Susan Rosenbaum, they generated a "new distrust" that "the rhetoric of sincerity sought to mediate."[15]

In public debates of the time, sincerity is foregrounded, for instance, in responses to radical changes in media usage. With the advent of book printing and professional theater, as Mieke Bal and Ernst van Alphen argue, "sincerity became entangled in medial forms that complicated . . . the integrated semiotic field where body and mind were believed to be one."[16] These new medial forms were not met with unequivocal enthusiasm. Media historians teach us that the launch of a new medium always triggers intense social dreams, fantasies, and fears[17]—and the same is true for the media transitions of this age, which spark fierce sincerity anxieties. The ubiquity of book piracy, for one, now presents print publishers with angry customers and credibility concerns. Early modern critics accuse print books of being "nonoriginal," "superficial"—and, by extension, less sincere—substitutes for handwriting.[18] As book historian Adrian Johns has shown, publishers resist their work's bad reputation by carefully "project[ing] authenticity in the domains of print."[19] To achieve this goal, they use refreshingly practical means: they willfully mimic scribal practices by using quasi-handwritten fonts. The resulting, emphatically imperfect-looking books emulate the "sincere" model that their customers buy most readily: the handcrafted manuscript.[20]

As I argue in chapter 4, this trend of projecting sincerity in specific media—and of foregrounding aesthetic imperfection as a guarantee for human sincerity within a new media technology—will become vital to Russian and global digitization discourses.[21] But early modern sincerity rhetoric also anticipates post-Soviet sincerity talk in another respect. I am speaking of its profound politicization. On the one hand, the term "sincerity" is part and parcel of private conceptualizations of self: the attempt to be true to oneself is an intimate, personal process. On the other, inquiries into sincerity's semantic origins immediately lead us into the public, and indeed political, arena.[22] In early modern culture the birth of the term "sincerity" coincided with that of "the idea of society,"[23] and the new word instantly surfaced in markedly public contexts. Historian John Martin has demonstrated how, in the Renaissance take on selfhood, citizens could either opt for an "outer," "prudential self"— one following the conventions of society or court life—or an "inner" "ideal of sincerity."[24] Sincerity was thus believed to originate from private spheres—but it was not supposed to remain there. For English Calvinist divines, for example, the privately oriented sincere ideal inextricably blended with the civic act of political opposition: they took much pride in publicly expressing their personal views on the powers that be.[25]

With its insistence on public personal expression, Calvinism continues a rhetorical tradition born in Greek parrhesia and medieval free speech. This tradition parallels sincerity and hypocrisy, respectively, with political opposition (on the part of either the intellectual elite or the common man) and the political status quo (embodied in stately authority, or in Catholic faith, for example). Apart from the self-view of English Calvinists, the same tradition informed a contemporary German cult of sincerity. Literary historian Ingo Stöckmann describes how in the early seventeenth century the so-called old-German opposition saw itself as a sincere counterideal to a deceitful French court; and how its representatives shoved forward sincerity as an answer to the challenge of building political communities.[26] Sincerity acquired a similarly consolidating function in the rise of the Dutch Republic. Here notions of sincerity and pretense were used to prove and test the sovereign's commitment to her or his people.[27] In France, finally, drama writers at the time constructed sincerity as a safeguard against the erosion of court life and its omnipresent hypocrisy.[28]

The last example—of French anticourt rhetoric—anticipates a drastically politicized cult of sincerity in late eighteenth-century France. To that cult of sincerity we shall turn shortly; but what matters here is that, together with the other examples mentioned, the French case marks the early modern birth of a rhetorical habit. This is the (drastically dichotomized) habit of locating sincerity and hypocrisy in opposing political groups, or in social strata whose mutual tension speakers seek to highlight. As we shall see in chapter 2, Russia's contemporary language of sincerity is unthinkable without this sociopolitical usage of the term. Before moving on to the present day, however, I want to continue our journey through time, and turn to the origins of *iskrennost'*—the Russian equivalent for sincerity.

OLD RUSSIA: *DERZNOVENIE* AND *ISKRENNOST'*

As I said, many well-known studies of sincerity rhetoric frame their topic as a self-evidently Western phenomenon, but anxieties about expressing one's inner feelings have, of course, never been limited to Western Europe and the United States. We witnessed them in China at the start of this chapter, and Russia is another case in point.

According to a team of Russian linguists led by Anna Zalizniak, one of the eight "core ideas" organizing the Russian linguistic worldview is "the thought that it is good when others know what a person feels."[29] Among the words used to articulate that thought, the linguists refer to the adjective *iskrennii*, or "sincere."[30] Zalizniak and her colleagues are not alone in suggesting that this word has a unique status in the Russian language. The prominent philologist Anna Wierzbicka claims that the Russian noun *iskrennost'* covers a much wider array of meanings than its common English translation of "sincerity" suggests: in her view, it includes notions of "kindness," "innocence," and "depth of feeling."[31] Finally, the renowned literary historian Svetlana Boym argues in a study of Russian everyday life that "the Russian word *iskrennost'* suggests kinship, proximity, closeness; it may be related to the word for 'root'—*koren'*—making Russian sincerity

appear more 'radical.' . . . [It] suggests kinship rather than purity; it mani-
fests itself in a number of familiar rituals that Russians deem sincere, but
which foreigners could perceive as theatrical."[32] Coupling etymology to
anthropological observation, Boym continues: "Russian codes of sincere
behavior are much more emotional and outwardly expressive than those
of their Western counterparts."[33]

The conclusions of Boym and colleagues confirm an old cliché
about the Russian's inner world. In cultural historian Catriona Kelly's
words, when foreigners speak of "Russian emotions," they often think of
"an expression of feelings that looks natural, sincere, unpredictable, coming from the very heart, or . . . 'from the soul's depths.' "[34] Emblematic of
this trend is the notion of a "Russian soul"—that enduring myth of an
intrinsically Russian national character that is supposed to be less rational and more spontaneous than the temperament of other nations.[35]

While the relationship of the stereotypical "sincere Russian" to real
life is wonky, the term "sincerity" did make its way into the Russian
language at a remarkably early stage. Contrary to its English or French
counterparts, the Russian word *iskrennost'* first appeared in written
sources in the eleventh century, when the country had barely learned to
write.[36] Etymological references suggest that, at this time, the term did
not carry any public or political connotations. In Church Slavonic, political associations did color the related concept of *derznovenie*. Designated
today as "boldness" or "impudence," in Old Russian this word mirrored
the Greek parrhesia—including its notions of constructive criticism
of the authorities. The word *iskrennost'* originally lacked such critical
overtones. In the earliest recorded appearances of its various grammatical hypostases—the noun *iskrennost'*, the adjectives *iskrennii, iskrenii,
iskrinii, iskren'nii*, and the adverb *iskreno*—the term denoted exclusively
positive notions of uprightness, truthfulness, nearness, and intimacy.[37]

In this initial set of meanings of iskrennost', the skeptical question
of whether a speaker is true to herself or himself had no central place.
And why should it have? This question was, after all, of little interest to
the writer of Old Russian texts: defined primarily by religious and ideological parameters, ancient Russian literature was supposed to deal
with fact not fiction, and to shun individual originality. In a culture that
lacked a Reformation and Renaissance experience, thinking about an
autonomous "self" was simply not a pressing issue.[38]

The situation changed with one of Russia's early literary milestones: the splendidly candid late seventeenth-century autobiography of Avvakum Petrov.[39] This archpriest was exiled and imprisoned for opposing the major reforms that Nikon—then patriarch of the Russian Church— was pushing through in Orthodox theology. In his *Life*, Avvakum describes both his hardships and his love for God's world. His narrative is conspicuously personal for the era in which it was written. It leaves room for such intimate and critical self-reflections as the following: "I am nothing. I have said and I repeat: I am a sinner, a fornicator and a ravisher, thief and murderer, friend of publicans and sinners, and to every man a wretched hypocrite. So forgive me and pray for me; and I must pray for you who read me or listen to me. I can do no better, and what I do, I relate to men; let them pray to God for my sake. On the day of judgment they shall know my actions, for good or evil. I am untaught in words, but not in knowledge; I am not learned in dialectic, rhetoric and philosophy, but I have Christ's wisdom within me. As the Apostle says: 'Although I be rude in speech, yet not in knowledge.' "[40]

If shot through with a solid dose of devout rhetoric, Avvakum's language of private emotion is unusually intimate for its age. Not coincidentally does Ulrich Schmid—author of a history of Russian autobiographical writing—call his story "the birth place of an individual consciousness in Russian cultural history."[41] The priest indeed brings to Russian literature a clearly recognizable sense of self and self-awareness. As the fragment above demonstrates, he cautiously stylizes this "self" as a social outcast with an unpolished diction.[42] His emphasis on roughness and illiteracy renders Avvakum an unmistakable forerunner of what will become a classic Russian literary type: the sincere, raw countervoice to the polished but hypocritical ruling class.

THE EIGHTEENTH CENTURY: THE DANGEROUS LANGUAGE OF THE HEART

Sincerity increasingly troubled intellectuals as a social problem in the course of the next century. Hypocrisy then became an acute political concern in especially (pre-)revolutionary France. Experts have demonstrated that the impact of eighteenth-century French vocabularies of emotion on the public sphere can hardly be overestimated: in contemporary thinking about politics and society, sincerity loomed unusually large.

Indeed, with the onset of Romanticism French *sincerité* gained mythical status. Jean-Jacques Rousseau—arguably literary history's most influential advocate of the concept—ardently resorted to the term in his confessional writings. In Henri Peyre's words, in Rousseau's hands it became "a substitute for almost any other quality, moral or aesthetic."[43] Rousseau lent the term a political charge, too: to him, it designated an immediate expression of the individual self as opposed to public dissimulation—that is, to the hypocrisy of societal or civilized life, of court life in particular.[44]

Rousseau is a leading name in the history of sincerity that we are unpacking here. Itself influenced by seventeenth-century debunkings of court hypocrisy, his notion of sincerity heavily colors French revolutionary thought. According to historian Lynn Hunt, French Republicans value the "unmediated expression of the heart above all other personal qualities." To them, "transparency was the perfect fit between public and private; transparency was a body that told no lies and kept no secrets. It was the definition of virtue, and as such it was imagined to be critical to the future of the republic. Dissimulation, by contrast, threatened to undermine the Republic: . . . it lay at the heart of the counter-revolution."[45] In the revolutionaries' ideal state, in short, the hearts and minds of the people and of the authorities sincerely side with each other.

French revolutionaries were not alone in their life-or-death preoccupation with sincerity. As the eighteenth century unfolded, the term took center stage in literary writings, and written language in general, in a number of European countries. According to one study of British poetry, in the course of the century "sincerity [emerges] . . . as something required of all artists."[46] As in early modernity, the word once again figured in domains where the private and the public blend; but the social groups onto which it was projected were now demarcated more sharply. In this age of growing travel possibilities, territorial wars, and increasing trade contacts, sincerity became a catchword of emerging nationalist discourse. Early British nationalists, for instance, presented sincerity as the ultimate English virtue. As historian Gerald Newman has shown, in early nationalist debates they gradually established a relationship of equivalence between "Sincerity" and the English "National Ideal itself."[47] Following the neat binary logic that typifies nationalist thinking, they consistently opposed "what is English-sincere-good" to "what is Frenchified-insincere-corrupting."[48]

English nationalist views of France coincided with visions of a "dis-simulative" French court among influential social actors *within* French society: the revolutionary-minded intellectual elite. French revolutionar-ies used the term in a way different from the way British nationalists did, however. The latter projected their ideals of a more "sincere" society onto their nation as a whole. French intellectuals envisioned this ideal trait in one specific component of French society: the common people. Galva-nized by literary developments and by then freshly emerging discourses on human rights, the intellectual elite began to employ a sentimentalist vocabulary that emphasized that the socially underprivileged had feelings, too. They started by locating feelings in all people—but soon they pro-jected human beings' nobler emotions—including sincerity—exclusively onto the lower (and, more often than not, rurally based) social strata.[49]

In a groundbreaking inquiry into the emotional language of histori-cal French elites, anthropologist William Reddy explores this "belief in the purity and sincerity of country people's emotions," and wonders: to what extent did it expedite the ultimate arrival of the Revolution?[50] An-swering his question is not easy, as Reddy himself acknowledges; but beyond doubt is the controversial political role that the "language of the heart"—and the word "sincerity" in particular—acquired once the Revolution and the Terror set in. In the court cases of the 1780s, the term migrated straight into the courtroom when "hypocrisy" became a formal crime. In legal documents of the time, injured and perpetra-tor were consistently portrayed as "sincere" commoners and "artificial" aristocrats, respectively.[51] With time, suspicions of insincerity turned into a forceful legal instrument: in some cases, such suspicions led as far as the death penalty. Attempting "to govern on the basis of sincerity, and to govern in such a way as to produce sincerity, even when using instru-ments of pure coercion," revolutionaries thus radicalized the rhetoric of sincerity to such an extent that it could, literally, kill.[52]

RUSSIAN SENTIMENTALISM: PUTTING *ISKRENNOST'* ON THE MENTAL MAP

The language of the heart may have been exceptionally perilous in revolu-tionary France; but sentimentalist vocabularies have, of course, impacted actively on many other liberation and democratization discourses. As is commonly acknowledged today, sentimental rhetoric played a major emancipatory role, for example, in eighteenth-century British-American debates on slavery and abolitionism.[53]

Spurred on by a mixture of those debates, Freemason ideals, Rousseau's legacy, and French revolutionary rhetoric, intellectuals in late eighteenth-century Russia similarly started expressing a dissent with social inequality. Along with other "refined" sentiments, they promoted the supremacy of a prerational (and principally sincere) "human nature" over such modern notions as civilization and culture. More pointedly, Russian sentimentalists joined a trans-European cult of self-exploration in which *chuvstvitel'nost'*—the ability to be emotionally moved—and social compassion were the norm.[54] Experts have demonstrated that this chuvstvitel'nost' and compassion were not devoid of inner contradictions. In practice, the sentimentalists' "spontaneity" was expressed in strictly regulated emotional rituals; and their insistence on intimacy went hand in glove with a sophisticated social and fashion consciousness. Oozing domesticity was all well and good, but one did have to look exactly right in doing so.[55]

Paradoxes between spontaneity and intimacy, on the one hand, and cultural regulation and sociability, on the other, did not diminish the social impact of the new public consciousness, however. Nor did they prevent the sentimentalist mindset from thoroughly converting one specific dimension of public consciousness: the Russian vocabulary. In a language that hitherto had paid little attention to articulating individual emotion, the sentimentalist turn eventuated in an introduction of new words; but also in a reappraisal and revision of existing terms that suited the new worldview. Among the revised terms, iskrennost' occupied a vital role.

Before we leave the eighteenth century, I want to take a closer look at this—to post-Communist Russia quite fundamental—modification of the concept of iskrennost'. As we saw, the word "sincerity" entered the Russian language long before sentimentalism hit Russian ground. In early usage it referred mainly to religious or familial relationships,[56] but occasionally it arose in political contexts as well. A Muscovite text labeled a *boiarin* a "sincere tsar," for instance;[57] and the eighteenth-century poet Mikhail Lomonosov forged an explicit link between sincerity and political power in an ode to Peter the Great, when Lomonosov lauded the "Russians' sincere love" for their tsar.[58] Lomonosov framed the concept as a positive notion; but—and here we land at the word's seman-

tic transition—not all contemporaries situated it in equally favorable semantic regions. The same (late) eighteenth century witnessed the start
of a gradual mood shift among Russian intellectuals, from state-oriented
toward antistate—or at least toward a highly critical stance to the reigning
authorities.[59] Their change of mood coincided with a reconceptualization
of the term "iskrennost' "—one without which both prerevolutionary
emancipatory discourse and (post-)Soviet sincerity rhetoric would be
unthinkable.

The conceptual transition was epitomized in Nikolai Karamzin's famous story "Poor Liza" ("Bednaia Liza," 1792). The narrator of this short
girl-meets-boy history projects sincerity emphatically onto the common
people; in one of Russian literature's most widely cited quotations, he
explains to readers that "peasant women can love, too."[60] As Catriona
Kelly rightly points out, contemporaries embraced Karamzin's narrative
not least for its iskrennost' rhetorics and their democratizing effects:
it was read as a critique on autocracy and as an "innovative manifesto
of sincere feelings" that propagated equal emotional rights for all
Russians.[61] (With his novella *My Confession* [*Moia ispoved'*, 1802] the
same author would later mordantly parody Rousseau's ideals of emotional transparency—but that social satire attracted substantially less
public attention.)[62]

A similar move toward a new, politically engaged conceptualization
of sincerity marked Aleksandr Radishchev's 1780s *Journey from St.
Petersburg to Moscow* (*Puteshestvie iz Sankt-Peterburga v Moskvu*). The *Journey* is a travelogue—a genre that, together with diaries and letters, ranks
among the favorite literary platforms of sentimentalists in and outside
Russia. In each, a deliberately unpolished writing style—one not wholly
unlike that of Avvakum a century earlier—served as hallmark for artistic and human candor. This conceptual nexus between conscious linguistic crudity and sincerity anticipates the post-Soviet writer-blogger's
insistence on imperfect language as guarantee for authenticity—but
that is a topic to which we return in chapter 4. What matters here is that
Radishchev's travelogue—which is the best-known sample of its genre
in Russia—presented a historical plea against autocracy and serfdom,
and that it firmly placed the word "iskrennost' " on the mental map of Russian critical political thought. (A lack of) sincerity, to Radishchev, was
directly related to Russia's social problems. In Radishchev's view, the

tsarist authorities lacked iskrennost',[63] and the intellectual elite suffered from the same shortfall.[64] Echoing French revolutionarism, this author located sincerity exclusively in the common—preferably rurally based— Russian people.[65] "If," Radishchev mused in a programmatic passage, "the regime . . . is founded on sincerity and a love of common well-being," then should it not love rather than punish its "sincere" citizens?[66]

In both Radishchev's *and* Karamzin's writings, the rhetoric of sincerity traveled to the same opposition spheres where it gradually landed in Western Europe. From Lomonosov's pro-government designation, it now morphed into a marker of discord between state and people. That, to Radishchev, the very *word* "sincerity" encapsulates that political discord suggests its repeated occurrence throughout his—admittedly not unsizable—travelogue. As an adverb or adjective, the word "sincere" occurs nine times, and the noun "sincerity" four. On ten of these thirteen occasions, the term appears in a distinctly political context.[67]

THE LONG NINETEENTH CENTURY: SINCERITY'S NEW MEANINGS

As Radishchev busied himself with putting sincerity on Russia's sociopolitical map and French Republicans enforced a "sincere" society, the late eighteenth century witnessed yet more semantic layerings of the term.

To start with, around this time the early modern "sincerity suspicion" toward new technologies underwent a revival. Just as Renaissanceera readers preferred the handwritten to the printed, so, in the Romantic age, industrialization and urbanization led to a favoring of the "natural" over the urban and the technologically sophisticated. Not coincidentally do Romantic thinkers and artists portray city life and standardized, machine-generated production as threats to human sincerity. Antitechnological rhetoric was not shared by all Romantic circles, but it was formative to the movement as a whole—and such influential Romantic texts as Hoffmann's *Sandman* (*Der Sandmann*, 1816) and Shelley's *Frankenstein* (1818) persistently contrasted nonanimated machines with human characters for whom sincerity is a middle name. In a not unrelated move, John Ruskin, the era's leading art critic, contrasted "engine-tuned precision" with "human intelligence" and "freedom of thought."[68] Ruskin—to whom "the greatest art represents everything with absolute sincerity"[69]—placed industrialized perfection in direct opposition to human creativity when he famously argued: "To banish imperfection is to destroy expression, . . . to paralyze vitality."[70]

In Ruskin and many others, industrialization triggered a preoccupation with sincerity as a prerequisite of the low-fi, the preindustrial, and the nonpolished. This is not the only shift in sincerity rhetoric that technological innovations sparked at the time. In the same age, growing urbanization and increased social mobility triggered an infatuation with sincerity in urban middle-class circles. Cultural historian Karen Halttunen has explored a "cult of sincerity" in American civic life in the mid-nineteenth century. In her words, "As the city gradually replaced the town as the dominant form of social organization, . . . the stranger became not the exception but the rule," and so-called advice writers hastened to uphold sincerity to their readers as a cure for "the problem of hypocrisy in the world of strangers."[71] The advisers' voices were heard: mid-nineteenth-century American fashion, social behavior, and literary texts all exuded an intense fascination with sincerity as an aesthetic and moral ideal. Europe was urbanizing with equal speed, and here, similar fascinations thrived. Emblematically, in the second half of the century the Danish philosopher Søren Kierkegaard used, in one expert's words, "the principle of 'human sincerity'" as foundation for "a new religion."[72]

In the same period, European notions of sincerity experienced yet one more semantic "thickening." With the institutionalization of property rights, a democratization of patronage, and an expanding literary market, the late eighteenth century witnessed the birth of a literary marketplace where authors attained celebrity status and writing became a commodity. These institutional changes set off a vivid debate on artistic integrity and sincerity.[73] If a writer sought to sell work, according to a common concern of the time, was that aim not incompatible with the desire for undiluted self-expression? With time, the "selling-out-versus-sincerity" anxiety became so ubiquitous that it turned into a literary trope of its own. In letters and biographic statements, the French poet Paul Verlaine famously posed as a cynic who was merely making affecting art for money. At one point, the poet bitingly described how he was producing a book of patriotic poems, which would be "very sweet and very touching . . . very naïve of course, and I shall do my utmost to be absurdly sincere."[74]

Verlaine's allusion to selling out foreshadows present-day art criticism, which—as we shall see in detail in this book—insistently ponders sincerity's strategic advantages. But Verlaine's parody takes to extremes yet another aspect of nineteenth-century sincerity rhetoric that I want to highlight here. I am speaking of a fundamental problematization of the term. If suspicions accompanied talk about sincerity from the start, from High Romanticism onward a self-critical, ironic stance toward the concept became a stock motif in literature and philosophy. Where some early Romantics idealized sincerity, others scrutinized the other side of the coin. For them, sincerity transitioned from an ideal to be actively striven for into a morally suspicious never-neverland.[75] As Romantic irony became the norm for the creative avant-garde of the day, sincerity turned into a principal impossibility—and with time, literature started to brim with almost coquettish assertions of one's own *insincerity*. "I am a sick man . . . I am a spiteful man": this is how, in a famous first line, Fedor Dostoevsky introduced the hero of his *Notes from Underground* (*Zapiski iz podpol'ia*, 1864)—a novella that presented humankind in fundamentally pessimist terms. Ubiquitous in Dostoevsky's and his contemporaries' notions of self were senses of an unsolvable inner division—between one's "true" self and a cold ratio that constantly analyzes that "sincere" self, which can therefore never act freely.

Sincerity thus ended up in highly contested spheres within literary-philosophical debates of the time. In other discourses, however, it preserved a stable semantic core. I described earlier how, over the course of the eighteenth century, sincerity began to take pride of place in a binary logic that contrasted "good England" with "corrupt France," or the "hypocritical" court/aristocracy with "honest" common people. In the course of the nineteenth and early twentieth centuries, the same trend—of placing sincerity exclusively in the domain of one's own nation or in nonprivileged social groups—was consolidated in nationalist and populist rhetoric. In late nineteenth-century Germany, nationalists employed the national stereotype of an innately "German sincerity" in the service of nation-building ideals (a stereotype that Nietzsche would parody when writing, "The German loves 'sincerity' and 'uprightness.' How comforting it is to be sincere and upright. . . . The German lets himself go looking the while with trustful blue empty eyes—and foreigners immediately mistake him for his shirt").[76] In related, but populist rather than nationalist, moves, Marx and Engels favored the working classes over a principally "hypocritical" bourgeoisie;[77] and nineteenth- and early twentieth-century French thinkers idealized sincerité as a duty of French democracy.[78] "If the charm of the ancien régime was to be polite," the French dramatist Ernest Legouvé explained in a rather categorical conclusion in 1878, "the duty of democracy is to be sincere."[79]

The habit of locating sincerity in concrete nations, social strata, or political systems; the fundamental skepticism toward the term; the acknowledgment that sincerity can be employed as a strategic device; and the preoccupation with human sincerity in response to technological sophistication: in the course of the nineteenth century, the notion of sincerity starred in a whole parade of semantic settings—settings without which present-day sincerity talk would be unthinkable. So far, I have sketched these transitions with a special eye for Western European and American developments. However, reflection on the term went through a similar set of radical changes in nineteenth-century Russia—the time and space to which we turn now.

THE LONG NINETEENTH CENTURY: RUSSIA

In his classic study of sincerity and authenticity, Lionel Trilling argues that while sincerity calls "the public end in view," authenticity's goal consists in inward-directed self-expression rather than external communication. Trilling believes that authenticity accommodates, to a larger extent than the notion of sincerity does, "much that culture traditionally condemned and sought to exclude . . . , for example disorder, violence, unreason."[80] With time, so he claims, this more inclusive ideal of authenticity has come to supersede that of sincerity.[81]

In making his claim, Trilling is thinking of Western cultures. How do the same two terms interrelate and interact in Russia? Some would argue that the answer to this question is plain: according to Svetlana Boym, there simply is no Russian word for authenticity.[82] I disagree: the term *podlinnost'* is today commonly used as its translation, and Boym herself discusses Russian notions of authenticity elsewhere (although in doing so, she rightly claims that in the Russian context, authenticity refers primarily to legal authentication and authorship).[83] At the same time, my findings confirm that in Russia the concept of authenticity does not enjoy the favored cultural status it has gradually acquired elsewhere. They imply the contrary: with time, it is the Russian concept of iskrennost', or sincerity, that has earned an increasingly strong foothold in public discourse.

Whence this ongoing Russian insistence on sincerity? For a full answer to this question, we need to turn to post-Stalinist Russia—a place and time that I examine later in this chapter. The local popularity of the term harks back further in time, however. It cannot be isolated from a continual tendency, between the late eighteenth century and today, to conceptualize Russia's national identity primarily in negative terms, as the West's "Other."[84] In a tradition where one's cultural superiority is relentlessly articulated in relation to an external force, speakers are more likely to foster ideals of (an addressee-oriented and morally normative) sincerity than authenticity (a concept that, if we follow Trilling, is more inward-oriented and tolerant toward social transgression).

Not surprisingly, in Russia the insistence on locating sincerity exclusively in one's own nation or people is not restricted to a relatively brief nationalist phase—as seems to be the case with the trend toward contrasting English sincerity with all things French. Between the late eighteenth century and today, the projection of sincerity onto Russia or the Russian people (and, ergo, of hypocrisy onto the West) has remained an immensely powerful cultural cliché. Throughout the nineteenth century, it shimmers all too obviously in the rhetoric of a range of different intellectual circles. In the century's early decades—I am citing Svetlana Boym—Russian intellectuals eagerly contrasted "the issue of taste, treated as a sign of Europeanization and superficial civility" with a purportedly Russian-to-the-bone "true spirituality, more important than a mere veneer of foreign politeness."[85] A little later—roughly between the 1830s and the 1860s—the retro-oriented thinkers of the Slavophile movement never tired of placing a sincere Russia in opposition to a hypocritical West. In the same era, radical Russian intellectuals cultivated an antibehavioral model where, in Catriona Kelly's words, "refinement and politeness were rejected entirely . . . and plain living and sincerity cultivated with assiduity."[86] By the second half of the century, Russian-sincerity/European-falsity oppositions had turned into such a cliché that they turned into objects of outright literary parody.[87]

That "Russian sincerity" was turning into a cultural stereotype did not, however, prevent Leo Tolstoy from recycling it, toward the very end of the century, in his seminal essay "What Is Art?" ("Shto takoe iskusstvo?" 1896). Tolstoy wrote the essay in old age, when he was embracing Christian and pastoral ideals with near-obsessive fervency. "What Is Art?" famously argues that the "infectiousness of art"—the extent to which an artwork strikes a public chord—depends first and foremost on "the sincerity of the artist—that is, on the greater or lesser force with which the artist himself feels the emotion he transmits."[88] Less famous is the geopolitical framework within which Tolstoy envisioned the capacity for artistic sincerity. In the same essay, he argued that, in defying religion, (Western) European artists such as Verlaine and Baudelaire had "stopped being sincere, but instead become artificial and calculating," and now "entirely lack . . . sincerity and plainness."[89] If Western Europe had thus turned into a home for "frivolous" art,[90] the cultural space that did offer potential for the production of sincere art was, to Tolstoy—surprise!—his homeland.

Nihilists similarly—and in the same period—constructed sincerity as being distinctive for their Russian brothers-in-arms rather than like-minded Western Europeans. As Russian anarchist Petr Kropotkin explained in his memoirs, written in 1899, "it is nihilism . . . , in its various manifestations, which gives many of our writers that remarkable sincerity, that habit of 'thinking aloud,' which astounds Western European readers."[91]

In short, throughout the nineteenth century political and philosophical thinkers and writers were keen on constructing sincerity as an exclusively Russian accomplishment. In the examples I have selected so far, they do so explicitly. The same trend resonated implicitly—but no less powerfully—in a rhetorical fashion that blends two stock motifs of Romantic thinking: first, that of glorifying common Russians as bearers of a national essence; and second, that of envisioning a woman as the embodiment of the national ideal.[92] Russian Romantic writers and philosophers fervidly contrasted the intelligentsia, as a Westernized, urbanized, inwardly divided male force, against a genuinely Russian, pastoral, "whole" female counterforce.[93] Writer and historian Aleksei Makushinskii has mapped the conceptual poles that this discursive tradition contrasts as follows:

MASCULINE	FEMININE
city	country (earth)
Petersburg	Russia
intellect	soul
reflection	intuition
reason	faith
dichotomy	wholeness
European	autochthonous
culture	nature
educated class	people
groundlessness	rootedness[94]

Needless to say, the components of each of the two separate lists blurred conceptually in the nineteenth-century mind. To some extent, the city at the time *was* masculine, and Russia *equaled* intuition.

My own studies of nineteenth-century intellectual culture suggest that Makushinskii's list should be supplemented with at least one additional pair:

hypocrisy	sincerity[95]

To understand why, one need only remember the classic Russian novel. From *Eugene Onegin* to *Fathers and Sons,* the classics of Russian prose display a formulaic structure, revolving around an amorous clash between a self-centered, overcivilized, Westernized hero, and a hyper-Russian heroine, who identifies with "the people" and is outspokenly spontaneous and sincere.[96] In Turgenev's novels, for example, readers stumble over the many conspicuously Russian heroines who possess a "sincere and rightful face" "Faust", a "sincere soul" (*Rudin*), or a "sincere expression" *and* the innocence of a "sincere child" (*Asia*).[97] In contrast, the Hamletesque heroes whom these honest creatures meet suffer from an excessively developed self-consciousness; *in*sincerity is their proverbial middle name.[98] "What you consider sincere"—thus the programmatic Turgenevian hero Rudin is criticized—"to us feels obtrusive and immodest . . . how are we supposed to understand you!"[99]

The emotional regime of Turgenev's world was common to, but not restricted to, literary production of the mid- to late nineteenth century. Historian Iuliia Safronova has shown that a similar regime underpinned public debates following Tsar Alexander II's murder. In these debates, a sincere Russian *narod* was opposed by an insincere cultural elite. Just as English nationalism opposed "what is English-sincere-good" against "what is Frenchified-insincere-corrupt," the participants of this debate consistently contrasted "what is Russian-sincere-good" with "what is Western(ized)-hypocritical-wrong."[100]

The debates over the tsar's murder and the sociopolitical metaphors of the Russian novel have much in common. Both partly reiterated traditional nationalist discourse—but both also differed from classic nationalist rhetoric in one crucial respect. Where nationalists typically identified with the "good" pole, Russian intellectuals increasingly represented their *own* social stratum (as well as that of the authorities) at the insincere end of the spectrum. Their intellectual discourse was one of guilt and critical introspection: it revolved around notions of social powerlessness, and of a failed responsibility on the part of the nobility and intelligentsia toward "the people."[101] In this discourse, intellectuals dislocated sincerity from themselves. More than nationalists, who often personally identified with their sincere ideals, they located sincerity exclusively outside the self, in the stereotypical Other—whether that was a woman, an idealized Russian people, or a blend of both.

The late eighteenth- and nineteenth-century Russian intellectual elite, put plainly, was convinced of its own hypocrisy. Not surprisingly, Russian *intelligenty* embraced the Romantic habit of problematizing sincerity. They inquired, first, how one should test an artist's sincerity in a commercialized creative world.[102] As we have seen, this question haunted cultural audiences elsewhere, too, at the time, in direct response to literary and artistic professionalization. Within Russia, sincerity doubts already emerged as a leitmotif in the reception of the country's best-known classicist poet: Gavriil Derzhavin. Literary historian Joachim Klein has analyzed how the famous composer of court odes repeatedly felt forced to respond to accusations of political flattery. He did so by insisting "obsessively . . . on the factual truth of his panegyric poems and the purity of his personal motives."[103] In doing so—so Klein argues—Derzhavin followed an Enlightenment-era "cult of sincerity," fueled by the writings of the Spanish Jesuit and philosopher Gracián. The latter's ethical manuals subtly assessed the behavioral norms of court life, advising readers to refrain from "pass[ing] for a Hypocrite, though such men are indispensable nowadays. Be considered prudent rather than astute. Sincerity in behavior pleases all, though not all can show it in their own affairs. Sincerity should not degenerate into simplicity nor sagacity into cunning. Rather be respected as wise than feared as sly."[104]

Gracián's views on public self-fashioning attracted an active following in Russia, and Derzhavin was a fan.[105] In his odes and metapoetic comments, the poet embraced a sincerity that exudes social and pragmatic anxiety. How—one might summarize his repeated concern—could a poet express wisdom and truth without falsely flattering his addressee? Derzhavin's heightened interest in this question was not fortuitous, argues Klein. Amid an ever-burgeoning interdependency between literary and court life and increasing literary commodification, late eighteenth-century (laudatory) poets are haunted by public distrust—a distrust that prefigures the suspicion thrust upon a writer such as Sorokin today. Contemporaries worried: could it be that writers, too, like all people, strive for commercial or social gain?

In Russia fears for artistic pragmatism are not exclusive to Derzhavin's life and work. They can be distilled from metaliterary and meta-artistic discourse throughout the nineteenth century, culminating in 1896 in an essay that I have already mentioned here: Tolstoy's "What Is Art?" Its author fiercely criticized the "calculating art" of his time. In his view, "as soon as art turned into a profession, it weakened substantially and the most important and valuable dimension of art— its sincerity—was partly destroyed."[106]

Apart from concerns about selling out, from Romanticism onward Russian intellectuals harbored more ontological worries about artistic honesty. With the same perseverance as their non-Russian colleagues, they pondered the question whether one can be sincere at all. Isn't the very idea of sincere self-expression—the conviction that a person can candidly convey private feelings to others—an illusion? Not by chance did the poet Fedor Tiutchev—as early as 1830, in his famous short poem "Silentium!"—propose total outward silence as the only proper strategy for dealing with intense inner feelings.[107]

Tiutchev problematized honest self-disclosure—but his poetry paid no special attention to the term "sincerity." That process, of problematizing the very concept of iskrennost', or sincerity, set in motion gradually.

In the first half of the century Russia's most famous writer—Aleksandr Pushkin—foregrounded the Romantic conundrum of a split between intimate feelings and outward appearance, but for him the *word* "sincerity" was not yet a troubled notion. Like Tiutchev, Pushkin employed the term relatively sparsely, and primarily in its conventional, positive meaning.[108] The word *iskrennost'* played no lead role either in the key novel of Russian Romanticism, Mikhail Lermontov's *Hero of Our Time* (*Geroi nashego vremeni*, 1839–41). Lermontov uses the term only twice, although, contrary to Pushkin, he does start utilizing it in more problematic settings. When the narrator introduces a set of excerpts from Pechorin's diary—the cynical upper-class hero whose writings form the book's core story—he explains: "Having re-read these notes, I am convinced of the sincerity of the one who exposed his own weaknesses and vices. Isn't the history of the human soul, even if of its very basest example, almost more curious and helpful than the history of an entire people, especially when it results from the self-observations of a ripe mind and when it is written without any vain wish to arouse empathy or surprise?"[109]

In this fragment, Lermontov takes the word "sincerity" to manifestly dark spheres. Pechorin is described elsewhere as "a portrait built up of all our generation's vices in full bloom"[110]—so for the "hero of our time," sincerity stands for truthfulness to a vexingly ugly, vain self. To Lermontov, ugly selves also thrive among Romantics outside Russia: he accuses even the French father of sincere rhetoric, Rousseau, of vainness.[111]

Lermontov, Tiutchev, and Pushkin, as I said, problematize sincerity—but they fostered no noteworthy interest in the *word* "sincerity." In the second half of the century, an infatuation with that particular term did start to haunt Russian writers. Iskrennost' then becomes a central term in a variety of discursive settings. The word is pivotal to the work of Russian radicals and nihilists, of which we saw a sample above; but also, for instance, to poet and critic Apollon Grigoriev and his essay "On Truth and Sincerity in Art" ("O pravde i iskrennosti v iskusstve," 1856). In this short text—which interrogates the link between art, ethics, and self-revelation—the word "iskrennost'" (including its adjectival and adverbial derivations) occurs thirty-eight times.

Like Pushkin and Tiutchev, Grigoriev used the concept of iskrennost' as a positive ideal—something that was "somewhere out there" and that an artist should strive for. Sincerity played an equally central but substantially less positive role somewhat later, in the work of Dostoevsky. Statistical dictionaries indicate that throughout his oeuvre, this leading name in Russian psychological realism resorted to the noun iskrennost' on 104 occasions; its adjectival and adverbial forms he employed nearly eight hundred times.[112] As his career went on, he turned to the term with increasing frequency.[113] Unlike predecessors, however, Dostoevsky framed the concept as an emotional category that was as momentous as it was untrustworthy. In especially his later fiction, he represents iskrennost' as a fundamentally unstable mental category.[114] In the human world, Dostoevsky asks with increasing skepticism, is sincere self-revelation something that can exist in the first place? In the novel *Demons* (*Besy*, 1872), sincerity acts as the proverbial greener grass on the other side: sincere is something this novel's characters *want* to or *claim* to be—but, in truth, they never are. When Petr Verkhovenskii tries to explain why he unexpectedly opens up to the novel's protagonist Nikolai Stavrogin, his explanation resembles a pointless mantra: this particularly unreliable nihilist repeats five times that he "seriously" means to do well—and, he adds twice, to act "sincerely."[115]

To Dostoevsky, in short, the existence of such a thing as iskrennost' is not a self-evident given. With his critical approach to the notion, we have arrived at the end of the nineteenth century. By this time the term "sincerity"—in Russia no less, if not more, than elsewhere—has acquired a prominent discursive position. Over the course of the century, as we have seen, the concept was used to project (nationalist, nihilist, radical, and/or artistic and literary) ideals onto Russia or "the Russian people"; it played a leading role in debates over artistic integrity, commodification, urbanization, and technological sophistication; and with time, its very existence was questioned. These sincerity concerns of the nineteenth century matter much to my story: they still make themselves felt in our own age's preoccupation with sincerity and memory, marketing, and media. Before we turn to this age, however, let us explore the era that followed after the nineteenth century. The sincerity anxieties of Dostoevsky, Tolstoy, and others were then taken on board in a series of fierce public discussions on society, selfhood, and truthfulness.

EARLY TWENTIETH-CENTURY (WESTERN AND EASTERN) EUROPE: "WHAT IS SINCERITY?"

Dostoevsky's Verkhovenskii preluded the late nineteenth and early twentieth centuries, when creative professionals across Europe were, in Trilling's words, preoccupied primarily "with the self" and, perhaps most important, "with the difficulties of being true to it."[116]

And how could they not? After all, the turn of the century was a time when, to cite historian Anna Fishzon, "the growth of media such as advertising and journalism . . . fostered the belief that language and images are constantly manipulated, throwing into question the locus of genuineness."[117] Early twentieth-century citizens found themselves in a world of increasing technological complexity—one where photography, film, and mechanized music technologies shook up existing views on the powers of realistic representation. The best-known contribution to these discussions was undoubtedly Walter Benjamin's essay "The Work of Art in the Age of Mechanical Reproduction" (1936). According to Benjamin, reproduction techniques sustain a world where people are surrounded by objects of art that lack the unique "aura" of the original. Benjamin used his essay to make a claim that is as bold as it has become famous: to him, "the sphere of authenticity" resides principally "outside technical . . . reproducibility."[118]

Reproduction technologies contributed to the emergence of a celebrity culture—one in which stories and images of public celebrities abounded, and which spawned heated debates on commercial success, authentic self-revelation, and "the disintegration of the self."[119] "Is artist X or Y sincere or is she or he driven by the sheer desire for mass sellings?" was a question that was posed eagerly at the time—particularly so in Russia, where the early twentieth century coincided with the emergence of a professional local consumer industry.[120]

Not surprisingly, sincerity anxieties were formative to contemporary views on language, art, architecture, and design. Malevich's black square, Mondrian's lozenge paintings, Le Corbusier's austere villas: all sprang from a fierce avant-garde desire to "produce sincerity," in the words of the renowned Russian art historian Boris Groys. "The modernist production of sincerity," to Groys, "functioned as a reduction of design, in which the goal was to create a blank, void space at the center of the design world, to eliminate design, to practice zero-design. In this way, the artistic avant-garde wanted to create design-free areas that would be perceived as areas of honesty, high morality, sincerity, and trust."[121]

It is not hard to see how the longing to move away from design interconnects with the drastic technological innovations of the time. Where standardized technologies now increasingly invaded daily life, art producers and consumers fiercely upheld the nonautomatized and the nondesigned as hallmarks of human sincerity. What this conceptual blending of the nontechnological with sincerity looked like in practice was nicely illustrated by public responses to Russia's newly born recording industry. The emergence of a mechanized record industry triggered a "discourse of sonic fidelity" whose participants persistently pondered over one question: did or did not performer so-and-so manage to transfer genuine musical pathos to recordings? In the words of Fishzon, in late imperial Russia "record reviews . . . often slid into judgment of a performer's ability to vocally convey pathos in a 'nuanced' and 'sincere' manner. Interrogating the recorded voice in an attempt to judge its approximation of live performance and emotional truth, these texts shared with celebrity narratives concerns and questions about affect, realism, and presence."[122]

In response to the demand for sincere expression in an increasingly automatized and mediatized world, record manufacturers acted not unlike the book publishers who mimicked handwritten fonts in early modern printing. They reduced surface noise and other acoustic distortions as much as possible, all in order to produce "records that did not sound mediated."[123]

Zero design was one expression of avant-gardists' longing for a nonautomatized sincerity; another was the contemporary preference for *imperfect* design. To the avant-garde artist, pseudo-clumsy or primitivist looks served as a token of sincere human creation. The linguistic and visual experiments of Futurist writers and artists are a case in point. Take the invented language of *zaum*—literally "transreason"—of Russian poets Velimir Khlebnikov and Aleksei Kruchenykh. The latter hailed zaum as an "organically, and not artificially," born language, whose very strength resided in its semantic indeterminacy—that is, in the fact that its words lacked clear meaning.[124] Or take the book designs that the Russian Futurist artist Nataliia Goncharova created for Kruchenykh and others (figures 1.1 and 1.2): these boasted a consciously

FIGURE 1.1 Book cover with quasi-amateurist sketch and fonts for collections of poems by the poets Kruchenykh and Khlebnikov, designed by Natalia Goncharova in 1912. Image courtesy of the Getty Research Institute, Los Angeles.

wonky design and semihandcrafted presentation. No matter how much these objects relied on and celebrated new printing technologies, at the same time their makers aimed at a nonpolished, "sincere" effect in the face of technological perfection.

The Futurists were, at the time, far from alone in linking sincerity with a move away from artificial or technological perfection. As contemporary record producers were busily eliminating surface noises, Theodor Adorno pleaded for a diametrically opposing musical strategy. In a 1927 essay he claimed—as rephrased by Fishzon—that it is "the residue of incidental noises and other imperfections" that "paradoxically, make the recordings sound human."[125] In a similar search for the nonpolished, jazz musicians now professed a style that music historian Ted Gioia has labeled an "aesthetics of imperfection"—one that leaves

FIGURE 1.2 Book cover with a deliberately non-
polished look for collections of poems by the poet
Kruchenykh, designed by Mikhail Larionov in 1912.
Image courtesy of the Getty Research Institute.

technical perfection for what it is and focuses on the "human element
in art."[126] Precisely this rhetoric habit, of reading imperfection as a
hallmark for artistic or human sincerity in the face of technological
sophistication, is embraced by new-media commentators today.

In fin de siècle culture, problems of selfhood and individual expression thus puzzled experts in design, art, and music. They also attracted the attention of professionals in other fields. Literary authors, for
instance, foregrounded sincerity anxieties in psychological writings and
in the popular press. The tensions between the conformist laws of civil
society and the individual's primitive instincts were at the heart of Sigmund Freud's study *Civilization and Its Discontents* (1929, published

1930)—although Freud did not employ a vocabulary of sincerity and hypocrisy to explain them. Sincerity also figured prominently in the writings of Oscar Wilde, who had famously stated earlier, in 1891: "A little sincerity is a dangerous thing, and a great deal of it is absolutely fatal."[127] Around the same time, Wilde put similarly provocative views on the concept in the mouth of his egregiously corrupt hero Dorian Gray (he joyously muses: "Is insincerity such a terrible thing? I think not. It is merely a method by which we can multiply our personalities").[128]

Wilde's nontrivial take on sincerity inspired numerous writers in the decades that followed. The Portuguese poet Fernando Pessoa tangibly echoed it when he confessed, in 1931:

> I want to be free and insincere,
> Without belief or duty of place.
> Even love I do not want: it attaches.
> Do not love me: that is what I hate.[129]

Pessoa is one among many self-professed Wilde adepts, and Wilde's views on self-revelation have done much to shape contemporary sincerity rhetoric. What matters to my argument is especially the impact of his take on sincerity as a strategic "method" on stardom and mediatization discourses —discourses that are formative to the reception of post-Soviet authors.

Wilde expressed his defiance of sincere expression in an artistic motif whose prominence in early twentieth-century culture can hardly be overrated: that of the mask which blocks "open" expression.[130] Wilde himself explicitly favored masks over human faces—and art over life— in "The Truth of Masks," published in 1891. "A Truth in art," so he concluded this influential essay, "is that whose contradictory is also true"; in other words, "the truths of metaphysics are the truths of masks."[131]

Slavonic scholar Irene Masing-Delic, who analyzed mask motifs in Aleksandr Blok's poetry, observed a similar infatuation with masquerading in early twentieth-century Russia. In her words, the mask was "a convenient symbol of [Russian Symbolist writers'] *Weltanschauung*. . . . The mask itself represented the apparent (the flat perspective), but through the slits of the mask . . . one could see or perhaps only suspect, the 'real' (the deep perspective). The mask is thus deceptive—'truth' is what it hides."[132] Russian Symbolists indeed highlighted a Platoesque split between the seeming and the real, although they did so without fore-grounding sincerity rhetoric. The Symbolist Blok, for one, seldom used the word in his poems.[133]

In early twentieth-century Russia, however, the Symbolists shared their love for masks and veils with many others. The "rich array of practices of masking and unmasking"[134] in early Soviet discourse—to which we return in a moment—is a case in point; and so are Russia's so-called religious-Renaissance thinkers. This loose collective of spiritually oriented philosophers and thinkers shared an intense focus not only on unveiling truths but also specifically on the notion of iskrennost'.[135] Philosopher Ivan Il'in's essay "On Sincerity" ("Ob iskrennosti," first published 1943) was wholly committed to defining the term and to explaining how one should evade hypocrisy;[136] and the problematic status of the concept in contemporary society was a major concern to the philosopher Nikolai Berdiaev. He claimed that his "philosophical autobiography" Self-Knowledge (Samopoznanie, first published 1949) was devoted entirely to "the problem of sincerity" and its historical development.[137] In a critical response to Rousseau, Berdiaev explained: "My theme is entirely different [from that of the Confessions], and in relation to this theme the problem of sincerity is posed in a different way. . . . [T]his is not a book of confessions, this is a book of comprehension, of knowledge of the meaning of life. I sometimes think that I could call this book Dream and Reality, because that is what defines something fundamental for me and my life, its basic conflict, the conflict with the world, related to the strong power of imagination, of evoking visions of another world."[138]

Berdiaev points to a relevant semantic transition. Early twentieth-century Russian thinkers and writers continued the Romantic tradition of problematizing sincerity—but their terminological frameworks differed from those used by their predecessors. As the quote from Berdiaev illustrates, they inherited nineteenth-century writers' binary logic, but they were concerned with the discrepancies between a "real" and a "dream" world rather than an inner versus an outer self. They thus neatly blended sincerity rhetoric into larger thematic preoccupations of the time—selfhood, truthfulness, and duality.

So far we have seen that the fin de siècle was an age of infatuations with "artificial" technologies, "badly designed" sincerity, and masks, veils, and dreams. It was also a period of continuing attributions of sincerity to specific social groups. In the work of such modernist writers as Virginia Woolf and Marcel Proust, the urban upper classes consistently adopt a troubled stance to sincere expression. The same writers just as persistently projected sincerity onto the domain of the poor and (geographically and socially) peripheral.[139] Characteristically, another famous name in modernist literature—the well-heeled heroine of Louis Couperus's novel *Eline Vere* (1889)—briefly finds undiluted "sincerity" in an idyllic country estate, but she ultimately collapses under the weight of an urban society life that "was one ongoing dissimulation!"[140]

Couperus contrasted urban high society and pastoral life as the ultimate sociospatial incarnations of hypocrisy and sincerity. To Ivan Il'in, hypocrisy and sincerity resided in two alternative sociospatial categories. In his essay "Against Russia" ("Protiv Russia"), Il'in contrasted "the average European," a person "ashamed of sincerity," with "the Russian man" and his inclination to expect "from people first of all . . . sincerity."[141] Il'in's views on a nationally defined iskrennost' were first published as late as 1948, in Germany; but they were emblematic for a broader neo-Slavophile trend toward—again!—presenting Russia (or the Russian people) and the West (or a Westernized Russian state and intelligentsia) as sincere versus insincere.

So far, in this overview of early twentieth-century sincerity talk I blend Russian with non-Russian examples—but with the consolidation of Bolshevik power, Russian sincerity rhetoric took an idiosyncratic turn. With the advent of a new regime, the gulf between the intellectual elite and "the common man" was officially proclaimed dissolved, and public attention shifted to a new million-dollar question: does citizen X or Y genuinely support the party ideology? Historian Sheila Fitzpatrick has shown how anxieties related to role-playing and performance—to sincere versus false self-representation—permeated early Soviet discourse, which revolved around notions of "unmasking" (*razoblachit'*) and defying "double identities" (*dvulichie, dvurushnichestvo*).[142] Her colleague Alexey Tikhomirov points in a similar direction when he claims that "the interplay of trust and distrust is the key to understanding the Soviet state's stability and its vital energy."[143] Tikhomirov sees in Soviet politics a "regime of forced trust," "based on simultaneously satisfying the basic human need for trust—in order to generate faith in the central power (above all, the leaders of state and party)—and maintaining a high level of generalized distrust."[144]

In Tikhomirov's "regime of forced trust," the question who was sincere and who not could clearly be of life-shaping importance, but the term "sincerity" is a pivotal concept neither in his nor in Fitzpatrick's analyses. Another expert on Soviet-era identity—historian Igal Halfin—does point out that at the time, specifically this notion turns into "a Communist obsession."[145] To be more precise, Halfin singles out sincerity as an "ultimate touchstone" for party-member autobiographies.[146] In his view, Soviet-era autobiographical testimonies exhibit—not unlike the court cases in revolutionary-era France—a strongly ceremonial dimension. "Normally considered one of the more private genres," Halfin writes, "autobiography became public because of the nature of the application process. Autobiographical interrogation was a ritualized procedure designed to evaluate the consciousness of the applicant. A certain presentation of the self could always be 'unmasked' and rejected as 'phony' (nepravdivaia)."[147] As described by Halfin, the Soviet interrogator to some extent echoed the eighteenth-century French revolutionary: both branded insincerity as a formal felony.

A similar preoccupation with formalizing and measuring sincerity underlay the socialist-realist doctrine. If, in the 1920s, members of the Russian Association of Proletarian Writers (RAPP) were highly critical of the term—in their words, "the slogan of 'sincerity' is the first mask of bourgeois liberalism"[148]—then it was in full demand again once socialist realism was introduced in the 1930s. This style's primary goal consisted of assessing: are our artists sincerely dedicated to official ideology? Not coincidentally, the newspaper that first articulated socialist realism's main tenets stressed how "the masses demand from artists *sincerity*, truthfulness, [and] revolutionary socialist realism in their representation of the proletarian revolution" (my italics).[149]

Sincerity thus complemented a wider complex of positive emotions used, as a recent study of Soviet Russia's emotional regime has it, to "cement the system."[150] Paradoxically but inevitably—in the words of literary historian Irina Paperno—the same sincerity-promoting system spawned "an emotional economy of duplicity, deception, and ambiguity (promoted by the need to hide one's thoughts and feelings and to con-

ceal one's parentage, ethnicity, and partnerships, or to form new loyal-
ties, identities, and partnerships without forsaking old ones)."[151]

In short, while the Soviet authorities advocated full-blown sincerity,
deceiving and hiding private emotions soon became second nature to
their citizens. This trend of duplicity did not mean that the regime
merely bred passive victims of top-down emotive regulation. Nor was
socialist realism as monolithic as some studies want us to believe. Scholars of Soviet-era literary journals, diaries, and personal documents have
convincingly demonstrated that moderate critics actively plead for more
"lyricism," "authenticity," and "sincerity" in socialist-realist literature in
the late 1930s;[152] and they have cogently proven that Soviet citizens did
not simply hide a politically subversive "true self" behind an ideologically loyal "public performance," as traditional studies of Soviet selfhood suggest.[153] In truth, commoners actively partook in Communist
self-fashioning. Whether citizens were sincere in their support for the
party ideology: this question was often no less of a concern to these citizens themselves than to the party at large. Both these personal and party-
level anxieties played a major role in the history that I am tracing here: in
the chapters that follow, we shall see how Soviet-era sincerity figurations
have remained a yardstick for contemporary Russian thinking about the
concept.

Taken together, the "travels" of the notion of sincerity in the early
twentieth century make for a turbulent ride. From the problematization
of the term in the "sincerity writings" of Wilde and others to the socialist-
realist insistence on sincerity, from Russian philosophers' infatuation
with mask motifs to avant-gardists' longing for imperfection as a token
of sincere human expression: this period was a time of ambivalent sincerity desires and concerns. Contemporaries longed at the same time
to be sincere *and*—in an age of intensifying mediatization, celebrification, commodification, and technological sophistication—to accept the
impossibility of that same wish. With time, this need to desist from
straightforward sincerity desires would only increase.

AFTER WORLD WAR II: DISCOMFORT, DECONSTRUCTION, DIGITIZATION

While becoming a gauge of correct living for Soviet citizens in Russia, in
mid-twentieth-century Western Europe and the United States sincerity

flared up as a concern for cultural critics. It did so especially after World War II. The relationship between (literary) sincerity and commerce then once again attracted heightened attention—attention that, as before, coincided with drastic institutional changes. Susan Rosenbaum analyzes how a cult of sincerity in the postwar United States interlinked directly with the rise of universities as patrons of poetry, the emergence of large publishing houses, and a heightened literary-celebrity cult.[154]

From the late 1950s onward, sincerity also became a ubiquitous term in humanist criticism. As in sentimentalism, the concept once again found itself in a rhetoric that foregrounded emancipatory and liberatory ideologies. In this time of renewed interest in Romanticism and its emancipatory bias, of feminism, neo-Marxism, antiracist activism, flower power, antiestablishment ideologies, intensified secularization, and beat culture, libraries were flooded with studies of literary sincerity, cultural histories of sincerity, and essays that asked what the term meant to contemporary culture.[155] Henri Peyre's wish, in his 1963 history of the concept, to establish "what literary sincerity should be, can be, and is,"[156] was programmatic.

As in earlier periods that foregrounded sincerity rhetorics, in the 1960s the concept was scrutinized with suspicion. As early as 1943, this highly critical definition of sincerity was anticipated by Jean-Paul Sartre. In the book-length essay *Being and Nothingness*, he explained the workings of the notion as follows: "A person appeals to another and demands that in the name of his nature as consciousness he should radically destroy himself as consciousness, but while making this appeal he leads the other to hope for a rebirth beyond this destruction. . . . Thus the essential structure of sincerity does not differ from that of bad faith. . . . Total, constant sincerity as a constant effort to adhere to oneself is by nature a constant effort to dissociate oneself from oneself."[157]

"Total sincerity," "bad faith": writing in the thick of World War II, Sartre presented sincerity as a contradictory and potentially damaging demand. The distrustful view on sincerity that his interpretation exuded intensified in the postwar era. "If we speak it, we are likely to do so with either discomfort or irony": thus Trilling voiced a much-heard concern of the time in 1970.[158] By then, sincerity suspicions were emerging not only in philosophical treatises. In the same period they permeated speech act theory, with its disavowal of the thought that words have a fixed meaning. In 1984 Jürgen Habermas famously argued that "claims to sincerity [*Wahrhaftigkeitsansprüche*] . . . can . . . be validated in actions," but not redeemed through interrogation—that hobby horse of the Soviet authorities—or other discursive procedures.[159] More than twenty years earlier, sociologist Erving Goffman had pointed in a similar direction while studying the performative aspects of human interaction. In his words, the borders between "cynical" performance—by one who "has no belief in his own act and no ultimate concern with the beliefs of his audience"—and "sincere" expression—by individuals who "believe in the impression fostered by their own performance"—are diffuse, to say the least.[160]

With the advent of postmodernism and its various linguistic and performative turns, yet more skeptical readings of sincerity entered public debate. The relatively stable mental concept that sincerity still was for speech act theorists—who accepted the notion of an autonomous sincere self—now made way for deconstructionist interpretations. To postmodern thinkers sincerity, like other philosophical notions, was, first of all, a cultural construct.[161] Such theorists as Judith Butler, Jacques Derrida, Michel Foucault, and Roland Barthes were convinced—and fervidly convinced others—that there is no such thing as a stable or transparent self. They problematized notions of "self-presence," "truth" (and the related notion of parrhesia), and "the 'I,' " and argued that the social demand to be true to oneself is unethical: if the language that we use is culturally constructed rather than neutral, attempts to give an account of oneself are by default "partial and failed."[162]

Postmodern takes on selfhood and subjectivity sit uneasily—and that is putting things mildly—with straightforward sincerity rhetoric. Barthes has gone so far as to claim that "one cannot write without burying 'sincerity' ";[163] and cultural theorist Efrat Tseëlon states that in a postmodern world—one "where appearances do not mask reality but *are* reality"—"sincerity as congruence between the private self and the public self is meaningless."[164] My chapters 2, 3, and 4 illustrate that the public impact of these and related postmodern readings of sincerity is hard to overestimate. Their lessons are taken home by psychologists and philosophers, who today claim that "there is no thing like 'the self' "[165] and who exchange discourse about a fixed "self" for talk about "self-experience" and "self-positions" that can be synthesized.[166] Postmodern sincerity logic is a point of departure for such historians as Geoffrey Hosking—the author of *Truth: A History*—who analyze and historically contextualize a "crisis of trust" in contemporary society and politics.[167] But postmodern insights have been incorporated, too, by the social stratum that is central to my argument. For today's creative professionals, postmodern discourse has radically undercut the possibility to treat the self as a fixed category—or a category that exists in the first place.

As postmodern deconstruction thrived, cultural critics started interrogating the view of art as a vehicle for undiluted self-revelation with increasing mistrust. In the 1960s and 1970s, conceptualists, pop art practitioners, and punks all searched for what one critic called a "refuge of authenticity [in] a low-fi, amateurish mode of production."[168] Many a creative pioneer of this age envisioned artistic sincerity exclusively in a quasi-homemade or amateur aesthetics—one that could be created by using deliberately sloppy technology or by working with nonprofessional performers. "Scars of damage and disruption are the modern's seal of authenticity": this was how Theodor Adorno voiced his age's aesthetic credo in the 1960s.[169] A decade later, Andy Warhol would go yet one step further. "No matter what a bad performer tries to do, it can't be phony": with these words he explained why, for him, aesthetic imperfection harbors artistic sincerity.[170] In his work and public self-fashioning Warhol consistently glorified artificiality, camp, and commodification. "Being good in business is the most fascinating kind of art," says one iconic Warhol wisdom; "I love plastic idols," another.[171] The artist knew how to provoke: here and elsewhere, he cherished precisely those domains (the commercial, the nonnatural) that traditionally rank both as emblems of bad taste *and* as diametric opposites of artistic sincerity.

The pop art infatuation with amateurism demonstrates how, for post–World War II artists, sincerity anxieties were at the same time very much alive and a constant object of dispute. Not surprisingly, around the same time that Warhol was promoting plastic and bad performance, Pierre Bourdieu gained fame with his take on the art world as a field of competing social forces. By the mid-1990s, every self-respecting intellectual across *and* beyond Europe was busy mastering this French sociologist's theory of symbolic and economic success. By implication, the possibility of artistic sincerity became an object of ongoing theoretical debate. With time, this debate entered into a consensus that American writer David Foster Wallace summarized this way: "There is, in writing, a certain blend of sincerity and manipulation, of trying always to gauge what the particular effect of something is gonna be."[172]

Wallace's pragmatic take on sincerity is not unprecedented: remember how Paul Verlaine insisted that he merely employed sincerity to reach a larger audience, and how Wilde discussed sincerity as a strategic artistic method. What *is* new is the extent to which Wallace's ideas are, today, commonly accepted. "In our days," said Boris Groys in 2008, "the romantic image of the *poète maudit* is substituted by that of the artist as being explicitly cynical—greedy, manipulative, business-oriented, seeking only material profit, and implementing art as a machine for deceiving the audience."[173] Our world, argues Groys, has grown accustomed to expecting that artists have a pragmatic agenda. In this world, artists who adopt the traditional image of lonely genius have a problem: today, it is outright pragmatism that is read as the most sincere pose.

As Verlaine and Warhol did before him, today an artist like Damien Hirst maximally exploits the pose that Groys outlines: that of the emphatically commercial "business-artist." Among other provocative gestures, Hirst has chosen to sell a complete show to Sotheby's, and to re-create a human skull in platinum and adorn it with diamonds worth 17.5 million euros. In the summer of 2007, *For the Love of God,* as the sculpture is called, was sold to an investment group for fifty million pounds sterling. Not surprisingly, critics often muse: Is Hirst only in it for the money? Or are his money-driven practices, and their shameless exhibition of the basest pragmatic mechanisms of art, an act of ultimate self-revelation?[174]

The road from Trilling to Hirst may seem long at first glance—but what they and many of the other postwar-era voices share is a fundamentally more skeptical approach to artistic candor than that of their predecessors. Between the mid-1940s and today, what artists and their critics have increasingly openly embraced is diffusion, plastic, imperfection, and commerce. Despite individual idiosyncrasies, their joint philosophy can be summarized as follows: if anywhere, it is in these unexpected domains that sincerity resides above all.

NEW, POST, POST-POST: SINCERITY TODAY

With Damien Hirst we have unambiguously arrived in the here and now. As the controversy around the British artist demonstrates, the

Bourdieuesque-cum-postmodern view of sincerity is today alive and kicking: by the mid-2010s, sincerity is a concept that only the lazy fail to approach with skepticism.

At the same time, the notion of sincerity has today traveled into new spheres. From the mid-1980s onward, the concept starts being fore-grounded in the post-postmodern and late postmodern discourse that interests me in this book. Visions of a new sincerity have circulated in-creasingly in discussions of novel trends in music, literature, film, new media, and the visual arts.[175] By the early 2000s, genres that rely on discourses of personal confession and sincerity began to hold sway—whether the talk show, the weblog, the memoir, or autobiography;[176] and toward the late 2000s, sincerity gained the renewed attention of leading philosophers and cultural and political theorists. Experts believe that it could "help us conceptualize what are today termed as fundamentalist movements" (Adam Seligman, Robert Weller, Michael Puett, and Bennett Simon);[177] or that it could be instrumental in "claiming" a contemporary "ethos of reason and argument" (Amanda Anderson).[178]

The above might imply that fixations on sincerity are today primar-ily a highbrow affair—but the opposite is true. With time, discussions on a reborn sincerity are increasingly firmly rooted in mainstream pub-lic debate. In fact, today especially Anglophone music fans, bloggers, and amateur poets appropriate the phrase "new sincerity"—in texts that employ it like a slogan rather than a full-fledged theoretical paradigm—for a dazzling variety of cultural practices. The expression is used in such wide-ranging contexts that, in November 2005, Californian writer Alex Blagg mockingly asked his blog readers to nominate "things you think might be considered New Sincerity." Blagg set the ball rolling with the following "official additions to the New Sincerity Movement": "Best Friends, High Fives, Lemonade Stands, Ron Popeil, Arena Football, Forts, Catapults, Retarded People, Hammer, Dodgeball, Camping Trips, Big League Chew, Backpacks, Andrew WK, Astronauts, Tenacious D."[179]

Blagg may take the current infatuation with new-sincerity rhetoric into absurd spheres—but he correctly diagnoses its near-compulsive ubiquity. Apart from numerous blog posts and literary-critical texts, by the early 2010s the Anglophone slogans "Neo-Sincerity," "New Sincer-ity," and "Cult of Sincerity" had figured in the titles of five recent and/or planned art exhibitions, two films, one book, one T-shirt design, and one punk-rock band.[180] Illustrative, too, is the public resonance of Christy Wampole's *New York Times* article. As I explained in my Introduction, Wampole's plea to exchange ironic social forms for a "cultivation of sincerity" spawned some 750 blog comments and more than 400 e-mails to the author.[181]

Today's almost maniacal interest in sincerity does not mean that the notion of a revitalized sincerity has remained unchanged over the past two decades. New-sincerity rhetoric first took flight in music, as I explain in detail in the next chapter. In the 1990s, the phrase emerged occasionally in film and literary criticism.[182] By 1999, the notion of a revived sincerity reached the *New York Times*, when contributor Marshall Sella detected a rebirth of "sincerity . . . in a world filled with rogues, punks and Wall Street sharpies."[183] In making his claim, Sella built on a book that some see as America's new sincerity Bible: *For Common Things: Irony, Trust and Commitment in America Today*. With *For Common Things*, the then twenty-four-year-old Yale student of law Jedediah Purdy berated contemporaries for an excessive insistence on irony, and he promoted instead "the qualities that would make us take another person seriously: the integrity of personality, sincere motivation, the idea that opinions are more than symptoms of fear or desire."[184]

The resonance of Purdy's book prefigured a public infatuation with irony and sincerity two years later. "The Age of Irony Comes to an End" and "Attacks on U.S. Challenge Postmodern True Believers": these programmatic predictions headed essays in, respectively, *Time* magazine and the *New York Times*, shortly after the traumatic World Trade Center attacks on September 11, 2001.[185] Not only did they fuel talk of a new sincerity in literature and art, they also gave rise to a neoconservative argument—one in which sincerity once again travels to sociopolitical spheres. Defying the multiculturalism of the 1980s and 1990s as "postmodern relativism," neoconservative sincerity adepts favor a "truthful" but substantially less tolerant political and philosophical outlook.[186]

In the same period, commercial anxieties emerged in reviews that applied the "new sincere" label to films, blogs, or exhibitions that protested against a market-driven cultural economy. Critic Christopher Gray spoke of a "'new sincerity'/anti-corporate movement" in American music launched by Kurt Cobain.[187] Simultaneously, in a diametrically opposed logic, cultural critics started to speculate whether new-sincere writers or artists did not consciously deploy sincerity as a strategic device—one that enhanced their symbolic or material status.[188] *New York Times* journalist Kelefa Sanneh, for instance, discerned an inseparability between sincerity and ambition among indie-music performers in the mid-2000s: "If they believe what they sing, maybe lots of listeners will, too."[189]

In other words, from the early 2000s onward, visions of a revived sincerity were underpinned both by post-traumatic concerns (the 9/11 aftermath) and by commodification rhetoric. In addition, new sincerity discourse today interlinks inextricably with discussions on digitization. In the past several years, new-sincerity rhetoric has been thriving particularly in blogs—and as I demonstrate in chapter 4, the rise of social media has prompted vigorous debates on digitization and sincerity among scholars, critics, and practitioners alike. Some frame the Web as the ultimate locus for sincere expression; others, on the contrary, portray the Internet as sincerity's ugliest enemy. What is more, our post-digital age boasts another topic that we shall explore in chapter 4: this is the growing current interest in deliberate aesthetic rawness, whether in the form of pseudo-wonkily crafted design, quasi-amateur art projects, or homemade food.

POSTWAR RUSSIA: "HOW CAN ONE BE SINCERE?"

Between World War II and today, then, sincerity has been persistently foregrounded in Western European and American critical thinking—whether in Peyre's interest in sincerity as a literary concept in the 1960s or in the "digital native's" desire for sincere craft in the 2000s.

In Russia, during the same period, sincerity has turned into even more of a public hobbyhorse. Here, the concept of iskrennost' has played a lead role in a public debate that kicked off in the 1950s, in the years immediately following Stalin's death. Historian Vladislav Zubok aptly portrays the intellectual elite of this age when he writes that "the most talented and energetic men and women in the postwar generation sought not only to express themselves professionally, in science, mass media, the liberal arts, and so on, but to create a new language of civic culture—a framework of social and moral responsibility, truth and sincerity."[190] Zubok and others mention sincerity as one in a longer list of prime cultural concerns of the age—but it is no overstatement to say that it is precisely the word "iskrennost'" that tops that list.

Whence the public Russian infatuation with specifically this term? In order to answer that question, we need to travel back in time to December 1953. It was then that former police investigator Vladimir Pomerantsev published an essay in the popular journal *Novyi mir* (*New World*), with the title "On Sincerity in Literature" ("Ob iskrennosti v literature"). The essay criticized the "insincerity" and moralistic "preaching" (*propoved'*) of socialist realism; instead, Pomerantsev proposed a literature of sincere "confession" (*ispoved'*).[191] As would later be the case in perestroika-era sincerity rhetoric, cultural memory and trauma were instrumental in Pomerantsev's argument: central to his essay was the view that the preceding Stalinist era was a period of insincerity, and that the search for a renewed sincerity would help in bringing that period to an end.

Pomerantsev's essay did not just call for sincerity on a thematic level: it also gave an unprecedented boost to the use of iskrennost', or sincerity, as an everyday lexical unit. In the text, the term "sincerity" occupies center stage: Pomerantsev uses variations of the word twenty-six times, thirteen of which consist of the noun—which is more emphatic than adjectival/adverbial derivations—and another six of its negative twin, the substantive *neiskrennost'* (insincerity). The noun "iskrennost'" plays the lead role in the title, and it is the term with which the text virtually opens. After a brief introduction, Pomerantsev famously asserts: "Sincerity—that is what, in my opinion, certain books and plays lack. Involuntarily you wonder: how can one be sincere?"[192]

I elaborate on these formal details for a reason: they demonstrate that *this* concept—not related notions such as authenticity and honesty—lies literally at the core of a text that opens the way for critical reflection on the Stalinist era. In the (slightly hyperbolic) wordings of critic Grigorii Svirskii, right after its publication "all thinking circles in Russia were talking about Vladimir Pomerantsev."[193] In leading intellectual forums of the time, his essay provoked fierce debates about artists' right to be sincere—or, to use another term popular at that moment, to avow lyrical "self-expression" (*samovyrazhenie*).[194] Iskrennost' became a prime value in various creative disciplines: literature is one, but in Thaw-era (early 1950s to early 1960s, that is) cinema, too, experts witness a fervent "concern with sincerity and naturalness."[195]

This book is not the first to argue that sincerity played a leading role in debates about coping with the Stalinist legacy. What fewer specialists have highlighted is that, in these debates, the concept of sincerity serves as anything but a word having to do strictly with the emotional and the private. Literary historian Beth Holmgren helpfully points out how private transformed into public when she explains that "the post-Stalin Thaw, which commenced as a public call for emotional sincerity and fresh individual expression, fomented a poetry revival of massive and public proportions."[196] I agree with Holmgren but would like to go further: Thaw-era sincerity rhetoric resides not merely in the *public* but also in the *political* arena in which Aleksandr Radishchev and others had placed it before, and in which it would land again in perestroika-era Russia.

Why am I saying that? First of all, Pomerantsev's initial discussion of the notion was rooted in political dissent: what he was attacking was the hypocrisy of Stalinist politics. His plea for a politically imbued, publicly professed sincerity remained central to the discussions that followed. "But all of this is about politics rather than literature" was how one reader summarized the literary-political fusion that characterized the discussion.[197] Second, Pomerantsev's essay endowed the term "sincerity" not only with political *connotations* but also with concrete political *impact*. Just how tangible this impact was, can be reconstructed from official reviews and reports on the essay.[198] In a decree that mentions Pomerantsev's text, Aleksandr Tvardovskii—the *Novyi mir* editor who had accepted the piece—was dismissed specifically for his "abstract understanding of sincerity."[199] Pomerantsev himself was berated for "prioritizing 'sincerity' over 'the party spirit [*partiinost'*]' "[200] and subjected to a publication ban. In itself, this chain of events—the appearance of a critical literary text, followed by political countermeasures—is, of course, far from unparalleled within Soviet reality. Unique to the Pomerantsev case, however, is the social charge that it loaded onto the word *iskrennost'*. In public discourse of the time, sincerity became a politically charged concept that could have outright legal implications.[201]

As the Thaw era drew to an end, the term preserved its political authority. Historians Petr Vail' and Aleksandr Genis explain in a study of Soviet life in the 1960s that, throughout this decade, sincerity remained "the key word."[202] Just as in the Pomerantsev case and, much earlier, revolutionary France, in the 1960s this central term possessed palpable political and legal powers. In 1961, the Moral Code of the Builder of Communism—a set of twelve moral rules with which each party and

Komsomol member had to comply—was formally implemented. As Vail'
and Genis point out, the Code included not only calls for honesty, consci-
entious labor, and collectivism but also an active "battle with displays of
contrary tendencies. Sincerity was obliged to be aggressive, annihilating
the principle of noninterference—a logical step given the general character of labor and [Soviet] life at large."[203] Sincerity operated in a rigid
emotional regime here—one that openly reprimanded citizens if they
were believed to lack this crucial feeling.

The Soviet regime of obligatory sincerity remained in place until as
late as 1978. In March of that year, the Soviet authorities refused to allow
the foreign staging of an Alfred Schnittke opera. The producers sent a
protest letter to the newspaper *Pravda,* which refused to publish the letter for one formal reason: "We are not convinced of Your sincerity."[204]
In fact, although sincerity rhetoric had enjoyed a Russian status apart
since the late eighteenth century, starting from the mid-1950s the concept of sincerity acquired buzzword status. The question of whether
writers related to Soviet reality without hypocrisy turned into a prime
concern in (metaliterary discussions of) such popular late Soviet literary
genres as Village Prose, confessional prose, youth prose, and silent
lyricism. "Sincerity, personal anxiety, confession": in Mikhail Epstein's
words, these notions epitomize the "moral searchings" that typified
Russian literary life between the 1950s and the 1980s.[205] The same notions were formative to both officially acknowledged and nonconformist
creative culture: a constant tension between irony and sincerity was vital, for instance, to *stiob* aesthetics—a popular parodic aesthetics of late
Soviet nonconformism on which we shall spend more time in the next
chapter.[206]

With late Soviet stiob we end our historical journey and arrive at the
starting point of this book's journey. Leaving Confucian, Renaissance-
era, and the many other historical and transnational rhetoric traditions
that I scrutinized here, we now enter Soviet Russia at the dawn of perestroika. The following pages demonstrate that visions of a new sincerity
then occupied the minds of several influential intellectuals both in and
outside Russia. The previous pages—whose leading voices return in the
next chapters—tell us something else. They teach us that the new sincerity that is so eagerly advocated today is, in many respects, not quite so
spanking new after all.

CHAPTER TWO

"But I Want Sincerity So Badly!"

THE PERESTROIKA YEARS AND ONWARD

WHILE WORKING ON THIS BOOK, I met a Dutch Ph.D. student who was studying Holocaust reworkings in contemporary Jewish-American fiction. According to Joost Krijnen, the "lessons of the Holocaust" underpin both the rise of postmodernism and "something sometimes referred to as 'post-postmodernism,' and . . . the 'new sincerity' in American literature."[1]

Krijnen's research picks up on a persistent trend, of reading (post-) postmodern paradigms as vehicles for coping with cultural trauma. This chapter outlines the genesis and development of that trend as it plays out in contemporary sincerity rhetoric. I start by monitoring the simultaneous emergence of North American and Russian new-sincerity discourses in the 1980s, before focusing on the trauma thread that permeates its Russian pendant from the very beginning. Central to my argument is poet-cum-performer and undisputed classic of recent Russian literature Dmitrii Prigov (1940–2007). Prigov is commonly seen as the spiritual father of a new or post-Communist sincerity in Russian culture. Here I interweave his personal creative story with that of late and post-Soviet sincerity rhetoric. In both, as we shall see, rather than as a private matter, artistic sincerity figures as a sociopolitical tool—one that is instrumental in digesting historical horror.

POST-PUNK AND THE NEW: NEW SINCERITY IN THE 1980S

"The elite reaction to 9/11," according to the American cultural critic Lee Siegel, "was an outburst of long-simmering discontent with the most frivolous aspects of American life"—in other words, a "call for a new sincerity."[2] Siegel's views are in tune with popular musings on the new sincerity. The concept's birth is often situated directly after the harrowing attacks on New York's World Trade Center. In the previous chapter I outlined how, according to a popular argument, the attacks triggered a collective longing to trade irony and cultural relativism in for a return to direct expression. In truth, visions of a reborn, late postmodern or post-ironic sincerity were formulated long before the 9/11 attacks—and they emerged more or less simultaneously in both the United States and Russia. I want to open this chapter by scrutinizing some of their earliest manifestations.

The journey starts in Texas. Here, in 1984, musician-cum-writer Jesse Sublett used the phrase in a pejorative context when he typified new developments in independent Texan rock music as a "New Sincerity."[3] Sublett employed this term to portray a loosely connected set of Austin-based rock bands that were protesting against "ironic" punk rock and New Wave. As rephrased by the bands' best-known historian, cultural theorist Barry Shank, Sublett accused "New Sincere" musicians of "championing 'content' over 'style' by their manner of not changing out of their daily clothing to perform, by their willingness to tune onstage, by their sloppy, unprofessional performances, and by their attempts to deconstruct the distinction between the musicians onstage and the fans in the audience."[4]

What irritated Sublett, in short, was an age-old device. In chapter 1 we saw how Renaissance-era publishers worked with deliberately frowsy fonts to project authenticity into the domain of print, and how early avant-garde artists crafted amateurish-looking books and illustrations in the face of technological perfection. The Texan bands that Sublett calls "New Sincere" share a similar habit: they insist on disorder and imperfection as markers of artistic sincerity in times of increasing technological sophistication.

In chapter 4 we revisit the nexus between sincerity and imperfection. Here we return to the 1980s. In this decade, visions of a post-

postmodern or post-ironic sincerity emerged not only in the United States. In Russia, the early 1980s saw the heyday of "group Mukhomor," a Moscow-based rock band launched in 1979. Mukhomor's initiators were professional artists Sven Gundlakh, Konstantin Zvezdochotov, Aleksei Kamenskii, and Vladimir and Sergei Mironenko—then a group of recent graduates from art college. On an album produced in 1982, the Mukhomor men presented themselves as founders "of New Wave in the USSR," whose "worldwide popularity" was sparked by nothing but "the sincerity of their songs!"[5]

Brief though it is, the Mukhomor citation provides useful insights into thinking on sincerity in 1980s Russia. Recall that in Sublett's musical universe sincerity was diametrically opposed to New Wave music. For the Mukhomor men, it was not: rather than presenting sincerity and New Wave as contrasting poles, they established a link between the two. What is more, the band members revisited (albeit with a wink, as I shall explain below) an ancient tradition: just as nineteenth-century novelists, nihilists, nationalists, and radicals saw Russia as the ultimate hotbed for sincere art, so these musicians now claimed that "sincere New Wave" was blossoming with special vigor in one geopolitical location: Soviet Russia.

In envisioning Russia as an ultimate locus for artistic, especially musical, sincerity, the Mukhomor members were not alone. In the early 1980s, for international audiences Russian rock and New Wave exuded a "heartbreaking sincerity, purity and clarity" (in the words of rock musician and firsthand witness Sergei Zharikov)[6]—one which local artists themselves actively promoted and exported. Their cautiously cultivated sincerity sometimes took on absurd dimensions—or so, at least, suggests an interview with musician Sergei Kuryokhin in a Russian-British talk show in the late 1980s. In a relaxed get-together of Russian and British pop musicians, Kuryokhin—then a cult figure in the Russian art scene—complained that Russian pop music was witnessing an "incredible growth of sincerity, sincerity simply to the level of pathology." Quasi-musing aloud, Kuryokhin asked singer Brian Eno and other talk-show guests: would it not be nice to team Russian music's "pathological sincerity" up with the "pathological sense of computization [kompiutizatsii]" and technological advancement that were now influencing contemporary Western music?[7]

Kuroykhin's question was underpinned by a conviction that is shared by many a defender of sincerity. As we have seen in tracing our topic's history, sincerity gains in social relevance—and is particularly urgently demanded from artists—in times of technological sophistication. Kuryokhin builds on this historical tradition when he draws an inversely proportional link between sincerity and technological sophistication: sincerity, in his citation, becomes the antidote or answer to "computization."

This is not to say that Kuryokhin's (or Mukhomor's) sincerity claims should be read too literally. Their comments are unthinkable outside the context of Moscow Conceptualism and Sots Art, the two major artistic movements in late Soviet nonconformist culture that (in retrospect) best represent the Russian postmodern experience. Their milestones include such world-famous installations as Ilya Kabakov's *Red Wagon* (1991), a trailer whose shapes evoke a Russian train carriage. Visitors are invited to enter the construction, take their place on benches along walls decorated with socialist-realist paintings, and listen to nostalgic music. On an affective level, the work is confusing: it both nostalgically reappropriates and demythologizes—or, put plainly, embraces and defies—the Soviet experiment. This confusion is at the heart not only of Kabakov's installation but also of Moscow Conceptualism and Sots Art at large. Both foregrounded discussions of sincerity within a distinctly deconstructivist discourse—one that builds upon the tension between irony and seriousness, but that fundamentally refuses to resolve that tension.[8]

Kuryokhin and Mukhomor are no downright Moscow Conceptualists, but this movement's view of art does feed their takes of sincerity. Moscow Conceptualist logic also feeds a series of new-sincerity projects by writer Dmitrii Prigov—the lead figure in this chapter—in the mid-1980s. An in-depth discussion of Prigov's work follows later in this chapter, but it is useful here to briefly assess his place in 1980s sincerity history. In 1984—the year when Sublett heralded a "New Sincerity" in Texan music—Prigov summoned a new series of poems he distributed in samizdat[9] to "run, run, gush out over this world of flowers, trees, sparkling skies, beasts, and creatures, tenderlegged and innocent humans and kiddies with sincerity."[10] A year later, Prigov employed the phrase "New Sincerity" (which he capitalized, just as the Texan music critics did at the time) to propose a new artistic philosophy. He did so in a lecture addressed to a colleague—one who plays a lead role in my next chapter. Vladimir Sorokin, a now famous Russian writer, was then mainly known in underground circles. In addressing this postmodern-to-the-bone peer, Prigov wondered aloud: instead of ironic distance, shouldn't today's writer opt for a "New Sincerity"—that is, for unashamed pathos and sincere expression? Confusingly, the tone of the lecture itself blended emotional commitment with analytical distance, without ever annihilating the tension between the two.

One year later, in 1986, Prigov used the same capitalized phrase "New Sincerity" as the title for another samizdat verse collection. In the poems of this collection, various lyrical heroes roam through Romantic settings—under cloudy skies, in twilit gardens, or through dusky forests. Around the same period, Prigov gave "New Sincerity" performances, in which he handed out home-printed feel-good messages to passers-by.

As this first introduction to Prigov illustrates, around the mid-1980s the poet did everything to morph "New Sincerity" into a full-fledged literary-theoretical paradigm. In doing so, he operated autonomously from his contemporaries in American music criticism—but the new paths that he opened up do partly overlap with theirs. Prigov's son Andrei told me that his father's preoccupation with sincerity was fueled by a fascination with New Wave music—the same music with which the Texan New Sincere bands engaged so eagerly (and which, simultaneously, the Mukhomor members embraced wholeheartedly).[11] What is more, Prigov and the Texan music critics shared a complex attitude to irony and performativity—one to which I return below when discussing Prigov's art and its roots in more detail.

Despite this conceptual overlap, the Russian and the American New Sincerity projects do not appear to have actively influenced one another. *Within* Russia, however, a range of pleas for (a new) sincerity did mutually influence each other at the time—and if, in the United States, appeals for a reborn sincerity were then largely limited to music industries, in Russia they extended far beyond that domain.

To understand the contemporary Russian infatuation with reviving sincerity, one needs to remember that the 1980s were, in Russia, the age of perestroika—a time whose infatuation both with the new and with sincerity was hard to miss. First of all, in the perestroika years previously censored works from the Thaw era were republished, and the Thaw generation, with its relentless infatuation with sincerity, sparked renewed public interest.[12] Second, the language of sincerity inevitably flourished in the glasnost—or openness—rhetoric that contributed to perestroika-era public discourse. As the country's new leader, Mikhail Gorbachev, famously asserted in a 1990 interview: "I detest lies."[13] Not surprisingly, until recently Russian literary historians have tended to portray the Gorbachev years—I am citing cultural historian Aleksandr Prokhorov—in terms of a downright "victory of the spirit of sincerity over Soviet oppression."[14] In doing so, they echoed a trend from an era when sincerity first became a major public concern: the sentimentalist epoch. Both then and now, hypocrisy was configured in stately authorities—then in tsarist autocracy and governmental institutions, as we saw in the previous chapter, now in the freshly dethroned Soviet authorities. By contrast, sincerity ideals were—again, both then and now—projected onto the "common people."

As we shall see below, this affective worldview, in which sincerity and hypocrisy tag onto concrete sociopolitical groups, was formative to Prigov's writings and performances. His art has proven particularly influential—but at the time, Prigov was merely one out of several creative professionals who either observed or promoted a contemporary revitalization of artistic sincerity. Apart from the musicians discussed above, early advocates included:

- artist (and then ex-Mukhomor member) Sven Gundlakh, who in a 1989 art catalogue diagnosed "the present state of culture" as a "*post coitus trista* . . . rooted in a striving for truth, clarity, and a new sincerity" (italics original);[15]
- poet Timur Kibirov, who, from the late 1980s onward, advocated a move away from what he would ultimately label postmodern relativism, toward a resurrected sentimentalism (and whose critical reception, as one expert argues, is dominated by the myth of "a poet who manages to return sincerity . . . to poetry");[16]
- and the poet Sergei Gandlevskii, who, in a 1991 essay, advocated a "critical sentimentalism" in post-Soviet writing.[17] Embroidering on classic sincerity rhetoric, Gandlevskii offered a revived sentimentalism as an alternative both to the "mockery" of what we now call postmodernism and to the "insincere" Soviet criticism of hard-boiled dissidents.[18]

The list is not long—but these early defenders of a newborn sincerity did strike a tender chord at the time. This is especially true of Sergei Gandlevskii's essay. Literary critic Sergei Chuprinin discusses it in detail in his widely used guide to post-Soviet literary trends, where he claims that, among other things, it inspired a full-fledged art exhibition entitled "Critical Sentimentalism, Sentimental Criticism" in St. Petersburg in 1992.[19] By the spring of 2009, when I visited Gandlevskii at his Moscow apartment, the poet even went so far as to complain about its impact. He looked disappointed when I told him that I wanted to visit him to inquire about this particular work. In his view, readers have promoted the text as an outright manifesto—an interpretation Gandlevskii never had in mind when writing it. While he lacks "any interest in critical sentimentalism as a conscious device," he explained over tea, vodka, and cakes, the essay has catapulted him into unwanted stardom as the father of a new sentimentality and/or sincerity (in discussions about his essay, the two concepts consistently conflate).[20]

At the time, it was not only Gandlevskii's support for a return to sentimentalism and sincere expression that beguiled readers. In perestroika-era Russia's intellectual in-crowd, debates over (a revived) artistic sincerity were as pervasive as they were vehement. With time, they became so ubiquitous that they turned into a laughing stock for contemporary writers. In 1989, Aleksei Slapovskii wrote a satire on contemporary artistic life that bore the programmatic title "The Sincere Artist: An Unwritten Novel." With Neiadov, the central character, Slapovskii portrayed a second-rate literary writer in perestroika Russia— one who shared with the heroes of Russia's great literary classics an infatuation with creating sincere art, with being sincere, and with connecting with "the people." Neiadov also shared with Russia's classic prose heroes a failure that I discussed in chapter 1: the failure to realize his striving for honest self-revelation. As literary historian Oliver Ready has explained, "Neiadov is . . . a descendant of a long tradition of hollow men in Russian literature. Like Onegin, he appears unable to love and his life seems scripted by cultural stereotype; like Count Nulin, he is defined in name and fate by what he is not."[21] Slapovskii himself similarly hints at historical continuity. On his website, he introduces the text in Gogolesque terms—terms that ooze ironic inversion—as a narrative "about an artist, who sincerely wanted to become sincere—and that's what he became."[22]

Slapovskii's, Prigov's, Gandlevskii's, and Gundlakh's creations and citations: all point to a perestroika-era preoccupation with sincerity— and with the difficulties of obtaining this classic ideal. The same is true of the many (emphatically capitalized) New Collectives and Institutions that nonconformist artist Timur Novikov launched in 1980s Leningrad. In the late Soviet and perestroika years, the city now known as St. Petersburg was the stage for his "new" initiatives—initiatives that were as much a mockery of existing institutions as symptoms of a longing to create new ones. Together with Sergei Kuryokhin—the same Kuryokhin who envisioned a "pathological sincerity" in Russian pop music—Novikov then founded:

- the New Artists, an art collective whose exhibitions and concerts promoted an influential blend of visual art, graffiti, music, alternative fashion, design, and writing (launched in 1982);
- the New (or Necrorealist) Cinema and New Theater—the label that the same collective used to refer to films and theater plays produced by its members;
- the New Composers, an avant-garde music group founded in 1983;
- and, in a "mock-conservatist" move,[23] the New Academy, a self-organized art institution founded by the New Artists (1989) that propagated Neoacademism—that is, the preservation of classical aesthetics in artistic practices.

I enlist Novikov's projects in relative detail here for a reason: the various initiatives occupied a central space in the story of late Soviet thinking on artistic sincerity. The creatives who united in them embraced the attitude to the absurdities of late and post-Soviet life that we have come to know as stiob. This parodistic aesthetic (akin to Moscow Conceptualist and Sots Art logic) left the answer to the question "Is this speaker sincere or not?" essentially unsettled. In fact, as anthropologist Alexei Yurchak explains in what has become a canonical study of the phenomenon, late Soviet stiob "required such a degree of *overidentification* with the object, person, or idea at which this *stiob* was directed that it was often impossible to tell whether it was a form of sincere support, subtle ridicule, or a peculiar mixture of the two. The practitioners of *stiob* themselves refused to draw a line between these sentiments, producing an incredible combination of seriousness and irony, with no suggestive signs of whether it should be interpreted as the former or the latter, refusing the very dichotomy between the two" (italics original).[24]

Novikov's and Kuryokhin's projects are unthinkable without stiob's ambiguous blend of seriousness and mockery. In art historian Ivor Stodolsky's words, their work exemplifies the insistence on make-believe in late Soviet nonconformist culture—a culture in which an artistic performance "was considered successful precisely when it duped the audience into believing something impossible or ridiculous."[25] Most famously, in 1991 Kuryokhin—in a hoax revolving around a subtly composed fake interview—convinced many a viewer of Leningrad Television that Lenin had, in fact, been nothing less than . . . a mushroom.[26]

Given their insistence both on "the New" and on this principal ambivalence toward sincere expression, it is not surprising that, in Novikov's initiatives, talk of a "New Sincerity" thrived. So, at least, commentators recall in retrospect. When I interviewed Dmitrii Golynko-Vol'fson—an expert on St. Petersburg's art scene and its history—he doubted whether Prigov was the one to coin the phrase. From Golynko's own recollections, rather than being a concept introduced by one individual author, the phrase arose as part of a casual code of conduct prevailing in circles around Novikov. Novikov himself, so Golynko remembers, spoke of a "New Sincerity" as if the term was his own find.[27]

Prigov's close colleague, the poet and nonfiction writer Lev Rubinstein, views Prigov's New Sincerity projects similarly, as products of a time when talk of the New was ubiquitous. In May 2009, in a downtown Moscow café, I interviewed Rubinstein about the period. In his words, it anticipated a "serious shift" from Moscow Conceptualism to whichever new artistic adagio would follow next.[28] Discussions of this shift, Rubinstein said, took place in distinctly informal spheres: he spoke of a period of "intense talks," when "all somehow influenced one another." The outcomes of these influential talks were rarely recorded. Symptomatically, in his 1985 New Sincerity manifesto Prigov wrote that Rubinstein himself had just "proposed a 'New Seriousness,' "[29] but in our interview Rubinstein denied ever having introduced this concept—although he considered it plausible that he used it in informal communication.[30] After all, at the time—in Rubinstein's own words—he "moved . . . from a very tough version of conceptualism" to what one could call a more serious style. In this new style, "I started allowing myself direct lyrical expressions within existing structures."[31]

As Golynko's and Rubinstein's observations testify, for the hardcore fact sampler the first steps in Russian new-sincerity debates are not a particularly pleasurable research object. They suffer from the same "common social amnesia" that cultural critic Irina Prokhorova has diagnosed in perestroika-era historiography at large.[32] Beyond doubt, however, is the insistent infatuation, in 1980s Russia, with protesting against (a not always concisely defined) tradition and with launching novel artistic schools. The New, in this cultural landscape, was a word that artists rarely used without a chuckle—but it was no less a magical epithet than it had been to early Soviet advocates of "new men" and "new worlds." In perestroika-era Russia there are few cultural domains whose leading representatives do not herald the dawn of New Trend So-and-So.[33]

Late Soviet and 1980s underground artists share another habit that is relevant to the argument of this book. They favor handmade, deliberately amateurish- or rickety-looking work—whether in the shape of Dmitrii Prigov's unreadable, torn, typo-ridden manuscripts; of Lev Rubinstein's habit of presenting his poems on sloppy library index cards; or of such intentionally flimsily edited artist's albums as Boris Mikhailov's *Unfinished Dissertation* (*Neokonchennaia dissertatsiia*, 1984–85), Timur Kibirov's *Poems on Love* (*Stikhi o liubvi*, 1993), and Vladimir Sorokin and Oleg Kulik's photo-cum-prose album *Deep into Russia* (*V glub' Rossii*, 1994). As I argue elsewhere, their makers' adherence to an aesthetics of imperfection is no random choice.[34] Each borrows heavily from a tradition to which Prigov, Rubinstein, and their contemporaries are all indebted: that of nonconformist text art of the 1960s. This trend's key representatives argued that all texts are staged—an observation that was particularly acute for propaganda-ridden Soviet Russia. In the late Soviet era, nonconformist writers inevitably produced and read manuscripts that circulated illegally and that were either photocopied or multiplied with the help of carbon paper. Wonky looks were, in short, unavoidable in samizdat Soviet practices—but with time, an unpolished design, typography, and spelling also started enjoying cult status in underground (and, later, post-Soviet) circles. Ultimately samizdat practices turned into objects of artistic reflection in their own right. Experts explain how samizdat "acquire[d] semantic potential and aesthetic significance . . . in the context of post-Soviet and international consumption"; but this process already starts in the late-Soviet artist's albums of Mikhailov and others, which consciously ponder and parody samizdat's raw aesthetics.[35] They evince how, with time, imperfectly written and designed books turned into a fashionable indicator of unofficial Soviet art's intellectual independence—just like archpriest Avvakum's autobiography once owed part of its success as a social critique to an emphatically slapdash writing style.

SINCERITY—POSTMODERNISM—TRAUMA

The preoccupation with raw aesthetics and novel cultural paradigms in 1980s Russia does not come out of the blue. It cannot be isolated from the sociopolitical transition that the country was undergoing at the time—and the intense focus on collective memory that accompanied it. In the 1980s and early 1990s, the late Soviet era made way for the noisy perestroika years. Acts of revisiting and reframing the Soviet experience then abounded in public discussion, and critical historical commentators stumbled over one another in popular journals, books, art galleries, the cinema, and on television.[36]

To Novikov's New initiatives, this historico-political dimension was marginal: according to Golynko-Vol'fson, they rather sprang out of a desire to catch up with "the history of twentieth-century Western art—that is, an attempt to inscribe itself into a foreign, already archived and museified past."[37] To debates specifically about a new *sincerity*, however, both politics and memory were pivotal from the start. These debates exemplify a reading of new-old binaries in which—according to a retrospective study of perestroika-era public discourse—" 'the new' stood for 'the good,' " and " 'the old' . . . was, firstly, Soviet . . . and, secondly, wrong."[38]

What the perestroika-era infatuation with the Soviet experience tells us is that in Russia the search for "new" and "heartfelt" alternatives to postmodern logic acquired idiosyncratic traits. In the Russian context, this search is both interwoven with and anticipated by another quest: that for a post-Soviet or post-Communist artistic creed. How these two different desires interrelated becomes clear when we revisit the statements on reviving sincerity that I cited earlier. Sven Gundlakh proposed his "new sincerity" in a 1989 exhibition catalogue that wholly revolves around a historical trope. *Art Instead of Art,* as the exhibition was called, offered one ongoing retrospective criticism of the Soviet experience.[39] Timur Kibirov's defense of sentimentalism similarly engaged with the Soviet experience. His poetic pleas for a rebirth of artistic sincerity were a direct response to the parodistic coping strategies that his colleagues employed in digesting the Soviet trauma.[40] And Sergei Gandlevskii foregrounded his "critical sentimentalism" as a tool specifically for dealing with the Soviet past. Despite Gandlevskii's irritation about the essay's cult status, I want to look into this, for our analysis, seminal text in a little more detail here.

Gandlevskii opens his essay with an idyllic portrayal of a relaxed morning on Labor Day, which ranked as one of Soviet Russia's prime national holidays: "spring, washed windows, sparrows chirping in the courtyard. 'Knives—scissors sharpened!' cries the last (perhaps) knife grinder. A holiday. Sardines and cheese on the table. A whole beautiful day ahead. A beret, short pants, and white socks with pompoms are ready to go out. Housemates squabbling off to the sides, and neighbors greeting each other. May 1st, happiness."[41] Gandlevskii goes on to describe how, with time, the innocent delight in everyday pleasures makes way for the gradual realization that "more so than anyone in the world, we were fooled. There was no holiday, instead there were blood, lies, general brutishness."[42] The author's desire for a newly sincere sentimentalism sprang out of the need to address precisely this historical disillusionment. It is no coincidence that the text—as Gandlevskii told me—was inspired by Aleksei German's film *My Friend Ivan Lapshin* (*Moi drug Ivan Lapshin*). Upon its first release in 1983, German's (pre-)perestroika-era classic thrilled viewers with its nuanced take on the recent Soviet past. Gandlevskii described to me how he watched the film together with his father. Afterward, father and son disagreed on whether it portrayed the Soviet era positively or negatively. As Gandlevskii now recollected, their dispute taught him an important history lesson: it showed him how the past could be viewed with "emotional ambivalence." In German's portrayal of the revolution and Soviet life, so the poet summarized, "warmth and shame coexist."[43]

Both Gandlevskii and his colleagues, when propagating a rebirth of artistic sincerity, pleaded for quite a specific sincerity—one that I call "curative sincerity." With this term I refer to a type of sincerity that, for its

defenders, has a near-medical therapeutic function: it is instrumentalized in healing historical trauma. I am not the first to point to this healing function of concrete emotions—or rather affective strategies—in
digesting the Communist experience. Most elaborately, perhaps, philosopher Maria Todorova elaborates on this function when reflecting on
post-Communist nostalgia. Todorova draws on the work of Svetlana
Boym and her popular (if not uncontroversial) notion of restorative nostalgia—a type of nostalgia that aches for tradition and seeks to reestab-
lish a lost home. Todorova agrees. "But," she adds, "one could distinguish
between restorationist (in the sense of the desire to restore the past) and
restorative or *curative* nostalgia" (my italics).[44] I find Todorova's distinction useful—but I have observed that nostalgia is not the only emotive
process that can act as cure for historical pains. In a similar vein, many
post-Soviet creative professionals frame *sincerity* as a healing emotive
force. This is why, in speaking of sincerity, post-Communist artists so
often speak of a traumatized cultural memory.

The insistence on memory—and I want to abandon our Russian
story and go transnational here for a moment—is not unique to post-
Soviet new-sincerity rhetoric. Nor is the belief that (literary) art is the
ultimate therapy for digesting collective trauma. Even a cursory glance
at history tells us that at times of artistic paradigm shifts the wish to
"solve" or "cure" traumatic sociopolitical experiences is never far away.
To mention but one historical example, was not the Romantic answer to
the Enlightenment partly fueled by the shocked reaction among intellectuals to the revolutionary events of the late eighteenth century?

The habit of foregrounding new artistic paradigms as a politico-
historical coping strategy resurfaces in the cultural era to which new-
sincerity rhetoric was responding: that of postmodernism. For all its
purported social detachedness, postmodern thinking brims with views
of the artist as society's personal doctor, and of art as a healing tool.
Gilles Deleuze already defined the artist as a "diagnostician" of society
in his *Logique du sens* (1969), which ranks among postmodernism's earliest philosophical manifestos.[45] And the influential cultural critic Jane
Flax finds in postmodern art "deeply political and ethical responses to
specific twentieth century horrors including the Holocaust, the gulag,
the Algerian War and other bloody exits from overt colonialism, and the
invention and use of the atomic bomb."[46]

With its inextricable interweavings with the Soviet experience, Russian postmodern art serves as a particularly forceful catalyst for historical horror. In Sots Art and Moscow Conceptualism, therapeutic prisms on art, politics, and history abound. On the one hand, Sots Art artists stress that their work is characterized by aesthetic or ironic distance, and ergo as far from direct social critique as possible. On the other, they analyze it in psychological terms, as a successful way of dealing with Russia's excruciating recent history. The renowned artistic duo Aleksandr Komar and Vitalii Melamid—composers of numerous life-size portraits of Stalin—explain the intricate interconnection between irony and nostalgia in their work as their only means of "accepting the past."[47] Another leading player in contemporary Russian art—the Medical Hermeneutics group, whose very name evokes curative spheres—saw its performances in Russia's difficult perestroika years as healing acts. "We felt our activity . . . would be helpful," Medical Hermeneutician Pavel Pepperstein explains in retrospect, "and even therapeutic for the situation."[48]

Not surprisingly, theoretical commentators on Russian postmodernism embrace equally therapeutically informed rhetoric. Authoritative critics define Sots Art and Moscow Conceptualism as a "liberating travesty from Stalinist aesthetics" (Ekaterina Degot') or an "overcoming of ideology" (Evgeny Dobrenko); and they claim that Russian postmodernism boasts one " 'basic' cultural function": "the reaction to the inevitability of living through a historical trauma" (Mark Lipovetsky).[49] Russian postmodernism is unthinkable without these and related statements on digesting a trauma of national scale.

Collective memory is thus formative to postmodern rhetoric. It is a sine qua non, too, for talk of a revived sincerity—again, both in and outside Russia. In the United States, the slogan "New Sincerity"—born, as we saw, in 1980s music criticism—attracted massive public attention in the wake of one of America's most painful cultural traumas: the attacks on the World Trade Center in September 2001. Cultural critics spoke at the time of a shift to a "post-ironic" "New Sincerity" as a response to the need to cope with the attacks.[50] "Attacks on U.S. Challenge the Perspectives of Postmodern True Believers" was the title of a programmatic essay by Edward Rothstein in the *New York Times* on 22 September 2001. Its author expressed the hope "that finally, as the ramifications sinks [*sic*] in, as it becomes clear how close the attack came to undermining the political, military and financial authority of the United States, the Western relativism of pomo [a popular designation for postmodernism] . . . will be widely seen as ethically perverse."[51]

The causal relationship between the 9/11 shock and (the renewed) sincerity that Rothstein and others forged also trickled down into European literature and art. Amsterdam-based literature professor Thomas Vaessens, for one, linked global new-sincere trends directly to what he labeled a "late-postmodern" response to the 9/11 attacks in Dutch literature.[52]

In other words, in the 2000s more than one cultural theorist framed a terrorist attack as a catalyst for a "new" or reborn public notion of sincerity. In the same decade the project of reviving sincerity was linked to more distant historical traumas. Joost Krijnen—in an early description of his Ph.D. dissertation[53]—maps a post-postmodern insistence on sincerity in American literature that he primarily traces to Holocaust memory, not the 9/11 attacks. In Krijnen's view, writers like Jonathan Safran Foer and Michael Chabon resort to a post-postmodern equivalent of traditional sincerity in order to make the Holocaust trauma "both meaningful and valuable."[54]

Krijnen, Vaessens, and Rothstein share a view on our age as post- or late postmodern; *and* they share with many others the conviction that its move beyond (early) postmodernism is informed, first and foremost, by collective memory. Similar memory-informed discourse on a late and post-postmodernism—we return to post-Soviet space now—emerged in the Russia of the early 2000s. In order to explain what I mean by saying that, I first want to recall the so-called Russian apartment bombings. In September 1999, four apartment blocks across Russia were destroyed in bomb attacks that killed 293 people and injured another 651. The blasts—staged, according to a popular interpretation, by the Kremlin—prompted the Russian authorities to launch a second war against the Republic of Chechnya.

In what some call a Russian analogy to 9/11,[55] the apartment bombings act as a tipping point in Russian debates about a late or post-postmodernism. How we should view that shift has been lucidly explained by Mikhail Epstein, the influential thinker whom I cited earlier, in an article published in 2006. Epstein argued that, together with other cultural traumas—he singled out the 9/11 attacks but also mentioned the three-day school siege in the North Caucasus town of Beslan in 2004, in which nearly four hundred people were killed—the explosions have sparked a Russian move away from postmodern relativism to a brand-new cultural paradigm. In his words, they have led Russians to take refuge in "the experience of the unique, the unrepeatable, the homemade, that which is not subject to any simulation."[56]

Epstein's explanation of the bombings illustrates once more how, in the 2000s, historical trauma colors discussions on a post-postmodern or new-sincere era—and how the sincerity that its defenders propagate is by definition a curative sincerity, one that is helpful in healing both recent and more distant historical wounds.

So far we have focused on curative-sincerity discourse as it developed in the twenty-first century. We have seen that cultural trauma has informed the global debate on a nascent sincerity from the early 2000s onward. I now want to take a leap back in time, to the nonconformist art scene of late Soviet Russia. A closer look at that scene—of which we caught a first glimpse on the previous pages—teaches us how in Russia a traumatized collective memory had been shaping attempts to reanimate sincerity long before the year 2000. In fact, in the art of Dmitrii Prigov it did so from as early as the 1970s onward.

WANTING SINCERITY BADLY: PRIGOV

Having gained fame in the vivid nonofficial art scene of 1970s Russia, the poet, painter, and performer Dmitrii Prigov gained global fame after the Soviet collapse. Both in Russia and abroad—thanks to some excellent translations and international exhibitions—he ranks as a master in artistically reappropriating Soviet clichés. Prigov's most celebrated creations include a series of quasi-hagiographical "Stories about Stalin" (1975–89), and theatrical performances in which the author mimics the (verbal and bodily) language of the Soviet authorities.

By the time of his death, in 2007, this status as a canonical figure in contemporary Russian literature was undisputed. So was his reputation in a spectacularly wide range of other artistic disciplines, including painting, sculpture, performance, rock music, dance, opera, and cinema.[57] From this plethora of artistic activities, what emerges as Prigov's best-known artistic achievement is the "behavioral project," "DAP," or "Dmitrii Aleksandrovich Prigov." "DAP" is perhaps best explained as Prigov's

consistent, long-term attempt to present the authorial persona—
including his work, his physical presence, and his biographical self—as
a discursive or cultural product. In the artist's own words, formative to
"DAP" was the idea of a "shimmering relationship between the author
and the text . . . , in which it is very hard to define (not only for the reader
but for the author, too) the degree of sincerity in the immersion into the
text and the purity and distance of the withdrawal from it."[58]

In its most tangible and easily accessible form, Prigov's "shimmering" behavioral strategy can be seen in a set of short video films
available on YouTube.[59] In the videos, Prigov adopts the identity of a
stereotypical representative of Soviet ideology—something between the
figure of the wise but stern leader and the prophetic writer-thinker. He
seems to embrace this identity wholeheartedly: for the viewer it is not
easy to determine the artist's affective relationship to his object of mimicry. Is it neutral? Tenderly affirmative? Mildly mocking? Not surprisingly, the "project DAP" has stirred heated metaliterary debates regarding
performativity, theatricality, and authenticity. I return to these debates
below—but first I want to take a closer look at Prigov's own voice in the
discussion.

Although it is by definition impossible to distinguish earnestness
from play in his authorial stance, Prigov himself consistently warned
against one-sidedly ironic, "nonserious" readings of his work. Among
"new sincerity" adepts, similar warnings often signal antipostmodern
sentiments—but although Prigov ranks as founder of a Russian "new
sincerity," he never explicitly opposed postmodernism. This is not terribly surprising. As I explain in this book's introduction, in pre-1990s
Russia the theoretical language of postmodernism was little used. Admittedly, the word "postmodernism" occasionally appeared in the early
1980s in such journals as *A-Ia* and *Iskusstvo* (*Art*)[60]—nonconformist art
journals in which Prigov also published. But it is unlikely that by the
mid-1980s, when this artist launched his "New Sincerity" projects, he
possessed the vocabulary to frame them as attempts to engage with—let
alone move beyond—postmodernism. In the 2000s, the poet did evolve
into an undisputed authority in postmodern theorizing—but even then
he chose never to define his pleas for (a new) sincerity as post-
postmodern. In retrospect, he even typified them as a step that marked
his transition from Moscow Conceptualism *to* postmodernism. The dif-

ficulty of "defining the degree of sincerity of an expression"—the core problem that his "New Sincerity" projects foregrounded—was for him inherent in "the postmodern consciousness."[61]

An emphasis on sincerity as a theoretical problem, a cautious approach to irony: these were interests that Prigov shared with many Western postmodern writers[62]—but among his postmodern colleagues, he went particularly far in hammering his insistence on the nonironic into readers. From the early 1970s onward he took meticulous care to explain that his relationship with irony was fraught, and that concepts such as sincerity and love were pivotal to his creations.[63] In a foreword to a collection dated 1971–74, the artist already claimed—in his, as always, somewhat hermetic wordings—that in his poetry he "wants to avoid the danger of a strictly horizontal time cut, which generates . . . pure irony. . . . What I need is a vertical, often taken and tracked and sincerely interpreted time cut from top to bottom." Instead of embracing irony as an artistic strategy, *this* poet—so Prigov assured readers—is "maximally serious" in his approach to life, which he sees as anything but "an object for humor."[64]

Readers who took these claims as straightforward statements of intent missed the point: in Prigov's hands, sincerity and irony never turned into unambiguous or unreflected sentimental categories. As a well-read critical intellectual in late Soviet Russia, Prigov undoubtedly knew his St. Augustine and Rousseau—but he was anything but their direct heir. It was no coincidence that, in a 1993 conversation with his colleague Gandlevskii, he claimed: "I write neither confessional nor personal poetry, and I do not have a personal language."[65] In his later writing, Prigov did make explicit attempts to write "personal poetry."[66] Even then, however, his notion of personal poetry should never be confused with classic self-revelatory lyrics. Invoking the postmodern claim that sincerity is nothing but a cultural construction, Prigov argued on one occasion that "sincerity has two modes[:] that of a truly sociocultural construct and that of some non-articulated principle. . . . The mode which I take up and which I experience and criticize, is the cultural mode."[67]

Undiluted self-expression, to put it somewhat differently, was never Prigov's primary aim. At the same time, Prigov defined his own "shimmering" strategy as an attempt to shift from the cultural mode to a more "generally human, prearticulated" type of self-revelation: in an interview, he explained that "if one correctly traces [sincerity's cultural mode], it evokes a classical response of sincerity. . . . In fact, at some point I sincerely enter into a discourse. The problem is not that of deceiving the reader. . . . The problem is that you yourself have to be beside yourself in that respect."[68]

The highly premeditated (but never jeering) form of sincerity that Prigov outlines here was pivotal to his artistic project—and the concept keeps emerging throughout his poetic and (pseudo-)theoretical writings. "But I want sincerity so badly!" he exclaimed, quasi-involuntarily, in the introductory text from which I borrowed this chapter's title.[69]

In pondering an avidly desired sincerity, Prigov was a child of his time *and* of historical tradition. In chapter 1, we saw how Dostoevsky's fundamentally unreliable characters incessantly expressed their craving for a sincerity that they tangibly lacked—remember how Verkhovenskii repeated over and over how "seriously" and "sincerely" he meant to do well. Prigov echoed their desire when he presented sincerity as something that the poet could never fully attain, and that, precisely for that reason, he sorely longed for.

But Prigov's sincerity project harked back to much more than Dostoevsky alone. In the previous chapter I outlined how, ever since early modernism, we have witnessed a transnational habit of locating sincerity and hypocrisy in opposing political groups—groups whose mutual tension the speaker seeks to highlight. Remember English Calvinism, which pairs sincerity with political opposition; late eighteenth-century French revolutionaries, who consistently framed "the common people" as sincere and court members as hypocritical; and the nineteenth-century Russian novel, whose authors projected truthfulness onto "the Russian people" and dissimulation onto the political powers that be. Or think of modernists' persistent association of moral corruption with the urban upper classes, and their just as persistent conviction that sincerity resides in the domain of the poor and geographically peripheral. In an ambiguous and often outright playful manner, Prigov, as we shall see below, revived this age-old trend of locating sincerity in specific sociocultural strata. He seemed to be well aware of it, too: it can hardly be a coincidence that he pointed to Maximilien Robespierre—intellectual father, one might say, of the French Revolution—when discussing the difficulty of dealing with sincerity in a politically turbulent age.[70]

What do Prigov's revisions of classic sincerity rhetoric look like in practice? That question is perhaps best answered by comparing sincerity à la Prigov with the tradition that has shaped it most directly. In chapter 1 I explained how Vladimir Pomerantsev's plea for sincerity after Stalinism paved the way for critical reflection on the recent past. We saw how, ever since the publication of his essay on the topic, sincerity has been at the heart of a post-Stalinist debate on the question: how should artists frame reality in the hypocrisy-ridden Soviet world? Prigov's work is unthinkable without this debate, which no critical intellectual in late Soviet Russia could have missed, and whose leading voices hold the artist responsible for reanimating sincerity in the face of deceitful Soviet rulers.

Like Pomerantsev and his contemporaries, Prigov was fascinated not by sincerity as such: his interest held specifically the curative sincerity that preoccupied Pomerantsev earlier. Just as Pomerantsev had, Prigov now framed sincerity as the ultimate answer and ailment to the "hypocrisy" of the Soviet experiment. And, as a diachronic overview illustrates, he did so with iron perseverance.

In 1980 Prigov presented sincerity as a cultural coping strategy in the lushly titled collection *Sincerity on Negotiated Terms or Tears of a Heraldic Soul* (*Iskrennost' na dogovornykh nachalakh ili slezy geral'dicheskoi dushi*). In the foreword to this collection, Prigov tells readers: "A poet is also human," and "I, too, have been wanting to say something direct, sincere, sentimental even." "As soon as I felt that longing," he continues, "from the dark-sweet layers of my soul the following lines surfaced: 'The weary sun silently sank into the sea . . . ,' 'On the edge a maple grew, in love with a birch the maple was . . . ,' 'Comrade, comrade, my wounds hurt. . . .' And I cried."[71]

In this fragment, what the desire for sincerity evokes in the poet are memories related specifically to mainstream Soviet culture: the quotations that make him cry are the titles of popular Soviet songs from the 1920s to the 1940s.

Soviet memory loomed equally large when Prigov launched the notion of "New Sincerity" in his 1985 lecture to Sorokin. "New Sincerity," he explained to his colleague, is unique in allowing artists to speak "clearly, sincerely and directly," but "without forgetting the entire scorching experience of what we have been through."[72] After all, Prigov concludes, "we need ideology!"[73] Prigov here coined his new poetic device as a creative therapeutic tool—one that would help the writer in coping with the Soviet heritage.

In his 1986 "New Sincerity" performances, Prigov put his theoretical plea into practice: in short notes that he printed out on strips of paper, he blended Soviet-era ideological speech with emotionally loaded calls for action. "Citizens! Let's sweep the apartment clean in the morning, let's open the door to the stairway and the wind of fresh changes will burst into our dwellings!" is one example. Another is: "Citizens! It is December already and our windows are covered in transparent ice, but on the other hand, it seems that it is cozier inside the apartment now!"[74] Taking his "New Sincere" credo literally to the streets, Prigov glued these and similar printed notes onto streetlights, walls, and fences and personally handed them to passersby. The KGB was not amused: just as sincerity pleas had concrete legal implications for Pomerantsev and Tvardovskii in the 1950s, so Prigov was now arrested and (a popular silencing measure of the times) briefly incarcerated in a psychiatric hospital.

The examples above confirm a claim that has often been made about Prigov: that in his hands, sincerity becomes an entity that intricately interweaves with—rather than strictly opposes—irony. Not without reason does Yurchak's study of late Soviet stiob—the parodistic aesthetic in which irony and sincerity blend—contain one section devoted entirely to Prigov and the ambiguities of his artistic project.[75] Scholars of Prigov's work have avidly studied these ambiguities—but his references to a "scorching" past, to the need for "ideology," and the ideological clichés in Prigov's "New-Sincere" performances also teach us something about his art that has received less attention from experts. They tell us that for *this* artist, reflections on sincerity are instrumental in rethinking Soviet history.

This is not to say that Prigov's neatly balanced "ironic sincerity" was directed strictly toward the Soviet experience.[76] Part of the confusion that "DAP" instills in readers and viewers stems from the very variety of poses that its conceiver strikes—here a Soviet policeman, there a woman in a Symbolist poem. "DAP" can engage passionately in historically nonspecific discussions of love, friendship, or death. In fact, if Prigov initially referred to himself as a "USSR-ish poet [*eseseserovskim poetom*]," in a later interview he called his art a "psychotherapeutic sublimation" that "project[s] [fears] onto large cultural themes"—that is, work that tackles cultural anxieties that are far from restricted to Soviet life.[77]

The Soviet experiment, in other words, was certainly not the only object of Prigov's "New Sincerity." When, however, he pondered the problem of sincere artistic expression, recent history was never far away. In fact, Soviet memory loomed large throughout Prigov's metareflections on sincerity right up to his death. Not long before he passed away, Prigov tried to answer the question "How can one be sincere?" in an essay published on the well-known news and commentary portal Polit.ru. In the essay, entitled "Sincerity: That Is What We Cherish Most of All" ("Iskrennost': Vot shto nam vsego dorozhe," 2005), Prigov mused: is the genuinely experienced trauma of victims of Soviet repression by definition more heartfelt than the equally earnest zeal of pro-Stalinist veterans? Or do the two relate in more complex ways?[78] With these questions, Prigov touched upon a particularly burdensome problem for post-Soviet intellectuals: how does one accept that countless Soviet citizens conducted dark deeds while meaning well? Recent studies—as we saw in chapter 1—contest that Soviet citizens hid a politically transgressive "true self" behind an ideologically loyal outward performance. Public intellectuals today drive home related observations. In Svetlana Alexievich's curated interviews with former Soviet citizens, for instance, she cites interviewees who insist that they "entered the party with a sincere heart," or that "sincere people" abounded "among Communists"; and literature theorist and politican Mikhail Lotman (son of the well-known semiotician) recently asked whether "people with a Communist past" are "sincere" when they express heartfelt grief about political developments in public, and concluded that the answer to this question is more complex than a simple yes or no.[79]

If one compares Lotman's interview, Alexievich's citations, and the rich set of Prigov quotations that I clustered here, it is hard *not* to see a consistent pattern. In each, whenever sincerity turns into an object of separate discussion, the speaker is responding to the trauma of the Soviet experience. Just as sincerity rhetoric was previously instrumentalized in liberating "the people" (French revolutionaries, Nikolai Karamzin), or in unraveling the suffocating limitations of socialist-realist and Stalinist dogmas (Pomerantsev), Prigov now employs it as a vehicle for digesting the Soviet trauma.

Prigov's take on sincerity thus goes a long way back. At the same time, he deviates from tradition in crucial respects. One we have already discussed: this is the intricate and all-pervasive interweaving of play and serious expression throughout Prigov's works.

Not unrelated to this principal ambiguity is another difference: where his forerunners project sincerity exclusively onto either "the people" or "the cultural elite," Prigov insists on exploring the potential sincerity of all sides: of the poet, but also the authoritarian figure or the Stalinist regime. As commentators have often argued, his performances of policemen and other representatives of Soviet power may unmask power players, but they also exude an unmistakable tenderness. And in "Sincerity: That Is What We Cherish Most of All," Prigov explicitly ponders the need to simultaneously respect the earnestness of repression victims *and* Stalin's defendants. "Yes," he argues in this essay, "but sincerity! Yes, but the bitter sincerity of the others! And one is not reproaching but rather complementing the other. Rather, it reproaches us, for the natural inclination of men to evade the complexities and complications that fill historical pictures."[80] Prigov here frames a concern that pervaded his work as a whole: the need not merely to revive but also to lend nuance to thinking on artistic sincerity in the traumatized world of post-Soviet Russia. In pleading for a fine-grained understanding of the term, he did not simply echo existing sincerity anxieties: he took them into new semantic territories, where hard dichotomies made way for unresolved tensions.

In Prigov's art, sincerity thus acquired novel dimensions, while preserving its classic function of being a curative artistic tool for collective traumas. Whether the notion is blemished by historical trauma or not, so one could summarize his credo, the post-Soviet artist can express himself only by embracing sincerity—even if today that sincerity is principally complex, and principally stiobesque.

"MADLY SINCERE": PRIGOV'S READERS

On a winter evening at her house in London, Prigov's widow, Nadezhda Bourova, told me that Dmitrii and his grandson Georgii had an intimate bond. Shortly before Prigov's death, Georgii, then seven years old, confided to his grandmother: "Dusia . . . when Dima [Dmitrii] plays with me, it's for real."[81] With the astute perception of an unprejudiced child, Georgii Prigov touched upon a major, if not the central, issue in critical discourse on his grandfather's poetry. Is the speaker serious? Is his frowned earnestness "for real"? Or are listeners and readers witnessing a parodistic attitude to language and life? Critics and scholars never tire of asking where this icon of contemporary Russian literature stands. Prigov himself eagerly toyed with their sincerity anxiety—and their longing to catch a glimpse of the biographical author. As the jacket description of a 2006 book-length interview teasingly states, where previous publications merely foregrounded the poet's "image," the new book offers readers "one ongoing personal utterance."[82]

In 2006, the promise of a "personal utterance" did not come out of the blue. It was a direct response to readings of (especially the early) Prigov as a hardcore postmodernist—one whose artistic strategies relied primarily on relativism and language play.[83] The author of an "absurdist text" that "parasitiz[es] on forms of a culture that has outlived itself" and that "is ready to look at [all Soviet-era social] stereotypes from a distance": this is how, in 1993, fellow writer Viktor Erofeev typifies Prigov and his late-Soviet work.[84]

Erofeev's portrayal echoes that of many a Prigov expert at the time. Coaxed in part by the poet's own metastatements on his writings (remember how he denied writing personal poetry in the early 1990s), his critics have incessantly returned to a set of sincerity-related queries, including questions about the relationship between the author and the person Prigov; about Prigov's image [*imidzh*] and public behavior as opposed to the idea of a "real Prigov"; and the question to what extent, in his work, the autobiographical author does or does not blend with his lyrical ego.[85]

Prigovedy—Prigov specialists—share another preoccupation that interests us in this chapter. This is the concern with the relationship between sincerity and cultural memory. As we saw in the previous chapter, Irina Paperno frames Soviet society as an "emotional economy of duplicity, deception, and ambiguity." When Prigov's work first reached a wide audience, readers felt that it responded to precisely this troubled emotional regime, by problematizing sincerity and by critically interrogating the possibility of honest self-expression. In the same 1993 review that I just cited, Erofeev portrayed Prigov's playful-"parasitic" stance toward the clichés of Soviet life as that of "a 'forester,' who helps to out-live in culture that which has turned into carrion. This is inevitable for the salvation of culture. . . . Prigov enhances a liberation of conscious-ness, his conceptual activity evokes in listeners a catharsis."[86] In other words, it was historical experience—specifically, so Erofeev argued to-gether with others, the *Soviet* experience[87]—that led Prigov to exchange genuine creative expression for playful parody.

The reading of Prigov's work that I am outlining here, as a hardcore deconstructive act, has long been popular—but not all critics always shared it. A prominent defender of an alternative view is literary histo-rian Andrei Zorin, who has typified the poet's writings as "traditional sentimental lyricism" ever since the 1980s.[88] To Zorin and other alterna-tive voices in early Prigov scholarship, memory is no less a central cate-gory than it is to those who insist on his parodistic-parasitic aims. In 2009 I visited Zorin in Oxford, the home base for his scholarship, to talk about his friendship with Prigov. Over lunch he told me that he had viewed Prigov's oeuvre through a sentimentalist lens ever since they first met in 1981. Predictably, for Zorin the "New Sincerity" projects did not come as a surprise. Nor did he envision them as a shift within the poet's oeuvre. To him, sincerity had always mattered to Prigov's art—and more specifically, to the artist's take on Soviet life. Zorin also be-lieved that the Moscow Conceptualist project—without whose complex stance on Soviet reality Prigov's work is unthinkable—displayed a mark-edly "Romantic nature."[89]

Zorin is alone neither in his insistence on Soviet memory nor in his reading of Prigov along sentimentalist and Romantic lines. His "lyrical" take on Prigov closely resembles that of Mikhail Epstein, for instance. Epstein frames Prigov's work in terms of "lyricality" and "serious-ness."[90] In 1999, he singled out the poet as the leader of a "new sincerity" in Russian writing—one that took the reader into spheres "foreign to both Modernism and Postmodernism." "As early as the second half of the 1980s," Epstein writes, "Dmitry Prigov, the leader of the Moscow Con-ceptualists, called for a change of direction, toward a 'new sincerity.' Turn-ing away from strict Conceptualist schemas, which parodied models of Soviet ideology, the new movement was to strive for a lyrical assimilation of these dead layers of being and consciousness."[91] As this short summary illustrates, Epstein portrays the new sincerity as a direct literary response to Moscow Conceptualist parodies of Soviet ideology—and hence, implicitly, as a response to the Soviet condition itself.[92]

Epstein may (unlike Prigov himself) see Prigov's preoccupation with sincerity as a markedly *un*postmodern step, but his and Zorin's readings of Prigov match an insistence on lyricism, romanticism, and ethics that resonates in postmodern theorizing from the start. As early as 1979, Boris Groys titled his groundbreaking essay on the Moscow Conceptualist movement "Moscow *Romantic* Conceptualism" (my italics)—and more than one scholar defends "the proposition that Postmodernism is yet another mutation of [Romanticism]."[93] In a different but not wholly unrelated discourse, Jean-François Lyotard criticized one-dimensional explanations of postmodernism as an "anything-goes" mentality in 1983; the 2004 *Cambridge Companion to Postmodernism* takes this criticism to its extremes when its author states that "postmodernism . . . is about ethics before it is about anything else."[94]

I return to this insistence on postmodern ethics, romanticism, and lyricism later—but what counts here is that the same notions resonated in Prigov's work throughout his career, including the early phase that is traditionally read as hardcore postmodern. In Prigov's reception in literary circles, "serious," "lyrical" readings have also been prominent, and with time, their number increased. In the 1990s and early 2000s, Zorin's and Epstein's takes on Prigov's work were exceptional—but after the poet died from a heart attack in 2007, the situation changed.

Those present at the poet's funeral—Zorin wrote contentedly in an obituary—had learned with surprise that Prigov had been a practicing Russian Orthodox believer. In Zorin's words, "DAP" now "turned out to be anything but the 'clown' for which he had always been taken."[95] In posthumous reviews, critics exchanged their views of Prigov as a playful relativist for tangibly less frivolous readings of his work. Experts now hastened to convince their audiences that Prigov had turned out to be a less jocular poet than previously acknowledged, and that he had been anything—*anything*—but a coolly relativizing postmodernist. Poet-cum-critic Mikhail Aizenberg stressed the "tender and oddly sensitive texture" of Prigov's prose; artist Ilya Kabakov called his colleague "madly sincere"; literary historian Brigitte Obermayr foregrounded his "postmodern sincerity"; and cultural historian Evgeny Dobrenko proposed focusing on Prigov's "deep sociality" rather than "the 'Russian postmodernism' made up by critics."[96]

Dobrenko made his claim in the foreword of *Non-Canonical Classic* (*Nekanonicheskii klassik*, 2010) the first edited scholarly volume devoted to the poet. This volume is exemplary for a new phase in Prigov's reception—one in which critics fervently defied such categories as postmodern play and radical deconstruction. The contributors, to mention a mere selection, asserted that Prigov's early poetry was in fact "tender," "pious almost" (Aleksandr Barash); that the same project should be read "also as a wholly serious (if citational) modeling" (Maria Maiofis); and that a postmodern reading of the "DAP" project was "unproductive" (Mikhail Iampol'skii) (Iampol'skii would later devote a book-length publication to the claim that Prigov's innovations lushly exceed the Moscow Conceptualist paradigm; but both Iampol'skii's study and the follow-up volume to *Non-Canonical Classic* appeared when this book was already in the copyediting phase).[97] Mark Lipovetsky, to conclude, approvingly cited Prigov experts Sabine Hänsgen and Georg Witte and their claim that "Prigov's authorial manner cannot be reduced to a cold, rational manipulation of linguistic stereotypes, just as one cannot claim that Prigov as a person wholly disappears behind the surface of the language's simulative tools."[98]

What followed on Prigov's untimely death, in short, was a manifest shift toward more "serious" or "sincere" interpretations of his art.[99] As the citations above demonstrate, many a critic placed this seriousness *outside* postmodernism, as Epstein had done before. I disagree: as this chapter illustrates, ever since the mid-1980s concerns about sincere expression have haunted a whole range of Russian intellectuals who traditionally rank as postmodern artists. Lev Rubinstein, Timur Novikov, and the Mukhomor collective are cases in point—and so, as we shall see in the chapter that follows, is Vladimir Sorokin, who ranks as another leading name in Russian postmodernism. Prigov's preoccupation with sincerity was no exception from a relativizing, "nonserious," or intrinsically ironic postmodern experience: it was part and parcel of that experience from the start.

To the Russian postmodern experience, to describe things a little differently, sincerity concerns are of perennial importance. As we saw, these concerns rarely stand by themselves: they cannot be isolated from the perestroika- and post-perestroika-era insistence on collective memory. A more detailed look at Prigov's reception confirms this insight. Once critics rediscovered Prigov's sincerity, they connected it to a classical cultural trope: that of the artist as society's doctor. What resonated throughout different posthumous analyses of his work is the image of the artist as therapist—of someone who helped contemporaries overcome the Soviet trauma. Ilya Kalinin, critic and editor in chief of the popular cultural-political journal *Neprikosnovennyi zapas* (*Inviolable Source*), read Prigov's writing and art as downright artistic "work with memory as therapy."[100] And Dmitrii Golynko-Vol'fson—to add a second example—highlighted the "glimmering signs of mysterious authenticity" in Prigov's depiction of Soviet life, seeing the artist's rendition of Soviet Russia as an attempt "to overcome the monster of ideology."[101]

This overview of recent developments in Prigov's reception history reiterates two insights that the poet's own work teaches us. It tells us that sincerity matters to Russian postmodern artists substantially more than early commentators acknowledged. It also confirms that for these artists, when sincerity is at stake, the Soviet trauma is rarely far away.

HANGOVER POETICS: PRIGOV'S CONTEMPORARIES

The last few pages have focused on Prigov, who is a particularly fitting example to unravel the "memory thread" in post-Soviet sincerity rhetoric. As I argued earlier, however, his is not a unique case. We have already spotted a similar insistence on cultural memory in the ideas of a handful of other early adepts of a revived sincerity. I am thinking especially of Sven Gundlakh and Sergei Gandlevskii, whose visions of a "new sincerity" and "critical sentimentalism" arose out of the perestroika-era need to address a conflicted, traumatic Soviet memory (remember how Gandlevskii presented critical sentimentalism as a tool to deal with simultaneously happy and brutal Soviet memories).

In more recent Russian new-sincerity discourse, the focus on digesting the Soviet experiment that these artists share does not vanish—quite the reverse. After the perestroika era, discussions on Soviet memory did lose some of their initial sharpness, but they remained formative to public reflections on honesty and artistic self-revelation. The list of examples is too long to sum up here—but in order to grasp the sheer width of the debate it is worth briefly tracing some of its noisier contributions.

To start with, collective memory is formative to the view of a reborn sincerity adopted by Mikhail Epstein—the same Epstein who singles out Prigov as one of the new sincerity's leaders. In his view, the words that "new sincere" thinking revitalizes have been tarnished by "centuries of traditional, official usage."[102] One historical period that, in Epstein's view, has particularly tainted our culture's "big words" is the mid-twentieth century and its Nazi and Communist experiments. At one point he goes as far as defining his "new sincerity" and "new sentimentality" as a "hangover poetics" that reclaims literary expression after a century that "makes us nauseous" with its "catastrophes and revolution."[103]

Since their appearance in print, Epstein's writings on a selfconsciously sincere "hangover poetics" have been widely cited in debates on post-Soviet literature. No less popular is literary critic Nataliia Ivanova's book *The Nostalgic Present* (*Nostal'iashchee*, 2002), which similarly links sincerity and Soviet memory. In *The Nostalgic Present* Ivanova observes a move away, in recent writing, from postmodern and stiobesque takes on Soviet reality. The critic forges an explicit link to Pomerantsev's essay on a post-Stalinist sincerity when she claims that "today, sincerity is perhaps even more revolutionary than in 1953."[104]

The Nostalgic Present is probably Ivanova's most famous contribution to post-Soviet literary scholarship—but the relationship between artistic sincerity and the Soviet past did not haunt her in this publication alone. Already in 1998 Ivanova discerned a "new sincerity" in Russian literature triggered by memory concerns. In her words, the rebirth of sincere literary expression was triggered by a "moral shift of a significant part of society toward acknowledging the ambivalence of the past."[105] More than a decade later, in 2011, Ivanova again connected sincerity and history when she mused, in an article entitled "Art in the Light of Sincerity": "Can a contemporary literary professional be sincere and open? Or is that fundamentally impossible in the age of postmodernism?"[106] The critic explained that she saw sincerity as a particular challenge in post-Soviet society, where the question of how to interpret the turbulent recent past was still unsettled.[107] "In the new Russia," writes Ivanova, "new people experience a mental clash: after all, their own fathers belong to the Soviet people. . . . Judge them? Justify them? What would they be doing if, in judging the [Soviet] authorities and society, they would continue to love their parents? Were these executioners or victims? Or both at the same time?"[108]

As in her other writings, Ivanova here firmly fuses thinking on artistic sincerity with commemorative concerns. In a quest that eerily resembles that of Prigov in one of *his* sincerity essays—the one where he pondered the sincere commitment that repression victims and Stalinist veterans share—Ivanova resorts to sincerity rhetoric to plead for a more nuanced take on the Soviet past.

Ivanova's most recent thoughts on sincerity and cultural trauma date back to the early 2010s. By then, the intersection of the two concepts had attracted much wider public interest than when sincerity was first proposed as a therapeutic cultural tool in the 1980s. In the course of the 2000s, creative professionals superimposed the same idea on a rich range of artistic and intellectual disciplines—think, apart from literature, of nonfiction writing, visual art, blogging, graphic animation, and music. I limit myself to a discussion of three representative samples.

The first was a show jointly hosted by three paragons of Moscow Conceptualist and Sots Art—Aleksandr Melamid and Ilya and Emilia Kabakov—at New York's respected Apexart Gallery in 2006. The show was entitled *Neo Sincerity,* and its name was inspired by an idea from Art Spiegelman.[109] Ever since the year 2000, this American comic artist has vowed that we are entering an age—in his words—of "neo-sincerity, which is sincerity built on a thorough grounding in irony, but that allows one to actually make a statement about what one believes in."[110] Borrowing Spiegelman's neologism, the exhibition emphatically configured sincerity as a sociopolitical tool: the makers saw it as an aesthetic strategy for coping with historical traumas such as the Soviet experiment and the Holocaust.[111]

Two years later, literary scholar Mark Lipovetsky similarly toyed with the idea of a curative sincerity, albeit with a solid dose of critical skepsis. In *Paralogues* Lipovetsky discerned a "late postmodern" trend in Russian writing that attempted to restore the grand narratives of the past. In nonfictional genres, Lipovetsky argued, this "late postmodern" tendency inclined "toward what D. A. Prigov . . . labeled a 'new sincerity.'"[112] If himself hesitant toward the concept of a "new sincerity," Lipovetsky does use this label in his book to cluster the essayistic writings of a number of contemporary authors. Crucial to his reading of purportedly "new sincere" writers are, once again, history and memory. Lipovetsky ascribes a downright healing historical function, for instance, to the memoirs of Grisha Bruskin—a Jewish Russian painter who gained fame in late Soviet nonconformist circles—and to the essays in prose of Lev Rubinstein, the writer whom I interviewed for this book in 2009. To Lipovetsky, Bruskin's autobiographical writings on his life as an artist in Soviet Russia "manage to conquer trauma as a trace of violence and systematic terror."[113] In a similar vein, Rubinstein's unique blend of personal-historical nonfiction writing is, says Lipovetsky, "for him the single accessible form of *historical consciousness*, which allows him to reconcile himself with trauma and to conquer it through laughter, while at the same time refraining from *identifying* . . . with the ideologicized discourse of 'grand history'" (italics original).[114]

In the passage from which this quote comes, Lipovetsky is crystal clear on the type of shock that the "newly sincere" essayist Rubinstein sought to overcome: rather than historical trauma per se, his battles targeted the Soviet trauma.

Memory-informed views of post-Soviet sincerity also resonate in the work of anthropologist Alexei Yurchak—my last example here and, together with Lipovetsky, a resonant name in post-Soviet cultural studies. In 2008, Yurchak turned from the study of stiob to the notion of a "post-post-Communist sincerity." In the mid- and late 2000s, Yurchak observed among younger Russian artists a local pendant of global "new sincere" trends. As he views it, their art testified to a "post-post-Communist," specifically Russian, brand of sincerity—one that favored rather than rejected Soviet myths.

This post-Soviet turn to Soviet aesthetics is often treated as reactionary nostalgia. Yurchak disagrees—and he also takes issue with his colleague Serguei Oushakine, an anthropologist who sees the post-Soviet trend of actively revisiting the past not as outright politicized behavior but as a mere "act of mechanical retrofitting."[115] Oushakine is convinced that the intense Russian interest in the Soviet past is fueled by a nostalgic longing for "activating old forms . . . and . . . inhabiting already existing structures"—not by a desire to restore the Soviet system.[116] Yurchak does discern a political dimension in post-Soviet nostalgia. Contrary to those who warn against political reactionism *and* to Oushakine, however, he prefers portraying this nostalgia in remedial terms. In his words, in contemporary Russian art we are witnessing deliberate attempts to engage with the Soviet past in order to "enable an aesthetic construction of the future."[117]

In analyzing this new-sincere engagement with the Soviet past, Yurchak draws on concrete works of (musical, visual, and animation) art and conversations with creative professionals with a Soviet-Russian background. In each, the memory thread I trace in this chapter is pervasive. Take the reception of the popular retro-Soviet band Kim and Buran: Yurchak explains how a reviewer noted in 2005 that their music "nostalgically immerses us into the great past of Soviet films about pioneers who dream of following in Gagarin's footsteps[. It evokes the] kind of untainted perception of life that is characteristic of a child. This is what *new sincerity* is all about!" (italics original).[118]

An unblemished look back on Soviet life: that is central, too, to work by the artist Dasha Fursey, whom Yurchak interviewed for his sincerity research when she was in her twenties. Fursey, who paints distinctly positive images of icons from Soviet culture (see figure 2.1 for an example), is currently represented, among other institutions, by London's prestigious Saatchi Gallery. In 2008 she professed to Yurchak how, starting from the early 2000s, she had felt a renewed interest in the "untaintedness and sincerity" of Soviet-era images and looks.[119] In Yurchak's view, Fursey and her contemporaries offer an "aesthetics [with] its own political potential . . . based on the redeemed categories of sincerity and idealism."[120] He concludes by proposing that both the turn toward a new sincerity in contemporary Russian art and the wider popular demand for that trend are "instances of the same contemporary phenomenon of reassessing the history of Soviet modernity, exploring its meaningful aspects, and separating the original ethical aspirations of that modernity from the political regime which relied on them for its own ends."[121]

Both here and in his other reflections on the topic, Yurchak not only discerns in post-Soviet Russia a persistent interest in sincere self-expression, he also frames that interest in manifestly historical terms—as an artistic attempt to grapple with the recent past.

No matter how much their individual takes on "a new sincerity" may differ, Yurchak, Lipovetsky, the Kabakovs, Ivanova, and Epstein all use this particular phrase—or close variations on it—to capture the

FIGURE 2.1 Painting from artist Dasha Fursey's "Pioneer Girls" series (2005), which Alexei Yurchak discusses as representative of a "post-post-Communist sincerity" in contemporary Russian art. Yurchak, "Post-Post-Communist Sincerity," 265ff. Image courtesy of Dasha Fursey.

same idea. Each voices the notion that sincerity can be used as a therapeutic social tool, a healing device in the struggle with historical horrors. Admittedly, a scholar like Lipovetsky takes a distrustful stance toward that idea: he doubts the possibility of reviving sincerity in a postmodern world. When he (skeptically) monitors public debates on a "new sincerity," however, he joins his colleagues in one crucial respect: all frame the new discursive trend as instrumental in curating cultural trauma.

STIOB GONE ROTTEN: REACTIONARY TURNS

In their fascination with a curative sincerity, Lipovetsky and the others are no pioneers, as we have seen. They inherit the logic and, in part, language of sincerity of Gandlevskii—and, even more important, of Prigov—but they adapt this language to Putin's Russia. I write "Putin's Russia" rather than simply "today's Russia" here on purpose: when memory and sincerity concerns intertwine, the question of what is happening in the Kremlin today is never far away. Contemporary politics is ubiquitous in Prigov's new sincerity projects; political engagement underpins Yurchak's notion of a post-post-Communist sincerity; but political concerns also shape the less liberal voices that, with time, entered post-Soviet sincerity debates. A closer look at these voices helps to assess why, in the course of the 2000s, the debates make a distinctly reactionary turn.

Under Putin, new memory paradigms take the place of the relentless historical revelations that characterized perestroika-era and 1990s public space. In Putin-era political culture, Stalin's name is rehabilitated on official holidays and on World War II memorials. It reappears in remarkably positive contexts in school textbooks on Russian history.[122] Official institutions promote a glorious Soviet myth—one whose powerful political legacy lives on in contemporary Russia, and whose geopolitical implications today frighten most of the Western world. The authorities revive and hail Soviet memory for a clear reason: the past is an indispensable tool in forging a patriotic public retromentality.

For the new sociocultural landscape, postmodern rhetoric is not unimportant. In Lipovetsky's words, what we are witnessing in Putin's Russia is an "aestheticization and secondary legitimization of Soviet culture"—one that instrumentalizes postmodern discourse by leading it "into the cultural-political *mainstream*" (italics original).[123] In Lipovetsky's view, this process of aestheticization is enacted by concrete social strata: Lipovetsky is referring both to reactionary politicians who borrow postmodern rhetoric to legitimize controversial measures and to artists who are well versed in postmodern rhetoric and use it to openly profess reactionary political ideas.

Illustrative of the new "Russian-Soviet identity," as some scholars call the mind-set that I am describing here[124]—and of the role that sincerity anxieties play in it—is the art of Aleksei Beliaev-Gintovt. Beliaev-Gintovt is both a painter of monumentalist canvases of Soviet *realia*— say, Red Square parades and socialist-realist statues—and a self-professed Stalin adept. In interviews, he marries a tone reminiscent of postmodern stiob to concrete nationalist-political engagement. He openly sympathizes with Putin and Stalin; he glorifies state institutions; and in recent years, he has applauded Russia's military interventions in Ukraine.[125] In one representative interview, Beliaev-Gintovt argues:

"It is impossible to imagine a nobler thing than Stalin's architectural project. The ideal reconstruction project for Tskhinvali [the capital of South Ossetia, a prime battleground during the Russo-Georgian war in 2008] would be the style of Stalin. City of the Sun, Stalin style. Stalinist architecture is the emanation of the Sun."[126]

Bearing in mind that Beliaev-Gintovt believes that a Caucasian "mountain road along which no Russian tanks move looks incompetent," it is easy to imagine just how controversial this figure is within the Russian art world. Not surprisingly, when he won the Kandinsky Prize—a prestigious international art award—in December 2008, both the local and the global art world expressed furious indignation. More than one art professional concurred with curator Andrei Erofeev when the latter called Beliaev-Gintovt a Russian Leni Riefenstahl.[127]

Beliaev-Gintovt is no isolated case. His work represents a neotraditional turn in post-Soviet (literary) art—one whose approach to the Soviet legacy is hard to place on a scale between downright seriousness and full-fledged parody. Not surprisingly, to the public reception of neotraditionalist works, sincerity anxieties are perennial. Most notably, perhaps, sincerity concerns surface in the numerous labels that academic commentators apply to the new stance to the past. Central to their definitions is the notion of stiob and the question to what extent individual artists or intellectuals are seriously identifying with the new patriotic ideology. Here are four examples:

- Lipovetsky launched the term "Post-Sots," which he defines as a communication mode in post-Soviet art "that allows the viewer/reader, on the one hand, to escape direct ideological identification with heroes, preserving the illusion of ironic distance ('stiob'), but on the other, . . . to be drawn into [the hero's] plot . . . on an irrational, *pseudo-deideologized* level" (italics original);[128]
- sociologist Mischa Gabowitsch speaks of "stiob fascism" and explains that, in contemporary Russia, "as long as the space of sincere political debate remains restricted, . . . fascism will remain—among other things—an object of stiob." In Gabowitsch's view, in the late 1990s stiob transformed into an intellectual "culture of cynicism" that proved a perfect breeding ground for Putin's political system. In chapter 4 we shall see that Russian

protest cultures of the 2010s have been read as a "sincere" response to precisely this system;[129]

- cultural historian Boris Noordenbos has introduced the phrase "imperial stiob," for "contradictory amalgams of postmodernism with restorationism" in post-Soviet literature that borrow from stiob aesthetics their "confusing blend of ideological seriousness and self-mocking irony";[130]

- and, in analyzing early manifestations of post-Soviet neo-traditionalism, art historian and curator Ivor Stodolsky talks of "stiob gone rotten," or a process "where the satirical act becomes what it satirises" and where the "sincerity" of artistic gestures becomes "questionable."[131]

Just how sincere is the political commitment, patriotism, and Stalin idolatry of Beliaev-Gintovt and his like? And what does sincerity even mean in the cynicism- and hypocrisy-laden Russia of Putin (a society where—as writer and producer Peter Pomerantsev puts it in a much-lauded recent analysis of "the new Russia"—"life is just one glittering masquerade, where every role and any position or belief is mutable")?[132] These two questions resound throughout the different definitions. In each, sincerity is a thorny term; and how, in present-day Russia, could it not be? Even to the same Yurchak who is known for his analyses of stiob and of (a politically productive) post-post-Communist sincerity, the notion of a revived sincerity has proven troublesome in recent years. When I presented a talk on this book in St. Petersburg in October 2014, Yurchak commented that any discussion of present-day sincerity talk in Russia should acknowledge its political twists. Under Putin, the concept had "mutated" into "something that paved the way for cynical purism," and for uncomplicated, collectivist patriotism.[133]

The examples above were all coined by academic commentators. Artists used less distanced wordings for similar worries about the increasingly neoreactionary memory culture that we witness in Putin's Russia. "This is sentimentalism, but not a critical one": that is how "critical sentimentalism founder" Gandlevskii summarizes a widely held concern about the artistic mode that artists like Beliaev-Gintovt epitomize. When we met in Moscow, Gandlevskii told me that he especially worried about the top-down memory culture within which the new credo emerges. "In today's 'official ideology of idealizing the past,'" he feels, "intimate feelings are stolen by the authorities" (in an odd twist of fate, in May 2016 the same Gandlevskii would briefly be incarcerated by these same authorities for tearing down a Stalin poster from a wall at the Lubyanka subway station in Moscow).[134]

Sentimentalism as a top-down instrument to cement the system: Gandlevskii's view on Putinist Russia calls to mind an emotional regime that reigned in Russia not so long ago. I am speaking of Soviet Russia and its insistence—discussed in detail in chapter 1—on civic sincerity and publicly testified honesty. In the words of historians Petr Vail and Aleksandr Genis, in Thaw-era Russia "sincerity was obliged to be aggressive" and pro-Soviet, and failure to display it in public could be publicly reprimanded.[135] In Putin's Russia, state authorities no longer measure the extent to which citizens sincerely support official ideologies (in today's Russia, experts claim, the need to trust citizens is replaced by an insistence on official documents);[136] but the self-professed sincerity of an artist like Beliaev-Gintovt *is* aggressive—and the public acclaim for his purportedly honest support of the regime inevitably evokes associations with the Soviet era.

In my talk with Dmitrii Golynko-Vol'fson, he expressed a concern regarding new-sincere discourse similar to Gandlevskii's. In his view, from the turn of the century onward new-sincerity rhetoric has gradually morphed into "neoconservatism."[137] Illustrative of Golynko's worry is the biography of the same Timur Novikov to whom Golynko ascribes such a major role in 1980s new-sincerity rhetoric. In the late 1990s, this artist started embracing openly reactionary-traditional political paradigms. He called for a "new seriousness" in Russia's "cultural ecology"—one reliant, to cite Novikov expert Ivor Stodolsky, on a "semi-ironic nostalgia for imperial glory."[138] In the course of the 2000s, radical-nationalist ideologists started glorifying a similar imperial nostalgia. In a programmatic interview in 2004, Russia's best-known promoter of neofascist and expansionist thinking—the political scientist Aleksandr Dugin—prophesied that the "main principle" of new Russian art "will be the absence of irony—that is, a new seriousness. A grin instead of a smile, a terrible instead of a funny joke."[139]

It is a long way from Epstein's optimistic "hangover poetics" to Dugin's grim "grin instead of a smile"—and in the context of the geopolitical tensions of the mid-2010s, the latter sounds ominous, to say the least. What matters to me here is this: together, these and the other examples monitored in this section illustrate that Prigov was not alone in linking sincerity to Russian collective memory. Naturally, pleas for a "new seriousness," "new sincerity," or "neo-sincerity" take on one guise when undertaken by liberal critics and quite a different one when embarked on by neoconservative politicians and artists. But the various appeals and efforts to breathe new life into sincerity rhetoric have things in common, too. What is most important is that they share the same trait that we discerned in Prigov's art earlier. This, as we saw, is the insistence to view sincerity as a tool to cope with collective—and especially Soviet—memory.

MEMORY, MARKETING, MEDIA: NEW TURNS IN THE DEBATE

In 2007, writer-cum-activist Kirill Medvedev published an essay that quickly captured international attention. Medvedev (not to be mistaken for his ex-presidential namesake) gained fame as a poet around the year 2000. In the mid-2000s he moved from literary activity to radically leftist activism. He is now known as the founder of a Marxist publishing house and as an organizer of neoleftist political actions—think literary solidarity evenings for striking workers, or a street protest against the staging of Brecht in a purportedly "bourgeois" theater.[140] Critics have repeatedly linked Medvedev's verse with a "new sincerity" in Russian poetry, and some also relate his recent turn to nonfiction directly to a post-postmodern craving for sincerity. In their view, the poet uses his "op-ed writing of the public intellectual" to reclaim sincere artistic language through political discourse.[141] Medvedev himself fuels such readings of his career shift in the essay that interests me here.

Written in 2008, "The Writer in Russia" couples a neo-Marxist protest against postmodernism to a fierce critique of present-day Russia. In Medvedev's view, under Putin Russia's artistic climate is defined "not so much by 'money' and 'celebrity' . . . , but by the 'new sincerity.' "[142] The poet sketches this "post-postmodern" mentality, with its foregrounding of "direct expression" and "biographical experience," in critical strokes. "It is President Putin and contemporary poetry and the broadcasters on television. It is [Belarusian president] Alexander Lukashenko admitting that his party falsified the elections—lowering Lukashenko's numbers from 93 percent to 80 percent—because, Lukashenko very sincerely confessed, 'the European Union wouldn't have accepted the results otherwise.' This is simultaneously unbelievable and symptomatic. The new sincerity is the blogosphere, with its absolutely sincere poets in one corner and its equally sincere Nazis in the other."[143]

Putin, Lukashenko, neo-Nazis: in Medvedev's vision of a new sincerity, poetry once again goes hand in hand with politics. Not surprisingly, Soviet history looms large over the "new emotionalism," as Medvedev occasionally calls the new mind-set. According to him, although arising partly as a reaction to postmodernism, "the new emotionalism" responds no less to another cultural condition: the "confused and conflicted (post-)Soviet consciousness" that marks today's Russia.[144]

Medvedev is yet another example of a writer for whom a "new sincerity" is by definition a curative sincerity. To him, the newly revived sincerity is "a tool that c[an] force open" existing cultural discourses— discourses among which "the rough, ideologized Soviet one" plays first fiddle.[145] Ultimately, however, the author concludes that, as it stands, "the new sincerity" fails to succeed in fulfilling that healing promise.[146]

But I am not paying attention to Medvedev's essay here in order to repeat my point on sincerity and memory. I am doing so because his text flags a diachronic change in post-Soviet sincerity discourse. "The Writer in Russia" echoes the concern with memory that still permeates Russian sincerity debates today—but it links that concern with new directions in which the debates gradually moved between the late 1990s and the late 2000s, and which will be central to the next two chapters of this book.

The first change of course is exemplified by the poet's reference to commodification. When Medvedev places "new sincerity" in opposition to "money" and "celebrity," he is responding to debates that fascinated an increasingly wide audience in the Russia of the 2000s. For creative professionals and their critics, the tension between artistic sincerity and commercial interests became a central anxiety at the time. I trace this "commodificatory turn" of the debate in chapter 3—but I want to use this moment to briefly return to Prigov and emphasize that commodification concerns have not been absent from Prigov's sincerity work and its reception either.

In the 2000s, both critics and Prigov himself repeatedly linked his interest in sincere expression to attempts to popularize—or, to use a less nuanced term, "sell" or "brand"—his art.[147] Most elaborately, Prigov toyed with the relationship between artistic sincerity and commercial pragmatism when describing his participation in an art project entitled "Crying Artists" (2005). In his own words, this project—a series of photographs of sobbing and weeping artists—aimed to "show artists in their genuine image and meaning—as sincere and deeply feeling creatures. But they, today's artists, are—understandably—although not all, not all!—but in general, they are cynics and pragmatics. . . . How does one draw that type into crying?"[148] Ultimately, Prigov continued, the authors of the project used onions to create a work in which "the artists' faces are wrought into a crying grin, their eyes flood with moisture, a treacherous tear crawls over their cheeks." "This," he concludes, "is the great deception of art and all sorts of artistry."[149]

In his take on the "Crying Artists" project, Prigov revived old concerns about sincerity and artistic pragmatism—concerns that I discussed in chapter 1 and to which we return in chapter 3—but he also played with classic views on crying as a pragmatic strategy. In a cultural history of tears, historian-cum-journalist Tom Lutz sketches how, throughout human history, the tear has been read both as "the ultimate mark of a sincere and truthful heart" *and* as "tactics in various petty power plays and deceptions."[150] Just how lively both readings still are today can be seen from the commotion over the teardrops that Vladimir Putin shed in March 2012 during his presidential election victory speech: both in social media and in the press, the million dollar question that they provoked was: "Are Putin's tears sincere or strategic?"[151]

Prigov would have loved the commotion over Putin's tears: tears form a persistent motif in both his visual works and his literary writings,[152] and in time, he started to openly connect this motif with reflections on commodification. He did so in the text on crying artists, but also in a section on his personal website called "online projects." As Andrei Prigov told me, for this section his father teamed up with a site administrator who composed a set of plain animated GIF pictures.[153] The images alternated with comments by Prigov—comments that mostly displayed the same feel-good tone as his New Sincerity messages of the 1980s, and that revolved wholly around notions of lyrical expression and weeping.[154] At one point the poet claimed: "I cry and tears overflow . . . the entire screen, what is more, the entire world." This assertion is followed by a kitschy image of a tear whose caption reads "Tear of a child: 8,5$."[155]

Prigov's online projects bring us to a second new direction—next to that of artistic pragmatism—in sincerity debates. After the 1990s, these debates intertwine inextricably with discourse on (new) media. Medvedev's "Writer in Russia" essay is again revealing of this change of course.

Among other things, Medvedev defined "the new sincerity" as "the blogosphere, with its absolutely sincere poets in one corner and its equally sincere Nazis in the other." This statement might look enigmatic to a reader with limited knowledge of the (Russian) blogosphere— but it refers to a popular vision of blogs and new media as the ultimate loci of a revived sincerity or post-postmodern social engagement. My chapter 4 explores that vision in detail—but it would be wrong to envision discussions on sincerity and media as wholly isolated from the memory-related thread I traced on the preceding pages. Sincere expression and new media interconnect in Medvedev's essay; but they also mingle in Prigov's art. On his website, the same Prigov for whom memory was so formative to sincerity eagerly (if never without a playful wink) used his "online projects" to echo readings of digital media as vessels for sincere expression. At one point on the page, he asks viewers of the "online projects" page to "try to enter all humanity's pains and sufferings onto the site"; at another, he expresses a desire to reflect the beauty of life on an "enormous screen. . . . To simply write down, as it is in the heart, in all its length and width: Life is beautiiiiifuuuuuuul! Bye, DAP."[156]

MEMORY, CONFLICT, AND CURATIVE SINCERITY: CONCLUSION

With Prigov's digital art and the "Crying Artists," we have lifted a tip of the veil for the chapters that follow—and that track discourse on sincerity, commodification, and digitization. In this chapter, memory took the lead instead. We have seen how a wide range of post-Soviet artists and critics read sincerity as a coping tool for the "scorching" Soviet experience, as a creative reassessment of Soviet history, or as a vehicle for digesting historical trauma. Together, they illustrate how in Russian literature, music, film, visual arts, and animation, thinking about a "post-postmodern" or "new" sincerity is inextricably intertwined with attempts to deal with the recent past. They also force us to change some of the views that currently predominate in studies both of post-Soviet Russia and of sincerity. By way of conclusion, let me briefly touch upon these scholarly interventions.

As I have argued, the nexus between sincerity and memory is not unique to Russia—but political history looms exceptionally large over new-sincere talk in post-Soviet artistic and literary debates. This should not surprise us, perhaps: in chapter 1 we saw that politics have permeated Russian (literary) sincerity rhetoric ever since the sentimentalist era.

Political history—and especially the Soviet trauma—is, moreover, formative to contemporary Russian literature. "What it emulates and struggles with, is history," says Alexander Etkind of post-Soviet litera- ture; and Rosalind Marsh argues that "Russian society's confrontation with its past" is a leitmotif of post-Soviet writing.[157] Etkind believes that the preoccupation with the Soviet past in post-Soviet writing is inevita- ble. In his view, since post-Soviet society lacks "hard memory" (this historian's metaphor for monuments, state laws, or court decisions that critically assess the recent past), reminiscences of Soviet terror tend to adopt "soft" forms (literary, historical, and other textual narratives).[158]

My findings confirm Etkind's views; they also expand them slightly. Apart from excursions into visual arts and film,[159] Etkind has explored "soft memory" primarily in literary and historiographical texts; but the memory-infused discussions on a "new sincerity" that I map illustrate how the Soviet trauma is commemorated in a yet wider range of soft cul- tural domains. Soft memory is Soviet memory as we find it in literature, nonfiction, film, and painting, but also in other audiovisual practices— such as animation art or music.

The story of Prigov and his colleagues, in short, further refines our understanding of (post-)Soviet memory. That artists single out sincerity as an artistic tool for dealing with that memory is not surprising either—and here we arrive at a second insight that my findings compli- cate. Sincerity experts Ernst Van Alphen and Mieke Bal have argued that the concept of sincerity is "firmly lodged" not only in personal relations but also "in public and political tensions." In their words, the notion is principally foregrounded "in times of intercultural tensions and con- flicts."[160] I agree—but I think that perestroika-era and post-Soviet liter- ary debates do compel us to slightly modify or rather stretch their view. These debates demonstrate that interrogations of the concept thrive at times not only of *intercultural* turbulence but also of *intracultural* tumult. In modern Russia, sincerity debates flourished after Stalin's death; and they revived during and directly after the downfall of the Soviet Union. Russian discussions on a post-postmodern, new sincerity developed emphatically in the aftermath of this—internal—political crisis. Both then and in the post-Stalinist era, in short, it was intracultural rather than intercultural social conflict that triggered discussions on sincerity in art.

Soft memory and sincerity as a postconflict emotion: my analyses thicken and redress existing ideas on both these paradigms. They ask us to rethink existing convictions on contemporary culture in one last, perhaps particularly fundamental way. From the mid-1980s onward, as Russian creative professionals started to assess the then waning Soviet period, they persistently turned to sincerity as a healing tool. On the pages above, I have touched upon a series of artists and critics who all isolate sincerity as an instrument in coping with the Soviet experience. Their insistence on a curative sincerity prompts us to fine-tune the dominant view of perestroika-era and post-Soviet creative culture—and specifically of the postmodern experiment that has been so central to this culture.

As I explain earlier in this book, existing studies emphasize Russian postmodernism's skeptical, ideology-weary nature; its nonserious, deconstructive stance; and its irony and playfulness. Admittedly, with time experts did start speaking of more "serious" or "sincere" strands within postmodernism. As we saw, some allocated a central place to "serious" dimensions of postmodernism from the start, by foregrounding the movement's principal romanticism, lyricality, and ethical commitment. But when it comes to sincerity rhetoric, what postmodern theorizing systematically foregrounds is the fundamental impossibility of straightforward uprightness. Meanwhile, the postmodern artist has not simply given up on sincerity. Postmodern artists display a tangible preoccupation with the concept: to them, it is a highly troublesome, but for that very reason also crucial and affectively charged, philosophical problem. In existing scholarship on postmodernism, this palpable postmodern fixation on the problem of sincerity—the "postmodern Romantic struggle with sincerity," as one Dutch colleague of mine puts it[161]—is often marginalized. It is either embedded in discussions on authorial distance and deconstruction or seen as part of a secondary, "late post-modern" phase.

My analysis in no way prompts us to dismiss the rich insights into Russian postmodernism that have been delivered so far. It is no attempt at demonstrating that Dmitrii Prigov was, in fact, more sincere than current studies claim. Neither do I suggest that deconstruction and play are irrelevant to the view on sincerity of Prigov and his contemporaries. Quite the contrary: this view is steeped in demythologizing, deconstructive logic. What my observations do imply is that, in the stories that we tell ourselves about postmodernism, the concept of sincerity merits closer attention. Rather than a random object of deconstructive wit—or an artistic trope that postmodern authors simply dismantle—sincerity anxieties are formative to these stories. Scholars correctly frame the (Russian) postmodernism experience as relativizing and playful; but its leading voices simultaneously insist on affective concerns whose importance to postmodernism is insufficiently captured by theories of deconstruction, play, and relativism. I am speaking of concerns about sincere expression, and the curative potential that this problematic notion has in digesting a troubled past.

CHAPTER THREE

"I Cried Twice"

SINCERITY AND LIFE IN A POST-COMMUNIST WORLD

A MEANS OF COPING WITH THE SOVIET TRAUMA: this post-traumatic function of sincerity has remained intact in recent years. In February 2010, for instance, critic Viktor Misiano defined the art of the renowned artists Vladimir Dubossarsky and Alexander Vinogradov as a "New Sincerity" that serves as a "second 'thaw' "—one that "is evidently nothing other than an attempt to simply discover at least some sort of values" in the face of Soviet history.[1]

At the same time, toward the end of the twentieth century the concept of sincerity began to emerge in very different—and less historically imbued—settings. This chapter opens with an overview of new directions in post-Communist sincerity discussions, before homing in on one particularly dominant rhetorical thread. I am speaking of the trend to embed sincerity in thinking about post-Soviet socioeconomic life. Amid a growing group of purportedly new-sincere artists, writers, filmmakers, and musicians, I devote special attention to one highly controversial cultural icon: the writer Vladimir Sorokin. Around the turn of the century and in the early and mid-2000s, his pleas for a move away from deconstructivist logic triggered fierce metaliterary debate. In the debate, sincerity-related anxieties played a crucial role. Rather than as a tool to help digest the Soviet past, the concept now featured heavily in a quest to understand the present—and to face the socioeconomic challenges of life in a post-Communist world.

THE 1990S AND 2000S: BUILDING A NEW SINCERE CANON

In this book's Introduction and in chapter 1, I outlined how the early 1990s witnessed the slow unfolding of a global post-postmodern debate. Between then and today, talk of a "new," "late," or "post-postmodern" sincerity has spread to an ever-widening transnational range of creative disciplines. Apart from those covered in the previous chapter—literature, music, animation, art, film, and journalism—they include TV, comics, new and social media, and product and fashion design.[2] Symptomatic of the wildly varying phenomena to which, with time, new-sincerity rhetoric was applied was an article on "a geeky 'new sincerity'" in the online journal *Wired* in 2010. *Wired* reporter Angela Watercutter used her text to simultaneously frame the popular American TV series *Glee*, singer Lady Gaga, and President Barack Obama as emblematic of a post-ironic sincerity.[3]

No less varied, from the 1990s onward, are the social contexts in which different new sincerities have cropped up across different world regions. Initially, a revived sincerity was proposed as an answer to postmodernism, but in time its defenders also presented it as a response to the 9/11 attacks, to celebrity culture, consumerism, and the financial crisis, and to mediatization and digitization.

In Russia, during the 1990s and 2000s I saw visions of a revived sincerity extend to an especially divergent plethora of cultural and artistic practices. Art works, literary texts, films, theater plays, classical concerts, pop songs, fashion boutiques, blogs, TV programs:[4] even Masiania—a popular Russian cartoon character—has repeatedly been typified as representative of a "new" or "post-post-Communist" Russian sincerity.[5]

How critics envision this emphatically cross-disciplinary revitalized sincerity is illustrated by an essay entitled "On Sincerity in Art" by author-cum-journalist Dmitrii Bavil'skii. "My strongest recent aesthetic experiences," wrote Bavil'skii in the newspaper *Vzgliad* (*Glance*) in 2005,

> are, in one way or other, linked to sincerity. . . . So it is time to
> speak of a "new sentimentality." Especially since that is exactly

how people try to characterize what, well, say, [the popular
writer, actor, and musician] Evgenii Grishkovets does. . . . First
Grishkovets had these soul-gripping dramatic monologues.
Then plays performed by others. Then he turned to records,
and now books. And everything Grishkovets does, he does very
sincerely. . . . Then [the equally popular singer-songwriter]
Zemfira's new record. . . . Her records are no "theater of songs,"
but a diary (that is why you believe them), a *ZhZh* in song and
in rhyme. . . . Having mentioned Zemfira, one cannot fail to
mention [actress and celebrity] Renata Litvinova . . . another
inveterate superhuman of the contemporary pop scene. . . . The
deliberate artificiality of her image, in which you nevertheless
glimpse a certain ingenuousness: yes, I am not a diva, but I
will be one. . . . Together, they form a series going by the
provisional name "To sincerity in art."[6]

Bavil'skii's essay is a good place to start this chapter's inquiry into 1990s
and early 2000s sincerity rhetoric. In simultaneously envisioning a new
sincerity in theater, music, writing, and film, Bavil'skii adopts the transdisciplinary approach that resounded throughout debates on the trend
in this period. But in building his own new-sincerity canon with prominent names in post-Soviet pop culture, Bavil'skii also interweaves sincerity with a cultural process that has my special interest throughout the
pages that follow—that of celebrification.[7]

LITERATURE: POST-POSTMODERN TURNS
AND NEW SINCERE LABELS

In the 1990s and early 2000s, post-postmodern rhetoric quickly gained
in popularity. In Russia, a particularly generous number of declarations
of "postconceptualist" or "post-postmodern" turns then resounded in the
field that is central to this book: that of literature. In the previous chapter
we saw how throughout the late 1980s and early 1990s a handful of Russian writers and critics promoted a "new sincerity" or "critical sentimentalism." From then on, the group of people advocating a new culture of
sensibility grew exponentially. They blended in with a broader group of
authors, critics, and scholars who all heralded the rise of a late or post-
postmodern age. Here in outline are some milestones in their debate:

- in 1993 the influential poet and critic Mikhail Aizenberg defined post-Soviet reality as "postconceptual," and the task of contemporary poetry as that of "overcoming quotation signs";
- in 1997, critic Viacheslav Kuritsyn signaled "the end of the heroic era of postmodernism" and the advent of a "post-postmodernism" in Russian literature;
- in 1999, literary scholar Mark Lipovetsky retrospectively diagnosed postmodernism's "crisis" and a "new humanism" in 1990s writing;
- and, in 2001, poet, editor, and critic Dmitrii Kuz'min—another leading name in twenty-first-century Russian literary criticism—mapped a "postconceptualist" canon in new Russian poetry that foregrounded "unmediated lyrical expression" while at the same time "acknowledging the impossibility of that expression."[8]

Many examples could be added: in recent years, in Russia as elsewhere, we have seen a gradual but unmistakable crystallization of the idea that postmodernism is in crisis, and that new literary paradigms are on the march.

Not unexpectedly, within a literary landscape colored in post-postmodern hues, (new) sincerity rhetoric is now becoming ever more persistent. In the 1980s and early 1990s, Prigov's and Epstein's pleas for a new sincerity were exceptions—but from the mid-1990s onward, the same phrase begins to circulate among a growing number of literary critics. With time, more and more literary experts use it to tag concrete writers or texts as counterreactive to postmodern mentality. Natal'ia Ivanova, the well-known literature specialist whom we also saw at work in the previous chapter, asserted in 1998 that postmodernism has proven to be "difficult, awkward, uninteresting" for Russian readers, and that she saw more potential in "a literature of 'free breath' and 'new sincerity.'"[9] Ivanova helpfully put forward poets Lev Rubinstein and Sergei Gandlevskii as advocates for the new brand of writing.[10]

In the course of the 2000s, the phrase "new sincerity" attracted yet more resonance among literary professionals. Illustrative of its buzzword status by the late 2000s were the responses I received when interviewing critics and poets for this book in May 2009, at a literary soirée at factory-turned-gallery Vinzavod.[11] Writer-cum-critic Ilya Kukulin thought of "the new sincerity" as a "not uninteresting" trend but found the phrase to be "systematically undertheorized" and "unresolved" as a literary-historical problem. Poet Danila Davydov suggested that we meet later that week, eager as he was to expand on it in detail. Both he and Kukulin had expressed their take on "the new sincerity" in influential critical journals some years earlier.[12] The meeting with Davydov somehow failed to take place, but I did receive minute elaborations on the theme from another guest of the same evening: prose writer Evgenii Popov, whose parodistic miniatures on Soviet life attracted international attention in the 1990s. Popov, who was in his early sixties when I spoke to him at Vinzavod, is today still active as a writer, editor, and blogger. To my inquiry he responded with enthusiasm: a new sincerity, in his view, was a major upcoming trend in contemporary Russian writing.

Later that year, Popov e-mailed me his foreword to a special literary section in the conservative literary journal *Oktiabr'* (*October*). In the e-mail he wrote that the thematic section would unite "a small circle of writers of 'new sincerity,' who let themselves be heard more and more confidently with each year."[13] The "new sincerity à la Popov," as it turned out, differs drastically from that of Prigov in the 1980s. Popov's sincerity defied a series of contemporary trends that ranged from satirical writing to post-Soviet glamour. It protested partly against pulp fiction, and partly—in an embittered attack on postmodernism's purported relativism—against "AS IF apocalyptic authors, [who] blink and whisper: I, ladies and gentlemen, describe horror and ghastliness, I am a cool intellectual, I use swear words, but you understand, of course, comrades, that I do all that on purpose and that it has little to do with reality, after all, you and I are enlightened, politically correct people, of one blood, right?" (capitals original).[14]

Borrowing Prigov's phrase, Popov recycled it in an antipostmodern tirade whose straightforward sarcasm takes us far from its original tenor. So, over time, do many other conceptualizations of a revived sincerity. In fact, by the mid-2010s, the literary tag "new sincere" has become so popular that critics repeatedly complain about its wildly diverging—and, by implication, theoretically inconsistent—usages. Kukulin did so when we met at the Vinzavod factory, as we saw. Kukulin was then voicing a concern that had haunted colleagues for some time. In the year 2000, critic Leonid Kostiukov already felt so irritated by the lack of semantic clarity in new-sincerity rhetoric that he snarled: "How am I to understand new sincerity now, as willing and inclined as I am toward a serious dialogue? . . . We are forced . . . to conclude that the word has undergone a final devaluation. . . . In this Lego-like word chaos one can exchange Skorodumova for Danilov [two poets whose names critics link with the term], and sincerity for humanism."[15]

In 2002, Dmitrii Kuz'min—the same Kuz'min who spotted a "post-conceptualist" turn in Russian writing around the same time—pointed to a similar inconsistency when he parodically used the term in the title of the poetry anthology *It's Easy to Be Sincere.*[16] Cultural historian Irina Kaspe—I shall limit myself to one last influential example—more or less echoed Kostiukov's and Kuz'min's objections a few years later. In an essay in the leading Russian humanities journal *Novoe literaturnoe obozrenie (New Literary Observer)*, she rebuked literary professionals for their neglect of the phrase's conceptualist roots. Once it landed in the hands of critics, Kaspe argued, it acquired downright " 'liquid' meaning." Over the course of time, she complained, they helped "new sincerity" morph from a complex conceptual notion into a tag for a poetry of unproblematic "literary self-exposure, a public demonstration of what is most intimate."[17]

Kaspe correctly pointed to an inflation in usage of the phrase. Between the early 1990s and today, new-sincerity rhetoric crops up persistently in literary scenes from Moscow to Cheliabinsk (where Bavil'skii is partly based). In the same period, the qualification "new sincere" has been bestowed on an increasingly diverse group of Russian writers. The list includes Evgenii Grishkovets, Lev Rubinstein, and Sergei Gandlevskii, as we have seen—but also, to mention some more examples, the poets Dmitrii Vodennikov and Vera Pavlova and prose writers Marta Ketro and Vladimir Sorokin.[18] To Sorokin we turn now.

SINCERITY AND SOROKIN

Around the time that critics were chiding "the new sincerity" as an increasingly confusing or "liquid" label, that same label was eagerly applied to the work of Vladimir Sorokin. The pages below home in on this internationally renowned Russian writer. More specifically, I scrutinize Sorokin's *Trilogy (Trilogiia)* and the fierce metaliterary debates that this prose work triggered in the early twenty-first century. Composed as a set of three novels—*Ice (Led,* 2002), *Bro's Way (Put' Bro,* 2004), and *23.000* (2005)—the *Trilogy* follows the pseudo-gnostic Brothers of Light sect. The Brothers, to whom ordinary men are no more than useless "meat machines," "awaken the hearts" of new members of the sect by striking their chests with magic ice hammers. Once all chosen Brothers are awake—thus goes the sect's founding myth—the earth dissolves, and the members turn into "Eternal Rays of Light."

The Brotherhood narrative and the discussions it has elicited, I believe, merit the attention of more than just the Sorokin specialist. They deserve exploration as a crucial stage in the burgeoning post-Soviet new-sincerity discourse of the early 2000s—the period when the *Trilogy* sees the light. Appearing in a time and place of drastic socioeconomic transformation, this work triggered debates that spotlight sincerity in discussions on a highly pragmatic matter: the practical challenges of post-Communist-era intellectual life. In monitoring these discussions in detail, the analysis that follows refines our knowledge of the post-Soviet literary field. It also helps us understand an important but as yet little studied question. This is the question of how this field has been shaped by—and, in turn, how it has shaped—the broader emotional anxieties and regimes of post-Communist life.

TRUE TO SELF: THE *TRILOGY*

From the moment that its first sections were made publicly available, Sorokin's *Trilogy* has confronted readers with a hermeneutic riddle. Its author is one of post-Soviet Russia's most famous writers, who started his literary career in the 1970s as a shrewd dissector of Soviet ideology and language. In early interviews, Sorokin explained that his work was inspired by postmodern thinking—he mentions Foucault and Derrida as sources of inspiration—rather than by any concrete social or moral interests. In a 1992 interview, he famously claimed to tire of questions about the ethical implications of his writings: "I do not understand that type of query: after all, these are mere letters on a piece of paper."[19]

"Mere letters": although we need not take Sorokin's statement as gospel (to the distinct pathos that seeps through in all his work I return in a moment), his comment does help to explain why his early texts in particular are filled with such a lush mixture of obscene and shocking detail. His fascination with cannibalism, graphic sexuality, violence, and death has raised dust, and not just among professional critics: in 2002 a novel in which he staged Stalin and Khrushchev engaged in anal copulation led to legal charges of pornography. At a public demonstration that drew worldwide attention,[20] protesters deposited nearly seven thousand copies of the book into an enormous papier-mâché toilet right outside the Bolshoi Theatre, in the heart of Moscow.

By the early 2000s, when the protesters staged their toilet stunt, considerations of Sorokin's "tough prose" tended to split into two categories: the nonspecialist, conservative reading (as "vulgar," "unnecessarily violent," "hermetic intellectualism") and the literary-expert, progressive interpretation ("linguistic play," "radically postmodern," "deconstruction of [Soviet] ideology").[21]

The *Trilogy* fails to fall into either division. Since the publication of *Ice* in 2002, reactions to the novels have been exemplified by what literary historian Dirk Uffelmann has called the "topos of a 'new Sorokin.' "[22] Critics had already observed a (late or post-postmodern) change in Sorokin's poetics a few years earlier, upon publication of his novel *Blue Lard* (*Goluboe salo,* 1998)—the same novel that later spawned the toilet protests—and of his scenario for the Russian gangster film *Moscow* (*Moskva,* Aleksandr Zel'dovich, 2000).[23] But with the *Trilogy*—which reached a much wider audience than *Moscow*—discussions about Sorokin's purported literary transformation became ubiquitous. The new Sorokin, readers never stopped marveling, produced accessible page-turners and released them through a best-selling publisher. The new Sorokin invoked esoteric fantasy worlds. The new Sorokin did not play with linguistic styles but wrote about people of flesh and blood, even if these people were a tad frightening (that they propagated the death of all humans who fail to rank as potential members of their sect made it somewhat hard to embrace them as positive emotional heroes).

Perhaps most important, though, was that the new Sorokin elaborated on a familiar literary-philosophical motif: that of being true to one's self. Evoking classic dichotomies, the *Trilogy* presents a narrative that persistently contrasts the "outer body" with the "inner soul," and "mind" with "heart"—and that classically highlights the latter as good poles. The plot revolves around the need to "awaken" human hearts; the members of the sect communicate with their hearts rather than language; and they stress the need to "tell the truth!" In other words, they plead for an all-pervading sincerity—a concept that is foregrounded when a prospective member's refusal to embrace his new life is interpreted as a "defense against sincerity. Which always frightened you."[24] "Ice—childhood—sincerity—power—light," is how Mark Lipovetsky, in an authoritative commentary, summarized the myth uniting the three texts.[25]

"UNMEDIATED SPEECH": THE *TRILOGY* AND SOROKIN

With its foregrounding of the "language of the heart," the *Trilogy* revolves around a motif that could not be more at odds with Moscow Conceptualism and postmodernism—or, to be more precise, with these philosophies as seen through popular lenses. I am speaking of the motif of direct, unmediated expression. It is precisely this motif that has sparked musings on a "sincere turn" in Sorokin's career—musings that are reinforced by his public performances during and after publication of the *Trilogy*.

Starting from the early 2000s, Sorokin's public self-fashioning has undergone a tangible shift. In interviews he gave at the time, he articulates views eerily resembling those of the members of his sect: contemporary humanity is a "totally isolated" "meat machine"; humankind has been "created by a higher mind"; and life's goal consists of "awakening" himself and others.[26] The same interviews indicate that Sorokin now thinks very differently about postmodernism to the way he did in his early years. He publicly reproaches critics who superimpose postmodern theory on his work: in the spring of 2005, in an open letter to the quality newspaper *Nezavisimaia gazeta* (*Independent Gazette*), he claims to have parted with "simulacrae and transgression" and asks readers to "forget . . . about deconstruction."[27] "Before, I created worlds and destroyed them"—he argues elsewhere—but in the *Trilogy*, "I simply create a world and admire it."[28] In this positive, postdeconstructivist poetics, politics matter. "As a storyteller," Sorokin told the German newspaper *Der Spiegel* in 2007, "I was influenced by the Moscow underground, where it was common to be apolitical. This was one of our favorite anecdotes: As German troops marched into Paris Picasso sat there and drew an apple. That was our attitude—you must sit there and draw your apple, no matter what happens around you. I held fast to that principle until I was 50. Now the citizen in me has come to life."[29]

In brief, in Sorokin's public self-comments during the 2000s, sociopolitical commitment and plain delight in creation completely replace his early infatuation with Derrida and deconstruction. The question whether this shift is inspired by a broader creative "school" or trend is not easy to answer. Operating at a time when manifesto-like post-postmodern statements are *en vogue,* Sorokin takes care to steer clear of obvious liter-ary labeling. When I asked him about his view on new-sincerity rhetoric in an interview in 2009, he cautiously avoided identifying his writings with this or any other literary ism in any way. "Maybe it's my age, Ellen," and "nostalgia for childhood": to questions on the theoretical labels that critics tag to his recent work, he answered with these and other general (and evasive) statements.[30]

Overt identification with a new literary school is clearly not So-rokin's goal—but in explaining his new poetics he does provide us with insights into their historical roots. I propose to halt at this historical lineage for a moment, as it teaches us much about the affective logic that underpins Sorokin's public self-fashioning.

In the same conversation I had with him in 2009, Sorokin ex-plained how much he appreciated a world-famous literary predecessor: Leo Tolstoy. In itself, this infatuation was not news to me. Sorokin has been referring to Tolstoy as a major source of inspiration throughout his career.[31] What *was* news was Sorokin's insistence on frankness as one of his precursor's lasting merits. He explained that he had recently bought Tolstoy's collected diaries, adding that "I have never read more open-hearted writers than him. He did not hide any detail from his diary."[32]

That Sorokin appreciated Tolstoy's candidness should surprise few readers who know Sorokin's interviews from the mid-2000s. In these interviews, he unmistakably reverted to the classical vocabulary of artis-tic sincerity that mattered so much to nineteenth-century writers—to Tolstoy in particular. In more than one interview, Sorokin foregrounded such terms as "direct" or "unmediated speech," "tears," and, indeed, "sincerity." *Ice,* for instance, he presented as his "first attempt at a direct utterance about our life."[33] Calling it a product of his "nostalgia for . . . the unmediated," he labeled the text "a novel on the search for a lost spiritual heaven."[34]

At times, the language that "the public Sorokin" of this period em-ploys visibly builds on new insights into cultural theory. An example is his statement in 2005 that literature is an experience that can "stir up sincere tears, the salty taste of which returns a feeling for the real to you."[35] This observation inevitably conjures up art critic Hal Foster's in-fluential plea, in the 1990s, for a "Return of the Real"—that is, a gradual return to an "art and theory that seek to be grounded in bodies and sites, identities and communities."[36] But the interviews and self-comments of the 2000s also lean on historical vocabularies of emotion—particularly the language of sincerity as employed in the nineteenth century.

Sorokin's affinity with nineteenth-century sincerity rhetoric makes itself felt especially when we remember how, ever since the start of his career, this writer has embraced the tradition of placing an irrational but emotionally authentic Russia in opposition to an overtly rational West. In a talk that we had in 2002, Sorokin treated me to a somewhat unexpected but, within his poetics, classical comparison. When I asked him to expand on one of his female characters, he contrasted the purportedly straightforward affective system of Western European women (he compared them to pears) to the emotional layeredness ("like that of an onion") of "the Russian woman."[37] In the mid-2000s, Sorokin returned to the same tradition from a less banal perspective. In his open letter on the *Trilogy* he specifically criticized "Western Slavists" and German and French icons of postmodernism for "play[ing] hide-and-seek behind citations."[38] The honest art that Sorokin propagates instead is of Russian making: the true force of literature, he argues, we find in "the sea of tears that millions of simple readers" have shed over Nikolai Gogol's heroes.[39]

Sorokin's letter, in short, implies that the world can learn a lot from an emotional regime that dominates *Russian* culture in particular. This conviction cannot help but evoke the emotional rhetoric of nineteenth-century Russian intellectual discourse—a discourse in which Sorokin is very much at home. In his early novels, he travesties the style of a range of nineteenth-century Russian writers—Tolstoy or Dostoevsky, for instance, but also such second-rate authors as the radical nihilist Nikolai Chernyshevskii. Sorokin re-creates their language with such virtuosity that it is sometimes hard to tell the mimicry from the original.[40]

To date, critics have mostly stressed Sorokin's infatuation with nineteenth-century Russian classics when pointing to his "metadiscursivity"—that is, to his skill in re-creating and toying with existing linguistic styles.[41] But Sorokin's interest in Russia's nineteenth-century legacy is not irrelevant to his self-view as a writer either. In chapter 1 we saw how—centuries before Sorokin gained fame—the same authors whose style he masters so brilliantly promoted a cocktail of Russian-only "true spirituality" (Boym on the intellectual culture of the century's early decades); of "plain living and sincerity" (Kelly on radical intellectuals in the mid-nineteenth century); and of contrasts between a Western insistence on intellect/reflection/reason and a Russian preference for soul/intuition/faith/sincerity (Makushinskii's and my own analyses of nineteenth-century literary and philosophical discourse). We also saw how Tolstoy, in his famous essay on sincerity in art, was a particularly explicit defender of "sincerity and plainness" as the Russian artist's answer to the "frivolity" and artificiality of Western European writers—a rhetorical move that Sorokin repeats almost literally when he contrasts Western Slavists with Russian writers.

Both in his texts and in his public self-presentation, in a word, "the new Sorokin" builds on Tolstoy's and other nineteenth-century rhetorical traditions. In our interview, he pointed to another source for his preoccupation with undiluted artistic sincerity. This was his recent immersion in Russia's contemporary music scene. More specifically, he attributed his changed poetics to a shift in personal contacts, from Moscow Conceptualist circles to "musicians—both composers and performers—and people from cinema and theater."[42] He linked his recent predilection for a rhetoric of sincerity specifically to the first of those categories. In his words, the language of sincerity is especially suited for music, which "does not need intermediaries" and "requires some sentimentality, some intense sensitivity."[43]

Sorokin is indeed at his most persistently sentimental when commenting on his first (and hitherto only) libretto, for Leonid Desiatnikov's opera *Rosenthal's Children* (*Deti Rozentalia,* 2005). "This is no postmodernism, no deconstruction," he has stressed in interviews:

- [the libretto] is . . . very moving and evokes sincere and exalted feelings among normal people . . . this is an opera about the exalted. I wanted to write a moving human story;
- this is a very human story with its own metaphysics. I think that quite a few tears will be shed over *Rosenthal's Children;*
- personally, I cried twice;
- I think [the libretto] has become quite moving, just as the opera as a whole, which ultimately provokes tears of empathy;
- I think this has become quite a moving and sincere production, which evokes feelings of sympathy among listeners.[44]

"Moving," "sincere feelings," "tears," "crying": some fifteen years after Prigov addressed friend and colleague Sorokin in his programmatic

plea for a "New Sincerity" (the plea that I discussed in chapter 2), Sorokin himself foregrounds sincere expression as the key to his poetics.

In his recent work and public statements, Sorokin could not have
moved further away from the image that is often ascribed to postmodern
writers: that of the cool, emotionally distant rationalist. Experts have eagerly used that image to frame Sorokin's early writings. Like Prigov, and
like many other post-Soviet authors, he is believed to have gradually
moved from "cold" postmodernism to the emotionally "warmer" spheres
of a new sincerity or seriousness. A closer look at his oeuvre, however,
shows that this diachronic reading does not fit easily with reality. In
chapter 2 we saw that Prigov was never the strictly distanced observer
that critics have so often made him out to be. Neither was Sorokin. In
1992—the same year he called his work "mere letters on a piece of
paper"—he spoke of his growing hesitation toward ironic modes. "I can't
use the same devices any more," he claimed in an interview. "At the moment I love reading very un-ironic things. Perhaps irony has started to
irritate me. . . . I think that irony has simply ceased to work here, as it
ceased to work a long time ago in the West."[45] In our interview in 2009,
Sorokin admitted in so many words that he had, in fact, defied ironic
distance as early as 1985. In this year, Prigov addressed his "New Sincerity" plea to Sorokin—who was present in person upon their first public
pronouncement. This is what his colleague said to him at the time: "In
accordance with the Russian literary tradition, I read in your texts some
lofty ideas . . . , a positive content and axiology, but then You yourself
have not so far admitted to anything of the kind! . . . Surely, Vladimir
Georgievich, we are not forbidden direct expression? Forever? . . . and
in general, Vladimir Georgievich, one wants tenderness! Sure, I can
read it from your face, that this is what you want! . . . After all, we need
ideology! . . . we need ideals!"[46]

That Prigov's plea did not lack playfulness is an observation that I
discussed in detail in chapter 2. What matters here is that Prigov used it
to ask Sorokin to give his readers precisely that which they later found in
the *Trilogy*: tenderness, ideals, and direct access to the author's worldview. When I asked Sorokin how he had responded to Prigov's questions
when first hearing them in 1985, he answered: "These questions did
not need to be answered. They already contained their own answer. He
already knew me well at the time."[47] If a little cryptic, his words do imply

that, in the mid-1980s, Prigov's sincerity anxieties were far from alien to him.

Sorokin's artistic biography, in short, contradicts the views of a radically divided "cool" early and emotionally committed or "sincere" late phase in his career. In truth, a concern for sincere expression resonated in it from the very start. Sorokin's readers have not been wholly indifferent to this concern. Experts of post-Soviet culture have insisted from an early stage that Sorokin's work exuded a "pathos of positivity and nationalism" that was less "external" and detached than the author himself professed (Ekaterina Degot'), and that his work, "for all its claims to detachment," was "a passionate response to a society that lived on hypocrisy and sham" (Sally Laird).[48] Their observations are in line with as resonant a voice in the debate on postmodernism as Linda Hutcheon; she detects in postmodern irony "an affective 'charge' . . . that cannot be ignored."[49] Their views concur, too, with those critics of Russian postmodernism and stiob who point at the complex relationship between irony and genuine emotional self-revelation; and, to mention another influential example, with Boris Groys's analysis of Sots Art—the late Soviet and post-Soviet art that today we call postmodern. In his seminal study *Gesamtkunstwerk Stalin*, Groys argues that irony and post-Stalinist Russian culture make a problematic match. After the Stalinist experiment, he argues, Russian artists have simply become too aware of their own involvement in ideological processes to wholeheartedly embrace an ironic or ridiculing mode.[50]

The sensitivity of Groys, Hutcheon, and others to the tension between irony and pathos, detachment and affective commitment, or mockery and sincerity has done much to refine theorizing on postmodernism. What they did not change, however, is the relative neglect, in leading studies of Russian postmodernism, of sincerity as something that artists strive or long for. As with Prigov's, a closer look at Sorokin's writings tells us that, to a greater extent and earlier than leading experts acknowledge, Russian postmodernists struggled with concerns about "direct expression" and "tenderness." Rather than being a prelude to a late or post-postmodern phase, these sincerity anxieties were pivotal to the Russian postmodern experience from the start.

Sorokin's interest in the sphere of "unmediated" sentiments—that much I hope to have made clear here—was, by the turn of the millennium, not an unexpected move. It has always resonated in his oeuvre and self-comments. What did change toward the late 1990s is the persistence with which Sorokin started promoting undiluted sincerity. What changed, too, is the means that he used to convey intimate self-revelation. Apart from literary texts and interviews, these tools—as we shall see next—now included mass media and visual tools.

"I MEAN IT": PUBLIC PROFILE

Sorokin's self-professed move toward the sphere of "unmediated" sentiments is no isolated case. It occurs in a cultural era that displays a growing concern with the mediatization of society—a concern to which we shall return in chapter 4. In Russia, the same concern has a tangible impact on literary metadebates. We saw that in 2001 Dmitrii Kuz'min mapped a "postconceptualist" canon in new Russian poetry that foregrounded "unmediated lyrical expression"—and from the mid-1990s onward, it has been difficult *not* to notice interest in unhampered personal expression thriving among former Moscow Conceptualists. We saw in chapter 2, for one, how Lev Rubinstein switched from verse to first-person journalistic writing around the mid-1990s; and how, in the early 2000s, a book-length interview with Prigov was presented as "one long personal utterance" by an artist who had earlier foregrounded a mere "image."[51]

But Sorokin's shift toward the emotive-personal sphere has been particularly hard to miss. This author has shared his new public profile with a mass audience, via a plethora of interviews and public appearances that have foregrounded his private self rather than the figure of the literary professional. In early interviews, Sorokin clung mostly to literary-technical spheres—but from the early 2000s onward, he began mentioning family members, expressing political views, and insisting on tropes of honesty and openness. "I want to frankly claim," "I mean it," "That truly excites me": these and similar metadeclarative observations now abound in his public statements.[52]

Each of these new features conveys the same message: rather than the inscrutable Sorokin of the 1990s, this is the *real* writer opening up to readers. From 2009 onward, the "real Sorokin" even acquired an independent publication platform when the author launched a blog for the elite social-media project Snob. Since then, first-person mini-narratives have frequently updated Snob readers on the writer's whereabouts and his views on, say, politics, food, or the literary scene.[53] When readers comment online, Sorokin often treats them to personal replies. His newly revamped website also features a personal blog (one that, admittedly, boasts very few actual posts) whose first entry explicitly solicits reader questions.[54]

The changes in Sorokin's verbal self-fashioning dovetail with a shift in his visual self-representation. Early photographs of the author convey a reserved, emotionally neutral physical presence;[55] on the spines of his first collected volume, an *en face* portrait looks equally restrained.[56] From the early 2000s onward, Sorokin has amended this impersonal public profile. His media appearances have now become tangibly more communicative (and, at times, downright intimate)—from glamorous photo sessions with his daughters and in domestic outfits that allow viewers a glimpse of a naked leg or chest, to online videos in which he leisurely chats away in his dacha garden, enjoys a vodka-tasting session, or revels in a sumptuous dinner.[57] When I suggested that we have a talk about his work—first in 2002, then again in 2009—he proposed meeting not in one of the many anonymous establishments that Moscow boasts but (on both occasions) in the posh place-to-be-seen Café Pushkin.

Sorokin's celebrity-style self-presentation culminated in 2008, when the author starred in a short film available on the online cultural news portal *OpenSpace*. While not devoid of ironic notes—the video is part of a video series on "outstanding and even very outstanding representatives of the scanty masters-of-culture tribe," and at one point Sorokin's dogs are shown copulating[58]—overall the film stays remarkably true to a classic trope: that of the grand writer opening up to his audience. Viewers see Sorokin, with a short beard and dressed all in white, in his stark green garden—birds twitter, birches gleam in the background—and at his wooden desk, a portrait of his ever-beloved Tolstoy at hand, this time with literary classics in the background. He expresses a firm disdain for city life and for the current Russian government. And he resorts, again, to outright sentimental terms when hailing the countryside: "I simply love to wander through the forest. And touch the trees with my hands."[59]

An emphatically nature-loving, openhearted, politically critical intellectual: Sorokin's self-stylization in the *OpenSpace* film toys with classical literary prototypes. Most notably, of course, they include the same Tolstoy whom Sorokin himself so prominently foregrounds in interviews and in the video. In the video, Sorokin's interest in Tolstoy resonates in the very clothes and surroundings in which he is filmed. His all-white attire, the (little) beard, and the stark green trees in the background: together they unavoidably evoke painter Ilya Repin's famous portrait of Tolstoy from 1901. In the Repin painting, we see a bearded Tolstoy against the greenery of his country estate—which, like Sorokin, this writer avidly glorified as the city's purer antipode.

POSTMODERNISM, POSE, PERSON: RECEPTION

Writer of a best seller on "awakening hearts," man with a longing for "the unmediated," interviewee with "frank" opinions, homebody in swanky bathrobe, and publicly proclaimed nature lover: rather than complying with the stereotype of the distant-ironic conceptualist, Sorokin's new public image fits in with post-Soviet utopias of glamour and celebrification. His consistent identification with Tolstoy reinforces rather than clashes with that highly cultivated status of public celebrity: in the words of literary historian Caryl Emerson, "Tolstoy's quest to simplify human nature and return us to nature coincided with the worldwide graphic revolution. . . . [He] became the world's first multimedia celebrity. . . . Not only photographers but cartoonists and newspaper columnists pursued him, or better stalked him, through telegraph, wax cylinder, color photo, newsreel, film."[60]

The paradox that Emerson points out—that between Tolstoy's love for the unmediated and his strong media presence—is not irrelevant to Sorokin's professional biography either. The social setting in which Sorokin expresses his interest in sincere creative expression is far from unimportant to its impact. He professes his love for "the real" in an increasingly mediated society—one that, as some argue, exchanges humanity's age-old insistence on irony and subjectivity for a near-exclusive preoccupation with appearance. Sociologist Harvie Ferguson, for instance, argues that contemporary society boasts a "non-ironic identity"— one that "is not based on trust, or on openness, but on superficiality—on the glamour of the modern personality and of modern identity."[61] In this new "age of glamour," so Ferguson muses, "appearance may well be "consecrated as the only reality in which both personal and social identities are assimilated to a new culture of consumerism."[62]

Consumerism, glamour, appearance: these were certainly productive social categories in the postsocialist, highly mediatized, semiauthoritarian society that Putin's Russia presented in the 2000s. In the words of cultural historians Helena Goscilo and Vlad Strukov, under Putin "Russia's political power . . . is hugely invested in creating glamorous new symbols."[63] This infatuation with glamour and celebrity in post-Soviet space does not come out of nowhere. In the Russia of the 2000s, so Goscilo and Strukov claim, "the discourse of glamour and celebrity has assumed the function of official ideology, with adulatory rituals replicating those of religious cults."[64]

Sorokin's public self-revelations fit perfectly into both the global and the Putin-era demand for glamour. In a move that could have been whispered into his ear by his one-time good friend Boris Groys, Sorokin in his public behavior stabilizes (I am citing Groys) "the celebrity system by confirming the suspicion to which it is necessarily already subjected."[65] Put somewhat differently, "the new Sorokin" models his public behavior in such a manner that it readily fuels those wishing to argue that he exploits public media.

Not surprisingly, Sorokin's recent work and public appearances have provoked heated public debates regarding performativity, artistic integrity, and literary and biographical self-fashioning. Is, readers wonder, the more open Sorokin that we see today a genuine presence, or is he a pretender, a Dorian Gray–like advocate of sincerity as a "method"—one that boosts social and economic statuses? In online chat forums, these and related questions are posed by the angry war veteran, the enthusiastic teenager, and the worried (or, in contrast, excited) parent; but in the 2000s, Sorokin's public self-fashioning is also discussed with increasing fervor in Russia's leading intellectual forums. My special concern here is these last debates, and their gradual shift of attention from the intraliterary to the extraliterary world.

Until roughly the turn of the twenty-first century, literary theorists were inclined to focus in the first place on the world within Sorokin's texts. The title of an influential 1999 edited volume on Sorokin was *Poetics of Metadiscursivity* (*Poetik der Metadiskursivität*); the titles of its individual chapters were mostly conceived according to the scheme "theme or linguistic strategy X in work(s) Y of Sorokin."[66] The same fascination with text-internal poetics and language experiments typifies entries and articles on Sorokin in 1990s literary handbooks and renowned literary-theoretical journals.

After the publication of *Ice*, however, this insistence on the inner world of Sorokin's writings waned, and critics focused more on "the man Sorokin." In the more personalized discussions that subsequently arose, sincerity concerns take center stage. Some critics worry that Sorokin "truly . . . feels" the way his violent characters did (Vasilii Shevtsov), or are disappointed in this Sorokin "without a mask," who turns out to lack a style "of his own" (Ostap Karmodi); others rejoice at the "honest" expression of "Sorokin's true voice" and try to unravel "the person Vladimir Sorokin" (Lev Danilkin), delighted that Sorokin's "new sincerity" allows him to finally "be himself" (Dmitrii Bavil'skii), or glorify him in retrospect as "Russian literature's most sentimental writer" (Vladimir Kukushkin); yet others read the texts through a more skeptical lens, as an attempt to tap into "the crisis of postmodernism" and charm the masses with "a genuine authorial voice" (Psoi Korolenko), or as a "pose," as "word theater" that simply continues the postmodern project and "fools" readers (Shevtsov, again, and Igor' Smirnov).[67]

Sorokin reacts by publicly protesting against parodistic readings of the works. He responds with indignation to the last skeptical reading I cited above, by Igor' Smirnov, a renowned Slavist and then close friend of the author. "Igor' Pavlovich, my dear chap, have a little vodka . . . ," Sorokin says in his open letter: "Believe me, I did not sit down to write the biography of Sasha Snegirev [one of the *Trilogy*'s main heroes] . . . to simply mock . . . our consumer society. How do you imagine such a process?"[68] But Sorokin's statements merely fuel the discussion. More than one commentator glimpses in his protests yet another playful postmodern gesture. "The brilliant stylist . . . threw his audience another bone [and] publicly enacted the role of the contemporary critic"—thus writer-cum-critic Maia Kucherskaia summarized a common, and highly disbelieving, response to the author's objections in the spring of 2005.[69]

The *Trilogy* not only triggers debate among literary critics, it also sets in motion a shift in Sorokin's reception by literary historians—a shift whose impact resonates clearly in the first full-fledged monograph devoted to Sorokin. Published by literary scholar Maksim Marusenkov in 2012, the study aims to demonstrate that, "rather than linguo-stylistic experiments," Sorokin's interests have always been *"ethical questions,* which the writer links tightly to the problem of the interrelationship between literature and real life."[70] In his analyses of Sorokin's work and "artistic manners," Marusenkov promotes "a critical attitude toward the deep-rooted view of [Sorokin] as a *radical* postmodernist." Instead, he sees in the author an "absurdist," whose "conviction of the monstrosity of the modern world and a profound disappointment in humankind accompany him throughout his entire creative journey."[71]

Marusenkov's defiance of rigidly postmodern views of Sorokin— and his defense of a more biographically inspired reading that accommodates ethical commitment and emotional anxiety—is no isolated case. From the publication of the *Trilogy* onward, the question "To what extent does Sorokin's 'true voice' resonate in his work?" has arrested more than one literary historian. Mark Lipovetsky critically maps the work's reception but extends its real-or-fake topos by discussing it as a "non-ironic" attempt to "truly recreate" traditionalist discourse.[72] Literary scholar Mariia Bondarenko, after critically unraveling existing readings of *Ice* and their preoccupation with authorial sincerity, links the text with "new sentimentalist" trends in Russian poetry—trends, she claims, that refuse to clarify the tension between postmodern deconstruction and a "breakthrough of [authorial] sincerity."[73] The German Slavist Dirk Uffelmann, while ultimately concluding that the question of whether the *Trilogy* is a parody or not "need not be solved," starts his analysis of the novels with the question: "Are we to believe Sorokin's 'self-reception' in interviews?"[74] Handbooks of post-Soviet literature engage in similar interrogations of Sorokin's true intent in their analyses of the individual *Trilogy* sequels. Some argue that, with *Bro's Way,* Sorokin has become a "classic without quotation signs: serious and correct"; others that *Ice* merely pursues the conceptualist project, "mystif[ying] not only credulous readers, but also suspicious critics."[75]

Fake or real? That question runs throughout the history of the novels' reception as a basso continuo. I dwell on the question here neither in order to decide whose voices in the discussion are right or wrong nor to suggest that Sorokin's critics all fall prey to binary true-false thinking. Many of them embed their comments in a much more complex perspective on reality than that classic dichotomy suggests. But the different readings of the texts (including Sorokin's own) do share something else: an emphasis on sincerity. This emphasis has my interest here. To be more precise, what interests me is not their preoccupation with authorial truthfulness as such but rather the important change in the post-Soviet sincerity discourse that the *Trilogy* debates elicit. What that change is, I shall now explain in more detail.

"MERCENARY INTERESTS": SINCERITY AND STRATEGY

In the previous chapter, we looked at discussions on a curative sincerity—or, to put it more clearly, at post-Soviet writers, artists, and critics who struggle with the question "How does one configure artistic sincerity after the Soviet trauma?" In the reception of the *Trilogy,* we occasionally encounter the same question. Soviet memory looms especially large when reviewers touch upon the fascination with violence and totalitarian ideology that pervades the text. In discussing this dimension, more than one reviewer has linked the novels to the neotraditionalist turn in twenty-first-century Russia that, as we saw in chapter 2, can be read as yet one more attempt at coping with the Soviet past.[76]

In the late 2000s, the trend toward relating Sorokin's "sincerity interest" to neotraditionalist sentiments increases. It is then fed by Sorokin's public appraisal of Ukrainian writer Mikhail Elizarov. Both in his books and in his behavior, this Sorokin protégé promotes a distinctly neoconservative view of reality. His writing and public rhetoric ooze what Boris Noordenbos calls "imperial stiob"—the "confusing blend of ideological seriousness and self-mocking irony" that I briefly mentioned in chapter 2. Elizarov's performance at the 2011 London Book Fair speaks volumes. According to Oliver Ready's *Times Literary Supplement* report on the fair, "after bewailing life in a postmodernist age deprived of sincerity and big emotions, Yelizarov went on to comment, with great feeling and apparent sincerity, that 'the Stalin problem has been somewhat exaggerated.' "[77] This and other public statements have triggered discussion over the stance toward the Soviet past of Elizarov—and, by implication, that of Sorokin.

In other words, questions related to collective memory matter to the debate about sincerity in Sorokin's work and public presentation. This is not surprising: as I explained in chapter 2, the interrelationship between sincerity and the Soviet trauma is still a vivid concern for many a writer and critic today. At the same time, from the early 2000s onward, Russian sincerity rhetorics have gradually moved away from *memory-related* concerns toward another quest: that of dealing with the post-Soviet *present*. Discussions on artistic sincerity journey into pragmatic spheres, as its participants begin to wonder: how do artists handle the new socio-economic reality with which post-Communist life confronts them?

To the reception of the *Trilogy,* this last question is imperative. The work was published when the muddled perestroika era had come to an end and a new status quo had supplanted confusion about the social, political, and economic transition. In this new era, the politics of honesty that Gorbachev practiced with such success in the late 1980s lost its attraction. Symptomatically, the slogan "Vote with Your Heart" that Russia's then leader Boris Yeltsin used to promote his presidential campaign in 1996 gradually turned into a mock phrase. Today, it sarcastically describes voters who refuse to see through Russian politicians' PR techniques.

The new social and economic realities of the late 1990s and early 2000s left a tangible stamp on Russian literary life. In the perestroika years, Russian writers were confronted with a free market—a development that, together with unrestricted freedom of speech, brought them inescapable social and financial insecurity. Initially, this insecurity was outweighed by the euphoria that followed the regaining of liberty. Over the course of the 1990s, however, the new social situation began to pose serious difficulties for highbrow authors from official and nonofficial backgrounds alike. Both now found themselves in a society in which literature played an increasingly marginal role: not only were state subsidies terminated, the difficult economic situation led to a decrease in consumer demand; authors had to compete with previously forbidden classics *and* with new contenders in the book market; and, to top it all, in the West post-Soviet titles now manifestly lacked the luster of "exotic" or forbidden Soviet-era literature.[78] "Remaining relevant after Communism," to cite cultural historian Andrew Wachtel's study of professional coping strategies among postsocialist writers, proved no easy task.[79]

It was in this complex socioeconomic landscape that Sorokin launched his *Trilogy* and turned to a more public-oriented self-presentation. He did so not only on a rhetorical level: if, in the early 1990s, he claimed in an interview "not [to] take a reader as such into account,"[80] he now launched his work with the popular publisher Zakharov and promoted it actively through numerous appearances in (inter)national media. He did so with success: its publication marked Sorokin's emergence as a key name in mainstream Russian literature. Today his name figures at the top of Russia's cultural hierarchy; he is a best-selling author who securely manages to live off his writing. On a financial questionnaire that I devised for him in 2009, he indicated that his writings have earned him a living since the mid-1990s. From the 2000s onward, he added informally, he was able to live off his work with considerable ease.[81]

Not coincidentally, a recurring question in the sincerity debates that have accompanied the *Trilogy* has been that of commercial commodification. Discussions of Sorokin's switch from a postmodern to an outspokenly sincere self-representation have kept returning resolutely to one and the same inquiry: is that switch literarily or socioeconomically motivated? Is it spurred by a desire for an alternative artistic or affective approach, or is it a strategic step that allows the author to reach a larger audience—and, by implication, to sell more books?

Reviewers keep returning to these and related questions, whether in traditional terms—of a moral dilemma between "selling out" and being "true to oneself"—or in more nuanced inquiries into the interaction between commodification and sincere expression. The philosopher Mikhail Ryklin voiced a popular perspective on his once close friend Sorokin when he plainly accused him of selling out. To his regret, Ryklin wrote in 2003, with *Ice* Sorokin had turned his work into a mere "commodity" and his name into a dubious "brand sign."[82] In 2009, Timur Kibirov expressed a similar view on his colleague when he told me over drinks that the *Trilogy* was Sorokin's attempt to write "the book that people wanted." Although, Kibirov emphasized, he understood the longing to "win as many reader souls as possible," he berated Sorokin for cold-heartedly "guess[ing] according to this principle what people want and then writing and publishing precisely that."[83]

Ryklin's and Kibirov's readings do not excel in theoretical sophistication—but the novels have also led to more complex considerations of the interplay between sincerity and commercial profit. In fact, the list of reviews that touch upon the tension between the two is so long that I can provide a mere selection here. It includes

- the conviction of Igor' Smirnov (the same professor whom Sorokin asked in his open letter to "have some vodka" and drop his skepticism) that *Ice* is a highbrow text "disguised as a commodity for literate idiots," and that *Bro's Way* is an intentionally repetitive sequel, whose dreariness mocks "consumer society, which is forced to buy the same goods today as it purchased yesterday";
- critic and poet Ilya Kukulin's discussion of *Ice* in terms of a tension between its author's "new sincere" interests and its status as an "intellectual best seller," "deliberately calculated to gain quick symbolic and material success";
- the interpretation of another critic and poet whose voice we have heard previously in this book, Dmitrii Golynko-Vol'fson, that the same novel is a "falsification [of discredited ideological truths] in pursuit of personal mercenary and career interests";
- critic Gleb Morev's interpretation of Sorokin's anti-ironic protests as strictly pragmatically motivated: more complex readings would "merely confuse . . . the readers of . . . the [popular] venues where Sorokin published his latest stories";
- and the reading from critic Oleg Zintsov that *Ice* is a sample of "that 'new sincerity' that . . . splendidly enhances the sales of cultural salesware."[84]

Zintsov, Morev, and the other commentators each have their individual take on Sorokin, but they share one thing: a focus on sociostrategic considerations. Sorokin is neither the first nor the only writer whose life and work trigger considerations of this kind—and I want to halt for a moment at the broader critical discourse into which the *Trilogy* reception blends.

In chapters 1 and 2 we saw that questions about a tension between sincerity and commodification tinged the public reception and self-fashioning of Gavriila Derzhavin, Paul Verlaine, and many other canonical names in literary history. The same questions can be distilled from theoretical reflections on some of twenty-first-century Russia's most popular poets. Prigov is a case in point, as we saw in chapter 2. So is Dmitrii Vodennikov, whom I discuss in more detail in chapter 4. Several critics see Vodennikov as the leader of a "new sincerity" in poetic writing—and more than one reader has accused him of using sincerity for commercial gain. Danila Davydov, for instance—the same Davydov who looked forward to telling me more about a reborn Russian sincerity in 2009—argues that Vodennikov embraces a "new sincere" poetics strictly in order to enhance his star status among poetry lovers.[85] In November 2010, journalist Konstantin Shavlovskii followed an analogous logic: he devoted a lengthy TV interview to "finding out from the poet Dmitrii Vodennikov" why in "the new sincerity," "openness is used more and more often by creatives to turn their work into salesware."[86] Vodennikov himself avidly fuels the confusion. Just like, in the nineteenth century, Lermontov and Pushkin exploited hyperstylized paint portraits to fortify their status as Great Romantic poets, so Vodennikov now adopts a cautiously designed Romantic pose in PR photographs and interviews (see figure 3.1 for an example). In his poetry, meanwhile, he simultaneously creates and undermines his reputation as a sincerity icon. "Dozens of articles have been written about me," he wrote in 2001 in "Men Can Also Fake an Orgasm" (a poem whose title firmly puts sincerity anxieties on the agenda):

> "Sense of an exalted cry"
> "Stormy flower of an unconsolidated neomodernism"
> "Word-subject in its polyphonic text"
> . . . and even
> "The new sincerity, the new sensitivity, the new word."
> My God, on what have you wasted
> my invaluable life.[87]

Sorokin, Prigov, Vodennikov: they are just three of a plethora of writers and artists who attract questions relating to sincerity and selling. Some critics even see honest self-revelation as a key to commercial victory in all of Russia's cultural scene today. Take Dmitrii Bavil'skii—the writer and journalist whom I cited at the start of this chapter. Bavil'skii considers (a revived) sincerity as an important factor in "success in today's mass art."[88] Art critic Vladimir Sal'nikov adheres to a similar belief, although he superimposes it primarily on the 1990s: he argues that "one of the . . . key ideas" of this decade has been the need for Russian artists to "look sincere" to avoid "remain[ing] unnoticed."[89] His colleague Ekaterina Degot' would probably nod upon hearing Sal'nikov: she

FIGURE 3.1 Photograph of poet and alleged "'new sincerity' leader" Dmitrii Vodennikov on Vodennikov's blog, by Ol'ga Pavolga. The photograph can be viewed online on Vodennikov's blog on http://vodennikov.livejournal.com/814683.html. Photograph courtesy of Ol'ga Pavolga.

claims that 1990s (Russian and global) art "performed under the slogan 'freedom and sincerity'" within "a wholly new market, in which not art works . . . but the artist himself was sold as a media figure."[90] Dmitrii Golynko-Vol'fson would shake his head in disagreement, though. In the Skype conversation we had in 2009, Golynko-Vol'fson presented not the 1990s but the 2000s as the decade when the new sincerity became entangled with commercial concerns. He believes that after the turn of the century, economic stabilization led the new sincerity away from its post-conceptualist roots into rigidly ideological spheres. In the relatively secure economy of Putinist Russia—so he argued—"new sincere" writing became the hobbyhorse of a markedly neoliberal, neoconservative intellectual elite.[91]

Golynko-Vol'fson targets a period different from the one his colleagues do, and he is more pessimistic than they are—but all of them spot a distinct link between economy and (sincere) emotion. This link interests not only cultural critics: so far I have focused on debates about sincerity and commodification in literary and art *criticism,* but similar debates resonate among artists and writers—that is, among the practitioners who are the target of this criticism. The same Timur Kibirov who accused Sorokin of selling out in our conversation in 2009 is a case in point. In a 2005 poem, Kibirov emphasized that he "has opted for a low-budget role" in refusing to actively market his own work[92]—but seven years earlier, he presented himself as a professional who embraced a sentimentalist stance as a conscious career strategy. In an interview he then argued that a sentimentalist pose had been his means of standing out and being published abroad. In 1998, Kibirov argued, "it was clear that publishing work was only possible in the West, and that one had to find some ways of sending one's poems there"; he continued to explain that his "strategy" (Kibirov's term) to attract foreign attention was to be different: he deliberately defended "the sentimentality that is considered so unworthy in contemporary culture."[93]

Artist Oleg Kulik is even more explicit than Kibirov. He outlined his strategic goals in a self-commentary that reiterates several of the historical samples that I analyzed in chapter 1—from Paul Verlaine's striving to treat readers to "absurdly sincere" work to Andy Warhol's insistence on kitsch as a magnet for success. In an interview with Ekaterina Degot', Kulik explained: "In the West I position myself as Russian, but always very understandable, very clear, very Western in form. Understandable to such an extent that, in some projects, nothing Russian remains except for the label. . . . Most of all, I fear losing people's interest in me. Because without that, everything is pointless in today's world. . . . I experienced that situation in the 1980s. *Degot':* One could say that you adapted your strategy somewhat when you understood that there was such a demand for anything Russian. *Kulik:* I did not adjust my strategy. It just became more conscious. By the way, there is no big demand for anything Russian. But there is a demand for sincerity and persuasiveness. And specifically the Russian issue can offer that sincerity and persuasiveness. That looks a whole lot more adequate than working with the Western canon, which hardly supports or feeds you."[94]

Loaded with such economically inspired terms as "label," "strategy," and "demand," Kulik's explanations seamlessly play into contemporary concerns with art and economic coping strategies. He blends these with the same historical stereotype that Sorokin revives—the notion that

FIGURE 3.2 Screenshot from artist Jason Mombert's performance *The New Sincerity*. Mombert's performance, which critic William Powhida summarizes as an attempt "to invent a new sincerity out of constructive irony," comments on social survival in the art world today. Mombert, *The New Sincerity*; and William Powhida, "Outpost."

Russia is the ultimate locus for sincere expression—by bringing in an additional dimension: that of selling "Russian sincerity" to a foreign audience.

Kulik may—like Sorokin—have been keen on presenting the longing to be sincere as an exclusively Russian affair, but we have seen in previous chapters that new-sincerity rhetoric thrives elsewhere, too. So does the trend to interrogate the relationship between sincere expression and commodification. The list of Anglo-American examples in particular is long; I limit myself to a mere two representative ones. One is Canadian artist Jason Mombert's 2001 video performance *The New Sincerity* (figure 3.2). In a five-minute video, Mombert uses footage of a dreary art-scene party—beautiful, well-off young people drinking and engaging, clearly bored, in childish outdoor games—to comment on celebrity identity and social survival. The second sample is critic Kelefa Sanneh's claim, in the *New York Times* in 2005, that, for so-called independent or alternative rock musicians, "sincerity is inseparable from ambition: if they believe what they sing, maybe lots of listeners will, too."[95]

The habit of linking a new sincerity to commodification processes, in short, thrives outside Russia, too. Once the two are linked, one cultural trope surfaces with force. I am speaking of a trope that, at first sight, appears to be diametrically opposed to the "Is new sincerity good for sales?" logic that we explored on the pages above. This is the trend to present the new sincerity as not a commercial but an *anticapitalist* paradigm. That trend merits some exploration before we move to this chapter's conclusions.

In a *Sunday Times* lifestyle article from 2009, Jessica Brinton tells readers that today "the rules of cool" dictate that we "forget splashing the cash," and that our times are best "described in such slogans as 'the new modesty', 'the new sobriety' or . . . 'a cultural return to sincerity.'"[96] "Who Needs Money?" as the article is called, is emblematic of a trend to present "the new sincerity" in terms of an ethos of anticonsumerism and DIY. DIY—"do it yourself," that is—is a popular shorthand for a practice that I ponder in more detail in chapter 4: that of engaging in independent building, crafting, and repairing practices as both a cost-saving and creative act. The representatives of this trend—which the financial crisis of the late 2000s has reinforced—present repair and craft practices as simultaneously sincere, post-postmodern, and postcapitalist. In doing so, they (unwittingly, often) build upon Fredric Jameson's by now canonical study of interconnections between postmodern and capitalist thinking. In Jameson's words, "The postmodern may well . . . be little more than a transitional period between two stages of capitalism, in which the earlier forms of the economic are in the process of being restructured on a global scale, including the older forms of labor and its traditional organizational institutions and concepts."[97]

Jameson and DIY fans operate on different levels of theoretical reflection—but they share an insistence on coupling postmodern logic to economic transition. Just as Jameson presents the postmodern as a new, "late" stage in capitalist development, so Brinton and like-minded people present a post- or late postmodern "sincere" anticonsumerist behavior as postcapitalist.

It might prove worthwhile to further explore the Jamesonesque heritage in post-postmodern DIY cultures—but that is not a path that I shall walk here. What I do want to highlight are the specific twists and turns that postcapitalist "sincerity talk" takes in Russian art.

Take Oleg Kulik—the same artist who claimed to use sincerity to target a Western audience. Kulik has explained his provocative nude performances—which have consisted, for instance, of physical attacks on museum audiences—as a "metaphor of [the artist's] sincerity and nakedness" that criticized Western Europe's "marketing approach to art."[98] Kulik advanced similar ideas when asked to curate the

Moscow Biennale in 2005. Both in press releases and in Kulik's self-commentaries, "I Believe"—as the art show was called—was promoted entirely in terms of "sincerity," "truth," and "authenticity."[99] Its organizer, curator Joseph Backstein, explained in an interview that the show's pre-occupation with sincerity was not random: he framed it as a "protest against . . . the transformation of art into a commodity. . . . We say: no, art is magic, sorcery."[100]

A not unrelated argument underpinned a last Russian example of postcapitalist sincerity rhetoric that I shall offer here. It stems from a February 2008 review of an art gallery on the Russian cultural news portal *OpenSpace*. Uhrwerk is a Berlin-based exhibition space for cutting-edge Russian art. The *OpenSpace* reviewer summarized Uhrwerk's credo as . . . "the new sincerity"—and then added that, "in the age of art's total commercialization," the Uhrwerk curators select "sincere artists, who do not see art as business."[101]

Uhrwerk and "I Believe" are intriguing cases. The initiators criticize capitalism—but their projects are commercially successful undertakings, staged in what we commonly label a post-Communist rather than post- or anticapitalist society. One of their curators, moreover, is self-proclaimed "sincerity seller" Oleg Kulik. Commentators have understandably picked up on this paradox—and sincerity anxieties resound in the reception of Uhrwerk and "I Believe" no less than in that of the *Trilogy*. Reviewer Sergei Khachaturov, for example, fails to believe in the authenticity of Kulik's biennale project. It feels to him "as if everything is a little bit on purpose and not for real"—an impression that does not subside when Kulik himself provides visitors of the chilly exhibition venue with warm blankets and tea. Even in this "touching concern" Khachaturov detects "the energy of a naughty pretender": "after all, Oleg Borisovich is an Artist above all else."[102]

Whether the anticommodification projects of Kulik and others *are* genuinely sincere is not the question that I seek to answer. What does matter to my argument is their unmistakable role in the debate I traced on the preceding pages: the debate on sincerity and commodification. This debate is vivid—but those readers who remember my historical chapter will also remember that its main concerns are not new. In concluding this chapter, I start by taking a step back to see how the post-Soviet picture blends in with larger historical patterns.

SINCERITY AND LIFE IN A POST-COMMUNIST
WORLD: CONCLUSION

Sincerity after Communism: these three words flawlessly recap the conceptualizations of sincerity I have traced in this and the preceding chapter. Post-Soviet intellectual debates, while marked by a heightened concern for the concept, rarely focus on sincerity per se. They invariably scrutinize a sincerity that follows *after the Communist experiment*. Together, this chapter and the previous one have shown that the debates do so in two respects. First, the new sincerity is envisioned in Russia as an artistic coping strategy for dealing with a historical trauma: that of the failed Soviet Communist experiment. Second, attempts to revive artistic sincerity arise emphatically within the capitalist, post-Communist society that Russia is today. In the next chapter, we turn to yet another discursive formation of post-Communist sincerity. Before we do so, I pause here to consider (a) what my analyses tell us about postsocialist culture and (b) how they relate to the history of sincerity rhetoric. I start with the second question.

In chapter 1, I adopted a panoramic view of the cultural history of sincerity. This bird's-eye view demonstrated that the question "How does artistic sincerity relate to commodification?" has a long history. This history is tracked in detail in a pioneering study by literary historian Susan Rosenbaum. Building on historical (meta)literary analyses, she argues that sincerity concerns originate in (mid- to late) eighteenth-century processes of literary commodification, and that they heighten at times of radical changes in the literary field.

Rosenbaum's insights are valuable—but she limits her empirical cases to Anglophone poets and their critics. The pages above can be read as an attempt to test Rosenbaum's "English-only" findings against a different, but internationally no less influential, local literary tradition: the Russian. Among Russian writers (and other creative professionals) and their critics, do we witness a historical pattern similar to that mapped by Rosenbaum? In other words, does Russian creative life witness an analogous intensification of sincerity anxieties in periods of drastic transition within the creative field?

Whether Rosenbaum's hypothesis is true of Russian literary history per se is a question that requires additional analysis—but in chapter 1 we did see how Derzhavin's adherence to a late eighteenth-century sincerity cult was a direct response to literary commercialization. We also saw how Tolstoy's plea for sincerity reacted to changes in the economy and mediascape of the late nineteenth century. In an age when successful literary professionals attracted unprecedented media attention, Tolstoy spotted and bewailed a negative correlation between commodification and sincerity: where the first flourished, the second withered. At the same time—in one of the many paradoxes that shape his biography—it was Tolstoy himself who ranked among Russia's first and most successful multimedia literary celebrities.

Both the Derzhavin case and the Tolstoy case confirm Rosenbaum's claim. This chapter shows that there is another Russian case that corroborates her findings. I am speaking of the early post-Soviet years. Russian debates over a new or reanimated authorial sincerity emerged precisely then, when the downfall of the Soviet Union forced authors to adopt new socioeconomic survival strategies. In metaliterary debates of the time, literary concerns entwined with pragmatic anxieties, and artistic decisions were readily linked to market-oriented considerations.

So far, my findings confirm Rosenbaum's hypothesis—but they vary from hers in one important respect. Rosenbaum's analyses focus on poetry of the Romantic and post–World War II periods. Much as they differ, these two eras have things in common, too. Most prominent of all, they share the public assumption that sincere behavior and commercial considerations are in fundamental opposition. Rosenbaum looks at poets and critics for whom sincerity and commodification are rock-hard opposites. A famous example is the poet Ted Hughes's attempt to persuade readers of the sincere intentions of his partner and fellow poet Sylvia Plath. In a foreword to a publication of her diaries, he sought—as paraphrased by Rosenbaum—"to persuade the reader that Plath's commercial instincts affected only her earlier writing and prose, resulting in an artifice that she would shed in her movement toward a 'real self' in her final volume of poetry."[103]

As Rosenbaum rightly adds, Hughes frames the poetry of his beloved in terms of a classic "commercial versus internal inspiration" distinction.[104] Contemporary theorizations defy that traditional dichotomous reading of sincerity. They configure self-revelation and strivings for self-profit as two sides of the same coin. In fact, argue current studies of sincerity rhetoric, "commercial culture combines sincerity and performance, rendering them indistinguishable practices."[105] In my introduction, I explained that these and related insights from the emergent discipline of emotion studies inform my approach to sincerity—but they are not just a useful tool for developing my own take on the topic. They also inform the empirical cases that we tackled in this chapter.

What do I mean when I say that? I do not mean, of course, that the critics and artists who were cited here all minutely follow and use developments in the emergent field of emotion studies. If nothing else, this field's boom simply started in Russia too recently to impact the *Trilogy* debates.[106] But the voices that we heard in this chapter do know and use somewhat related lessons—lessons that both they and today's leading theorists of emotion have learned from another relatively young theoretical tradition. Post-Soviet commentators on a new sincerity may frequently defy postmodern logic, but all operate within an intellectual culture that has been permeated by postmodern theorizing. None of the commentators whom we cite in this chapter has been left entirely unaffected by the postmodern experience, whether they embrace it or take it as a rock of offense. Nor are they likely to have missed its main message: that sternly dualistic worldviews distort reality, and that binary oppositions are too schematic to help us truly understand the world and its makings.

A similar lesson is taught to "my" subjects by literary sociology. At the time that Sorokin's *Trilogy* appeared, this new research paradigm offered the latest fashion in Russian humanities. In the early 2000s, the country's leading intellectual forums enthusiastically debated Pierre Bourdieu's socioliterary theories, and literary professionals published a number of Bourdieu-inspired studies.[107] In the same essay collection in which Igor' Smirnov (the professor whom Sorokin mocked in his open letter) discussed *Ice* in socioeconomic terms, he reviewed one of these "Russian Bourdieus," literary historian Mikhail Berg. "Why should one deny a literary historian the right to concentrate on the tactics of literary competition?" Smirnov asked in 2003, in what boiled down to an outright defense of sociologically inspired literary theory.[108]

Similar pro-Bourdieu pleas could be heard throughout the European and American humanities at the time; this very book might not have seen the light of day had its author not referred to Bourdieu in a grant application. But sociohistorical literary theory has struck a special chord in Russia: in the early 2000s, what could be a more forceful tool to analyze a field that had just undergone such radical social and economic changes? A field, moreover, whose dynamics were tangibly impacted by the post-Soviet infatuation with glamour and celebrity—an infatuation to which the same socioeconomic transitions have been imperative?[109] And once it had sprung to life as a critical-cum-academic discipline, how could socioliterary theory not impact discussions of artistic sincerity? In a literary profession where symbolic and economic success was on the tip of everyone's tongue, it was inevitable that the very possibility of artistic integrity became an object of fierce theoretical debate.

Both literary sociology and postmodernism have nuanced contemporary understandings of what it means to be sincere. Both emphasize that sincerity and commercial gain do not relate to one another as black and white: they are, always, by default, intertwined. It is these lessons that participants in the Sorokin debate have taken on board—and it is in this respect that they differ from the Anglophone voices mapped by Rosenbaum. In the Romantic and post–World War II literary field, fake and real were two rigidly opposing poles. In post-Soviet Russia, critics are still intrigued by the tension between fake and real, as the fierce debates on Sorokin's narrative and its public presentation illustrate. Participants in the debate rarely seek to eliminate the same tension, however—remember Uffelmann's claim that the question of parodistic dimensions "need not be solved" for Sorokin's prose in *Ice*. That sincerity and theatricality are inextricably linked rather than diametrically opposed is today a truth that intellectuals, in Russia as elsewhere, embrace rather than deny.

In short, for Rosenbaum, new, postbinary views on emotion are external instruments that help her in tracking sincerity discourse; but in my analyses they have (while remaining helpful methodological tools) become part and parcel of the discourse in question. With this insistence on postbinary thinking, my findings expand and lend nuance to existing thinking on sincerity. Most important, they demonstrate that in recent years the historical pattern that Rosenbaum outlines—socioeconomic changes trigger sincerity anxieties—has been in place but that moral accusations of selling out are less common than they were in earlier historical periods. Today, many a critic and cultural commentator unpicks rather than scorns the interplay between self-revelation and salesware.

Deepening existing scholarly reflection on sincerity and "good business": that is one intervention that my findings prompt. A second intervention that they trigger pertains to literary-sociological research—especially to its post-Soviet pendant.

Existing scholarship has done much to deepen our insight into post-Communist Russia's literary and creative fields and into the social and economic dynamics that shape them. For post-Soviet Russia, Bourdieu-inspired studies by Andrew Wachtel, Birgit Menzel, Mikhail Berg, and others have contributed to important debates on artistic coping strategies, and on creative production as symbolic or economic capital.[110] Without their work the chapter that you have just read would have looked quite different.

What the same studies do not (or only marginally) bring into the discussion, however, is the category of emotion. Which artistic coping strategy works? Which cultural object acquires symbolic or economic capital? These questions cannot be answered without considering how emotional norms, communities, and regimes shape a particular cultural-historical period. My analysis of the *Trilogy* controversy (and of the discursive landscape in which it emerged) aims to do precisely that—to devote minute attention to affective categories in analyzing the Russian literary field. I am not embarking on a scholarly solo expedition in doing so: one literary-historical study that relies on affective dynamics in monitoring social and economic gain is Joachim Klein's study of sincerity in Derzhavin's work;[111] another is a prize-winning essay by sociologist Adi Kuntsman, on camp authors' usage of homophobic imagery to gain symbolic capital.[112] But they are mere first steps in boosting our sensitivity to emotion as a driving force in creative production and consumption processes.

This chapter takes one more step in the direction that Klein and others have started exploring. It demonstrates how emotion informs creative production in post-Soviet space. More pointedly, my analyses unpack the emotional community formed by creative professionals of late 1990s and early 2000s Russia. They demonstrate that within this community, creative labor is—to cite the title of Boris Groys's influential study on media and sincerity—constantly "under suspicion."[113] The literary and art professionals who belong to this scene are by default skeptical toward sincere artistic expression. They live and work in a society which has just reembraced capitalism, and whose cultural life has been shaken to its foundations by radical social and economic transitions. With the Communist economic doctrine still fresh in their minds (and, from the late 1990s onward, amid the Putin-era "culture of cynicism"),[114] it is inevitable that they share a preoccupation both with hypocrisy and with the commercial gain that unfiltered affective openness can bring in art. That Russian creatives operate in an increasingly mediatized society—a factor to which we return in the next chapter—only reinforces this preoccupation. Within the "sincerity-doubting" emotional community they form, the speak-from-the-heart rhetoric of Sorokin's *Trilogy* and its public presentation were bound to provoke a heated debate.

The *Trilogy* was likely to "work"—to attract massive public attention—within the emotional regime of turn-of-the-century intellectual Russia: this conclusion demonstrates how emotional norms shape social interaction among post-Soviet creative professionals. Emotional norms are formative to that interaction in yet one other respect. As sociologists of emotion argue, "people do not emote simply because the animal within responds instinctively to certain predicaments. Rather, people intelligently guide their . . . displays of emotions to fit what is expected."[115] Social expectations also (albeit, as emotion-studies experts have argued, not exclusively)[116] inform the voices that I have tracked in this chapter. All are well versed in postmodern and literary-sociological theorizing. Both theoretical paradigms, with their insistence on defying black-and-white moral judgments, create social expectations: they breed emotional communities where tensions and paradoxes are a norm rather than a taboo. The emotional norm of accepting contradictions—of pointing them out, but without displaying negative emotions—is imperative to the debate on post-Communist sincerity and commodification. Exceptions notwithstanding, the rule among the critics and artists whom we heard on the pages above is the acknowledgment that sincere expression and commercial interests go together like peas and carrots. Emblematic of this acquiescence is the review by Ilya Kukulin that I cited earlier. Kukulin sees no harm in simultaneously embedding *Ice* in a trend to revive sincerity in Russian literature and labeling it an "intellectual best seller," "calculated to gain quick symbolic and material success." He does so in a text that adopts a decidedly neutral, morally nonjudgmental tone. That he does so is no coincidence: it has everything to do with the emotional norms reigning in his (and, I should add, our and my) age.

In the next chapter, I trace yet one more socioeconomic thread in the ongoing debate on post-Communist sincerity. I am referring to the trend of reading contemporary cultural practices as markers of a new engagement and social commitment—one spurred by the same increasing mediatization and digitization that I assessed marginally in the pages above. But before turning to new media, let me briefly recapitulate what Sorokin's *Trilogy* and its public presentation and reception teach us. Together they demonstrate that, around the turn of the millennium, Russian sincerity talk is dominated by explorations of the interrelation between sincere expression and economic coping strategies. They epitomize how these explorations work in practice—*and* they illustrate how, after the history-oriented sincerity concerns I tracked in chapter 1, from the late 1990s onward sincerity has been central to a very different debate. The concept plays a prominent role in discussions about dealing with the present, and with the socioeconomic challenges faced by a distinct emotional community: that of post-Communist creative professionals.

CHAPTER FOUR

"So New Sincerity"

NEW CENTURY, NEW MEDIA

IN THE COURSE OF THE 2000S AND THE EARLY 2010S, the visions of sincerity I traced in the preceding chapters have remained in force. Sincerity as a therapeutic tool for cultural trauma, and sincerity as an economic coping strategy: both these views on artistic self-revelation are easy to trace in the many online references to a new sincerity that crowd the Internet.

Over time, however, that same Internet has started to function more and more as an object of discussion in its own right. Both in Russia and elsewhere, from the 1990s to the present day, the relentless advance of new technologies has turned into a topic for theoretical reflection—on the postdigital aesthetics and logic that dominate our age, for instance. As I explained in my Introduction, defenders of this notion refuse to contrast "old" and "new" media: are not, they ask, our everyday lives today by default computational? Critics also harbor a growing interest in the interconnections between mediatization, authenticity, and intimacy—and one recurring concern in these discussions relates to sincerity. Some commentators argue that digital media are fostering a previously unheard-of flourishing of sincere expression. Others believe that new technologies are leading to a dehumanizing trend—one that must be fought by foregrounding sincerity *within* digitally mediated art, design, or writing. Still others use the notion of a revived sincerity as a social-identity marker in social media. While working on this book I found plenty of blog, Twitter, Instagram, and Facebook posts where web users either portrayed themselves as spokesmen of "the new sincerity" or used the phrase as a label for their favorite films, books, or, say, corporate brands (remember, in my Introduction, the blogger for whom pretty girls at Starbucks epitomized "the new sincerity").

The following pages trace debates on sincerity and digitization as they evolved from the early 1990s onward, with a special emphasis on the first decade of the twenty-first century—the Web 2.0 age, with its staggering rise in the use of social media. As in the other chapters, I track transnational developments, but with a special interest in post-Soviet sincerity discourse. I open this chapter by tracing global and Russian discussions on sincere expression and mediatization. Next I focus on debates specifically about the nexus between (artistic) sincerity and *new* media—that is, digital media platforms in particular. These debates take us into the world of social-media users, of bloggers in particular: in blogs and other social media, debates on a new sincerity flourish with special vitality. After mapping the outlines of these online discussions, in the final pages of this chapter I zoom in a little further, on the role that craft, amateurism, and imperfection play in a digitized age.

Contrary to chapters 2 and 3, the story that follows does not focus primarily on literature. I do look at professional writers and artists—and poet Dmitrii Vodennikov could be called the central literary "hero" of this chapter, just as Sorokin and Prigov were key names in the previous two chapters. But next to Vodennikov, my special interest here is in the digital "produser"—a term coined by media expert Axel Bruns to reflect that, online, the distinction between producers and consumers of (literary as well as other) content blurs. Social-media cultures are, to Bruns and others, by default participatory cultures, whose "users are . . . necessarily also producers."[1]

This chapter does not blindly inherit the feel-good logic that permeates especially early scholarship on produsage and participatory cultures—but it does trace precisely the type of online produser to which Bruns refers. More specifically, I follow the countless online critics and bloggers who have their say on the topic of sincerity. I do so with special attention to local idiosyncrasies. As my findings attest, the online debates of Russian-speaking sincerity adepts overlap with and at the same time differ from those of their non-Russian counterparts. As we shall see, in Russian discussions about new media and sincere expression the propaganda-ridden Soviet mediascape still looms large. It does so particularly in Putin-era Russia, when state media and Kremlin propaganda resurface as realities of life. More important still, if non-Russian critics hold a special interest in the interrelationships between digitization and *authenticity,* then in Russia critical debates on "the digital" consistently emphasize the nexus between new-media technologies and the concept that I trace throughout this book: sincerity.

MASS MEDIA, POPOMO, TRUTHINESS: WAITING FOR SINCERITY

Among the many critics who claim that our culture has moved from postmodern to post-postmodern paradigms, quite a few link this shift to society's increasing (mass-)mediatization. In a joint essay, literary scholar Katherine Hayles and architect Todd Gannon argue that postmodernism died with the advent of Netscape in 1995, and that digital technologies have facilitated a "renewed emphasis on the materiality of surfaces" in literature and architecture.[2] In their view, "postmodernism has not so much disappeared as been swallowed up . . . by the flood of data, associations, information, and cross-references unleashed by the World Wide Web."[3] In a less positive vision, literary historian Alan Kirby believes that with mobile media we have moved from postmodernism to the "frightening" world of a technology-induced "pseudo-modernism," "whose content and dynamics are invented or directed by the participating viewer or listener."[4]

Hayles, Gannon, and Kirby's visions of a post-postmodern condition blend in with a wider debate, on the impact of mediatization on such concepts as reality, identity, and truthfulness. In past decades, scholars, thinkers, and other cultural commentators have gone to considerable lengths to demonstrate how we now live in a fundamentally "mediated" society (Thomas de Zengotita); how a focus on entertainment is turning our existence into *Life: the Movie* (Neil Gabler); how our media-saturated world is composed of "simulacra"—references that lack referents in real life (Jean Baudrillard); and how media today are spawning the rise of a "post-fact society" (Farhad Manjoo), where a preference for truthfulness makes way for a focus on "truthiness" (Stephen

Colbert)—a feeling that something is true that requires no backing up with hard facts.[5]

Given their infatuation with questions of reality, truth, and trust, it is not surprising that critical commentators of media culture have eagerly pondered the interrelationship between mass mediatization and, specifically, sincerity. In chapter 1 we saw that this trend toward foregrounding sincerity at times of radical changes in media usage goes back a long way. Remember how sincerity emerged as a prime cultural concern in early modernity, for instance, at a time when the printed book was gaining popularity; or how sincerity anxieties intensified in the early twentieth century, following the introduction of new printing and reproduction technologies.

In our age of mass mediatization, sincerity is in the limelight once again. In 2009 Ernst Van Alphen and Mieke Bal wrote, in their book-length study of the concept, that today sincerity is to an increasing extent a "media effect."[6] They hastened to add that, if sincerity is now more and more framed in and by media, this "media framing" does not make the concept "any less culturally powerful": "far from being dismissed, it must be taken extremely seriously."[7] In the course of the 2000s, Boris Groys drove home a similar point in a series of publications on sincerity and media. In his words, "In observing the media's many designed surfaces, one hopes that the dark, obscured space beneath the media will somehow betray or expose itself. In other words, we are waiting for a moment of sincerity, a moment in which the designed surface cracks open to offer a view of its inside."[8]

Groys, I believe, is right in claiming that today's mediated society displays an obsessive interest in honesty and (self-)exposure. I now devote some more attention to this media-induced preoccupation with sincerity.

MEDIATIZATION AND "THE *NEW* SINCERITY"

Groys does not frame the sincerity that media observers crave as a fundamentally novel emotion—but other critical theorists do detect an interrelationship between mediatization and the emergence of a previously nonexistent or new sincerity. As early as 1993, film historian Jim Collins observed a "New Sincerity" in contemporary cinema that "purposely evad[es] the media-saturated terrain of the present in pursuit of an almost forgotten authenticity, attainable only through a sincerity that avoids any sort of irony or eclecticism."[9] In the exact same year, the American writer David Foster Wallace (whom I mentioned briefly in chapter 1) argued in an influential essay that a world where TV reigns is a world where "sincerity and passion [are] 'out.'" America's "next real literary rebels," he argued, would be those new voices that dare to move beyond TV-induced irony toward a life view that many will consider "too sincere"; those, in other words, who do not shun "old untrendy human troubles and emotions" and who are "willing to risk . . . accusations of sentimentality."[10]

Collins and Wallace were early advocates of a conceptual link that several cultural commentators would defend in the 2000s: the nexus between changing mediascapes and a radically transformed, new notion of sincerity. In the United States, for instance, the logic that underpinned Wallace's essay about TV was swiftly extended by a currently still growing army of Wallace experts. In a much-cited analysis published in 2010, literary historian Adam Kelly presented Wallace as the founder of an American "New Sincerity" that was responding directly to mass-mediatization.[11] In the same year, an essay in the new-media journal *Wired* invoked Wallace's ideas to argue that contemporary media culture is moving away from sarcastic detachment toward, again, a "New Sincerity." According to *Wired* contributor Angela Watercutter, such wide-ranging media phenomena as singer Lady Gaga's popularity, the unexpected success of the TV series *Glee,* and Barack Obama's 2008 election all epitomize a revival of sincerity in contemporary media culture. "Neo-sincerity," as Watercutter labels the new public mentality, replaces an age in which "we were trained in irony by the very instrument that is usually the target of its ridicule: TV."[12]

Wallace fans are particularly keen on pointing to the link between mediatization and honest self-revelation—but they are not alone. In 2002 art critic Glenn Mannisto had already pointed in a similar direction when, in a manifesto-like article entitled "The New Sincerity," he spoke of a search for sincerity and truth in art that was responding both to the 9/11 attacks *and* to mass-mediatization. Mannisto's "New Sincerity" sought to "reclaim the individual's expressive capacity from the corporate monolith of mass-media entertainment."[13] In 2008 poet Jason Morris envisioned a similarly techno-shy "New Sincerity" in various artistic disciplines. "Drawing is the new old thing in visual art," Morris believed; and in new filmmaking, he envisioned a "New Sincere" tradition that consciously moves away from technological sophistication. "In their use of the long take," Morris argued, "Wes Anderson and a few other young filmmakers (maybe quoting Dogme, Expressionism or Neo-Realism), nod toward the medium's first promise—to be an 'honest' representation of reality."[14] Morris is merely one among many European and United States–based film and TV commentators who envision a "new," or "quirky," and often emphatically atechnological, sincerity in the films of Anderson and, say, Michel Gondry, or Lars von Trier; in empathically low-fi films by so-called mumblecore directors;[15] and in drama and reality TV series such as *Girls* or *The Bachelorette*.[16]

The discussion about sincerity and technocriticism in TV and film cannot be isolated from recent developments in American literary life. In the early 2010s, our current infatuation with online and social media was fiercely criticized, in novels and public statements, by Jonathan Franzen and Dave Eggers. That precisely these two writers defy digitization is relevant to my argument: they are not only immensely popular—Franzen is an Oprah Winfrey selection, Eggers shares with Bill Clinton the status of TED prize winner—but critics and scholars also eagerly frame them as harbingers of an American "new sincerity."[17]

The examples above mostly stem from American art and media criticism, where attempts to link the digital and the sincere prosper. Critics either demonstrate that contemporary media spark a newborn sincerity or emphatically locate sincerity outside the digital. A similar logic flourishes outside the United States. In 2008 literary historian Thomas Vaessens, to mention one example, observed a move in contemporary Dutch writing toward a "late postmodern" or "new sincere" paradigm—one that he sees as a direct response to "this mediatized world of standardized emotions."[18] At the time, more than one colleague beyond Dutch borders would have nodded in agreement upon hearing his claim. Vaessens's claim would have met with approval among cultural historians and critics in Western Europe, but also—I am moving back to Russian spheres now—among their colleagues in Moscow, St. Petersburg, and post-Soviet Russia's other creative and academic hubs.

By the late 2000s, Russophone new-sincerity and new-authenticity rhetoric had acquired near-cliché status. In 2008 journalist Varvara

Babitskaia claimed that "the 'new sincerity' had managed to become our poetic mainstream."[19] In this new "poetic mainstream," the concept of sincerity was, as elsewhere, avidly co-implicated in discussions on mediatization. After the collapse of the propaganda-ridden media empire that the Soviet authorities were continually constructing,[20] the post-Soviet era saw a more pluralistic and, in the 2000s, increasingly digitized and user-led mediascape. Under Putin, however, the authorities have started exerting more and more control over both print and digital media—and experts have framed the Putin-era media model as "neo-authoritarian" or even "neo-Soviet."[21]

Critics have eagerly pondered the sociocultural implications of these (part local, part global) media transitions. Next to more politically informed queries, throughout the late 1990s and 2000s Russian new-media commentators have insisted on unpacking the relationship that interests us here: the one between mediatization and sincere expression. How, they have asked, does straightforward self-revelation relate to our age's continually increasing mass mediatization and technological sophistication? In 1999, for instance, art historian Valerii Savchuk unraveled an emphatically unmediated "new sincerity" among St. Petersburg–based nonconformist artists. In his view, theirs was a "postinformational sincerity"—one that asserted the supremacy of the artist's body over politics and that responded directly to the "mass-mediatization" of the right to self-expression.[22] In the previous chapter I cited art critic Ekaterina Degot', who came to a similar conclusion in 2004: she stated that (Russian and global) art of the 1990s was created "under the slogan 'freedom and sincerity.'" In her view, this age's insistence on what is real or authentic (Degot' also speaks of a preoccupation with the artist's body) responds first and foremost to the mediatization of society and art.[23]

Savchuk and Degot' focus on visual arts—but in the late 1990s and early 2000s, cultural historians Mark Lipovetsky and Birgit Beumers signaled a not unrelated trend in theater. In a study of new Russian drama they highlighted the documentary drama of Moscow's Teatr .doc—a hugely popular theater collective in the early 2000s that built on real-life stories and verbatim acting techniques.[24] Its founders coupled a firm, mumblecore-like longing for the authentic and nonfictional—one that answered (I am citing Teatr.doc artistic director Mikhail Ugarov) a post-Soviet need for "a theatre where one does not act"[25]—to an equally firm move away from the technologically mediated. It is no coincidence that Teatr.doc, as Lipovetsky and Beumers pointed out, is inspired by the Dogme movement in Danish cinema:[26] in both projects, a defiance of technological intervention ranks as a hallmark for artistic sincerity in a hi-tech age.

Savchuk, Degot', and Beumers and Lipovetsky are mere tips of an iceberg: the list of post-Soviet statements and projects that relate mediatization to sincerity is long. Rather than synthesizing the different and often incompatible views on this interrelationship, by way of conclusion I limit myself to two very different last samples here. The first is the public presentation of the 2005 Moscow Biennale, "I Believe." In interviews and PR brochures, curators framed this event not only as a protest against consumerist views on art, as we saw in chapter 3. They also presented the show as a "serious, deep" response to our information and entertainment age—one, they emphasized, that was marked "by a high level of sincerity."[27] My last example stems from political spheres. In a news article published in October 2014, journalist Andrei Pertsev described how Russian journalists openly justified doctored images of fights in the city of Donetsk: Ukraine, after all, was in need of Russian defense. This trend to bluntly defend Kremlin media propaganda, Pertsev argued, emblematizes a state-induced "new sincerity"—one that is paradoxically honest in refusing to hide its rhetorical goal.[28]

NEW SINCERITY AND NEW MEDIA

Up to this point, I have focused on critics who link (new-)sincerity rhetoric to relatively broadly framed notions of mediatization. The examples that I monitored are responding to shifts in media usage of all kinds—whether it be the growing sophistication of today's hi-tech devices, our increasing exposure to media images, or the growing popularity of TV in the 1990s.

My special interest in this chapter rests with a narrower strand within this broader discussion on mediatization. On the ensuing pages, I examine public discourse not on media as such but on *digital* media in particular. More specifically, I scrutinize how cultural commentators interrogate the complex relationship between technological sophistication and human self-revelation—and how, in doing so, they simultaneously revive and revise old sincerity anxieties.

Where do we find debates on sincerity and digitization? As with the other debates I have been following in this book, discussions on the interplay between the digital and the sincere are taking place on a transnational scale. We shall see next that they are resonating in the United States, the Netherlands, and Russia—but they are also recognizable elsewhere. At the 2006 Indonesian Poetry and Sincerity Festival I mentioned in my Introduction, the organizers presented poetic sincerity as an antidote to the purported superficiality of a digitized world.[29]

Discussions on sincerity and new-media innovation, in short, are flourishing in various world localities. They are also blossoming across various media. The Indonesian example stems from a print publication, but figurations of sincerity as a response to digitization are also resonant within digital media. In a 2009 online column for the *National Post*, for example, writer Kate Carraway traces demands for "the new sincerity"—a trend that she discerns in the revival of such traditional social practices as bowling—directly to a digitization of her daily life. In her words, "Interacting honestly and meaningfully with colleagues, friends and partners has more cachet, and is more natural to people for whom expressing their loves and likes and fears via Twitter and Facebook has become not only ubiquitous but basically required for friendship, dating and networking."[30] Carraway here uses *online* media to present an emphatically *offline* sincerity as a new behavioral strategy. She is not alone. Visions of the new sincerity as a tool for coping with a digitized world are circulating online in bewildering quantities. Twitter and Instagram users adopt the hashtag #newsincerity to identify (often remarkably low-tech) trends in, say, music, or photography, as "new sincere"; bloggers have expressed a strong interest in the topic throughout the 2000s and (first half of the) 2010s; Wikipedia editors engage in ongoing discussions on "the New Sincerity's" outlines in film, philosophy, art, and music (by the mid-2010s, Wikipedia featured lengthy Wikis on the notion in English, Estonian, and Italian). It is these online voices that are of special interest to me in this chapter.

I started this section by asking where we might find discussions on sincerity and digitization. If it is hard to answer this question comprehensively, two things are clear from the above: the discussions are taking place on a transnational *and* transmedial scale, and they flourish with particular force in online media. In the pages that follow, I study this blossoming online debate on "the sincere and the digital" in more detail.

"BUZZ ON BLOGS": ONLINE (NEW-)SINCERITY DISCOURSE

In order to understand online discussions on sincerity, we need to understand both who partakes in them and what they deal with. Let us start with the first question.

My findings—based on roughly monthly repeated Google and Yandex searches for the term and on extensive readings of blogs, chat forums, and other social media between the early 2000s and 2015—imply that those web users who engage in new-sincerity rhetoric tend to be relatively young urbanites. Most are under fifty, many are twenty- or thirty-somethings; many live in urban hubs.[31] Upon closer scrutiny, the majority of the numerous bloggers who present their take on the new sincerity turn out to be either creative professionals (literary, art, film, design critics, writers, journalists) or students of the humanities or the social sciences. The online dialogue between ASh and bordzhia with which I began this book is a case in point. This chat on "the new sincerity" is conducted between two web users who, to judge from their language use and sociocultural references ("wha' a nightmare," "hawk on," the mention of a roommate, literary seminars, and poets), are likely to be literature or language students in their late teens or early twenties.

In short, rather than a blueprint of contemporary society at large, the group whose digital discussions I trace in this chapter consists of the socioculturally privileged and the urbanized. This is a limited group—but its numbers substantially outmatch the literary, artistic, and musical in-crowds I traced in my preceding two chapters. While Groys's claim that today "the production of sincerity and trust has become everyone's occupation" may be somewhat bold,[32] the publicly archived debates on sincerity that we find online *are* conducted by substantial numbers of web users. The search hit numbers I mentioned in my Introduction illustrate how, with the rise of social media, the trend of framing (one's place in) society in terms of a new sincerity visibly travels into pop-cultural spheres. Online discussions on the notion are fought out between an ever-increasing corps of sincerity adepts, whose visions of the notion cover a rapidly expanding cultural domain.

This last observation—that online new-sincerity fans are discussing a swiftly widening cultural territory—brings us to my second question. We now know more or less *who* is involved in online (new-)sincerity talk, but not what digital sincerity advocates are talking *about*. I explore this question by first mapping global—especially Anglophone—online talk of a new sincerity, before focusing on its Russian pendant.

By the spring of 2012, English-language online talk of a new sincerity could adopt different guises. To begin with, prominent cultural commentators and professional critics were using their blogs and sites to promote "the New Sincerity" as a coherent cultural paradigm. A groundbreaking example stems from the blog of American radio show host Jesse Thorn. In 2006 Thorn published a "Manifesto on the New Sincerity" on his blog, which offered what has become a much-quoted attempt at a formal definition for the concept. "What Is The New Sincerity?" Thorn rhetorically asked his blog readers, before answering: "Think of it as irony and sincerity combined like Voltron [the Super Robot who was a central character in the American animated television series of the same name], to form a new movement of astonishing power. Or think of it as the absence of irony and sincerity, where less is (obviously) more."[33] In his own blog, Thorn frequently employs his self-defined slogan to refer to, say, interesting new films or music worth hearing. "Wow," he wrote in December 2006, for example, of a new composition by much-loved comedians, "this song is . . . about to EXPLODE with New Sincericism."[34]

In blog discussions about "the New Sincerity," Thorn is often presented as the trend's intellectual father. Another name bloggers invoke as the founder of "the New Sincerity" is that of Mikhail Epstein, the Russian cultural theorist whose name has come up often in the course of this book. Contrary to the cliché that has Russia following the West in its cultural orientations,[35] Epstein's post-postmodern theorizing has tangibly impacted American cultural criticism—and a decisive factor in its cultural transfer has been Epstein's decision to provide unrestricted online access to most of his writings. In the course of the 2000s, Anglophone bloggers eagerly linked to the online PDFs of the Russian professor's English-language essays on reviving sentimentality and sincerity. They did so in posts that are as well informed as they are informally toned ("What is this new sincerity business?").[36]

Thorn and Epstein both use online media to present "New Sincerity" as a prominent new trend or movement, and both do so with success. Other online new-sincerity aficionados have different goals in mind. Some make quite an effort, for instance, to theorize the media specificity of the trend—or, put more plainly, to convince others that the concept persistently resides inside digital media. Just as letters were once catapulted into the ultimate expressive outlet for Russian sentimentalist sincerity, writers now use online platforms to frame these same platforms as formative to contemporary sincerity. More than one observer of recent Anglophone writing has, for instance, signaled a new poetic sincerity sparked by Flarf—a collaborative poetry movement whose members use digital search tools to compose poems.[37] Others envision the blogosphere as the ultimate discursive platform of a new sincere movement. Its diary-like setup (in blogging expert Jill Walker Rettberg's words, "Most blogging is to some extent self-representational, and as such a form of life-writing or autobiography");[38] its reputation as a vehicle for making private communication public; its status as an accessible publishing tool for amateur writers; its potential for active audience participation: many an online commentator claims that these blogging features were bound to generate a revival of sincere self-expression.

Illustrative of the habit of envisioning a reborn sincerity specifically in weblogs is a 2008 blog post on "the New Sincerity" by British social-media expert Roo Reynolds. Reynolds singled out the video blog (2006 to 2007) of online artist Ze Frank as the ultimate incarnation of the new cultural paradigm. As he was "obsessively watching [Frank's] popular (and highly interactive) video podcast 'the show' last year," he writes, "I was repeatedly struck by his genuine joy in the strangeness and creativity of the world. . . . Ze Frank may never even have heard the term, but he exudes the New Sincerity like flying a kite with Bruce Lee on a sunny day."[39] Reynolds, in other words, selects as the gold standard for "the New Sincerity" a—"highly interactive"—blog. He does so *in* an interactive blog, too. In the comments section of his entry, Reynolds and his readers make a communal attempt at further defining "the New Sincerity" and its relationship to digitization.

Andrew Chen, a student in American literature, is another advocate of blogs as the prime platform for a newborn sincerity. "New Sincerity," Chen writes in an open-access paper, "is . . . notable for its medium—

blogs. Massey, Mister, and Robinson [three contemporary American poets] . . . routinely publish new poems on their well-kept blogs and receive feedback from one another as well as from their sizeable reader-ships. Furthermore, the evolution of New Sincerity is quite traceable through their cyberspace interactions. After Massey finished his manifesto—which, like those of the other New Sincrerists [sic], took the form of a blog entry—he received an enormous influx of responses and incited a great deal of buzz on blogs and internet forums, which, as the New Sincerists themselves will attest, are in a large part responsible for New Sincerity's growth as a movement."[40]

Chen shares with Thorn, Epstein, and Reynolds a habit of using online media to debate—in partly colloquial, partly theoretically dense terms—the outlines of a present-day sincerity. In the "buzz on blogs" (to use Chen's term) that they observe, however, new-sincerity rhetoric also circulates in less analytically refined contexts.

"Basically Luchador is so new sincerity that you can't get sick of it," wrote blogger Roundhouse Kicks in September 2006 in an emblematic post; rather than a highbrow poet or art-house film, this blogger was referring to a new sneaker model introduced by Nike.[41] In 2013 the En-glish Wikipedia entry entitled "New Sincerity" devoted a full separate section to "Bronies"—tech-savvy male adult fans of the animation show *My Little Pony,* whom *Wired* portrays as "internet neo-sincerity at its best."[42] Together with other pop-cultural references to present-day sincerity (for two more examples, see the "sinceriod" and Honest Tea Bottles in figures 4.1 and 4.2), Roundhouse Kicks's Nike assessment and the Bronies section nicely illustrate how, with time, Anglophone new-media users have come to appropriate the phrase "new sincerity" in a range of cultural and commercial contexts so wide that it inevitably starts attracting parody. In chapter 3 I outlined how, from the early 1990s onward, advocates of a revived sincerity have projected the notion onto an ever-growing variety of cultural domains and practices; and in chapter 1 we saw how this drastic variety prompted writer Alex Blagg, in 2005, to mockingly invite his blog readers to nominate random things for being "the New Sincerity." A year later, Chicana poet Lorna Dee Cervantes made a similar parodistic move. Cervantes ridiculed the discursive formats of news and social media by offering readers of her blog a nonsensical "Ten Top Trivia Tips about The New Sincerity!" ("The

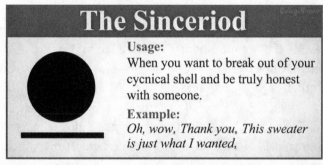

The Sinceriod

Usage:
When you want to break out of your
cycnical shell and be truly honest
with someone.

Example:
*Oh, wow. Thank you. This sweater
is just what I wanted.*

FIGURE 4.1 In February 2013, the *sinceriod*—an underscored full
stop—was introduced as one of "8 New Punctuation Marks We
Desperately Need" on the comic video site CollegeHumor. It now
circulates on a number of social media platforms. Its definition as a
mark that allows an author to "break out of your cynical shell and be
truly honest" hints at post-postmodern rhetoric. "8 New Punctuation Marks We Desperately Need," a 2013 CollegeHumor post by
Mike Trapp (http://www.collegehumor.com/article/6872071/8-new
-and-necessary-punctuation-marks, accessed 5 January 2015).

New Sincerity once lost a Dolly Parton lookalike contest," for example,
and "Dueling is legal in Paraguay as long as both parties are New
Sincerists!")[43]

Cervantes's and Blagg's persiflage is more than corny joking. It tells
us, more than any statistic overview could, just how many web users today
are engaging in new-sincerity rhetoric. Their parodies also reveal how in-
tensely online commentators invest the term affectively; *and,* to conclude,
they show us the near-grotesque heterogeneity of the set of social and
cultural practices on which social-media users superimpose the term.

"PUBLIC SINCERITY": NEW SINCERITY IN RUSSIAN
NEW MEDIA

The samples that I have discussed so far mainly originate in English-
language digital platforms. It would be a mistake, however, to treat
online new-sincerity rhetoric as an exclusively Anglophone affair. I also
encountered multiple hits when I conducted online Google blog searches
for "new sincerity" in a random set of other languages, including Bulgarian, Estonian, German, French, and Italian.

Russia is another case in point. In Russia, from the early 2000s
onward, writers and bloggers have been expressing an interest in sin-

FIGURE 4.2 "Honest" tea bottles. Blogger Drawn2Design
mentioned the brand in a 2008 blog post to illustrate how
product packaging "has been moving more towards the
socially responsible, the environmentally sustainable . . .
you know, the more *ethical* end of the spectrum for a good
while now." In Drawn2Design's view, this shift emblematizes a "new sincerity" in package design. ("Package Design:
Huggable Japanese Stuff, Junk Food Design, and the New
Sincerity," a 2008 blog post by Drawn2Design at http://
drawn2design.wordpress.com/2008/10/24/package_design
/, accessed 5 January 2015). Image courtesy of Honest Tea
Ltd. and the Coca-Cola Company.

cerity and digitization that is as persistent as, if not more than, that of
their Anglophone counterparts. Admittedly, as we saw in chapter 3,
cultural critics are today still turning to the Soviet experiment and the
post-Communist transition as formative experiences for a Russian new
sincerity. With time, however, a new cultural generation emerges—one
whose members try, in cultural historian Rosalind Marsh's words, "at

the same time to conserve their cultural legacy and to liberate themselves from it."[44] As elsewhere, from the 2000s onward this generation has started pointing more and more to digitization when pondering present-day sincerity.

Take Dmitrii Kuz'min—the poet, editor, and critic whose views on new, "postconceptualist" literary and behavioral trends I reviewed in chapter 3. To Kuz'min, digital media are a decisive factor in the formation of the new trends, in which longings for "authentic lyrical expression" take center stage.[45] In 2006 a handbook on new Russian writing developed a not unrelated argument. Its authors argued that "interactivity" and "virtuality" were imperative to post-postmodern Russian literature; they singled out "neosentimentalism," with its insistence on sincere expression, as one especially persistent post-postmodern paradigm.[46] Two years earlier, the journal *Online Poetry* (*Setevaia poeziia*) had already devoted a special issue to "Truth and Sincerity in Art" ("Pravda i iskrennost' v iskusstve"); among other contributions, this special venue for online writing boasted discussions of "the social aspects of 'the new sincerity' " and of the history of the term "new sincerity."[47]

From the early 2000s onward, these and many other public reflections on sincerity probe the nexus between sincere expression and digitization. Their authors often focus on literary production, but the interconnection between the sincere and the digital is also explored in spheres that take us well beyond the literary domain. *New Sincerity: A Manifesto* (*Novaia iskrennost': Manifest*), for example, is a film about a Russian-Ukrainian "Innovative Marketing Communication" forum held in 2011. The film consists of short interviews with forum participants about the need for genuine emotion in promotional media strategies. In a YouTube teaser text for the film, the makers link this need for what they call "new sincere" PR to the rise of social media. "The Internet"—so they warn marketing specialists—"has shown your true face to the world. The consumer can now choose. One tiny mistake—and they destroy your image, trample your brand like an insect."[48]

The Russian-Ukrainian marketeers and their like are taking the notion of a revived sincerity to new lands. To them, sincerity today is thriving for a fairly specific reason: sincere communication cannot be isolated from interactivity, online disclosure, and social-media sharing—in short, those features that together shape the digital spheres that are increasingly invading our daily lives. This is not to say that, for the Russian commentators in question, "the digital" is an amorphous whole. Like their Anglophone colleagues, Russian media commentators argue that, within online media, some services form more fruitful vehicles for reviving sincerity than others. Many point to blogs—which enjoy disproportionate popularity in Russia—as particularly fertile breeding grounds for self-revelation. In a 2004 article in the newspaper *Nezavisimaia gazeta* (Independent Gazette), for instance, journalist and writer Katia Metelitsa argues that it may be hard to define "what the 'new sincerity' is," but that "everyone is talking about it"—and that its blogging proponents experience "more thrill and relaxation as a result of public sincerity . . . than from a truly secret confession or a visit to a psychoanalyst."[49] In 2007 a (rather speculative) sociological study of trendsetting young Russians in the 2000s singled out the blogosphere as the "main channel for the distribution of trends," in which a renewed longing for "Romanticism," "genuine values," and "sincerity" occupy pride of place.[50] Journalist Igor' Shevelev trod similar discursive paths in 2008 when he ascribed the popularity of blogs to a "stagnatory tendency toward sincere expression" in post-perestroika Russia.[51]

The habit of hailing blogs as ultimate vehicles for honest expression may be thriving in various parts of the world, but it has come as no surprise in Putin's Russia. Under his reign, as I said, many offline media operate under rigid official restrictions. An online genre like the blog offers a welcome space for relatively free—and, contrary to the microblogging services Facebook and Twitter, elaborate—public expression.

Especially from the late 2000s onward, Russian blogs have been more than a mere outlet for free speech, however. Against a backdrop of growing citizen activism, several bloggers started framing their medium as a tool for outright civic engagement. In the late 2000s and early 2010s, they unmistakably formed a "participatory culture." In media theorist Henry Jenkins's words, participatory cultures are (sub)cultures "with relatively low barriers to artistic expression and civic engagement."[52] To the participatory culture of civically engaged Russian bloggers, sincerity is no random concept: they operate in an oppositional scene that, in political scientist Mischa Gabowitsch's words, inherits

from the "informal, closely knit and justifiably paranoid milieu" of traditional Russian dissidents a preoccupation with "personal character traits
such as decency and honesty."[53]

Not coincidentally, in metacomments on their weblogs Russian
bloggers persistently interweave talk about digitization with reflections
on both social commitment and sincerity. Take Moscow-based filmmaker
Elena Pogrebizhskaia, who produces documentaries about the socially
underprivileged. Pogrebizhskaia ardently promotes her films in her
blog—an online medium she uses because, as she explained in an interview, "I love it when people are sincere."[54] In 2009 Pogrebizhskaia used
her blog to advertise a fundraising concert for terminally ill patients. In
her words, both the concert and her documentaries are attempts to "be
braver than cynicism, more naive and more open."[55]

Pogrebizhskaia presents her work in terms of a post-postmodern
civic engagement—one that outbraves mockery—and her blog as a vital
tool to share it. In a broader social context, journalist Andrei Loshak
leans on the same logic. In November 2010, Loshak published an article
on the online culture-news portal *OpenSpace,* which, with nearly two
hundred thousand views, used to rank among the site's most-read contributions.[56] He argued that in Russia new technologies facilitate a new public mentality. In the new-media age, he explained, discontented Russian
citizens send their president an online message or (in an example that
captured national media attention) put an end to dire living conditions in
a nursing home by blogging about it.[57] "Set against [the] sincere human
impulse" of these online initiatives, he concluded, "the perversity of
[state] representatives stands out with particular clarity."[58]

At this point, let me turn from Pogrebizhskaia and Loshak—for
whom (post)digital sincerity is a catalyst for social activism—back to the
wider debate on the nexus between sincerity and digitization. In the
course of the 2000s, this debate gains both in strength (in 2006 Dmitrii
Golynko-Vol'fson even went so far as to brand mobile texting a technology
that fosters "new-sincere" writing)[59] and in polemical acumen. In an
analysis of the Russian blogosphere, cultural historians Irina Kaspe and
Varvara Smurova argue that for blogs the term "new sincerity" is "un-
suitable"; meanwhile, critic Sergei Kostyrko states that, in blogs and online forums, rather than sincerity and unmediated expression, readers
are facing strictly literary authorial images.[60] When I asked poets Lev

Rubinstein and Timur Kibirov about the purported link between blogging and (a new) sincerity, they claimed not to see any connection whatsoever.[61]

Whether these critical voices are right is a question that warrants separate discussion—as I said earlier, what interests me here is the discourse itself. But Kostyrko's reference to literature does bring us to a special voice in the debate on sincerity and social media. I am referring to the professional Russian writer. Compared to non-Russian colleagues, a disproportionately large share of Russian-speaking authors host a personal weblog.[62] Critics have framed several of these blogs as the ultimate products of their hosts' "new sincere" literary stance.

Dmitrii Vodennikov's blog and its public reception are a case in point. In chapter 3 we saw how this writer's critics had stumbled over one another in trying to establish whether the alleged "leader of the 'new sincerity' movement" was genuine in his infatuation with artistic integrity.[63] In the spring of 2009, at a Moscow café, I interviewed Vodennikov about his blog and about readings of his works as emblems of a Russian new sincerity. His stance toward this notion was ambivalent. Yes, he claimed, it was he who first coined this term in the late 1990s (he had never heard of Prigov's "New Sincerity," he said when I asked), but now he embraced a different cultural paradigm.[64] Blogs, to him, exemplified the new paradigm: their "openness," he believed, shows us that "the new sincerity has ended, and the new honesty has started."[65]

I found Vodennikov's discursive comments on (a new) sincerity somewhat elusive, and detected in his body language a similarly ambivalent preoccupation with sincere expression. Making flirtatious comments and talking rapidly and exaltedly, during our conversation he often spoke with half-closed eyes and trembling hands ("When I like someone, I start quivering," he explained), posing as a vulnerable *Einzelgänger* who was opening up his most secret thoughts to me.[66]

In public interviews *and* on his blog and his Facebook page, Vodennikov adopts a similar pose. In blog and Facebook posts, he creates an emphatically intimate self-image through autobiographically imbued lyrical texts, occasional active communication with his (mostly female) readers in the comments section, and dramatic self-portraits (the preceding chapter's figure 3.1 is a case in point). At the same time, the poet's tangible pleasure in linguistically and visually constructing a romantic image gives rise to constant doubts among his audiences. Just how truly private, I have often seen viewers wonder in comments, is the glimpse that social media afford us into this artist's life? As usual, Vodennikov merely deepens the confusion. Openly toying with his status of "sincerity icon," he once quasi-casually mentioned in his blog that, with a friend, he had been talking "about the new sincerity, which is, of course, a little funny. When I let my conscience speak."[67]

Vodennikov plays with the notion of the blog as the new sincerity's ideal literary medium, and he is not unique in doing so. I asked writer and social-media pioneer Sergey Kuznetsov during a visit to his downtown Moscow apartment about the link many critics see between (writers') blogs and a "new sincerity." Kuznetsov agreed that such a link exists. After all, he explained:

> The idea of a "New Sincerity" culminated in around the year 2000, at a time when blogs were becoming popular. At that time, there was a lot of talk about a "New Sincerity." The link interested me personally, too. . . . I started blogging mainly for myself—as a means of expressing personal, private utterances. . . . After a while the blog became very successful, and it began to attract a large readership. That was the phase in which I gradually came to realize that my blog was more public than I had originally intended. At some point, this public popularity became problematic, [and] I started writing for friends only, which I had done for years. Attempts at a personal utterance then shifted more to my books, and I used my blog less for that purpose. However, in the private mode I was still writing for about seven hundred readers. So just how private was blogging for me really, at that time? I began wondering about this question, and at the same time I was still interested in using my blog publicly—for personal expression, but in a new way: a social way. As precisely that—a space for "social personal expression"—is how I see my blog today.[68]

"Social personal expression": this notion is close to the function that media expert Henrike Schmidt discerns in blogs. Relying on extensive monitoring of writers' blogs, Schmidt argues that, when blogging, Russian writers adopt an "aesthetics of nearness" that is marked by a constant wavering between "mystification" (in the form of borrowed user identities, for instance) and a post-postmodern "sincerity," or frank author-reader communication.[69]

Schmidt's and Kuznetsov's statements—and here I turn back from the writers to my broader argument—highlight an important concern in discourse on sincerity and social media: that of a shift in the relationship between private and public discursive space. Just as urbanization, social mobility, and industrialization did during the Renaissance and the Romantic era, so digitization now triggers sincerity anxieties to which private/public tensions are formative. Media expert Nancy Baym recently diagnosed a "cultural turmoil" in online discourse "regarding how much disclosure is appropriate to whom under what circumstances, and its flip side, how much privacy must be protected."[70] The turmoil continues to this day. In the early 2010s, a team of Harvard experts explored the sensations of fulfillment that disclosing personal information activates in our brains. They claimed that this activity sparked a sense of satisfaction similar to that triggered by earning money, eating food, or having sex. The researchers concluded that the neural preference for sharing information about oneself at least partly explains social media's booming popularity. Its users want to share—so much so, that they accept the risks of hacking, fraud, and data tracking. In the words of philosopher of technology Esther Keymolen, "When it concerns the Internet, our default setting is trust."[71]

The blogger-writer's search for candid contact with readers, Pogrebizhskaia's insistence on noncynical online engagement, the view of blogs as tools for an unprecedented public sincerity and trust: I have used this section to bundle together those threads within discussions on sincerity and digitization that have created the greatest public resonance in Russia. In doing so, I have paid special attention to the voice of the professional: that of the writer, the critic, the cultural theorist, the journalist. This group is influential—but it forms only one part of a much larger group of online Russian produsers who are advocating a revival of sincerity. For a full grasp of the debate, it is vital that we take a look at that larger choir of online voices.

"TOO MUCH, MR. PRIGOV!": THE NONPROFESSIONAL'S TAKE

Earlier we saw how Anglophone bloggers are using the notion of a re-born sincerity to hail a wild variety of cultural practices. These can range from pop singer Lana Del Rey to *My Little Pony* TV shows. Russian online media accommodate similarly vivid popular discussions on "the new sincerity." Students, school kids, office workers discuss their take on the term in blogs, on Twitter, and on a range of online forums and social networking sites. Just like their non-Russian counterparts, they are embracing the paradigm of a new sincerity not so much as a full-fledged theoretical paradigm but rather as a tool in constructing a desired online (political, social, intellectual, and/or countercultural) identity. Put more plainly, web users are adopting the phrase to demonstrate to others where they stand in life.

This is not to say that online commentators are unfamiliar with the professional debates that I have traced so far. Just as many of "our" American bloggers were perfectly aware of theoretical discussions on postmodernism and post-postmodernism, so Russian online fans of reviving sincerity are often thoroughly versed in post-Soviet critical theory. Blogger cyrill_lipatov makes this clear in a post written in the summer of 2012: "Let me first make clear that I do not ascribe the status of paradigm to the new sincerity. *Too much, Mr. Prigov!* . . . The gesture of the new sincerity is highly impoverished. It turns its back on pathos, does not know irony, lacks subtlety, defies complexity[:] . . . the auto-matized writing of blogs, the discourse of likes. . . . The new sincerity is introvert to an autistic extent. With it, in our post-post circumstances, we naïvely seek to attain some stable self-identification. And it is pre-cisely naïveté that permits us these searches. . . . And that is why, for twenty years already, the new sincerity has been the best brand. In poli-tics, art and marketing."[72] In this brief comment, cyrill_lipatov—whose user details tell us that he is a Russophone Ukrainian student based in Budapest—manages to bundle all the debate lines I am tracing in this book. He couples sincerity concerns to thinking on memory, but he also links it to commodification and to digitization.

The last part of cyrill_lipatov's statement also brings us to a field onto which Russian social-media users project sincerity concerns with even more fervor than their non-Russian counterparts. I am speaking of the field of present-day politics. In Putin's Russia—as plenty of journal-ists and researchers have demonstrated—social media are a locus for a rapidly growing political engagement.[73] Russian social-media users are eagerly employing online platforms as political tools—to launch concrete civic activity, as we saw, but also to discuss ongoing political developments. In doing so, they often turn to sincerity rhetoric. In August 2009, for example, blogger fragmaker wondered: "Will Putin's snobbism be replaced by Medvedev's new sincerity?"[74] After the stormy parliamentary and presidential elections of 2011 and 2012, similar-sounding posts on (the absence of) a new sincerity in Russian politics abounded. In the spring of 2012—to mention merely two representative examples— users yury_zagrebnoy and romcola debated how "the new sincerity" of the 1990s was making way for the cynical careerism of Putin's electorate,[75] and blogger space_ulysses complained that the "cheap" PR devices of popular blogger-cum-political-activist Aleksei Navalny were incarnating "the new sincerity[:] good old hypocrisy, only sincere."[76]

We are by now very familiar with the anxieties about sincerity that these web users and bloggers revive. When they locate hypocrisy and sincerity, respectively, in Russia's official and alternative political camps, they echo the views on the state and the people of a writer like Alexander Radishchev. When they specifically place a *novel* sincerity in opposition to state pretense, they are reviving—whether consciously or not—both Vladimir Pomerantsev's criticism of socialist-realist hypocrisy and (among others) Prigov's glorifications of a post-Communist sincerity. And when they berate opposition leaders for a "new sincerity" that is not to be trusted, they call to mind Sorokin's—and many other writers'— distrustful critics. Our online political commentators eerily mirror these critics when they use the phrase "new sincerity" to pose the question: is politician X or Y truly reviving sincerity, or is he or she merely embracing the concept as an effective spinning strategy?

In this overview, I have limited myself to mapping and historically contextualizing the infatuation with sincerity witnessed among online lovers of politics, and, earlier, of literature. In truth, the online debate on a reborn sincerity is of course far from confined to literary and political spheres. As with non-Russian new media, over time the range of phenomena onto which new-sincerity paradigms are being superimposed has widened so radically that it has become practically interminable. Russian social-media users employ the phrase to typify such drastically differing phenomena as checkered summer dresses, an alcohol-drenched scooter ride, a new recording of Bach's St. John's Passion, and Moscow socialite Ksenia Sobchak.[77] Not coincidentally, satirical and derogatory takes on "the new sincerity" are flourishing in Russian online discourse as much as they are in Anglophone—remember how Nikolai Ushkov claimed wearily in 2009 that the new sincerity, "if not entirely waggish, is surely beyond being new, almost old."[78]

WIRED AUTHENTICITY AND SINCERITY: CREATIVE IMPERFECTION

"You want the stripped-down, lo-fi version of life, the kind that feels vintage, handmade or home grown. You want authenticity." In an article published in the *Los Angeles Times* in December 2003, journalist Gina Piccalo uses these words to summarize a craving for "the real" in an age when people are "always online."[79] She supports her argument by pointing to the popularity of products such as Aveda's organic shampoos packaged in recycled paper or Ikea's paper lamp shades.

Piccalo's reference to the "handmade" and "home grown" evokes a major component of the debates we are tracing—one whose importance, in fact, can hardly be overrated. This is their insistence on notions of craft, amateurism, and imperfection. The handmade, the deliberately non-professional, the wonky: without these categories, public discourse on new technologies is unthinkable. The imperfect figures as the prime ingredient in an argument whose century-old roots I traced in chapter 1: that of linking technological advancement to dehumanization, and of transforming sincerity or authenticity into a repair tool for this dehumanization. The printed book, industrialized machines, and later new printing and reproduction techniques: all, as we saw, sparked a counterdesire for sincere or authentic human expression—one that cultural critics incessantly sought in the emphatically handcrafted and the unpolished.

The same infatuation with—a usually cautiously stylized—imperfection affects debates on our postdigital age. Ours is the age of Photoshop and online spellcheckers—an age in which the number of tools with which we can perfect our daily lives is amplifying exponentially. In response to this growing technological perfection, creative professionals are increasingly embracing what I call *sublime imperfections:* creative practices that hail imperfection as a hallmark of authentic, sublime, or sincere human expression in a digitized age. In doing so, they are displaying the same infatuation with human craft and imperfectness that earlier intrigued such cultural commentators as John Ruskin and Walter Benjamin. As we saw in chapter 1, Ruskin felt that "engine-tuned precision" was lethal to genuine human expression; Benjamin presented authenticity and technology as irreconcilable domains.

In our techno-driven age, Ruskin's and Benjamin's views on an emphatically atechnological authenticity and sincerity resonate across different parts of the world. I provide a set of representative examples here, starting with non-Russian sources.

In (literary) writing—the art form to which this book has devoted most attention—cultural historian Nicholas Rombes today discerns a renewed preoccupation with "human authorship—with its mistakes, its errors, its slippages." In his view, this preference for human imperfection is fueled by the "hegemony of digital technologies."[80]

A similar desire for creative imperfections underpins a recent fetishization in amateur photography of hit-or-miss snapshots, oversaturated colors, or blurring. Users of the online apps Instagram and Hipstamatic, owners of lomo cameras, plus a range of professional photographers: many of them are embracing the nonpolished, quasi-clumsy shot.[81] That deliberate imperfections have a long history in photography is a different story; what interests me are the cultural longings that they answer in our digitized age. Lomography adept (and Lomography Society International's Cross Channel marketer) Tomas Bates summarizes these longings juicily when he explains why he prefers lomo's technology to digital photography: "Consider the process when you take an analogue photo. You load the film into the camera. You take a photo and light shoots through the shutter and hits the film. You hold the print in your hands once it's been developed. You feel the paper, you see the grain. You are holding something real. Something original. Something Authentic."[82] Today Bates's comments bear near-cliché status. Rare, by 2016, is the trend-conscious youngster who does *not* favor rickety analogue pictures' "authenticity" or "sincerity" over digital photography— even if digital media are considered the ultimate outlet for sharing the same wonky photographs. Politicians and PR advisers have discovered the strength of shaky images, too: a study of Barack Obama's "Yes We Can" campaign attributed its success partly to the campaign's quasi-amateurist on-the-go feel.[83]

Clumsily shot amateur videos now enjoy a similar cult status. Their popularity resonates with an old love for conscious technical flaws in professional filmmaking—one that has tangibly increased in our digitized age. Earlier I cited film historian Jim Collins; as early as 1993 he observed in recent filmmaking a "new sincerity" that moved "back in time away from the corrupt sophistication of media culture toward a lost authenticity." Collins emphasized the complex relationship of this filmic new sincerity with hi-tech spheres: just as the Instagrammer hails the technically nonadvanced primarily via digital channels, so the cinematographic "search for lost purity and authenticity," in truth, depended "on dazzling special effects and the blockbuster budgets they entail." Collins signaled the new (post)digital sincerity in a selection of Hollywood productions—but experts have recently spotted cravings for a deliberately nontechnologically perfected "authenticity" in a much wider range of films, from blockbusters to art-house movies, from both the 1990s and the 2000s.[84]

The current search for authenticity and sincerity in imperfection makes itself felt in film, photography, and literary criticism—but even more than these disciplines, it haunts twenty-first-century design. In a 2002 book on contemporary design, Renny Ramakers—cofounder and director of the leading Dutch design company Droog—spoke of a "trend in imperfection" in design that responds "to the all-pervading perfectionist technology of our time."[85] Ramakers argues that "in a world of smooth industrial perfection and canned one-dimensional beauty designers and artists are searching for authenticity"[86]—a desire that she historically tracks back as far as Ruskin's love for the nonpolished. Illustrative of the desire is the exhibition "Misfit," held in 2010 in Rotterdam's prestigious Boijmans van Beuningen Museum. Curators presented this overview of Hella Jongerius's deliberately overbaked pottery and handcrafted vases as a celebration of rickety forms in response to our hi-tech society (figures 4.3 and 4.4),[87] and design writer Claire Barrett explicitly linked Jongerius's infatuation with "misfits" to today's "vogue for the handcrafted" and "desire for authenticity."[88]

With Jongerius, I conclude my overview of creative imperfections here—but in the Amsterdam-based research project *Sublime Imperfections*, two Ph.D. students and I examine how wonky responses to digitization flourish in a whole range of additional cultural spheres, from

FIGURES 4.3 and 4.4 Vases, handmade flowers, "Artificial Flowers," and pottery "B-set" by Hella Jongerius. The latter is presented on Jongerius's website as an "imperfect set of tableware." By firing the clay too hot, Jongerius disfigures each item slightly, as a result of which "individuality is created within serial production." Hella Jongerius, production descriptions on http://www.jongeriuslab.com/site/html/work/b _set/ (accessed 5 January 2015). Photographs courtesy of Hella Jongerius Design.

FIGURE 4.5 Garments by German fashion
collective Correll Correll. Their collections feature in
a recent publication on handcrafted art and design
to whose compilers "the omnipresence of technology" is fueling an "emergence of handmade . . .
practices [which expose] the processes of fabrication
as gestures of sincerity." Hung and Magliaro, eds., *By
Hand*, 11–12. Photographs courtesy of Daphne and
Vera Correll from Correll Correll.

animation and music to food culture and fashion (for an example from
the latter sphere, see figure 4.5).[89] What interests me here is not so much
this abundance of the trend in itself (or its complex legacy to thinking
about the sublime) as the terminology that its adherents adopt.

All the sources that I cite here—with the exception of Collins—
connect digitization with a desire for a handcrafted or consciously imperfect *authenticity* rather than *sincerity*. They confirm communication
expert Nancy Baym's claim: in her words, "The discourses around

technology . . . tell us that, millennia after the invention of the first communication technologies, we remain oriented towards preserving the
authenticity of human connection and of ourselves."[90] My samples cor-
roborate both Baym's conclusion and a similar one drawn by writers and
consultants James Gilmore and Joseph Pine. In their view, "the emergence of new technologies triggers [a] longing for authenticity: where
automated systems take over, consumers increasingly embrace 'authentic,' human interaction."[91] In an influential argument, Gilmore and Pine
state that today's economy is an experience economy, whose central consumer sensibility—replacing traditional paradigms of availability, cost,
and quality—is that of authenticity.[92]

The insights that Baym and Gilmore and Pine provide are helpful
in understanding digitization discourse, and I agree with them that
technological sophistication goes hand in hand with longings for such
categories as "the human" and "the real." Their work does have one not
irrelevant drawback, however. It makes universal allegations while relying mainly on Anglophone sources. My studies of digitization indicate
that these do not offer the exhaustive global picture that the authors
claim to give. A more inclusive transcultural glance evinces that while
Western European and American critical commentators of new media
insist primarily on *authenticity*, their Russian pendants tend to foreground the concept that this book traces: *sincerity*.

Before turning to Russian spheres, let me stress that I am not
claiming that sincerity concerns are nonexistent in Anglo-American
discussions on digitization and imperfection. Collins and his filmic
"new sincerity" argument are a case in point. So is Nicholas Rombes—
the same Rombes who sees a rebirth of the human author in digitized
writing. Rombes discerns in recent auteurist cinema a trend to hail "deliberate imperfections that . . . remind viewers that human beings made
[them]"—and he labels this trend a "post-ironic" "new sincerity."[93] Erik
Kessels, art director of the world-leading Dutch advertising agency KesselsKramer, makes a not unrelated claim in a 2008 publication on creative marketing: in his view, "despite the lack of high-end technology
that lends so many productions their veneer of professionalism," it is a
lo-fi "sincerity" that lends contemporary amateur (art)work its charm.[94]
Gilmore and Pine blend authenticity with sincerity, too, when they state

that today's technology-fueled experience economy is "all about being real. Original. Genuine. Sincere. Authentic."[95]

Sincerity, in short, is no invisible category in the global debate that I am tracing here. In its Anglophone version, however, it is authenticity, not sincerity, that is transformed into a first-aid tool for digital sterility. Gilmore and Pine helpfully explain why they favor this particular term. They refer to Lionel Trilling's seminal analysis of sincerity and authenticity as, respectively, externally and inwardly oriented, and, paraphrasing Trilling, argue that authenticity has come "to suggest the deficiencies of sincerity and to usurp its place in our esteem," to morph into the "marvellous generative force" that the experts see in it today.[96] I am not convinced, however, that authenticity "usurps" the place of sincerity in the current discourse on human, nontechnically mediated contact. It may do so in Anglophone discussions, as the samples we observed in this section demonstrate. But a look at their Russian equivalents—and it is to Russian debates on digitization and imperfection that we now turn—provides a very different picture.

"NEW SINCERITY XXXL": LO-FI IMPERFECTION
IN A POST-SOVIET WORLD

My previous examples might suggest that responding to digitization with imperfection is a strictly Western move. Nothing could be further from the truth. I demonstrate elsewhere that the nonperfect is today being lauded by creative professionals from a plethora of local backgrounds—think of countries like Brazil, Korea, and Iran.[97] In Russia, too, the wonky is a popular safe haven from technological sophistication. What follows is a short overview of Russian sublime imperfections—one that highlights not only their popularity across different disciplines but also the idiosyncratic terminology that dominates the Russian debate.

In the year 2000, art historian Marina Koldobskaia discerned among Russian artists a revitalization of "sincerity, sensibility and sensitivity"— one that was not only responding critically to postmodernism but also embracing a sometimes ostentatiously clumsy craftsmanship.[98] Cultural critic Viacheslav Kuritsyn articulated an analogous vision—although without using the term "sincerity"—in the conclusion to an influential monograph on Russian postmodernism, published a year earlier. In recent Russian art Kuritsyn diagnosed a mainly digitally mediated "post-postmodernism." This post-postmodern visual art, Kuritsyn believed, foregrounded "everyday life," by celebrating the consciously wonky looks of homemade albums, by fetishizing private letters, or by lauding the feeble aesthetics of amateur photographs.[99]

In photography, Russian lomo aficionados are also embracing aesthetic imperfection as the hallmark of a novel and, to some, post-postmodern cultural logic. They are transforming "sincerity" into the new aesthetic's buzzword just as eagerly as non-Russian fans connect imperfection with authenticity. Photographer Irina Osaulenko—to cite one representative voice in the debate—puts it this way: lomography's shaky aesthetics satisfy a longing "for the sincerity and unmediated expression that we have lost. After all, they are what many of us long for most of all."[100]

The wobbly and shaky are similarly being transformed into a hallmark for sincerity in Russian graphic design and architecture. A love for a quasi-handcrafted, sketchy style is what emanates from the posters of Ostengruppe—an internationally acclaimed design lab that unites five of Russia's top graphic designers. In Russian architecture, raw looks and ostentatiously man-made constructions resonate no less firmly. For the world-renowned architect Sasha Brodsky—he represented Russia at Venice's Architecture Biennale and was a visiting critic at Cornell University—deliberate chaos and incompletion are a signature device. When I interviewed Brodsky for the architecture journal *Mark* in 2008, I asked what sources inspired him most. He linked lo-fi nonprofessionalism with sincerity when he answered: "Constructions made by nameless architects, the spontaneous architecture you find in the areas around Moscow. Structures composed unprofessionally, from whatever was at hand, but exuding a specific truth or sincerity. People built these not for the sake of form, but strictly for their own goals, without architectural training, without a budget."[101]

Amateurism is celebrated as a token of a non-tech-savvy sincerity, too, in recent Russian music and music criticism. Sergei Zharikov—the same music critic who attributes the global repute of perestroika-era pop to its "heartbreaking sincerity" (see chapter 2)—argues that new technologies have shaped a new generation of proudly amateurist Russian artists. As a prime example of what he labels their "artefacts of 'the new sincerity,'" Zharikov singles out Sergei Beliak. In 2001 Beliak—a famous Moscow-based attorney—released his debut album *Erotic Hallucinations of a Russian Lawyer* (Eroticheskie galliutsinatsii russkogo advokata). Beliak's emphatically amateurist self-presentation—in the ensuing PR campaign, the lawyer emphasized his lack of music training—only fueled the album's success.[102] Two years later, the debut album of singer and celebrity icon Stas Baretskii resembled Beliak's in its celebration of amateurism—an amateurism that critics again read as a sign of a revived sincerity in a mediated world. In the words of critic Denis Boiarinov, Baretskii—"a mountain of a man, formerly a bodyguard at a food market in Rambov, self-made poet and only son of an old mummy"—incarnated with his music "the illustrious new sincerity size XXXL."[103]

The examples above disentangle debates on digitization and aesthetic imperfection mainly in the audiovisual arts. Most important, they demonstrate that, in hailing the technically flawed, contributors to the debate insist on sincerity rather than authenticity. The same discourse—including the preoccupation with sincerity—is flourishing in another cultural domain: that of literature and creative writing. Sincerity and the nontechnological are linked conceptually, first of all, in the very design of certain contemporary books. In 2006, for example, Moscow-based poet Vera Pavlova published a collection of poems entitled *Letters to the Neighboring Room* (Pis'ma v sosedniuiu komnatu). All are written by hand rather than typeset in digitized fonts. According to the jacket text, Pavlova's choice of human handwriting and its inevitable occasional slips of the pen is a conscious artistic device rather than a random selection. The handwritten, the text explains, heightens the work's "sincerity."[104] The book thus caters to a heightened transnational interest in (to cite the subtitle of a study on the subject) "handwriting in the age of new media"—but, as in other disciplines, the transnational debate on handwriting today primarily hails authenticity, whereas this Russian example revolves around sincerity.[105]

The technically imperfect may be embraced in book *design*, but it is also highlighted as a guarantee of nonmediated honesty *within* literary texts. As Henrike Schmidt has demonstrated, reflections on literary dilettantism, amateurism, and graphomania have been formative to the development of the Russian-language Internet.[106] Schmidt draws a historical parallel with a late eighteenth- and early nineteenth-century preference for unpolished writing among Russian sentimentalists.[107] Indeed, just as the sentimentalist saw in a not unduly perfected style an indication of genuine emotion, so today's discussions on "imperfect" writing—typos, aberrant punctuation, or other norm-deviating linguistic practices—evince a tangible concern with unmediated sincerity. Most famously, linguistic imperfection has been transformed into a guarantee for sincere expression in padonki language. Padonki—a misspelled version of the Russian word for scoundrels—is an online jargon that thrived in Russia in the middle of the last decade and playfully defied orthographic and grammatical correctness. Among padonki's arguments against linguistic etiquette, a prominent concern was protesting against digital flawlessness. In their "Anti-gramar Manivesto," the padonki (as the users of the language are known) stated that "the bettir the digital spelchekkurs, the moor the rusian languich losiz its spontuneitie." By way of solution, they called for "A FAIGHT WID THE SOWLLEZ CAMPUTIR CORECTNIZ wich nastie robut-accupantz enfors upon us!!!"[108]

Elsewhere I have illustrated how an analogous preoccupation with linguistic and stylistic imperfection characterizes the blogs of many influential Russian writers.[109] What their blogs share is an aesthetic strategy—expressed either through linguistic practices or in metastatements—of embracing an unpolished writing mode as the norm for online authorship. What the padonki experiment and many writers' blogs share, too, is a conviction that, in digitized times, imperfect writing serves as hallmark of a writer's artistic integrity. Human "spontaneity": that is what padonki project onto erratic language. A similar philosophy emerges from poet Dmitrii Vodennikov's views on blogging. In our interview, he told me that, when blogging, he makes "constant typos"—but these typos, he said, merely reinforce his weblog's "artlessness."[110] With me Vodennikov used the term "artlessness" (*nepoddel'nost'*), but, as we saw, the same poet has also envisioned in blog writing a very specific type of artlessness—a "new honesty," that is—in Russian online writing.

Sincerity is central, finally, in journalistic musings on the (often quasi-)amateurist, error-tolerant aesthetics of Russian e-writing. In the early 2000s, journalist Marina Mitrenina linked online experiments with erratic language to the ongoing debate on a post-postmodern "new sincerity." In her words, in online writing, postmodern relativism makes way for the nonedited, "unmediated text," and for a "priority of sincerity over grammatical correctness."[111] The when and where of Mitrenina's claim are not unimportant: she published it in 2003 in *Russkii zhurnal* (*The Russian Journal*)—a major publication platform for Russia's web pioneers, and a journal that many of the creative professionals whom we discussed here zealously read at the time. Its publications, including Mitrenina's analysis of online writing, are still circulating on the web, often in more than one version.

Together, the statements and examples above make one thing clear: several of Russia's leading creative professionals harbor an interest in imperfection as a safe haven for automatization. They point at yet another distinctive feature of Russian sublime imperfections. As a rule, the journalists, practicing artists, and critics whom I cited point to imperfection as a hallmark of *sincerity* rather than authenticity—the term that dominates Western discussions on creative imperfection.

This Russian insistence on sincerity does not, of course, point to an intrinsic cultural preference for one concept or the other. It harks back to the inordinate significance with which the notion of iskrennost' has historically been endowed in Russia. In chapter 1 we saw how the term acquired buzzword status in a social-identity crisis among intellectuals in late-eighteenth century Russia. We also saw how (and why) the trend of defending an emphatically sincere Russian otherness toward the West has persisted ever since. In the same chapter we witnessed next how, in the post-Stalinist Russia of the 1950s, intellectuals presented sincerity as a counterresponse to socialist-realist hypocrisy—and in the subsequent two chapters I traced the near-obsessive interest in the same concept in perestroika-era and early post-Soviet Russia. Together the three preceding chapters illustrated how, while Trilling believed that authenticity has superseded sincerity as a Western model, the more normative and outward-directed ideal of sincerity has preserved a dominant cultural status in Russia.

In today's new-media age, this disproportionate Russian interest in the notion has not relented. Not surprisingly, when Russian commentators laud the imperfect or the handcrafted in a wired age, they rarely present these categories as a hallmark of authenticity. The sincere, not the authentic: that is what they hunt for in the unpolished and the wonky.

SINCERITY AND AUTHENTICITY: CONCLUSION

In post-Soviet Russia, my sources indicate, we witness an infatuation with imperfection in online writing. This insistence on the nonperfect in literary spheres is not surprising. Not only is Russia—according to a persistent literaturocentric myth—"the world's most reading country," its reading habits are also clearly shaped by the highly normative language culture of the Soviet era.[112] Post-Soviet creative writing subverts, but is at the same time formed by, this culture—and in the semiotic space in which its practitioners move, deviations from the norm are prime markers of subcultural identity. Not coincidentally did we see in chapter 1 that creative imperfections—and the current infatuation with craft, purportive amateurism, and the homemade—were already permeating nonconformist Soviet- and perestroika-era literature and book art long before the advent of digital media. Set against this longer-standing literary and artistic interest in lo-fi aesthetics, the preoccupation with imperfection in Russian digital discourse comes as little surprise. Rather than that insistence on imperfection in itself, however, what mattered to me in the present chapter is the terminology that contributors to the debate use in defending the rickety. I shall turn to this terminology in a moment; let me first assess this chapter's place in the story of my book.

By unraveling the post-Soviet insistence on sincerity in times of media change, the previous pages have highlighted a third component of sincerity rhetoric after Communism. In chapters 1 and 2 I demonstrated that the local and temporal idiosyncrasies of post-Communist life trigger a heightened preoccupation with sincerity. I indicated how, in the years following the fall of Communism, sincerity anxieties intensified in Russia in response both to politico-historical commotion (chapter 2) and to economic turmoil (chapter 3). This chapter has illustrated how the drastic media transitions that Russia is witnessing today are further enhancing the post-Communist preoccupation with sincerity.

As I have explained, I am not the first to observe a link—in Russia and elsewhere—between drastic changes in media usage and cravings for genuine human interaction. The preceding pages do, however, force us to lend nuance to existing views of this link. More specifically, they urge us to question whether the prime cultural concern of our rapidly automatizing experience economy is indeed authenticity. It is true that today's rise of new technologies triggers cravings for lo-fi, authentic human interaction, as the productive analyses of Gilmore, Pine, and Baym claim. But digitization also fuels different cravings—cravings that reverberate modestly in Western public discourse but instantly catch the eye in a part of the world that Gilmore, Pine, and Baym do not study.

My findings in this chapter illustrate that experts adopt a limited scope when they claim that "what consumers really want" is authenticity. Yes, authenticity is in great demand today—but when we move beyond Western paradigms, we see that what cultural consumers crave right now is not authenticity alone. Blogger cyrill_lipatov, journalist Mitrenina, and the many other commentators who had their say on the preceding pages believe in the dawn of a related but fundamentally different cultural and consumer sensibility. This alternative sensibility, which has a particularly burdened rhetorical history in Russia, is sincerity. An inclusive take on our experience economy needs to reckon with this alternative longing. A truly transnational gaze on our time and age—to put it somewhat differently—acknowledges that, in some cultural settings, what consumers really want today is sincerity rather than authenticity.

Sincerity Dreams

Poems after osventsim poems after gulag poems after google
self-tribunal of unexpected maturity
flowery heat melting ice-cream
new sincerity
factory of meanings

Aleksandr Pivinskii, "Coquetting with Cuff Links" (2012)

When I told colleagues—academics, but also artists, writers, curators—
that I was writing this book, I was sometimes met with enthusiasm but
just as often encountered skepticism or outright irritation. Few of my
addressees took new-sincerity rhetoric seriously, even though all knew
about its existence or had a story to tell about it. Surely, many a conversation partner argued, I did not want to analyze that inflated hobbyhorse
of post-postmodern discourse called "the new sincerity"? Surely I real-
ized that the notion of a *novaia iskrennost'*, or reborn sincerity, had already been defined and exploited ad nauseam by artist so-and-so, writer
this and that, and curator X or Y? Over time, my conversations with
skeptics yielded an almost limitless "to-check" list of names, articles,
books, essays, artworks, films, weblogs, TV programs, and music, and
fashion and design trends that people today connect to talk of reanimating sincerity. Many examples never even made it into this book.

My colleagues' responses aptly illustrate the prominent status of the
cultural trend that interests me. I understand why it makes them vexed.
At times today's dreams of renewing or revitalizing sincerity are unduly
repetitive, and more than one new-sincerity advocate has conjured up
theoretically shaky visions. But I do not share the belief that these visions are outdated or unworthy of our attention. On the contrary: their

omnipresence proves just how topical sincerity dreams still are—despite the social and philosophical disillusions that mark the twentieth century—in the twenty-first century.

I am not alone in believing that contemporary sincerity models warrant close attention. As recently as 2012, the renowned publisher Norton launched a book-length monograph on sincerity. Its author, the journalist and freelance writer R. Jay Magill Jr., elegantly, if somewhat pompously, explained that "the ideals of sincerity and authenticity—twin ideals that insist you say what you feel and be true to who you are in order to live a satisfying life—continue to hold enormous and undeniable sway over our lives, even absent their religious origins. . . . The ideal of sincerity, born five hundred years ago as a moral imperative, abides in us in ways silent and compelling, drawing the secular mind inward like a strange magnetic north."[1]

My findings confirm Magill's claim that sincerity is anything but obsolete in twenty-first-century popular culture. They also demonstrate that today's strivings to renew sincerity have not been neglected by scholars. (New-)sincerity rhetoric has been tackled in thoughtful analyses of contemporary culture that have helped me enormously in crafting this book. Magill is one example; so is the work of Epstein and Yurchak. Together with a limited set of other scholars, they offer fruitful insights into present-day sincerity—but their analyses also have limits.

Take Magill. Just like Trilling and Peyre, he confines his analyses to the concept's "deep impact . . . on the Western soul."[2] His study does much to unravel the American infatuation with sincerity—but his interrogations of the concept rarely if ever venture into non-Western territories. Epstein and Yurchak do look at non-Western developments: they share with my book a focus on (late and) post-Communist experience. Like most other explorers of new-sincerity rhetoric, however, they limit themselves to article-length publications. Their studies offer short introductions to a topic that—as Epstein and Yurchak themselves acknowledge—fully merits in-depth investigation.

This book is my attempt at subjecting contemporary sincerity discourse to the more integral and transnationally devised study it deserves. The stories of Sorokin, Prigov, and the bloggers each help to craft a comprehensive and geographically inclusive analysis of present-day sincerity rhetoric. They also fine-tune our existing knowledge of the transnational debate on post-postmodern sincere expression. The twists and turns that present-day sincerity discourse is taking in Russia complement the Western light that experts like Magill shed on it.

What, then, are the newly gained insights which my non-Western sincerity study offers? In order to answer this question, let us take a closer look at the lines with which I opened this Conclusion. In his 2012 poem "Coquetting with Cuff Links" ("Koketnichaia zaponkami"), Aleksandr Pivinskii—not an unknown in Russia's contemporary poetry scene—unites three threads running through the post-Soviet debate on sincerity. The poet observes a "new sincerity" in contemporary culture that is inextricably interwoven:

- with collective memory: Pivinskii's "new sincerity" consists of poems that emerge "after osventsim"—Auschwitz, that is—and "after [the] gulag";
- with (post)digital media: this poet's "new sincerity" finds its expression in the digitally mediated poetry as we know it "after google";
- and with commodification: the poet borrows a metaphor from the language of commercial production when claiming that "the new sincerity" offers a "factory of meanings."

After chapter 1's historical prelude, I traced the three discursive threads that Pivinskii interlaces. I focused on sincerity rhetoric as employed by Russian creative professionals—the group, that is, that constitutes Russia's creative and intellectual vanguard. This group today foregrounds sincerity for at least three reasons.

The preoccupation of Russian creative professionals with sincerity is, first, a response to attempts to cope with the Soviet experience of the stormy perestroika era and its aftermath. Ernst van Alphen and Mieke Bal claim that, as a rule, sincerity rhetoric intensifies during times of intercultural troubles.[3] The Russian story teaches us that it also heightens during periods of *intracultural* turmoil. What should post-Soviet artistic sincerity look like? And what does sincerity mean in an age that is busy digesting the traumatic and morally corruptive Soviet experiment? Chapter 2 proved that these questions are more central to creative culture in perestroika-era and early post-Soviet Russia than existing studies acknowledge. Dmitrii Prigov's longing for what I call a *cura-*

tive sincerity—sincerity as a therapeutic tool to deal with a conflicted social memory—is especially pressing. But Prigov is not alone. Several leading creative voices of our time insist on affective concerns that merit a more visible place in the postmodern story. I am speaking of concerns about sincere expression, and about the healing potential of sincerity in digesting the historical horrors of the past century.

In post-Communist Russia, creative professionals thus turn to sincerity in reaction to political turbulence—but they also ponder sincerity ideals in response to economic unrest. Chapter 3 traced discourse on cultural life in the Russia of the late 1990s and early 2000s. At that time, creative professionals were fiercely debating the socioeconomic challenges that they faced now that the Communist experiment had collapsed. When writer Vladimir Sorokin chose, in precisely this period, to foreground a speak-from-the-heart rhetoric both in his prose and his public self-fashioning, he triggered vivid discussions on sincerity and commodification. Sorokin's story tells us that, to understand the post-Soviet literary field, we need to understand its emotional dynamics. In the past decades, sociologically inspired literary scholars have made worthy attempts to map the literary market of post-Communist Russia.[4] What these scholars rarely do, however, is bring in emotion as an analytical category. Which artistic coping strategy works, which cultural object acquires symbolic or economic capital: the *Trilogy* controversy teaches us that these questions cannot be answered without considering how emotional norms, communities, and regimes shape a particular cultural-historical period. It also teaches us that postmodernism and literary sociology have left indelible theoretical marks on current thinking on sincerity and commercial gain. Contrary to the historical takes on artistic integrity and "good business" that existing studies of sincerity rhetoric examine,[5] critics and art professionals today shun binary schematizations. In Russia as elsewhere, most progressive critics today agree that sincere self-revelation and strivings for self-profit are, in fact, two sides of the same coin.

Russian developments demonstrate, in short, how sincerity anxieties impact creative life at times when political and socioeconomic vectors shift. The same anxieties play up in periods when mediascapes mutate. In post-Soviet Russia, Soviet-era, propaganda-ridden press practices have made way for a more pluralist, part-digitized mediascape—even if we do witness neo-authoritarian media modeling in Putin's Russia. In the past two decades, Russian creative professionals and social-media users with widely varying social backgrounds engaged in heightened debates on new media and its impact on selfhood, human expression, and interpersonal contact. I tracked their discussions and embedded them within the transnational debate on digitization and sincerity. Leading—Anglophone and Russian—voices in this debate, we saw, foreground sincerity as an attractive human ideal in an age of increasing machine-driven standardization. They eagerly engage with *sublime imperfections:* the making of hand-shot films, of scrap-wood design, typo-ridden texts, and other creative products that embrace rather than shun the aesthetically nonperfected as a token of genuine human expression in a digitized age.

Russian imperfection adepts fetishize sincerity—and in doing so, they contradict James Gilmore and Joseph Pine's famous assertions on the experience economy. According to Gilmore and Pine, "what consumers really want" in our hi-tech world is authenticity.[6] In Russia, cultural consumers today indeed express cravings for an emphatically nontechnological realness, but to express that craving they do not (or rarely) talk about authenticity. They use a different concept—one that has a special meaning for the post-Soviet mind. What they are searching for in the nontechnologically perfected is sincerity.

Do my findings tell us what, at this moment, the term "sincerity" means in Russia? Pivinskii's verses offer cues for a possible response, and so do recent analytical takes on the concept. One is a 2009 article in the *New York Times by* journalist Sophia Kishkovsky. She argued that in the late 2000s, Russian "kvartirniki, or 'apartment concerts,' a staple of the Soviet underground, are undergoing a revival, and invitation-only salons are competing with nightclubs. Glossy magazines talk of the 'new sincerity' and 'new spirituality,' reporting that well-to-do Russians, licking wounds from the crisis, would rather sit at the kitchen table than patronize another fancy restaurant."[7] Kishkovsky frames the financial crisis as new-sincerity trigger—but critics have also pointed to Putin's reelection and the detention of the punk-rock collective Pussy Riot as catalysts of "a demand for a 'new sincerity.'"[8]

These and Kishkovsky's readings of a "new sincerity" partly confirm, partly contradict my own observations during recent Russia
trips. In Moscow and St. Petersburg, I saw how—amid the at times
fervid civic engagement that we are witnessing in Russia today—an
underground aura could tangibly heighten the "sincerity factor" of new
cultural spaces or events. Both cities boast new creative hubs (Fligel,
Taiga, ArtPlay, and Vinzavod are cases in point) whose austere aesthetics
vaguely evoke the late-Soviet, sincerity-loving kitchen-table culture at
which Kishkovsky hints. At the same time, they attract a socioculturally
highly privileged (and only mildly politically engaged) crowd much like
those at postindustrial sites outside Russia.

It is tempting to use these and other recent visions to craft a watertight definition of Russian sincerity in the 2010s—but such a definition
would rely precisely on those speculative conjectures on the state of contemporary culture that I have tried to avoid here. In outlining the "travels" of sincerity rhetoric in perestroika-era and post-Soviet Russia, I have
not attempted to unravel what the eagerly discussed revived sincerity
"really" is. This question is unproductive in a world where creatives fundamentally distrust and deconstruct stable (theories of) selves. In that
world, the question of how to be sincere is a question that they either
cannot or do not want to answer, or refuse to theoretically ground or af-
firm. A simple dismissal of new-sincerity rhetoric as shallow or cynical,
however, would miss the point, too. After all, as the voices that populate
this book demonstrate, sincerity today remains a vital preoccupation for
writers, bloggers, and other creative professionals.

My aim is different. As the preceding reflections on memory, commodification, and media illustrate, I have sought to understand what
the relentless popularity of sincerity models teaches us about contemporary society—post-Communist and global alike. The longing to
digest a traumatic past, to cope with an economically tumultuous present, and to preserve interhuman connections in a postdigital age—
these cultural cravings are what really underpin the story of sincerity
after Communism.

The foregoing chapters unraveled how present-day sincerity talk
feeds into these larger cultural preoccupations. In doing so, they bring
nuance to Western studies of late and post-postmodern rhetoric. Cultural commentators who locate this type of rhetoric exclusively in West-

ern European and Anglophone spheres are mistaken. Not only has the postmodern project itself been anything but limited to Europe and the United States, the "What comes *after* postmodernism?" (or "Into which new forms does it morph?") question has also been pondered in a much wider range of geopolitical settings than current analyses suggest.[9] Post-Communist Russia is a case in point. Existing studies in English— today's academic lingua franca—persistently overlook something that my analyses prove: in this region, debates on a shift to late or post-postmodern cultural paradigms are thriving with at least as much fervor as, and possibly more than, in Western Europe or the United States.

"In the 1990s, everyone started talking about sincerity," the curator and critic Alla Mitrofanova argued at a conference on the perestroika years in 2007.[10] By the summer of 2016, as I was finishing up a complete draft of this book, it was clear that "the new sincerity" was not the new "honest" cultural mainstream that some envisioned at the time. But the preceding pages also demonstrate that the perestroika-era infatuation with sincerity has ended neither in Russia nor elsewhere. On the contrary. The precise meaning of the phrase "new sincerity" remains as obfuscated as it has been from the start, but fans continue to (re)construct and (re)define the phrase with relentless fervor. In poems, in art catalogues, in PR films, in fashion brochures, in TV shows, in blogs, on Twitter, in Instagram, *dreams* of reviving sincerity continue to haunt us as we speak.

NOTES

PREFACE

1. Korthals Altes, "Blessedly post-ironic?"
2. Epstein, "A Catalog of the New Poetries," 209.

INTRODUCTION

1. Dialogue between two bloggers on December 8, 2007 (blogs.yandex.ru
/cachedcopy.xml?f=89015cb1fea4bfd51c0c7ad775f1e155&i=108&m=http://blogs
.mail.ru/mail/magda20/15B76C2458988D5.html&text="Новая%20
искренность", accessed 4 September, 2010; no longer available).

2. For a transnational perspective, see Van Alphen, Bal, and Smith, eds., *The
Rhetoric of Sincerity;* for the United States, the United Kingdom, and France,
see Korthals Altes, "Blessedly post-ironic?" and "Sincerity, Reliability and
Other Ironies," 107–28; for the United States and the Netherlands, see Vaes-
sens, *De revanche van de roman;* for the United States see also Den Dulk, *Over
de drempel* and *Love Me Till My Heart Stops;* for China, Chung and Jacobi, "In
Search of a New Sincerity?"; for Estonia, the Estonian Wikipedia entry "New
Sincerity" (undated), online at http://et.wikipedia.org/wiki/Uussiirus; and for
Germany, Kirchmaier, "Die Verdichtung der Sinne."

3. The search tool I have used to browse Russian blogs is the Russian search engine
Yandex (blogs.yandex.ru), as well as—occasionally—Google's search engine. I
used these tools through lack of more perfect digital search tools—which are costly
and difficult to master for non-IT-specialists—but in the full awareness of their
bias and theoretical pitfalls. On the methodological problems inherent in digital
search tools, see Rogers, *The End of the Virtual;* on the challenges of using Google
for scholarly ends, see, among others, Jeanneney, *Google and the Myth of Universal
Knowledge;* on the biased results that it renders, see Pariser, *The Filter Bubble.*

4. For examples, see Ashkarov, "Pussy Riot—iznanka kazionnosti"; and Pertsev, "Novaia iskrennost'."

5. Yurchak, "Post-Post-Communist Sincerity."

6. Kulik, "Artist's Favourites." In the English version, the term "new honesty" is used—but when I asked him, Kulik explained that he used "sincerity" (*iskrennost'*) in the original (Facebook message from the author, January 11, 2012).

7. Epstein, "Katalog novykh poezii," "O novoi sentimental'nosti," and "Proto-, ili konets postmodernizma" (I cite these works here as reprinted in *Postmodern v Rossii*); Boym, *Common Places*, 102; Lipovetsky, *Russian Postmodernist Fiction*, 247, and *Paralogii*, 575ff.

8. Guyer, *Romanticism after Auschwitz*.

9. Hutchings, "Editorial," 1–2. Hutchings provides a brief but helpful overview of the theoretical problems inherent in academic usage of both terms.

10. On the "post" discussion in Slavic studies, see, among others, Rogers, "Post-socialisms Unbound," 1–16; Buckler, "What Comes after 'Post-Soviet' in Russian Studies?"; and Platt, "The Post-Soviet Is Over."

11. Hoerschelmann and Stenning, "History, Geography and Difference in the Post-Socialist World," 322.

12. For two samples, see Boev's "Remodernism?" and Dalakchieva-Lerinska's poetry review "Sreshchu vsevlastieto na khorizontalite."

13. Chung and Jacobi, "In Search of a New Sincerity?"

14. Hesmondhalgh, "Cultural and Creative Industries." For critical approaches to creative-industries scholarship, and to Richard Florida's (in Russia as elsewhere) popular but controversial study *The Rise of the Creative Class*, see, apart from Hesmondhalgh's analysis, especially Peck, "Struggling with the Creative Class," and Trubina, "Tramvai, Polnyi Wi-Fi."

15. Wachtel, *Remaining Relevant after Communism*.

16. Marsh, *Literature, History and Identity in Post-Soviet Russia*, 17.

17. Notable English-language examples include *Third Wave* (1992), an anthology of Russian poetry in translation that familiarizes Anglophone readers with "sentimental" and other alternatives to Moscow Conceptualist thinking, albeit without explicitly framing these as late or post-postmodern developments (Ashby and Johnson, eds., *Third Wave*); and the following analyses, which all contain discussions of Russian post-postmodern trends at chapter or article level: Epstein, *After the Future*; Epstein, Genis, and Vladiv-Glover, eds., *Russian Postmodernism*; Lipovetsky, *Russian Postmodernist Fiction*; Shneidman, *Russian Literature 1988–1994*, 205; Weststeijn, "After Postmodernism," and Weststeijn's valedictory lecture, Amsterdam, October 31, 2008 (unpublished). Raoul Eshelman's *Performatism* discusses post-postmodern trends in an internationally oriented study, but with a special eye for Russian cinema, visual art, and architecture.

18. I am referring to the terms as used by Nancy Fraser (in her article "Transnationalizing the Public Sphere") and Jürgen Habermas (most notably in *The Postnational Constellation*).

19. Groys, "The Other Gaze," 87.

20. Ilya Kukulin in discussion with the author, May 12, 2009. Transcription available upon request from contact@ellenrutten.nl.

21. I thank the anonymous Yale University Press reviewer who offered helpful comments on and input for my definition as outlined here.

22. Wu et al., "On the Trend, Detrending, and Variability of Nonlinear and Non-stationary Time Series."

23. Buckland, "Wes Anderson," 1–5.

24. Hebdige, *Hiding in the Light*, 181–82.

25. Epstein, "Conclusion," 457.

26. Ibid.

27. The outcomes of this joint project were collected in Vaessens and Van Dijk, eds., *Reconsidering the Postmodern*.

28. Thomas Vaessens, e-mail correspondence with the author, June 6, 2009.

29. Epstein, "Conclusion."

30. See, for representative examples, Arkhangel'skii, "Novaia ser'eznost'," on a Russian "new seriousness"; for a more political, neoimperialist use of the term, see Dugin, *Geopolitika postmoderna;* see Gubailovskii and Rodnianskaia,"Knigi neobshchego pol'zovaniia"; Markova, "Novyi-prenovyi realizm," on "new realism"; and Leiderman, *Postrealizm,* on "postrealism."

31. On the substantial methodological problems that cling to digital search tools, see note 3 in this chapter.

32. On this date, "new authenticity" spawned a mere 3,120. With 55,600 results, "new realism" again delivered a much higher score, but both here and in the Russian translation its double meaning—it also refers to a canonical phase in French film history—distorts the search results. The blog search services that I used were Google Blog Search and Yandex Blog Search (see also notes 3 and 35). The former was discontinued in 2011—but until March 2016, one could use an alternative search route to force Google to display the results (on this alternative strategy, see http://www.netforlawyers.com/content /google-kills-blog-search-engine-109, last accessed May 25, 2016). Yandex Blog Search was reduced to a two-month-only backtrack option in 2015.

33. "New Sincerity," Wikipedia, last accessed 2 March 2015, en.wikipedia.org /wiki/New_Sincerity.

34. See, for instance, Gross, "Alter Protest in neuen Klamotten"; Thumfart, "Das Kulturphänomen 'New Sincerity'"; Sanneh, "Mr. Sincerity Tries a New Trick"; Williams, "The Final Irony"; Maher, "If You're Unhappy And You Know It . . ."; and Saltz, "Sincerity and Irony Hug It Out."

35. The numbers were rendered by searches on blogs.yandex.ru, search option "all blogs and forums." I focus on blog and forum usage here, as they tell us much about popular use of the term—but I want to add that outside these platforms the picture is more ambiguous. A similar search in Cyrillic, on the same date, in Google delivered 7,160 hits for "new sincerity" ("*novaia iskrennost'*"). This score was much higher than the meager 1,680 hits the

Russian translation of "new authenticity" ("*novaia podlinnost'*") generated—but humble when compared to the 28,500 hits for "*novyi realizm*" (the Russian pendant of "new realism"). Indicative of the problems inherent in online search tools were the results for "*novaia iskrennost'*" that I collected in Yandex in January 2012: according to result page 1, the phrase (entered in Cyrillic) then yielded merely twenty-eight hits; but when I moved to page 2 and further pages, the term turned out to generate approximately 1,340 hits (the numbers varied from page to page).

36. Strictly speaking, new-sincerity discussions thus emerged when Soviet authorities were still in power; I nevertheless speak mostly of a post-Soviet discourse, as they went public only after the USSR had formally dissolved.

37. Prigov, "Preduvedomleniie," in *Novaia iskrennost'*. I am grateful to the poet's widow, Nadezhda Bourova, and Dmitrii Golynko-Vol'fson for providing me with a copy of the manuscript.

38. On Jimmy, see nikadubrovsky, post and comment 27 May 2009 (nikadubrovsky.livejournal.com/649798.html?thread=9542726, accessed 5 January 2015); on Starbucks, flippi754, post 3 March 2009 (flippi754.livejournal.com/151341.html); on hipster cafés, *Time Out*'s vkontakte.ru page, post 20 May 2015 (http://vk.com/wall-28845160_22474).

39. Most, *Doubting Thomas*, xi–xii.

40. Greenblatt, *Learning to Curse*, 14.

41. "Discourse Studies," *Centre for Discourse Studies*.

42. Plamper, "Vvedenie I," 31. Plamper defends his claim in detail in ibid., 31–33.

43. Medvedev, "The Writer in Russia."

44. All citations ibid.

45. Etkind, *Warped Mourning*, 237.

46. Among others, Cambridge-based initiatives—all launched in the 2000s—include the workshops Cultural Memory in Russia and Research Methods in East European Memory Studies, both held at King's College; the Interdisciplinary Research Group on East European Memory Studies and the anthropology-focused research reading group Telling Memories (2007–9), which had a strong post-Soviet component; and the HERA-funded Memory at War project (2010–13), which explored memory discourse in Poland, Russia, and Ukraine, and in which I coordinated a subproject on East European memory and new media (see www.web-wars.org for details).

47. On this view, see Van Alphen and Bal, "Introduction."

48. Etkind, *Warped Mourning*, 10. Among others, for more on the problems of post-Soviet memory culture see Nowak, *History and Geopolitics*.

49. Etkind, *Warped Mourning*, 192–93.

50. Skoropanova, *Russkaia postmodernistskaia literatura*, 5.

51. Lipovetsky, *Russian Postmodernist Fiction*, 14–15.

52. Man'kovskaia, *Estetika postmodernizma*, 12.

53. On the notion of "late postmodernism," see Fokkema, "The Semiotics of Literary Postmodernism"; and Green, *Late Postmodernism*. Within Russia, the

division between a hardboiled early and a less relativistic "late" postmodernism is defended most notably in Lipovetsky's *Paralogii*.

54. I am aware that I am not the first scholar to propagate more nuance in theorizing on Russian postmodernism; but existing pleas for the "sincerity problematization" that I defend incline to be discussed in passing or not to be
explicitly addressed (this is the case, for instance, in Epstein's book-length
studies of postmodernism, mentioned above, and in Lipovetsky's *Paralogii*).

55. He famously claimed in 1992 that his texts are "mere letters on a piece of
paper" (Sorokin, "Tekst kak narkotik," 121).

56. Sorokin, "Vladimir Sorokin ne khochet byt' prorokom."

57. Sorokin in Sokolov, *Moia kniga o Vladimire Sorokine*, 129.

58. Kibirov, personal conversation, Moscow, 13 May 2009. Transcription available upon request from contact@ellenrutten.nl.

59. Rosenbaum, *Professing Sincerity*.

60. Apart from Rosenbaum, I am thinking especially of Reddy, *The Navigation
of Feeling*; Van Alphen, Bal, and Smith, eds., *Rhetoric of Sincerity*; and the
take on sincerity in a number of essays (especially Kelly's, Safronova's, and
Sirotkina's contributions) in Plamper, Elie, and Schahadat, eds., *Rossiiskaia
imperiia chuvstv*.

61. See Bourdieu, *The Field of Cultural Production*, and Sapiro, *La guerre des
écrivains*.

62. Most helpful to me have been Wachtel's *Remaining Relevant after Communism* and Menzel's *Bürgerkrieg um Worte*. For canonical contributions to the
Russian discussion, see also Dubin and Gudkov, *Literatura kak sotsial'nyi institut*, and Berg, *Literaturokratiia*.

63. A sample of a literary-historical study that does rely on affective categories in
monitoring socioeconomic processes is Klein, "Derzhavin."

64. Berry and Dieter, *Postdigital Aesthetics*; Leiby, "I Am Such a Failure."

65. While acknowledging the problematic status of the concept of generation
(for a helpful discussion of the term and its theoretical slipperiness, see
Strauss and Howe, *Generations*), I do position, on the one hand, Prigov,
Sorokin, and a number of their contemporaries (Timur Kibirov, Lev Rubinstein, Sergei Gandlevskii) and, on the other, Vodennikov, and a selection of
writers of approximately the same age (Sergey Kuznetsov and Kirill Medvedev,
for instance), and the bloggers discussed in chapter 4 as two successive
generations.

66. Roth-Ey, *Moscow Prime Time*.

67. Bruns, *Blogs, Wikipedia, Second Life, and Beyond*, 2. On participatory cultures,
see Jenkins et al., "Confronting the Challenges of Participatory Cultures."

68. de Zengotita, *Mediated*.

69. On Colbert's usage of the notion "truthiness," see Zimmer, "Truthiness or
Trustiness?"

70. Nancy Baym foregrounds this notion in her *Personal Connections in the
Digital Age*; so do James H. Gilmore and B. Joseph Pine II in *Authenticity*.

71. The first large-scale scholarly intermingling in the debate took place in 1991, in Stuttgart, at the first Stuttgart Seminar in Cultural Studies, entitled The End of Postmodernism: New Directions (for the proceedings, see Ziegler, ed., *The End of Postmodernism*). Other representative studies include: Smith, Enwezor, and Condee, eds., *Antinomies of Art and Culture;* Turner, *City as Landscape;* Scharg, *The Self after Postmodernity;* Braidotti, "A Cartography of Feminist Post-Postmodernism"; Harris, ed., *Beyond Poststructuralism;* López and Potter, *After Postmodernism;* Rebein, *Hicks, Tribes, and Dirty Realists;* Stierstorfer, ed., *Beyond Postmodernism;* Brooks and Toth, eds., *The Mourning After;* Hoberek, ed., *After Postmodernism* (thematic issue of *Twentieth-Century Literature*); Timmer, *Do You Feel It Too?;* and Vaessens and Van Dijk, eds., *Reconsidering the Postmodern.* For theoretical discussions that touch upon a post-postmodern sincerity, see Cioffi, "Postmodernism, Etc."; Caputo, "The Weakness of God"; Eshelman, *Performatism,* excerpts of which were published from 2001 onward (his thoughts on sincerity Eshelman foregrounds in the essay "Performatism" in 2001); Gilmore and Pine, *Authenticity;* and Den Dulk, "Voorbij de doelloze ironie."

72. Following is a selection of representative examples that tackle the last three terms: Anton, *Selfhood and Authenticity;* Gilmore and Pine, *Authenticity;* Straub, ed., *Authenticity;* Foster, *The Return of the Real;* Farrell, *Subjectivity, Realism, and Postmodernism;* López and Potter, *After Postmodernism;* Rebein, *Hicks, Tribes, and Dirty Realists;* Polanyi and Rorty, "Postmodern Ethics"; Thacker, *Postmodernism and the Ethics of Theological Knowledge.*

73. I discuss a number of studies in chapter 1—but most important among the ones I have in mind are Trilling, *Sincerity and Authenticity,* and Peyre, *Literature and Sincerity.*

74. Among others, see Korthals Altes, "Sincerity, Reliability and Other Ironies"; An, *The Idea of Cheng;* and Sim and Bretzke, "The Notion of Sincerity (*Ch'eng*) in the Confucian Classics."

75. Van Alphen, Bal, and Smith, eds., *The Rhetoric of Sincerity;* Seligman et al., *Ritual and Its Consequences;* Milnes and Sinanan, eds., *Romanticism, Sincerity, and Authenticity;* Magill, *Sincerity;* Beeman, "Emotion and Sincerity in Persian Discourse"; An, *The Idea of Cheng;* Assmann, "Authenticity"; Benthien and Martus, eds., *Die Kunst der Aufrichtigkeit im 17. Jahrhundert;* Den Dulk, *Over de drempel;* Kelly, "David Foster Wallace and the New Sincerity in American Fiction"; Korthals Altes, "Blessedly post-ironic?" and "Sincerity, Reliability and Other Ironies"; Rosenbaum, *Professing Sincerity;* Tseëlon, "Is the Present Self Sincere?"; Jackson, *Real Black;* Collins, "Genericity in the 90s"; Wallace, "Ed Unibus Pluram"; Gross, "'Brooklyn Zack Is Real'"; Garlinger, "All about Agrado"; Barton Palmer, "The New Sincerity of Neo-Noir"; Wikander, *Fangs of Malice;* Chung and Jacobi, "In Search of a New Sincerity?"; Ashton, "Sincerity and the Second Person"; Chen, "New Sincerity in a Postmodern World"; Anderson, *The Way We Argue Now;* Groys, *Unter Verdacht;* Markovits, *The Politics of Sincerity;* Myers, "Entitlement and Sincerity

in Broadcast Interviews about Princess Diana"; Wampole, "How to Live without Irony"; Fitzgerald, *Not Your Mother's Morals;* Corcoran, "The New Sincerity"; Klosterman, "The Carly Simon Principle"; Gountas and Mavondo, "Emotions, Sincerity and Consumer Satisfaction."

76. This is the case for Magill, Den Dulk, Korthals Altes, Kelly, Collins, Gross, Barton Palmer, Chung and Jacobi, Ashton, Chen, and Corcoran.

77. Chung and Jacobi's workshop on the concept (mentioned above) took place at Tate Liverpool; the new-sincerity studies that I enlist were published by Oxford University Press, Routledge, the University of Kentucky Press, and the University of Texas Press, among others.

78. In the late 2000s the new sincerity was touched upon in B.A. and M.A. classes by Thomas Vaessens at the University of Amsterdam, by Liesbeth Korthals Altes at the University of Groningen, and by Robert MacFarlane at the University of Cambridge; at the University of Leiden, it received attention during the Rhetoric of Sincerity conference which resulted in Van Alphen, Bal, and Smith, eds., *Rhetoric of Sincerity;* and in the same period, at the University of Bergen it was discussed in at least two guest lectures, one by Alexei Yurchak and one by Dirk Uffelmann, within the framework of a research project on post-Soviet language culture (for abstracts, see www.hf.uib.no/i/russisk/landslide/guestlectures.html).

79. For the Slavic Forum, see the conference announcement at http://www.aatseel.org/resources/resources_research/2001_conf_details. The AAASS panel—cancelled for logistic reasons in 2008 and reorganized in 2009—was entitled "Sincerity and Voice: Contemporary Russian Poetry on the Page and in Song," with presentations on sincerity in Boris Ryzhii's poetry (Stuart Goldberg and Martin Daughtry) and on "new paradigms" in Russian poetry (Brigitte Obermayr) (for the full panel description, see the online conference programs at www.fas.harvard.edu/~aaass/convention/2008-program.pdf and http://www.fas.harvard.edu/~aaass/convention/2009-program-preliminary.pdf). Even more than in my own field, an incident in Dutch Studies indicates just how firmly rooted in academic and literary institutions the concept is becoming. The incident revolved around Amsterdam-based literature professor Thomas Vaessens, who is an advocate of a late postmodernism, which he links with debates on a reborn sincerity. Vaessens is also president of a prominent Dutch literary jury. In 2009, he was publicly accused of misusing academic power by nominating for "his" prize only books that matched his own ("late-postmodern" or "new-sincere") criteria (for details, see Peters, "Een rebelse mandarijn").

80. For a helpful overview of the new field of the history or sociology of emotions (both internationally and within Slavic studies), see Plamper, "Emotional Turn?" As a greeting to the new-sprung discipline, my book's title blinks at the name of a groundbreaking work in the field—Joanna Bourke's *Fear.*

81. Beeman, "Emotion and Sincerity."

82. Much attention is devoted to the concept, for one, in Reddy, *The Navigation of Feeling*; and—to mention a Russian example—in Safronova, "Smert' gosudaria."

83. Ahmed, *The Cultural Politics of Emotion*, 9, 12. See also Reddy, *The Navigation of Feeling*; and Williams, *Emotion and Social Theory*.

84. Van Alphen and Bal, "Introduction," 3.

85. For programmatic discussions of this shift in thought, see ibid., 3–6, and Rosenbaum, *Professing Sincerity*, 12–13.

86. Van Alphen and Bal, "Introduction," 16.

87. Sarjono, "Poetry and Sincerity," 9.

88. In the words of literary critic Viacheslav Kuritsyn, postmodern was "the main theme of [Russian] literary critics" in the first half of this decade (Kuritsyn in the conclusion of his *Russkii literaturnyi postmodernizm*).

89. I borrow the quote from Kukulin and Lipovetsky, "Post-Soviet Literary Criticism," 293. In this article, Kukulin and Lipovetsky provide a helpful overview of 1990s debates over postmodernism in Russia (ibid., 292–95)—although without mentioning Lipovetsky's own substantial role in these debates.

90. Among other publications, see Leiderman and Lipovetsky "Zhizn' posle smerti"; Aizenberg, "Vozmozhnost' vyskazyvaniia"; Epstein, "Proto-, ili konets postmodernizma"; Kuritsyn, "Vremia mnozhit' pristavki." For a discussion of a shift beyond literary postmodernism in which conservative criticisms prevail, see the contributions by Ivanova and others to the round-table discussion "Literature of the Last Decennium" in the journal *Voprosy literatury* in 1998 (Biriukov, "Literatura poslednego desiatiletiia").

91. My information is based on a recounting of the event by Maks Frai (aka Max Frei) on the "Salon intellektual'nogo obshcheniia" chat forum dating from 10 April 2000; the text is available online at www.teneta.ru/archive-chat-2000/Apr10.html.

92. Among others, see Mezhieva and Konradova, *Okno v mir*, 10–11; Skoropanova, *Russkaia postmodernistskaia literatura*, 528.

93. See, for instance, Lipovetsky, *Russkii postmodernizm*; Man'kovskaia, *Ot modernizma k postpostmodernizmu* and the section "Postpostmodernizm" in *Estetika postmodernizma*, 307–28; the conclusion of Kuritsyn, *Russkii literaturnyi postmodernizm*; reproductions of Epstein's essays on "postpostmodernism" and the end of postmodernism in his *Postmodern v Rossii*. For English translations, see Lipovetsky, *Russian Postmodernist Fiction*, 244–47; Epstein, *After the Future*; and Epstein et al., eds., *Russian Postmodernism*.

94. On late postmodernism, see Fokkema, "The Semiotics of Literary Postmodernism."

95. Lipovetsky, *Paralogii*.

96. Epstein, "Katalog novykh poezii"; Man'kovskaia, *Estetika postmodernizma*, 326–27; Boym, *Common Places*, 102; Lipovetsky, *Russian Postmodernist Fiction*, 244, 247.

97. Lipovetsky, *Paralogii*, 572–613, passim.

98. Apart from mid-1990s articles by Epstein and Lipovetsky that wound up—
in reworked versions—in their books, these include, among many others,
Natarov, "Timur Kibirov"; Kostiukov, "Postoronnie soobrazheniia"; Kukulin,
"Every Trend Makes a Brand"; Ulanov, "Sny o chem-to bol'shom"; Davydov,
"Dmitrii Vodennikov, Svetlana Lin"; Vezhlian, "Pamiat' momentam";
Kaspe, "Govorit tot, kto govorit 'ia' "; Kulle, " 'Novaia iskrennost' " po-
ital'ianski." An openly critical or derogatory view is expressed, among
others, in Ivanova, "Molodaia poeziia v poiskakh zhivogo slova." For positive
interpretations, see, for instance, Ivanova in Biriukov, "Literatura poslednego
desiatiletiia," 12–13; and Bondarenko, "Roman V. Sorokina 'Led.' "

99. Willem Weststeijn mentions it in "After Postmodernism," 219–20; Allard
den Dulk uses Epstein's ideas on the term for a discussion of a "New Sincerity" in American culture in Over de drempel (135, 137). "New sincerity" is
discussed in Bogdanova's Postmodernizm v kontekste sovremennoi russkoi literatury, 448–557. For Chuprinin, see Zhizn' po poniatiam, 188–90.

100. Sofronov, "Shto-to proiskhodit"; Savchuk, "Ideologiia postinformatsionnoi
iskrennosti"; Dudina, Epstein, and Savchuk, "Svetloi pamiati postmoderna
posviashchaetsia"; Degot', "Die russische Kunst in den 1990er Jahren," 41;
and Koldobskaia, Iskusstvo v bol'shom dolgu, 267–68.

101. Yurchak, "Post-Post-Communist Sincerity."

102. See Corcoran, "The New Sincerity."

103. Eggers's Heartbreaking Work of Staggering Genius was published by Zakharov in 2007 as Dusherazdiraiushchee tvorenie osheolomliaiushchego geniia
(trans. Evgenii V. Kuleshov). Erlend Loe's Naiv. Super (Naive. Super) was
published by Azbuka-klassika in 2004 as Naivno. Super (trans. Inna Stre-
blova). For an example of how these and other non-Russian sources are incorporated into Russian-language discussions of a new-sincere age, see
Burenkov, "Novaia iskrennost'."

104. For online texts on postpostmodernity by Epstein, see http://www.focusing
.org/apm_papers/epstein.html and http://www.emory.edu/INTELNET/e
.pm.erofeev.html (accessed 5 January 2015). For exemplary reactions, see
"The New Sincerity as a Response to Postmodernism," a 2005 blog post by
the American-Canadian poet Neil Aitken (http://blog.boxcarpoetry.com/?p
=67, accessed 5 January, 2015); or "post-postmodernism an abridged [sic]
introduction" (noncapitalized title original), a 2008 blog post by travisshaf-
fer (http://postmeaningful.blogspot.nl/2008/10/post-postmodernism
-abbridged.html, accessed 5 January 2015).

105. For the sources that inform my post- or transnational gaze, see my earlier
remarks on geopolitical labels such as "post-Soviet" and "postsocialist." In
addition, I am inspired by Jan Plamper, who sees a transnational perspective as the only thinkable approach to the discipline from which this book
takes its cues: the history of emotions (Plamper, "Vvedenie I," 35).

106. flippi754, "Ania Goodnight," March 9, 2009 (flippi754.livejournal.com
/151341.html, accessed January 5, 2015).

107. See, for examples, a selection of blog posts by user emylie on 22 November 2008 (http://emylie.livejournal.com/427364.html), by hasisin on 12 November 2008 (http://hasisin.livejournal.com/140620.html), and for the last citation, see Ushkov, "Fishka 'dukhovnost.'"
108. Wampole, "How to Live without Irony."
109. Ashbrook, "The Case against Irony" (radio interview with Wampole).

CHAPTER 1. HISTORY

1. Berg, *Literaturokratiia.*
2. Beumers and Lipovetsky, *Performing Violence,* 180.
3. For two groundbreaking publications advancing these insights, see Rosenwein, "Worrying about Emotions in History" and *Emotional Communities in the Early Middle Ages.* An analysis of emotional communities in Russia is provided in Kelly, "Pravo na emotsii, pravil'nye emotsii."
4. "Demonstrate," "show," and "doubt" are the three verbs that fall under "sincerity" in *The BBI Combinatory Dictionary of English;* the same verbs recur repeatedly in the historical sources that I discuss below.
5. Assmann, "Authenticity," 36. In the citation with which this chapter opens, Trilling also marks sincerity as a defining feature of post-Renaissance culture specifically in the West (in *Sincerity,* 6).
6. An, "Western 'Sincerity' and Confucian '*Cheng.*'"
7. Assmann, "Authenticity," 37.
8. Markovits, *The Politics of Sincerity,* 67. On parrhesia see also Foucault, *Fearless Speech.*
9. Korthals Altes, "Sincerity, Reliability and Other Ironies," 110. Korthals Altes cites Aristotle, *Rhetoric* 2, 1, 5–7: 78a6–20 (italics original).
10. I am referring to Irene van Renswoude's dissertation "Licence to Speak," which won the Heineken Young Scientists Award for Historical Science in 2014. For the citations, see van Renswoude cited in Spiering, "In de vroege Middeleeuwen was kritiek nog welkom," 10, and van Renswoude, "Licence to Speak," 49 (the 2012 speech, not the dissertation).
11. See on this Peyre, *Literature and Sincerity,* 17. The interrelation between an inner and outer self does surface as a concern in Plato's dialogues, where Socrates prays to Pan that "[I] may become beautiful within and that my external possessions may be congruent with my inner state" (Plato, *Phaedrus,* 75).
12. Trilling, *Sincerity and Authenticity,* 12–13.
13. Greenblatt, *Renaissance Self-Fashioning,* 1.
14. On the status of sincerity in early modern culture, see, among others, Trilling, *Sincerity and Authenticity;* Van Alphen and Bal, "Introduction"; Korthals Altes, "Sincerity, Reliability and Other Ironies"; Martin, "Inventing Sincerity, Refashioning Prudence." "Willing and sincere" (*prompte et cincere*) was the text inscripted in the handheld heart that formed Calvin's emblem (Martin, "Inventing Sincerity, Refashioning Prudence," 1327).

15. Rosenbaum, *Professing Sincerity*, 5–6.
16. Van Alphen and Bal, "*Introduction*," 2–3.
17. See, for instance, Boddy, *New Media and Popular Imagination*.
18. See on this argument, among others, Schmid, ed., *Russische Medientheorien*, 15–16.
19. Johns, *The Nature of Books*, 174.
20. See on this—although without literal reference to the term "sincerity"—Febvre and Martin, *The Coming of the Book*, 77–78.
21. Imperfection, here, should be understood in the so-called emic sense, as a term relating to the perspective of the participants in the culture at stake.
22. Trilling already speaks of the "political considerations" inherent in historical explorations of sincerity in *Sincerity*, 26; and as we saw, the Greek forerunner of the concept—the speech figure of parrhesia, or speaking one's mind openly to the authorities—is an emphatically public notion.
23. Ibid., 20.
24. Martin, "Inventing Sincerity," 1333.
25. Trilling, *Sincerity and Authenticity*, 21–23.
26. Stöckmann, "Deutsche Aufrichtigkeit" and "Bismarcks Antlitz," 18–19.
27. Korsten, "The Irreconcilability of Hypocrisy and Sincerity."
28. Peyre, *Literature and Sincerity*, 51.
29. Zalizniak, Levontina, and Shmelev, eds., *Kliuchevye idei russkoi iazykovoi kartiny mira*, 11.
30. Ibid.
31. Wierzbicka, "Russkie kul'turnye skripty i ikh otrazhenie v iazyke."
32. Boym, *Common Places*, 97 and 100. In a footnote Boym adds: "Max Vasmer also suggests the relation between iskrennost' and the old Russian iskren meaning close or nearby, from iz and the root of the word koren' (root)" (ibid., 315). The Vasmer edition to which Boym refers is Vasmer, *Etimologicheskii slovar' russkogo iazyk*, 2: 140–41.
33. Boym, *Common Places*, 101.
34. Citation from Kelly, "Pravo na emotsii," 51.
35. For a detailed (if itself occasionally mythologizing) analysis of the "Russian soul" myth, see Williams, "The Russian Soul."
36. For definitions and examples of early usage, see Vasmer, *Russisches etymologisches Wörterbuch* (vol. 1); Sreznevskii, *Materialy dlia slovaria drevnerusskogo iazyka* (vol. 1); and Barkhudarov, ed., *Slovar' russkogo iazyka XI–XVII vv.*
37. Dal', *Tolkovyi slovar' zhivogo velikorusskago iazyka* (vol. 2).
38. On this difference with Western European conceptualizations of subjectivity and self see also Schmid, *Ichentwürfe*, 37.
39. In his *Ichentwürfe*, Ulrich Schmid points out the testament of Vladimir Monomakh and the correspondence of Prince Kurbsky as predecessors to this autobiographical text (43).
40. Avvakum, "The Life of Archpriest Avvakum by Himself," 174.
41. Schmid, *Ichentwürfe*, 37.

42. On the (seemingly) unblemished, quasi-oral language of Avvakum's narrative, see Bortnes, *Visions of Glory*, 244ff. In the context of his emphatically nonpolished self-stylization, see on Avvakum also Schmid, *Ichentwürfe*, 55–57; and Brouwer, "Avvakoem," 27–30.

43. Peyre, *Literature and Sincerity*, 80.

44. On Rousseau's notion of sincerity—and its political impact—see also Trilling's *Sincerity and Authenticity*.

45. Hunt, *The Family Romance of the French Revolution*, 96–97.

46. Perkins, *Wordsworth and the Poetry of Sincerity*, 1. Christina Lupton has shown how eighteenth-century literary critics already departed from sophisticated views of sincerity rhetoric to a much greater extent than critiques of Enlightenment ideology acknowledge (see Lupton, "Sincere Performances"). On sincerity in eighteenth-century British culture, see also Guilhamet, *The Sincere Ideal*.

47. Newman, *The Rise of English Nationalism*, 127ff.

48. Ibid., 127ff. Guilhamet also touches upon the trend to oppose English "sincerity" to French "hypocrisy" in *The Sincere Ideal*.

49. On these developments, see, among others, Hunt, *Inventing Human Rights*.

50. Reddy, *The Navigation of Feeling*, 184–85. See also ibid., 326.

51. Ibid., 171. See also ibid., 196–98.

52. Ibid., 326.

53. Carey, *British Abolitionism and the Rhetoric of Sensibility*.

54. Andrei Zorin eloquently—and correctly, I believe—argues for defining the emotional culture of Russian sentimentalism as a "pan-European bond of sensitive hearts" (Zorin, "Import chuvstv").

55. On the self-controlling mechanisms that structured Russian rhetorics of emotion from the seventeenth century onward, see Kelly's "Pravo na emotsii" and *Refining Russia*. On the tense relationship between the sentimentalist culture of intimacy and its insistence on sincerity and public transparency, see Schönle, "The Scare of the Self."

56. For concrete examples, see Sreznevskii, ed., *Materialy dlia slovaria;* and Barkhudarov, *Russkii slovar' XI–XVII vv.*

57. Sreznevskii, ed., *Materialy dlia slovaria;* and Barkhudarov, *Russkii slovar' XI–XVII vv.* The example stems from the late fourteenth- or early fifteenth-century *Paisievskii sbornik*.

58. He does so in his "Ode to the Arrival from Holstein and to the Birthday of . . . Archduke Petr Fedorovich"; see Lomonosov, *Polnoe sobranie sochinenii*, 63.

59. Among many newer sources, a still reliable and detailed discussion of this increasing dissociation between intelligentsia and state is offered in Riasanovsky, *A Parting of Ways*.

60. Karamzin, *Sochineniia*, 1: 507.

61. Kelly, "Pravo na emotsii," 53.

62. For a reading of *My Confession* as "directed against both Rousseau's *Emile* and his *Confessions*," see Lotman, "Puti razvitiia russkoi prozy 1800–1810-kh godov," 31. For a critique of this parodic interpretation of the story, see Kanunova, "Evoliutsiia sentimentalizma Karamzina."

63. Radishchev, *Puteshestvie iz Peterburga v Moskvu*, 81.

64. Ibid., 73.

65. Ibid., 21, 23, 25, 36, 60–61, 81.

66. Ibid., 81.

67. Ibid., 21, 23, 25, 36, 48, 55, 60–61, 73, 81.

68. John Ruskin cited in Guy, ed., *The Victorian Age*, 333–34.

69. Ruskin, *The Laws of Fésole*. My translation relies on the online reproduction of this text at http://www.victorianweb.org/authors/ruskin/atheories/1.3 .html.

70. Ruskin cited in Black, *The Broadview Anthology of British Literature*, 429.

71. Halttunen, *Confidence Men and Painted Women*, 34–35.

72. Heckel, *Werke*, 1: 573.

73. See also Rosenbaum, *Professing Sincerity*, 8.

74. Paul Verlaine cited in Peyre, *Literature and Sincerity*, 158.

75. See on this shift also ibid., 47.

76. On this trend, see Stöckmann, "Bismarcks Antlitz." For the Nietzsche translation, see Nietzsche, *Beyond Good and Evil*, 244.

77. In their *Communist Manifesto*, for instance, Marx and Engels claim that socialism "laid bare the *hypocritical* apologies of economists" and call bourgeois marriage a "*hypocritically* concealed" system "of wives in common"; to "the proletariat," by contrast, they ascribe such sincerity-invoking adjectives as "infantlike" and "undeveloped" (Marx and Engels, *Manifesto of the Communist Party* [my italics]).

78. See Bergeron, "Melody and Monotone" (especially the section "Republican Sincerity," 57–58).

79. Legouvé cited in ibid., 58 (Bergeron cites the dramatist as quoted in Philip Nord, *The Republican Moment*, 230).

80. Trilling, *Sincerity and Authenticity*, 11.

81. Ibid., 9 and passim.

82. Boym, *Common Places*, 96.

83. Ibid., 99.

84. See on this trend among others Groys, *Die Erfindung Russlands;* and, for an analysis of the same trend in contemporary Russian culture, sociologist Lev Gudkov's concept of "negative identity" as discussed in Gudkov, *Negativnaia identichnost'*.

85. Boym, *Common Places*, 98.

86. Kelly, *Refining Russia*, 104. On Russian radicals' antibehavior see also, among others, Paperno, *Chernyshevsky and the Age of Realism*.

87. Kelly, *Refining Russia*, 145–46.

88. Tolstoy, *Sobranie sochinenii v 22 tomakh*, 15: 165. My translation builds on that by Alymer Maude (1899), excerpts from which can be read online at http://www.csulb.edu/~jvancamp/361r14.html.
89. Ibid., 15: 99, 15: 115.
90. Ibid., 15: 115.
91. Kropotkin, *Zapiski revolutsionera*. My translation relies on the online reproduction of Kropotkin, *Memoirs of a Revolutionist* on http://nihilpress.subvert.info/kropot.html.
92. George Mosse observes a "romantic tendency to perceive the unknown and the eternal in actual objects," whereby "a beautiful woman . . . exemplified the romantic utopia just as she represented the national ideal" (Mosse, *Nationalism and Sexuality*, 99). The two categories blur when nineteenth-century writers and thinkers represent the *narod*, or common people, as a feminine force or as embodied in a concrete woman.
93. If these rhetorical trends permeated Romantic thought as a whole (among others, see on this Böröcz and Verdery, "Gender and Nation"; Yuval-Davis, *Gender and Nation;* and Mayer, ed., *Gender Ironies of Nationalism*), then they took on particular force in Russia. For details, see Brouwer, "The Bridegroom Who Did Not Come"; chapter 1 of my *Unattainable Bride Russia;* Makushinskii, "Otvergnutyi zhenikh"; and, for a brief but influential discussion of the same trend, Lotman, "Siuzhetnoe prostranstvo v russkom romane XIX stoletiia."
94. Makushinskii, "Otvergnutyi zhenikh," 37.
95. Rutten, *Unattainable Bride Russia*.
96. On the systematic, consistent repetition of this plot scheme see also Brouwer, "The Bridegroom Who Did Not Come."
97. Turgenev, *Polnoe sobranie sochinenii*, 6: 339, 7: 15, 7: 113, 7: 184.
98. Ibid., 6: 316. On the opposition between Turgenev's "literary," "aestheticized" heroes and the Turgenevian heroine, see also Dukkon, "Problema 'literaturnosti' i original'nosti' v proizvedeniiakh Turgeneva," and Markovich, "'Russkii evropeets' v proze Turgeneva."
99. Turgenev, *Polnoe sobranie sochinenii*, 6: 316.
100. Safronova, "Smert' gosudaria."
101. Among many others, see on this somber public discourse Riasanovsky, *A Parting of Ways*. On the many social groups that contribute to it see Kimerling Wirtschafter, *Social Identity in Imperial Russia*.
102. On the impact of literary commercialization on nineteenth-century Russian authors and their sense of self, see Greenleaf and Moeller-Sally, eds., *Russian Subjects* (esp. 14ff. and chapter 4, "Encroaching Modernity: The Public and the Subject," 275–347).
103. Klein, "Deržavin," 50.
104. Gracián, *Oráculo manual y arte de prudencia*, aphorism 219. My translation relies on the online reproduction of Gracián aphorisms on http://www.online-literature.com/gracian/art-worldly-wisdom/13/.

105. Klein, "Deržavin," 41. As Klein explains, starting from 1741 Gracián's "El discreto" was published in Russian three times.

106. Tolstoy, *Sobranie sochinenii*, 15: 138.

107. Tiutchev, *Lirika v dvukh tomakh*, 1: 46.

108. I base these observations on automatized searches for (grammatical derivations of) the word "iskrennost'" in Tiutchev's and Pushkin's poetry. A possible exception is *Eugene Onegin*, where Pushkin puts the word in the mouth of Russian literature's most famous aesthete when Eugene turns down the love of his life: in a manifestly ironic occurrence of the term, he declares himself "endeared" by the lovesick Tat'iana's "sincerity," which reawakened in him "long silent feelings" (EO IV 12.7). On Pushkin and sincerity, see also Vinogradov, ed., *Slovar' iazyka Pushkina*, 2: 254.

109. Lermontov, *Sobranie sochinenii*, 4: 339. For my English translations of Lermontov, I rely on Nabokov's translation (see Lermontov, *A Hero of Our Time*).

110. Ibid., 4: 276.

111. "Rousseau's confession," in the narrator's perspective, "already has the shortcoming that he read it to his friends." Ibid., 4: 339.

112. Shaikevich, Andriushchenko, and Rebetskaia, eds., *Statisticheskii slovar' iazyka Dostoevskogo*, 132.

113. Ibid.

114. In his nonfiction, he joined the trend to locate sincerity in distinctly sociopolitical and national spheres—by asking whether the intelligentsia "sincerely wants to acknowledge the common people as its brother," for instance (Dostoevsky, *Sobranie sochinenii*, 14: 478). Here and elsewhere in his essays, Dostoevsky frames the term as a positive notion.

115. Ibid., 7: 211–12.

116. Trilling, *Sincerity and Authenticity*, 7.

117. Fishzon, "The Operatics of Everyday Life," 800.

118. Benjamin, *Illuminations*, 220.

119. Fishzon, "The Operatics of Everyday Life," 800. On this newly emerged celebrity culture see ibid. and Dyer, *Stars*.

120. West, *I Shop in Moscow*.

121. Groys, "The Production of Sincerity," 43.

122. Fishzon, "The Operatics of Everyday Life," 810.

123. Ibid.

124. Kruchenykh, "Declaration of Transrational Language," 183.

125. Fishzon, "The Operatics of Everyday Life," 817.

126. Gioia, *The Imperfect Art*, 70.

127. Wilde, *Intentions*.

128. Ibid., *The Picture of Dorian Gray*.

129. Pessoa, "I want to be free and insincere (20 August 1930)," in *A Little Larger than the Entire Universe*. On the kinship between Pessoa's and Wilde's "art of lying," see De Castro, "Oscar Wilde."

130. On the early twentieth-century cultural preoccupation with masks, see, among others, Trilling, *Sincerity*, 119–20. Irene Masing-Delic discusses their prominence in Russian literary culture of the same period in "The Mask Motif in A. Blok's Poetry"; see also the section "Veiled Brides" in my *Unattainable Bride Russia* (pp. 74–77).

131. Wilde, "The Truth of Masks."

132. Masing-Delic, "The Mask Motif," 81.

133. I used online search tools to scan Blok's collected poetry (at http://az.lib.ru), and found only one reference to (a nonproblematized) "lost sincerity," in the poem "Tired Souls Suddenly Feel" ("Ustalym dusham vdrug sdaetsia," 1900) (available and searchable online at http://az.lib.ru/b/blok_a_a/text_0340 .shtml, accessed 5 January 2015).

134. Fitzpatrick, *Tear off the Masks!*

135. Rutten, *Unattainable Bride Russia,* 99.

136. Il'in, *Poiushchee serdtse.*

137. Berdiaev, in chapter 12 of *Samopoznanie*. See also ibid., "Tsarstvo dukha i tsarstvo kesaria" (first published in Paris 1949) and the extended footnote on the term in his "Filosofiia svobodnogo dukha" (1927).

138. Berdiaev, chapter 12 of *Samopoznanie.*

139. Sincerity is persistently problematized and presented as a virtue that the upper classes desire but rarely possess, for instance, in Proust's *In Search of Lost Time* or Woolf's *To the Lighthouse* and *Mrs. Dalloway,* as can easily be verified with a keyword search for "sinc" or "sincer" in the online versions of the texts made available by the University of Adelaide (at http://ebooks .adelaide.edu.au/p/proust/marcel/p96d/ and http://ebooks.adelaide.edu.au /w/woolf/virginia/w91t/).

140. Couperus, *Eline Vere,* 279 and 449.

141. Il'in, "Protiv Rossii."

142. Fitzpatrick, *Tear off the Masks!*

143. Tikhomirov, "The Regime of Forced Trust," 80.

144. Ibid.

145. Halfin, *Terror in My Soul,* 271.

146. Ibid., 222.

147. Ibid., 59.

148. Gel'fand, *Protiv burzhuaznogo liberalizma,* 47. The translation I borrowed from Dobrenko, "Literary Criticism and the Transformations," 53. For a more extensive discussion of sincerity rhetoric in early postrevolutionary literary life (and in the literary worldview of RAPP and writer group Pereval, in particular), see ibid.

149. "Za rabotu!" *Literaturnaia gazeta,* May 29, 1932.

150. Delaloi, "Emotsii v mikromire Stalina," 450.

151. Paperno, *Stories of the Soviet Experience,* 209.

152. See on this Clark and Tihanov, "Soviet Literary Theory," 119.

153. Apart from Fitzpatrick and Halfin, I am thinking especially of Hellbeck, *Revolution on My Mind*.

154. Rosenbaum, *Professing Sincerity*, 5, 8.

155. The problem of defining sincerity in literature and philosophy was central to the work of several scholars at the time; representative studies include Peyre's *Literature and Sincerity* (1963); David Perkins's *Wordsworth and the Poetry of Sincerity* (1964); Davie's article "On Sincerity," published in the journal *Encounter* in October 1968; and Read's *Cult of Sincerity* (1968). The concept was pivotal, too, to the thinking of the influential critic F. R. Leavis; for a summary of his views on the topic, see Bell, "Poetry and Sincerity." As additional factors in the persistent philosophical interest in sincerity at this time, Herbert Read singles out the reaction to psychoanalysis, which "made us all suspicious of 'the objective truth,'" and the popularity of confessionary genres and autobiographies at the time (Read, *The Cult of Sincerity*, 15, 22).

156. Peyre, *Literature and Sincerity*, 306.

157. Sartre, *L'Être et le néant*. For the English translation, I relied on Sartre, *Being and Nothingness*, 56.

158. Trilling, *Sincerity and Authenticity*, 6.

159. Habermas, *Vorstudien und Ergänzungen zur Theorie des kommunikativen Handelns*, 113.

160. Goffman, *The Presentation of Self*, 10.

161. On this shift—and for (postmodern) criticisms of speech-act-theory notions of sincerity—see Korthals Altes, "Sincerity, Reliability and Other Ironies"; and Markovits, *The Politics of Sincerity*.

162. Butler, *Giving an Account of Oneself*, 78. This short summary builds particularly on postulates from the following works: Butler's *Giving an Account of Oneself*; Derrida's *De la grammatologie*; Barthes's *Fragments d'un discours amoureux*; and Foucault's *Fearless Speech*.

163. Barthes, *Fragments d'un discours amoureux* (English citation from Barthes, *A Lover's Discourse*, 98).

164. Tseëlon, "Is the Present Self Sincere?" 123–24 (italics Tseëlon's).

165. Metzinger cited in Taft, "An Interview with Thomas Metzinger." See also Metzinger, *Being No One*.

166. For relevant publications that illustrate this point, see Hermans and Kempen, *The Dialogical Self*; and Lysaker and Lysaker, "Narrative Structure in Psychosis."

167. Hosking, *Trust*.

168. Rugoff, "Other Experts," 11.

169. Adorno, *Aesthetic Theory*, 32.

170. Warhol, *The Philosophy of Andy Warhol*, 83.

171. Ibid., 92 and 53, respectively.

172. Wallace cited in Lipsky, "The Lost Years & Last Days of David Foster Wallace," 156. Here and elsewhere in his writings, Wallace takes much care to

demonstrate that—to cite Wallace expert Adam Kelly—"no artistic gift can exist without economy" (Kelly, "David Foster Wallace and the New Sincerity in American Fiction," 140).

173. Groys, "The Production of Sincerity," 44.

174. For an illustrative example, see Murray, "Fuck You Damien Hirst!"

175. Representative sources include Shank's discussion of 1980s Texan bands in his *Dissonant Identities*, 120, 146–51, 249; Collins, "Genericity in the 90s"; Kelly, "David Foster Wallace and the New Sincerity in American Fiction"; Mannisto, "The New Sincerity"; Sanneh, "Mr. Sincerity Tries a New Trick"; Robinson, "A Few Notes from a New Sincerist"; and Morris, "The Time between Time."

176. See on this Rosenbaum, *Professing Sincerity*, 1, 233.

177. Seligman et al., *Ritual and Its Consequences*, 123.

178. Anderson, *The Way We Argue Now*, 17.

179. 4 November 2005 blog post by Alex Blagg (http://blaggblogg.blogspot .com/2005/11/new-sincerity.html, accessed 11 November 2007; no longer available).

180. I am referring to the 2007 exhibition on new Chinese art at Tate Liverpool ("In Search of a New Sincerity?") and to "Neo-Sincerity (The Difference be- tween the Comic and the Cosmic Is a Single Letter)" (an exhibition at Apex- art New York, 2006); Adam Browne's art-house film *The Cult of Sincerity* (2008) and a T-shirt with the same slogan (2008) (both available for pur- chase at www.amazon.com); Jonathan D. Fitzgerald's book *Not Your Mother's Morals: How the New Sincerity Is Changing Pop Culture for the Bet- ter;* a purported "new sincerity" project within "the New York Biennale" (at http://www.complaintsboard.com/complaints/ny-biennale-art-c120356.html several artists complained that the show, scheduled for September 2009, was a hoax, but relevant to my argument is the ample public attention that it received online [at http://nybiennaleart.blogspot.com/2009/05/new -sincerity.html, for instance]); Telly Ramos's short film *New Sincerity* (2009); "New Sincerity: A Touring, Travelling, Collaborative Group Exhibi- tion on Wheels" (a website without references to actual exhibitions, United States, 2010, http://newsincerity.wordpress.com/about/); "New Sincerity" (an exhibition that traveled from Berlin / London Future Gallery to Beach London, 2011); and "The New Sincerity" (a rock-punk band whose online home is http://www.myspace.com/newsincerity).

181. Wampole, "How to Live without Irony."

182. For Anglophone examples, see Collins's 1993 text "Genericity in the 90s"; Olsen, "If I Can Dream"; and Epstein, "Conclusion."

183. Sella, "Against Irony." For Purdy's—not-amused—response, see Purdy, "The State of Irony."

184. Purdy, *For Common Things,* 6.

185. Rosenblatt, "The Age of Irony Comes to an End"; Rothstein, "Attacks on U.S. Challenges the Perspective of Postmodern True Believers."

186. See on this shift also Markovits, *The Politics of Sincerity,* 41, 82; and Vaessens and van Dijk, "Introduction."

187. Gray, "Something in the Way"; among others, see also Mannisto, "The New Sincerity."

188. See on this trend Barker and Taylor, *Faking It,* x ("Sincerity and authenticity are techniques one can employ in the service of personal authenticity").

189. Sanneh, "Mr. Sincerity Tries a New Trick."

190. Zubok, *Zhivago's Children,* 161–62.

191. Pomerantsev, "Ob iskrennosti v literature."

192. Ibid.

193. Svirskii, *A History of Post-War Soviet Writing,* 77.

194. For exemplary publications, see Sel'vinskii, "Nabolevshii vopros"; Gribachev and Smirnov, "'Violonchelist' poluchil kanifol'"; Berggol'ts, "Protiv likvidatsii liriki"; and Gribachev's reply to that article, "O samovyrazhenii v lirike." I thank Evgeny Dobrenko for directing my attention to some of these titles.

195. Prokhorov, "Inherited Discourse."

196. Holmgren, "Introduction," xxix.

197. Cited in Katsva, *Istoriia Rossii.*

198. Examples include Skorino, "Razgovor nachistotu"; Zapiska, "Zapiska Otdela nauki i kul'tury TsK KPSS"; Vasilevskii, "S nevernykh pozitsii"; and Tarasov, "Ob oshibkakh zhurnala 'Novyi mir'."

199. Kolesnikov, "O neiskrennosti v literature."

200. Aleksei Surkov cited in Svirskii, *Na lobnom meste.*

201. On the Thaw-era preoccupation with sincerity, in cinema in particular and in intellectual culture in general, see also Prokhorov, "Inherited Discourse."

202. Vail' and Genis, *60-e,* 14.

203. Ibid., 14–15.

204. Citation from Kotykhov, "Al'fred Shnittke."

205. Epstein, "After the Future," 425–26.

206. Yurchak, *Everything Was Forever,* 249ff.

CHAPTER 2. "BUT I WANT SINCERITY SO BADLY!"

1. Krijnen, project description for "Impious Renewal," e-mailed to the author, 21 April 2009. For the book version of Krijnen's dissertation, see Krijnen, *Holocaust Impiety in Jewish American Literature.*

2. Siegel, "As You Were."

3. Apart from Shanks, Michael Corcoran discusses the same trend (using the same "New Sincerity" label) in *All Over the Map,* 150–56.

4. Shank, *Dissonant Identities,* 149.

5. Mukhomor, *Zolotoi disk.*

6. Zharikov, "Terra Inc."

7. Sergei Kuryokhin in the talk show Leningrad-London in 1988 (the fragment in question can be viewed online at https://www.youtube.com/watch?v=CzBA4d1rG-A, last accessed 5 January 2016).

8. Among others, on Moscow Conceptualism and its members' complex relationship with irony see Jackson, *The Experimental Group*.

9. Samizdat—literally "self-publishing"—was a popular Soviet-era form of informal, hand-to-hand publication and distribution that aimed to circumvent censorship.

10. Prigov, *Sbornik preduvedomlenii*.

11. Andrei Prigov, personal conversation with the author, 26 February 2009, London. Notes available upon request from contact@ellenrutten.nl.

12. Hartmute Trepper has explored how a debate on the role of the Thaw generation was sparked in 1987 by publications in *Znamia* and *Novyi mir* of a popular Tvardovskii poem (see Trepper, "Die Auseinandersetzung um die Zeitschrift 'Novyj mir'," 24–26, 34).

13. Mikhail Gorbachev cited in *Time* magazine, June 4, 1990, 19.

14. Prokhorov, "The Unknown New Wave."

15. Gundlakh cited in Solomon, *The Irony Tower*, 201.

16. The critic whom I am citing is Evgenii Natarov in "Timur Kibirov," 39. The wish to revive literary sentimentalism is central to such early Kibirov poems as "On the Question of Romanticism" ("K voprosu o romantizme," 1989) and "To Seriozha Gandlevskii" ("Serezhe Gandlevskomu," 1990) (Kibirov, *"Kto kuda,"* 110–15 and 135–43); the former appeared in a collection with the then provocative title *Sentiments* (*Santimenty*, 1989). On postmodernism, see, among other poems, Kibirov's "The Postmodern" ("Postmodern," 1999) (*"Kto kuda,"* 395).

17. Gandlevskii, "Razreshenie ot skorbi," 226. For my English translations of the essay, I rely on Gandlevsky, "An Attempt at a Manifesto."

18. Gandlevskii, "Razreshenie ot skorbi," 226–28.

19. Chuprinin, *Zhizn' po poniatiam*, 263–65.

20. Sergei Gandlevskii, personal conversation, 14 May 2009, Moscow. Transcript available upon request from contact@ellenrutten.nl.

21. Ready, "Aleksei Slapovskii," 1111.

22. Book description accessed on 1 July 2012, http://slapovsky.ru/content/view/69/41 (no longer available).

23. Stodolsky, "A Multi-Lectic Anatomy."

24. Yurchak, *Everything Was Forever*, 249–50.

25. Ibid.

26. On the Kuryokhin hoax, see, for instance, Brigid McCarthy's interview with Alexei Yurchak (McCarthy, "Soviet Era Dark Humor").

27. Skype interview with Golynko-Vol'fson on 29 April 2009.

28. Personal communication with the author on 14 May 2009, Moscow. Transcript available upon request from contact@ellenrutten.nl.

29. Prigov, *Sbornik preduvedomlenii*, 297.

30. Personal communication with the author on 14 May 2009, Moscow. Transcript available upon request from contact@ellenrutten.nl.

31. Ibid.

32. Prokhorova, "Nedavnee proshloe kak vyzov istoriku."
33. On the preoccupation with "the new" of the time see also Golynko-Vol'fson, "Strategiia i politika vsego novogo." On the broader, transnational infatuation in the arts with newness into which new-sincerity rhetoric taps, see Groys, *On the New.*
34. Rutten, "Judge a Book by Its Cover."
35. See on these developments Engel, "Vom Tauwetter zur postsozialistischen Ära," 391–92; Küpper, "Präprintium"; and Komaromi, "The Material Existence of Soviet Samizdat." The citation is borrowed from the last source (618).
36. On the memory culture of the time (and of the ensuing Yeltsin years), see especially Smith, *Mythmaking in the New Russia.*
37. Golynko-Vol'fson, "Strategiia i politika vsego novogo."
38. Mikhailovskaia, "Politicheskie slova kak veshchi," 185.
39. For a discussion of some of the memory-oriented works at *Art Instead of Art*—as this exhibition was entitled—see the description of Sergei Mironenko's painting *Homo Sovieticus,* which was first displayed there, and its "use of idological clichés," on the auction website http://www.arcadja.com /auctions/en/mironenko_sergey/artist/313380/ (accessed 5 January 2015).
40. Gregory Freidin eloquently outlines the memory dimension in Kibirov's work when he explains that the cultural niche the poet occupies is located "in the imperfect fit between, on the one hand, the meaningful sentimental nostalgia experienced by an average post-Soviet citizen and, on the other, the sots-art aesthetic game" (Freidin, "Transfiguration of Kitsch," 128).
41. Gandlevskii, "Razreshenie ot skorbi," 226.
42. Ibid.
43. Personal conversation with the author, 14 May 2009, Moscow. Transcript available upon request from contact@ellenrutten.nl.
44. Todorova, "Introduction," 8. For Boym's original concepts, see Boym, *The Future of Nostalgia;* for an influential critical reading of her distinction between reflective and restorative nostalgia, see Nadkarni and Shevchenko, "The Politics of Nostalgia."
45. See Deleuze, *Logique du sens.*
46. Flax, "Soul Service," 79.
47. Komar and Melamid cited in Ratcliff, *Komar & Melamid,* 40.
48. Interview with Pepperstein in Von den Brincken, "Medical Hermeneutics."
49. Degot', "Kinostsenarii Vladimira Sorokina," 225; Dobrenko, "Preodolenie ideologii," 183; and Lipovetsky, *Paralogii,* 530.
50. Among others, see on this trend Markovits, *The Politics of Sincerity,* 82, and Vaessens, *De revanche van de roman.* One influential propagator of a post-9/11 New Sincerity is the American radio show host Jesse Thorn; for details see Thorn, "A Manifesto for the New Sincerity."
51. Rothstein, "Attacks on U.S. Challenges the Perspective of Postmodern True Believers."

52. See Vaessens, *De revanche van de roman.*
53. Krijnen, project description for "Impious Renewal," e-mailed to the author, 21 April 2009. In the final version (Krijnen, *Holocaust Impiety in Jewish American Literature*), Krijnen moves away from new-sincerity rhetoric to other developments in recent American fiction.
54. Krijnen, project description (see previous note).
55. Lipovetsky, *Paralogii,* 470.
56. Epstein, "Nulevoi tsikl stoletiia."
57. For an overview of Prigov's artistic output, see Dobrenko et al., eds., *Nekanonicheskii klassik,* 711–70.
58. Prigov, "What More Is There to Say?" 102.
59. For some samples, see http://www.youtube.com/watch?v=q_-l2h5mNYs &feature=related or http://www.youtube.com/watch?v=npRiTk6Bn6c &feature=related (both accessed 5 January 2015). Examples of Prigov adopting alternate identities also appear on his personal websites www.prigov.com and www.prigov.ru (under "performances" and "photos"); but these do not necessarily refer to Soviet stereotypes and clichés.
60. Menzel, *Bürgerkrieg um Worte,* 307.
61. Prigov and Shapoval, *Portretnaia galereia,* 13.
62. Among others, Thomas Vaessens and Yra van Dijk demonstrate how postmodern writers always viewed downright irony with hesitance—and critically attacks readings of postmodernism as one-sidedly ironic and relativistic—in Vaessens and van Dijk, "Introduction."
63. In introductions to his own collections, Prigov already protested against overironic and overrelativistic readings of his poetry in the early 1970s. For examples, see Prigov, *Sbornik preduvedomlenii,* 8–11.
64. Ibid., 8.
65. Gandlevskii and Prigov, "Mezhdu imenem i imidzhem," 5. On Prigov's complex relationship to the personal, to image, to behavior, and to the figure of the author, see Bogdanova, *Postmodernizm,* 458–59.
66. On his "attempt to write the most personal poetry" and related statements, see Zorin and Prigov, "Prigov kak Pushkin," 122.
67. Prigov and Epstein, "Popytka ne byt' identifitsiirovannym," 69.
68. Ibid.
69. Prigov, *Sbornik preduvedomlenii,* 222.
70. Prigov, "Iskrennost'," 172.
71. Prigov, *Sovetskie teksty 1979–1984,* 206.
72. Ibid., 300.
73. Ibid., 301.
74. Prigov, citations from New Sincerity performances, 1986. Citations taken from Katsov, "V luchshikh svoikh obraztsakh."
75. Yurchak, *Everything Was Forever,* 266–67.
76. Mikhail Iampol'skii rightly criticizes the trend to view Soviet reality as the prime object of Prigov's "parodism" in "Vysokii parodizm," 191.

77. Prigov, *Sovetskie teksty 1979–1984*, 24; and Prigov and Shapoval, *Portretnaia galereia*, 28.

78. Prigov, "Iskrennost'."

79. Alexievich, "Vremia sekond-khend;" Lotman is cited in Kugel', "Iskrennost' lzhetsov."

80. Prigov, "Iskrennost'."

81. Nadezhda Bourova, personal conversation with the author, 26 February 2009, London. Notes available upon request from contact@ellenrutten.nl.

82. Prigov and Shapoval, *Portretnaia galereia*, inside jacket flap.

83. Literary historian Olga Bogdanova discusses this view in an extensive analysis of the poet's work and reception in Bogdanova, *Postmodernizm*, 454–87.

84. Erofeev, "Pamiatnik dlia khrestomatii."

85. For a set of representative examples, see the discussions of Prigov in Bogdanova, *Postmodernizm*, 454–87 (esp. 458ff.); and Skoropanova, *Russkaia postmodernistskaia literatura*, 210–19.

86. Paperno, *Stories of the Soviet Experience*, 209; Erofeev, "Pamiatnik dlia khrestomatii" (here cited in Skoropanova, *Russkaia postmodernistskaia literatura*, 215; page of Erofeev citation not indicated).

87. Erofeev specifically refers to Soviet memory in "Pamiatnik dlia khrestomatii."

88. Zorin, "Slushaia Prigova," 430.

89. Personal conversation with the author, 24 February 2009, Oxford; and Zorin, "'Al'manakh'," 271.

90. Epstein, "Afterword," 277.

91. Epstein, "Conclusion," 457.

92. Ibid.

93. Groys, "Moskovskii romanticheskii kontseptualism." For the quotation on postmodernism and Romanticism, see Larrissy, *Romanticism and Postmodernism*, 1.

94. Lyotard, *Le Différend;* and Eaglestone, "Postmodernism and Ethics," 183.

95. Zorin, "Slushaia Prigova," 450.

96. Aizenberg, "Slyshite vy—Prigov"; Kabakov, "D. A. Prigov i ego 'bezumnaia iskrennost'"; Obermayr, "Semantic Poetry"; Dobrenko, "Byl i ostaetsia," 11.

97. Barash, "Prigov kak deiatel' tsivilizatsii," 269; Iampol'skii, "Vysokii parodizm," 181; Maiofis, "D. A. Prigov i G. R. Derzhavin," 299.

98. Lipovetsky, "Prigov i Batai," 338. For the citation, see Witte and Hänsgen, "O nemetskoi poeticheskoi knige."

99. A similar posthumous shift typifies the reception of other authors who recently pondered the problem of postmodernism and sincerity. Literary historian Adam Kelly has mapped how "new-sincere" readings of the work of American writer David Foster Wallace—mentioned briefly in the previous chapter—increased directly after his suicide at the age of forty-six in 2008 (Kelly, "David Foster Wallace and the New Sincerity in American Fiction," 131). Susan Rosenbaum speaks of "the elegiac nature of posthumous criticism" (Rosenbaum, *Professing Sincerity*, 202).

100. Kalinin, "Dmitri A. Prigov."
101. Golynko-Vol'fson, "Totalitarian Laughter as Magic Ritual" and "Chitaia Prigova," 170.
102. Epstein, "Conclusion," 458.
103. Ibid., 456, and "O novoi sentimental'nosti," 225.
104. Ivanova, *Nostal'iashchee.*
105. Ivanova in Biriukov, "Literatura poslednego desiatiletiia," 15.
106. Ivanova, "Iskusstvo pri svete iskrennosti."
107. Ibid.
108. Ibid.
109. The exhibition's full title was "Neo Sincerity: The Difference between the Comic and the Cosmis Is a Single Letter," and it was curated by Amei Wallach (at Apexart, 22 February to 8 April 2006).
110. Art Spiegelman cited in Reid, "Art Spiegelman and Françoise Mouly."
111. For details see the exhibition description on the Apexart site, available at http://www.apexart.org/exhibitions/wallach.php (accessed 5 January 2015).
112. Lipovetsky, *Paralogii,* 575.
113. Ibid., 610.
114. Ibid., 591.
115. Oushakine, " 'We're Nostalgic but We're Not Crazy'," 453.
116. Ibid., 482.
117. Yurchak, "Post-Post-Communist Sincerity," 257.
118. Ibid., 262. For the original citation, see Luchistyi, "Slava Zav'ialov."
119. Fursey cited in Yurchak, "Post-Post-Communist Sincerity," 265.
120. Ibid., 276.
121. Ibid.
122. For a thorough English-language discussion of the Putin-era reappraisal of Stalin and its impact on Russian intellectual/creative culture see Noordenbos, *Post-Soviet Literature.*
123. Lipovetsky, *Paralogii,* 469, 467 (italics original).
124. Etkind, "Putin's History Lessons"; and Scherrer, "Anciens/Nouveaux lieux de mémoire."
125. For exemplary interviews, see Kanishchev, "Beliaev-Gintovt," and Dremliugin, "Aleksei Beliaev-Gintovt."
126. Kanishchev, "Beliaev-Gintovt."
127. For my (Dutch-language) analysis of Beliaev-Gintovt's work and responses to his receipt of the prestigious Kandinsky prize, see Rutten, "Flirten met Stalin."
128. Ibid., 497.
129. The second citation is from Gabowitsch, *Putin Kaputt!?;* the first from Gabowitsch, "Fascism as *Stiob.*" Gabowitsch is not only critical of contemporary stiob: elsewhere he argues that late-Soviet underground culture—the birthplace of stiob—was unproductive and replete with empty

words. In 2014, against a backdrop of hardline and expansionist Kremlin politics, Marina Davydova situates contemporary oppositional failings in a similar historical framework. In her view, the "New Sincerity" of the 1960s (Davydova's term) lacked "clearness, clarity, energy of thought and of action" (Davydova, "1960-e").

130. Noordenbos, *Post-Soviet Literature*.
131. Stodolsky, "A Multi-Lectic Anatomy."
132. Pomerantsev, *Nothing Is True and Everything Is Possible*, 4.
133. Personal conversation with the author, 17 October 2014, St. Petersburg.
134. Personal conversation with the author, 14 May 2009, Moscow. Transcript available upon request.
135. Vail' and Genis, *60e*, 14–15.
136. Kaspe, ed., *Status dokumenta*.
137. Skype interview with the author, 29 April 2004.
138. Stodolsky, "A Multi-Lectic Anatomy."
139. Dugin, "Aleksandr Dugin."
140. For a comprehensive interview with Medvedev on his political views and activities, see Tsvetkov, "Kirill Medvedev."
141. For both views, see Meindl and Witte, "Die neue Aufrichtigkeit." The citation on the public intellectual is taken from ibid., 176.
142. Medvedev, "The Writer in Russia." The Russian original appeared a year earlier as "Literatura budet proverena: Individual'nyi proekt i 'novaia emotsional'nost'" in Medvedev, *Reaktsiia voobshche*.
143. Ibid.
144. Ibid.
145. All citations ibid.
146. Ibid.
147. For examples, see Kochetkova, "Dmitrii Prigov"; Ryklin, "Proekt dlinoi v zhizni" (see especially page 90); Golynko-Vol'fson, "Chitaia Prigova"; and Obermayr, "Semantic Poetry and Sincerity Revisited." The "selling" citation comes from Obermayr's analysis; in exploring Prigov's work on sincerity, Obermayr emphasizes that "whenever there is a call for sincerity, it will not come without a claim for the reader. Sincerity sells." Zorin speaks of Prigov's highly recognizable "brand" in Zorin, "Dmitrii Aleksandrovich Prigov," 80.
148. Prigov, "Pirogovskii narkoz."
149. Ibid.
150. Lutz, *Crying*, 54 and 56.
151. For two representative contributions to the ensuing national *and* international debate on the (in)sincerity of Putin's tears, see Harding, "Putin's Tears"; and a Russian-language forum discussion devoted to the question "Were Putin's Tears Sincere?" ("Slezy Putina byli iskrenni?"), conducted in March 2012, on the website www.mail.ru, available online at http://otvet.mail.ru/question/72276601/.

152. On the tear as a prominent theme in Prigov's visual art, see Zakharov, "Du-maia o nastoiashchem," 704. My observations imply that it is equally promi-nent in his literary writings: in the (not terribly voluminous) collection of poetry of his first ten years alone, I found seventeen references to tears and crying, and the same theme permeated several of his numerous writings on sincerity (for the references in question, see Prigov, *Sobranie stikhov,* 1: 4, 10, 15, 26, 39, 50, 59, 64, 67, 70, 89, 99, 184).

153. Facebook conversation with Andrei Prigov, 15 April 2012.

154. The address of the "Online Projects" section is http://www.prigov.ru/ac-tion/goglus.php.

155. To see the image, visit the "Online Projects" ("Setevye proekty") page on Prigov's website (http://www.prigov.ru/action/goglus.php, accessed 15 Janu-ary 2015).

156. Ibid.

157. Etkind, *Warped Mourning,* 237; Marsh, *Literature, History, and Identity,* 13.

158. Etkind, *Warped Mourning,* 192–93.

159. I am speaking of the more (audio)visually informed analyses that Etkind in-cludes in ibid.

160. Van Alphen and Bal, *"Introduction,"* 1.

161. I borrow the citation from media studies Ph.D. student Eva Sancho-Rodriguez's paper "The Merit of Genre."

CHAPTER 3. "I CRIED TWICE"

1. Misiano, "Dubossarsky and Vinogradov's 'New Sincerity.'"

2. Examples include Reid, "Art Spiegelman and Françoise Mouly"; Mannisto, "The New Sincerity"; Chung and Jacobi, "In Search of a New Sincerity?"; Sar-jono, "Poetry and Sincerity"; Groys, "The Production of Sincerity"; Collins, "Genericity in the 90s"; Olsen, "If I Can Dream"; Barton Palmer, "The New Sincerity of Neo-Noir"; Watercutter, "Sincerely Ours"; ABC, "A Clue to Style"; Korthals Altes, "Blessedly post-ironic?"; Reynolds, "Welcome to the New Sin-cerity"; and Williams, "The Final Irony."

3. Watercutter, "Sincerely Ours."

4. Apart from the ones discussed below and elsewhere in this book, repre-sentative transdisciplinary examples include Ivanova, "Iskusstvo pri svete iskrennosti"; Savchuk, "Ideologiia postinformatsionnoi iskrennosti'"; Pospelov, "Novaia iskrennost' na chetverykh"; Metelitsa, "Igra v otkrovenie"; Bavil'skii, "Ob iskrennosti v iskusstve"; Radzievskii, "Moskou: Nieuwe opre-chte kunst"; Semionov, "Novaia iskrennost'"; Koldobskaia, *Iskusstvo v bol'shom dolgu;* Koretskii, "Takaia vot 'novaia iskrennost'"; Kurliandtseva, "Absurd spaset mir"; Mikhailovskaia, "'Novaia iskrennost'."

5. Petrovskaia, "Dusha Pautiny"; and Yurchak, "Post-Post-Communist Sincerity."

6. Bavil'skii, "Ob iskrennosti." ZhZh is the Russian abbreviation for blogs hosted by LiveJournal—a brand that translates into Russian as *Zhivoi Zhurnal.*

7. On the post-Soviet "process of 'celebrification'" see especially Goscilo and Strukov, eds., *Celebrity and Glamour in Contemporary Russia.*

8. Aizenberg, "Vozmozhnost' vyskazyvaniia"; Kuritsyn, in the conclusion of his *Russkii literaturnyi postmodernizm;* Lipovetsky, *Russian Postmodernist Fiction,* 244, 247; Kuz'min, "Postkontseptualizm," 471.

9. Ivanova in Biriukov, "Literatura poslednego desiatiletiia," 12.

10. Ibid.

11. All personal communication, 12 May 2009, at an evening in remembrance of the poet Aleksei Parshchikov at the Vinzavod factory, Moscow.

12. Davydov, "Dmitrii Vodennikov, Svetlana Lin"; Kukulin, "Every Trend Makes a Brand."

13. The text was later published in the journal *Oktiabr'* (see Popov, "Priznaius' . . .").

14. Popov, "Priznaius' . . ."

15. Kostiukov, "Postoronnie soobrazheniia."

16. Kuz'min, ed., *Legko byt' iskrennim.*

17. Kaspe, "Govorit tot, kto govorit 'ia.'"

18. For examples see: on Vodennikov (to whom I return in more detail in the next chapter), Davydov, "Dmitrii Vodennikov, Svetlana Lin"; on Ketro, Popov in "Priznaius' . . ."; on Pavlova, Zavialov, "Kto eti liudi v chernykh plash-chakh?"; and on Grishkovets, his "Evgenii Grishkovets o 'novoi iskren-nosti.'"

19. Sorokin, "Tekst kak narkotik," 121.

20. See, for instance, the CNN report on the protests (Chilcote, "Russian Sex Row Author Summoned").

21. The first explanation of Sorokin's work was central to public protests and the threats of legal prosecution for Sorokin's allegedly pornographic writing by the youth movement Marching Together in the early 2000s; the second reading is elaborated most extensively in Lipovetsky's early writings on Sorokin (see Lipovetsky, *Russian Postmodernist Fiction*), and in Burkhart, ed., *Poetik der Metadiskursitivät.*

22. Uffelmann, "Led Tronulsia," 106.

23. Lipovetsky sees the novel *Blue Lard*—published a year earlier than *Moscow*—as a first marker of Sorokin's move away from hardcore postmodern toward a (revived) modernist poetics (Lipovetsky, "Russian Literary Post-modernism"; Lipovetsky revisits the same argument in *Paralogii,* 407ff.) On the *Moscow* scenario as a marker of a break in Sorokin's career/poetics, see, for instance, Kuritsyn, *Russkii literaturnyi postmodernizm;* Degot', "Kinostse-narii Vladimira Sorokina"; and Berg, *Literaturokratiia.*

24. Sorokin, *Trilogiia,* 292.

25. Lipovetsky, *Paralogii,* 619.

26. Sorokin, "Vladimir Sorokin ne khochet byt' prorokom," "Mea Culpa?" and "Pravila zhizni."

27. Sorokin, "Mea Culpa?"

28. Sorokin, "Vladimir Sorokin ne khochet byt' prorokom."
29. Sorokin, "Interview with Author Vladimir Sorokin."
30. Personal communication with the author, 12 May 2009, Moscow. Transcript available upon request from contact@ellenrutten.nl.
31. For an early example see Sorokin, "Tekst kak narkotik," 124.
32. Personal communication with the author, 12 May 2009, Moscow.
33. Sorokin, "Vladimir Sorokin ne khochet byt' prorokom."
34. Sorokin in Sokolov, *Moia kniga o Vladimire Sorokine*, 129.
35. Sorokin, "Mea Culpa?"
36. Cover text for Foster, *Return of the Real*.
37. Personal conversation, 3 September 2002. Transcript available upon request from contact@ellenrutten.nl. See also Sorokin and Wituchnowskaja, "Nichts leichter, als ein Held zu sein," 67–68. In this interview, Sorokin presents Russia as an "unpredictable zone" and "the West's antipode."
38. Sorokin, "Mea Culpa?"
39. Ibid.
40. I am thinking especially of the novels *Roman* and *The Blue Lard*.
41. The term "metadiscursivity" is introduced and applied to Sorokin's work in Burkhart, *Poetik der Metadiskursitivät*.
42. Personal communication with the author, 12 May 2009, Moscow. More specifically, Sorokin mentioned the following "warm" personal contacts: the composers Leonid Desiatnikov, Ol'ga Raeva, and Anatolii Pereslegin, pianist Aleksei Goribol, music critic and composer Petr Pospelov, film directors Aleksandr Zel'dovich and Il'ia Khrzhanovskii, and theater producer Eduard Boiakov.
43. Ibid.
44. Citations collected from Sorokin, "Po Bol'shomu"; "Idushchie vmeste' protiv 'Deti Rozentalia'"; "Vladimir Sorokin"; and "Ia v sovok opiat' ne khochu."
45. Laird, *Voices of Russian Literature*, 161.
46. Prigov, *Sbornik preduvedomlenii*, 298–301.
47. Personal conversation, May 2009.
48. Degot', "Kinostsenarii Vladimira Sorokina," 225; Laird, *Voices of Russian Literature*, 160.
49. Hutcheon, *Irony's Edge*, 15.
50. Groys, *Gesamtkunstwerk Stalin*.
51. Prigov and Shapoval, *Portretnaia galereia*, book jacket.
52. Sorokin, "Mea Culpa?," "Ia v sovok opiat' ne khochu," and "Pravila zhizni."
53. See http://www.snob.ru/profile/blog/5295 (accessed 5 January 2015) for Sorokin's profile page.
54. The blog can be read on www.srkn.ru/blog (accessed 5 January 2015).
55. Consider, for instance, the pictures of Sorokin in Kulik and Sorokin, *V glub' Rossii*, and in Sorokin, *Mesiats v Dakhau*.
56. Sorokin, *Sobranie sochinenii*.
57. See Ponomareva, *"Neonorma"*; the pictures and videos of Sorokin by Aleksei Kudenko in Sorokin, "Kogda nachinaet ottepel'"; in Akimov, "My s Vladimi-

rom Sorokinym" and "Kak my s Vladimirom Sorokinym"; and a 2009 photo series of Sorokin by photographer Serge Golovach in the journal *Snob*, 17 (2009): unpaginated first page and 2; the photo accompanying Danilkin, "Serdtse Sorokina" (photographer not indicated).

58. Copulating dogs act as something akin to a logo for "the new Sorokin": since the mid-2000s, portraits of the author flanked by his two dogs—brothers Fomka and Romka—in coition have also appeared in photo sessions by Pavel Samokhvalov for the journal *Time Out* (accessible online at http://www .timeout.com/london/things-to-do/time-out-moscow-heroes-2 [accessed 1 June 2015]), and by Golovach (see previous note).

59. Sorokin, "Vladimir Sorokin v proekte 'Velikany.'"

60. Emerson, *The Cambridge Introduction to Russian Literature*, 132.

61. Ferguson, "Glamour and the End of Irony," 11.

62. Ibid., 14.

63. Goscilo and Strukov, *Celebrity and Glamour*, 2.

64. Ibid., 14.

65. Groys, "The Production of Sincerity," 45.

66. See Burkhart, Poetik der *Metadiskursitivät*.

67. Citations collected from Shevtsov, "Put' moralista"; Karmodi, "Sorokin vyvel sebia v raskhod"; Danilkin, "Serdtse Sorokina"; Bavil'skii, "Sorokin forever!"; Kukushkin, "Mudrost' Sorokina"; Korolenko, "Put' Bro"; Smirnov, *Filosofiia na kazhdyi den'*, 209, and "Vladimir Sorokin."

68. Sorokin, "Mea Culpa?"

69. Kucherskaia in *Polit.ru*, "V gostiakh u tsiklopov."

70. Marusenkov, *Absurdopediia russkoi zhizni Vladimira Sorokina* (italics original).

71. Ibid., 297–99 (italics original).

72. Lipovetsky, *Paralogii*, 637, 672.

73. Bondarenko, "Roman V. Sorokina 'Led.'"

74. Uffelmann, "Led Tronulsia," 121, 124.

75. Mezhieva and Konradova, *Okno v mir*, 36; and Bogdanova, *Postmodernizm*, 425.

76. Mark Lipovetsky, for example, places the novels squarely within Russian late postmodernism—a literary tradition that, as we saw earlier, he sees as a direct "response to the necessity of living through historical trauma" (Lipovetsky, *Paralogii*, 530). For another example, see also Golynko-Vol'fson, "'Kopeika' i iznanka ideologii."

77. Ready, "Saplings in the Jungle," 14.

78. Wachtel, *Remaining Relevant after Communism*.

79. Ibid.

80. Sorokin, "Tekst kak narkotik," 121.

81. A PDF of the form is available upon request at contact@ellenrutten.nl.

82. Ryklin, *Vremia diagnoza*, 183.

83. Personal conversation with the author, 13 May 2009, Moscow. Transcript available upon request from contact@ellenrutten.nl.

84. Smirnov, *Filosofiia na kazhdyi den'*, 209, and "Vladimir Sorokin"; Kukulin, "Every Trend Makes a Brand"; Golynko-Vol'fson, "'Kopeika' i iznanka ideologii"; Morev in *Polit.ru*, "V gostiakh u tsiklopov"; and Zintsov, "Chitai serdtsem."

85. Davydov, "Dmitrii Vodennikov, Svetlana Lin."

86. 5-TV, "Noch' na piatom." For a while, in my own research I also worked with the hypothesis that both Sorokin's and other writers' choice for (either a provocative or) a "new sincere" authorial pose was likely to involve economic considerations (see Rutten, "Strategic Sentiments" and "Where Postmodern Provocation Meets Social Strategy").

87. "Muzhchiny tozhe mogut imitirovat' orgazm," as reprinted on Vodennikov's webpage (http://vodennikov.ru/poem/muzhchiny.htm, accessed 5 January 2015).

88. Bavil'skii, "Ob iskrennosti v iskusstve."

89. Sal'nikov, "Authorship and the Artwork."

90. Degot', "Die russische Kunst in den 1990er Jahren," 41.

91. Skype interview with the author, 29 April 2009.

92. Kibirov, *Kara-baras*, 43.

93. Kibirov cited in Kulle, "Ia ne veshchaiu," 14.

94. Degot' and Kulik, "Russkii—eto sotsial'naia kategoriia."

95. Mombert, "The New Sincerity."

96. Brinton, "Who Needs Money?"

97. Jameson, *Postmodernism*, 417. Jameson speaks of late capitalism; for a leading source on the postcapitalist logic that I discuss, see, in addition, Gibson-Graham, *A Postcapitalist Politics*.

98. Kulik in *Oleg Kulik* (DVD).

99. See Kulik, "Beseda s Olegom Kulikom"; and the press release on http://www.winzavod.ru/believe/.

100. Backstein, "Ia optimist po nature," 49.

101. Sigutina, "Berlinskaia koloniale."

102. Khachaturov, "Prisiaga na 'Veriu.'" For a second example, see Luzhetskii, "Sermiazhnaia pravda russkogo iskusstvo."

103. Rosenbaum, *Professing Sincerity*, 131.

104. Ibid.

105. Ibid., 4, 12.

106. The three publications that together marked the launch of this new academic field in Russia all date from the years 2009–11, when the *Trilogy* had long been published (Plamper, "Emotional Turn?"; Plamper, Elie, and Schahadat, eds., *Rossiiskaia imperiia chuvstv*; Steinberg and Sobol, eds., *Interpreting Emotions in Russia and Eastern Europe*).

107. Among others, see Dubin and Gudkov, *Literatura kak sotsial'nyi institut;* Berg, *Literaturokratiia;* and "After Bourdieu" ("Posle Bourdieu"), a special section on Bourdieu and the Russian humanities in the renowned Russian

humanities journal *Novoe literaturnoe obozrenie,* 60 (2003), accessible on http://magazines.russ.ru/nlo/2003/60/ (accessed 5 January 2015).

108. Smirnov, *Filosofiia na kazhdyi den'*, 129.

109. Goscilo and Strukov, *Celebrity and Glamour.*

110. Wachtel, *Remaining Relevant after Communism;* Menzel, *Bürgerkrieg ohne Worte;* Berg, *Literaturokratiia.*

111. Klein, "Deržavin."

112. Kuntsman, "'With a Shade of Disgust.'"

113. Groys, *Unter Verdacht.*

114. Gabowitsch, *Putin Kaputt!?*

115. Heisse and Calhan, "Emotion Norms in Interpersonal Events."

116. On the "synthesis" between universal and culturally defined emotion dynamics, see Plamper, "Vvedenie I," and Smail, *On Deep History.*

CHAPTER 4. "SO NEW SINCERITY"

1. Bruns, *Blogs,* 2.

2. Hayles and Gannon, "Mood Swings," 99, 110.

3. Ibid., 118–19.

4. Kirby, "The Death of Postmodernism and Beyond."

5. Gabler, *Life: the Movie;* de Zengotita, *Mediated;* Jean Baudrillard, *Simulacres et simulations;* Manjoo, *True Enough;* on Colbert's use of the word "truthiness" in his satirical show *The Colbert Report* in October 2005 and its roots, see Zimmer, "Truthiness or Trustiness?"

6. Van Alphen and Bal, "Introduction," 5.

7. Ibid., 15.

8. Groys, "The Production of Sincerity," 43. For Groys's view on sincerity and media, see also *Unter Verdacht.*

9. Collins, "Genericity in the 90s," 257.

10. Wallace, "E Unibus Pluram," 178, 192.

11. Kelly, "David Foster Wallace and the New Sincerity in American Fiction."

12. Watercutter, "Sincerely Ours."

13. Mannisto, "The New Sincerity."

14. Morris, "The Time between Time."

15. Mumblecore is the label used for a low-budget film genre that has flourished in the 2000s and 2010s; canonic mumblecore films feature nonprofessional actors, naturalistic dialogue, and, often, improvisation.

16. For representative reviews, see Macdowell, "Wes Anderson" (on the "'quirky' sensibility of recent American indie cinema" and its "tone which balances ironic detachment with sincere engagement"); Filippo, "A Cinema of Recession" (on "the sincerity . . . missing from so much postmodern media" of mumblecore films); Thurber Stone, "Summer Musings" (on the "retreat to New Sincerity" of *The Bachelorette*); and Thumfart, "Das Kulturphänomen 'New Sincerity'" (on the extent to which Lena Dunham "has . . .

overstrained" "the stylistic devices of the 'New Sincerity'" in her film *Tiny Furniture* and her TV series *Girls*).

17. For representative readings, see Fitzgerald, "Sincerity"; and Hamilton, *One Man Zeitgeist* (Hamilton does not merely present Eggers as representative of a "new sincerity" but sees his novel *A Heartbreaking Work of Staggering Genius* as "an Urtext for new sincerity" (ibid., 52)).

18. Vaessens, "'Ik ga met je mee ik durf het.'" See also Vaessens, *De revanche van de roman*.

19. Babitskaia, "Shto takoe 'Novyi epos.'"

20. Roth-Ey, *Moscow Prime Time*.

21. Oates, "The Neo-Soviet Model of the Media"; Becker, "Lessons from Russia," 139. For a more recent study, see also the updated version (2014) of Ognyanova, "Careful What You Say."

22. Savchuk, "Ideologiia postinformatsionnoi iskrennosti."

23. Degot', "Die russische Kunst in den 1990er Jahren," 41.

24. Beumers and Lipovetsky, *Performing Violence*.

25. Ugarov cited in ibid., 213 (for the original citation, see Petrushanskaia, "Mikhail Ugarov," 186, 187).

26. Beumers and Lipovetsky, *Performing Violence*, 236.

27. The quotations that I cite are collected from interviews with cocurator Zurab Tsereteli and others in a 2007 issue of the journal of the Moscow Museum of Contemporary Art devoted to this event (*Veriu*, 50, 52, 53).

28. Pertsev, "Novaia iskrennost'." See also Medvedev's essay in chapter 3.

29. Sarjono, "Poetry and Sincerity," 8–11.

30. Carraway, "Playing Nice: The New Sincerity." See also "The New (New New New) Sincerity," a 2011 blog post by Carraway (katecarraway.com/post /3778300882/the-new-new-new-new-sincerity, accessed 5 January 2015).

31. This profile matches recent surveys on new-media usage in Russia (for an exemplary recent survey, see Mail.ru Group, *Sotsial'nye seti v Rossii*.

32. Groys, "The Production of Sincerity," 42.

33. "Flava in Ya Ear," a 2006 blog post by Jesse Thorn (http://www .maximumfun.org/tags/flava-ya-ear, accessed 5 January 2015).

34. "Staying Up on the Wire," a 2006 blog post by Jesse Thorn (http://www .maximumfun.org/node?page=591, accessed 5 January 2015; capitals original).

35. For a publication that challenges this stereotypical view, see Menzel and Schmid, eds., *Der Osten im Westen*.

36. The citation comes from "You're So New Sincerity . . . ," a 2011 blog post on "the new sincerity" by benstones (http://benstones.tumblr.com/post /4060292499/youre-so-new-sincerity, accessed 5 January 2015), which cites Epstein, among other theorists, as benstones's source of inspiration.

37. For an example, see Ashton, "Sincerity and the Second Person." The Wikipedia entry "New Sincerity" refers to another analysis on new-sincerity discourse and Flarf (one enlisted as "Katy Henriksen. 'Drunk Bunnies, The

New Sincerity, Flarf: How Blogs Are Transforming Poetry.' *EconoCulture*, January 23, 2007"), but the link to the actual article fails to work.

38. Rettberg, *Blogging*, 111.

39. "Welcome to the New Sincerity," a 2008 blog post by Reynolds (http://rooreynolds.com/2008/05/28/welcome-to-the-new-sincerity/, accessed 5 January 2015).

40. Chen, "New Sincerity in a Postmodern World."

41. "Luchador Flyer Dunk High," a 2006 blog post by Roundhouse Kicks (http://rhkicks.blogspot.com/2006/09/luchador-flyer-dunk-high.html, accessed 5 January 2015).

42. See the Wikipedia entry "New Sincerity" and—for the neo-sincerity citation—Watercutter, "My Little Pony Corrals Unlikely Fanboys Known as 'Bronies.'"

43. "The New Sincerity (Don't Flog Blog the Messenger!)," a 2006 blog post by Lorna Dee Cervantes (http://lornadice.blogspot.com/2006/01/new-sincerity-dont-flog-blog-messenger.html, accessed 5 January 2015).

44. Marsh, *Literature, History and Identity*, 559. My (hesitant) use of the term "generation" I explain in note 65 of this book's Introduction.

45. Kuz'min, "Russkaia poeziia v nachale XXI veka."

46. Mezhieva and Konradova, *Okno v mir*, 10.

47. *Setevaia poeziia, Pravda i iskrennost' v iskusstve*.

48. Khersonskii, *Novaia iskrennost'*.

49. Metelitsa, "Igra v 'otkrovenie.'"

50. Bezdenezhnykh, Efimov, and Sheikhetov, "Eto nasha molodeZhZh."

51. Shevelev, "Slediashchie za slediashchim."

52. Jenkins et al., "Confronting the Challenges of Participatory Culture."

53. Gabowitsch, *Protest in Putin's Russia*.

54. Pogrebizhskaia, "Elena Pogrebizhskaia o lichnom balanse," 5.

55. Ibid.

56. Loshak, "Prozhivem bez gosudarstva." When still online, the same webpage featured a column with *OpenSpace*'s most-read articles: Loshak's was ranked as the tenth-most-read text.

57. For the story of the nursing home incident, see *Russia Today*, "Russia Shocked."

58. Loshak, "Prozhivem bez gosudarstva."

59. Golynko-Vol'fson, "SMSte iskrenne."

60. Kaspe and Smurova, "Livejournal.com, russkaia versiia"; and Kostyrko, "WWW Obozrenie Sergei Kostyrko."

61. Lev Rubinstein, personal conversation with the author, 14 May 2009, Moscow. Transcript available upon request from contact@ellenrutten.nl. Timur Kibirov, personal conversation with the author, 13 May 2009 Moscow.

62. I write in more detail about Russian writers' blogs (and their cultural prominence) in Rutten, "(Russian) Writer-Bloggers."

63. The citation stems from a 2010 blog post by the organizers of the poetry festival Poemania (http://poemania.livejournal.com/1269.html, accessed

5 January 2015); see also the announcement of the poet as "the leader of 'the new sincerity' " in Vodennikov, "Iz knigi 'Chernovik' "; and the discussions of Vodennikov's reception as a "new sincere" writer in Ivanova, "Molodaia poeziia v poiskakh zhivogo slova" and in Davydov, "Dmitrii Vodennikov, Svetlana Lin."

64. Personal conversation with the author, 14 May 2009, Moscow. Transcript available upon request from contact@ellenrutten.nl.

65. Ibid.

66. Ibid.

67. 5-TV, "Noch' na piatom." For a more detailed analysis of Vodennikov, social media, and self-fashioning, see Rutten, "Sincere e-Self-Fashioning."

68. Personal conversation with the author, 14 May 2009, Moscow. Transcript available upon request from contact@ellenrutten.nl.

69. Skype conversation with Schmidt during a Skype lecture for students by the author on digital Russian writing, University of Hamburg, May 30, 2011.

70. Baym, *Personal Connections in the Digital Age*, 146.

71. Keymolen, "Esther Keymolen Wondered." On trust and technologies, see Keymolen's dissertation "Trust on the Line." For the Harvard study, see Tamir and Mitchell, "Disclosing Information about the Self."

72. "Ulybaiushchiisia baklazhan," a 2012 blog post by cyrill_lipatov (http://cyrill-lipatov.livejournal.com/331842.html#comments, accessed 5 January 2015; italics original).

73. Among other publications, see on this development *Digital Icons, Russian Elections and Digital Media*.

74. Comment by fragmaker, 15.08.2009 (http://evil-ninja.livejournal.com /671903.html, accessed 5 January 2015).

75. "Ochen' interesnyi publitsisticheskii analiz . . . ," a 2012 blog post by yury_zagrebnoy (http://yury-zagrebnoy.livejournal.com/201622.html, accessed 5 January 2015).

76. "Zachem ia vel ZhZh esli mne za nego ne khotiat dat' aktsii Aeroflota?" a 2012 blog post by space_ulysses (http://space-ulysses.livejournal.com/852 .html, accessed 5 January 2015).

77. The examples in question I collected from reine_claude, post 20 December 2011 (http://reine-claude.livejournal.com/245677.html, accessed 5 January 2015); bronepoezd, post 17 August 2010 (http://bronepoezd.livejournal.com /606385.html?thread=8032433, accessed 5 January 2015); notterrier, post 8 July 2008 (http://notterrier.livejournal.com/47110.html?thread=552710, accessed 5 January 2015); and artelectronicsf, post 28 February 2012 (http:// artelectronicsf.livejournal.com/117542.html, accessed 5 January 2015).

78. Ushkov, "Fishka 'dukhovnost.' "

79. Piccalo, "Looking for 'Real.' "

80. Rombes, "The Rebirth of the Author."

81. I discuss a set of examples in Rutten, "Vintage_Russia."

82. Bates, "Photography, Philosophy and Authenticity."

83. Alexandrova, *Using New Media Effectively.*

84. Collins, "Genericity in the 90s," 259, 260. On the broader development, see, among others, King, *Spectacular Narratives*, 122 (on authenticity in so-called unsteadicam cinema); and Rombes, *Cinema in the Digital Age.*

85. Ramakers, *Less + More*, 159.

86. Ibid., 164.

87. This view resonates palpably in the different contributions to the exhibition catalogue by design theorist Louise Schouwenberg (Schouwenberg, *Hella Jongerius*).

88. Barrett, "Hella Jongerius."

89. See Rutten, "Vintage_Russia," for a more extensive (Dutch-language) publication on this topic. On www.sublimeimperfections.org, we share updates and news about the Sublime Imperfections project (2015–2019), which is funded by the Netherlands Organization for Scientific Research (NWO).

90. Baym, *Personal Connections in the Digital Age*, 155.

91. Gilmore and Pine, *Authenticity*, 14–16.

92. For a detailed version of this argument see ibid. For arguments on authenticity and its paradoxes as central ingredients of modern Western thinking, see also Adorno, *The Jargon of Authenticity;* Banet-Weiser, *Authentic^{TM};* Ferrara, *Reflective Authenticity;* Funk, Gross, and Huber, eds., *The Aesthetics of Authenticity;* and Potter, *The Authenticity Hoax.*

93. Rombes, "The Razor's Edge of American Cinema," jacket text.

94. Kessels, *Amateurism.*

95. Gilmore and Pine, *Authenticity*, 1.

96. Ibid., 12.

97. Rutten, "New-Media Language."

98. Koldobskaia, *Iskusstvo v bol'shom dolgu*, 267.

99. Kuritsyn, *Russkii literaturnyi postmodernizm.*

100. Osaulenko, "LOMOgrafiia."

101. Brodsky cited in Rutten, "Deliberate Incompletion," 114.

102. Zharikov, "Terra Inc."

103. Boiarinov, "Pop-protsess."

104. Pavlova, *Pis'ma v sosedniuiu komnatu.*

105. Neef, Van Dijck, and Ketelaar, eds., *Sign Here!* Throughout the *Sign Here!* contributions, authenticity emerges as a central concern; sincerity, by contrast, is discussed only once, and exclusively as a contrasting term with authenticity (ibid., 51).

106. Schmidt, "Russische Literatur im Internet."

107. Ibid.

108. The manifesto can be read online at http://www.guelman.ru/slava/manifest /istochniki/shelli.htm (accessed 3 June 2015); capitals original. See on padonki counterculture and its erratic semantics Zvereva, "Iazyk padonkaf"; Gusejnov, "Berloga vebloga" and "Instrumenty opisaniia nepolnoi kommunikatsii v blogosfere."

109. Rutten, "(Russian) Writer-Bloggers."
110. Personal conversation with the author, 14 May 2009.
111. Mitrenina, "Netneizm i traditsionnaia kul'tura."
112. The citation comes from Bykov, "Dostoevskii i psikhologiia russkogo literaturnogo interneta." How post-Soviet culture subverts, but is at the same time shaped by, Soviet Russia's highly normative language culture is elaborately explained in Lunde and Paulsen, eds., *From Poets to Padonki*. Philosopher of culture Virgil Nemoianu argues that imperfection is, in general, a pivotal conceptual category for literary writing (see, for instance, Nemoianu, *Imperfection and Defeat*, for his argument that literature is defined by a "discourse of warning, of imperfection, and of defeat" (4)).

CONCLUSION

1. Magill, *Sincerity*, 22.
2. Ibid., jacket text.
3. Bal and Van Alphen, "Introduction."
4. Among other studies that I cited in the previous chapters, see Wachtel, *Remaining Relevant*; and Berg, *Literaturokratiia*.
5. I am thinking especially of Rosenbaum, *Professing Sincerity*.
6. This reference to Gilmore and Pine recalls their book *Authenticity*—which I discuss in detail in chapter 4.
7. Kishkovsky, "A Cultural Awakening."
8. Arshakov, "Pussy Riot."
9. Among other sources, I am thinking of the following studies, which all tend to focus on Western European and American literatures: Brooks and Toth, eds., *The Mourning After*; Turner, *City as Landscape*; López and Potter, eds., *After Postmodernism*; Stierstorfer, ed., *Beyond Postmodernism*; Hoberek, ed., *After Postmodernism*; and Timmer, *Do You Feel It Too?*
10. Personal conversation with Mitrofanova, 30 November 2007, Helsinki. The conference to which I am referring is the Revisiting Perestroika conference, hosted by Helsinki's Aleksanteri Institute from 29 November to 1 December 2007.

ABC. "A Clue to Style: Nancy Drew and the New Sincerity." ABC Local. 1 June 2007, online at http://abclocal.go.com/wls/story?section=resources&id =5354287.

Adorno, Theodor. *Aesthetic Theory*. London: Bloomsbury, 2013.

———. *The Jargon of Authenticity*. New York: Routledge, 2002.

Ahmed, Sara. *The Cultural Politics of Emotion*. Edinburgh: Edinburgh University Press, 2004.

Aizenberg, Mikhail. "Slyshite vy—Prigov!" *OpenSpace*. 6 August 2008, online at http://www.openspace.ru/literature/projects/130/details/2286/.

———. "Vozmozhnost' vyskazyvaniia." *Znamia* 6 (1994): 191–98.

Akimov, Boris. "Kak my s Vladimirom Sorokinym skhodili k Anatoliiu Kommu." *Snob,* 13 June 2010, online at http://snob.ru/selected/entry/20014.

———. "My s Vladimirom Sorokinym vybrali luchshuiu v Rossii vodku." *Snob,* 29 October 2009, online at http://snob.ru/selected/entry/8326.

Alexandrova, Ekaterina. *Using New Media Effectively: An Analysis of Barack Obama's Election Campaign Aimed at Young Americans*. New York: Fordham University Press, 2010.

Alexievich, Svetlana. "Vremia sekond-khend: konets krasnogo cheloveka." *Druzhba narodov* 8 (2013), online at http://magazines.russ.ru/druzhba/2013 /8/2a.html.

An, Yanming. *The Idea of Cheng (Sincerity/Reality) in the History of Chinese Philosophy*. New York: Global Scholarly Publications, 2008.

———. "Western 'Sincerity' and Confucian '*Cheng*.'" *Asian Philosophy* 14 (2004): 155–69.

Anderson, Amanda. *The Way We Argue Now: A Study in the Cultures of Theory.* Princeton, N.J.: Princeton University Press, 2006.

Anton, Corey. *Selfhood and Authenticity.* Albany: New York University Press, 2001.

Arkhangel'skii, Andrei. "Novaia sereznost'." *Vzgliad,* 25 August 2008, online at http://www.vz.ru/columns/2008/8/25/200033.print.html.

Arshakov, Andrei. "Pussy Riot—iznanka kazennosti." *Vzgliad,* 15 March 2012, online at http://vz.ru/politics/2012/3/15/567975.html.

Ashbrook, Tom. "The Case against Irony." WBUR: Boston's NPR Radio Station, 3 November 2012, online at http://onpoint.wburg.org/2012/11/30/the-case -against-irony.

Ashby, Stephen M., and Kent Johnson, eds. *Third Wave: The New Russian Poetry.* Ann Arbor: University of Michigan Press, 1992.

Ashton, Jennifer. "Sincerity and the Second Person: Lyric after Language Poetry." *Interval(le)s* 2 (2)–3 (1) (2008–9), online at http://www.cipa.ulg.ac .be/intervalles4/8_ashton.pdf.

Assmann, Aleida. "Authenticity—the Signature of Western Exceptionalism?" In *Paradoxes of Authenticity: Studies on a Critical Concept,* edited by Julia Straub, 33–57. Bielefeld: Transcript, 2012.

Avvakum. "The Life of Archpriest Avvakum by Himself." In George Fedotov, *The Way of a Pilgrim and Other Classics of Russian Spirituality,* 137–82. Translated by Helen Iswolsky. Mineola, N.Y.: Dover, 2003.

Babitskaia, Varvara. "Shto takoe 'Novyi epos'." *OpenSpace,* 20 February 2008, online at http://os.colta.ru/literature/events/details/1249/.

Back, Joseph Laurence. *The Broadview Anthology of British Literature. Volume 5: The Victorian Era.* Toronto: Broadview, 2006.

Backstein, Joseph. "Ia optimist po nature, ia veriu. Interv'iu s Iosifom Baksh-teinom." *Zhurnal moskovskogo muzeia sovremennogo iskusstva* 2 (2007): 47–50.

Banet-Weiser, Janet. *Authentic™: The Politics of Ambivalence in a Brand Culture.* New York: New York University Press, 2012.

Barash, Aleksandr. "'Da ia ved' shto, da ia s liubov'iu . . .': Prigov kak deiatel' tsivilizatsii." In *Nekanonicheskii klassik: Dmitrii Aleksandrovich Prigov (1940–2007),* edited by Evgeny Dobrenko, Ilya Kukulin, Mark Lipovetsky, and Mariia Maiofis, 263–79. Moscow: Novoe literaturnoe obozrenie, 2010.

Barker, Hugh, and Yuval Taylor. *Faking It: The Quest for Authenticity in Popular Music.* New York: Norton, 2007.

Barkhudarov, Stepan, ed. *Slovar' russkogo iazyka XI–XVII vv.* 6th ed. Moscow: Nauka, 1979.

Barrett, Claire. "Hella Jongerius." *Idfx Magazine* (undated), online at http://www .idfxmagazine.com/story.asp?storycode=3552.

Barthes, Roland. *Fragments d'un discours amoureux.* Paris: Seuil, 1977.

———. *A Lover's Discourse: Fragments.* Translated by Richard Howard. New York: Penguin, 1990.

Barton Palmer, R. "The New Sincerity of Neo-Noir: The Example of the Man Who Wasn't There." In *The Philosophy of Neo-Noir,* edited by Mark T. Conard, 151–67. Lexington: University Press of Kentucky, 2006.

Bates, Tomas. "Photography, Philosophy and Authenticity." *Lomography.nl,* 25 March 2011, online at http://www.lomography.nl/magazine/lifestyle/2011 /03/25/photography-philosophy-and-authenticity.

Baudrillard, Jean. *Simulacres and simulations.* Paris: Galilée, 1981.

Bavil'skii, Dmitrii. "Ob iskrennosti v iskusstve." *Vzgliad,* 20 June 2005, online at http://www.vz.ru/columns/2005/6/20/892.html.

———. "Sorokin forever! Znaki prepinaniia No. 56: Glavnaia kniga oseni— Vladimir Sorokin 'Put' Bro', roman. Izdatel'stvo Zakharov." *Topos,* 14 September 2004, online at http://topos.ru/article/2746.

Baym, Nancy. *Personal Connections in the Digital Age.* Cambridge: Polity Press, 2011.

Becker, Jonathan. "Lessons from Russia: A Neo-Authoritarian Media System." *European Journal of Communication* 19 (2) (2004): 139–63.

Beeman, William O. "Emotion and Sincerity in Persian Discourse: Accomplishing the Representation of Inner States." *International Journal of Sociology of Language-publication* 48 (2001), online at www.brown.edu/Departments /Anthropology/publications/Emotion.htm.

Bell, Michael. "Poetry and Sincerity: Leavis on Yeats." In Bell, *F. R. Leavis.* New York: Routledge, 1988.

Benjamin, Walter. *Illuminations: Essays and Reflections.* Translated by Harry Zorn. New York: Harcourt, 1968.

Benson, Morton, Evelyn Benson, and Robert Ilson, eds. *The BBI Combinatory Dictionary of English.* Amsterdam: John Benjamins, 1986.

Benthien, Claudia, and Steffen Martus, eds. *Die Kunst der Aufrichtigkeit im 17. Jahrhundert.* Tübingen: Niemeyer, 2006.

Berdiaev, Nikolai. "Filosofiia svobodnogo dukha" (1927), online at http://www .vehi.net/berdyaev/fsduha/.

———. *Samopoznanie: opyt filosofskoi avtobiografii* (1949), online at http://www .vehi.net/berdyaev/samopoznanie/index.html.

———. "Tsarstvo dukha i tsarstvo kesaria" (1949), online at http://www.vehi.net /berdyaev/carstvo.html.

Berg, Mikhail. *Literaturokratiia. Problema prisvoeniia i pererasredeleniia vlasti v literature.* Moscow: Novoe literaturnoe obozrenie, 2000.

Bergeron, Katherine. "Melody and Monotone: Performing Sincerity in Republican France." In *The Rhetoric of Sincerity,* edited by Ernst van Alphen, Mieke Bal, and Carel Smith, 44–60. Stanford: Stanford University Press, 2009.

Berggol'ts, Ol'ga. "Protiv likvidatsii liriki." *Literaturnaia gazeta,* 28 October 1954.

Berry, David M., and Michael Dieter. *Postdigital Aesthetics: Art, Computation and Design.* Basingstoke: Palgrave Macmillan 2015.

Beumers, Birgit, and Mark Lipovetsky. *Performing Violence: Literary and Theatrical Experiments of New Russian Drama.* Chicago: University of Chicago Press, 2009.

Bezdenezhnykh, Ivan, Konstantin Efimov, and Sergei Sheikhetov, "Eto nasha molodeZhZh." *Ekspert Online,* 12 July 2007, online at http://expert.ru /russian_reporter/2007/08/nasha_molodezh/.

Biriukov, Sergei. "Literatura poslednego desiatiletiia—tendentsii i perspektivy." *Voprosy literatury* 2 (1998): 3–83.

Boddy, William. *New Media and Popular Imagination: Launching Radio, Television, and Digital Media in the United States.* Oxford: Oxford University Press, 2004.

Boev, Khristo. "Remodernism?" *Liternet* 12 (145) (2011), online at http://liternet .bg/publish9/hboev/remodernizym.htm.

Bogdanova, Olga. *Postmodernizm v kontekste sovremennoi russkoi literatury (60–90e gody XX veka—nachalo XXI veka).* St. Petersburg: Filologicheskii fakul'tet S.-Peterburgskogo gosudarstvennogo universiteta, 2004.

Boiarinov, Denis. "Pop-protsess. Ot krizisa do krizisa: glavnoe." *OpenSpace,* 25 December 2008, online at http://os.colta.ru/music_modern/projects/112 /details/7080/.

Bondarenko, Mariia. "Roman V. Sorokina 'Led': Siuzhet-attraktsion—ideologiia— novaia iskrennost'—kataficheskaia dekonstruktsiia." *Literaturnyi dnevnik,* May (2002), online at www.vavilon.ru/diary/020518.html.

Böröcz, József, and Katerine Verdery. "Gender and Nation." *East European Politics and Societies* 8 (2) (1994): 223–316.

Bortnes, Jostein. *Visions of Glory: Studies in Early Russian Hagiography.* Oslo: Solum, 1988.

Bourdieu, Pierre. *The Field of Cultural Production. Essays on Art and Literature.* Cambridge: Polity Press, 1993.

Bourke, Joanna. *Fear: A Cultural History.* London: Shoemaker & Hoard, 2005.

Boym, Svetlana. *Common Places: Mythologies of Everyday Life in Russia.* Cambridge, Mass.: Harvard University Press, 1994.

———. *The Future of Nostalgia.* New York: Basic Books, 2001.

Braidotti, Rosi. "A Cartography of Feminist Post-Postmodernism." *Australian Feminist Studies* 20 (47) (2005): 169–80.

Brinton, Jessica. "Who Needs Money? Forget Splashing the Cash: Happiness Now Lies in Austerity." *Sunday Times,* 22 February 2009, online at http://women.timesonline.co.uk/tol/life_and_style/women/the_way_we _live/article5747047.ece.

Brooks, Neil, and Josh Toth, eds. *The Mourning After: Attending the Wake of Postmodernism.* Amsterdam: Rodopi, 2007.

Brouwer, Sander. "Avvakoem: De afscheiding van de Russische oudgelovigen." In Avvakoem: *Het leven van aartspriester Avvakoem door hemzelf geschreven,* 7–43. Antwerp: Benerus, 2001.

———. "The Bridegroom Who Did Not Come: Social and Amorous Unproductivity from Pushkin to the Silver Age." In *Two Hundred Years of Pushkin. Volume 1: "Pushkin's Secret": Russian Writers Reread and Rewrite Pushkin,* edited by Joe Andrew and Richard Reids, 49–65. Amsterdam: Rodopi, 2003.

Browne, Adam. *The Cult of Sincerity.* Video. Directed by Adam Browne. 2008. YouTube: Amazon Video on Demand.

Bruns, Axel. *Blogs, Wikipedia, Second Life, and Beyond: From Production to Produsage.* New York: Peter Lang, 2008.

Buckland, Warren. "Wes Anderson: A 'Smart' Director of the New Sincerity?" *New Review of Film and Television Studies* 10 (1) (2012): 1–5.

Buckler, Julie. "What Comes after 'Post-Soviet' in Russian Studies?" *PMLA* 124 (1) (2009), online at http://dash.harvard.edu/bitstream/handle/1/4341694 /Buckler_WhatComes.pdf.

Burenkov, Aleksandr. "Novaia iskrennost'." *Be-in,* January 9, 2007, online at http://be-in.ru/journal/index.php?phenomena/9.

Burkhart, Dagmar, ed. *Poetik der Metadiskursivität: Zum postmodernen Prosa-, Film- und Dramenwerk Sorokins.* Munich: Otto Sagner, 1999.

Butler, Judith. *Giving an Account of Oneself.* New York: Fordham University Press, 2005.

Bykov, Dmitrii. "Dostoevskii i psikhologiia russkogo literaturnogo interneta." *Oktiabr'* 3 (2000), online at http://magazines.russ.ru/october/2002/3/byk -pr.html.

Caputo, John D. "The Weakness of God: A Theology of the Event." In *The Mourning After: Attending the Wake of Postmodernism,* edited by Neil Brooks and Josh Toth, 285–302. Amsterdam: Rodopi, 2007.

Carey, Brycchan. *British Abolitionism and the Rhetoric of Sensibility: Writing, Sentiment, and Slavery, 1760–1807.* London: Palgrave Macmillan, 2005.

Carraway, Kate. "Playing Nice: The New Sincerity." *National Post,* 9 March 2011, online at http://news.nationalpost.com/arts/playing-nice-the-new-sincerity.

Chen, Andrew. "New Sincerity in a Postmodern World." *The Midway Review: A Journal of Politics and Culture* 4 (2) (2009), online at http://midwayreview .uchicago.edu/archives/WQ09.pdf.

Chilcote, Ryan. "Russian Sex Row Author Summoned." *CNN.com,* 25 July 2002.

Chung, Yupin, and Thomas Jacobi. "In Search of a New Sincerity? Contemporary Art from China." Workshop for Tate Liverpool, 21 April 2007.

Chuprinin, Sergei. *Zhizn' po poniatiam: Russkaia literatura segodnia.* Moscow: Vremia, 2007.

Cioffi, Frank L. "Postmodernism, Etc.: An Interview with Ihab Hassan." *Style,* 22 September 1999, online at www.articlearchives.com/humanities-social -science/literature-literature/1535105-1.html.

Clark, Katerina, and Galin Tihanov. "Soviet Literary Theory in the 1930s: Battles over Genre and the Boundaries of Modernity." In *A History of Russian Literary Theory and Criticism: The Soviet Age and Beyond,* edited by Evgeny Dobrenko and Galin Tihanov, 109–44. Pittsburgh: University of Pittsburgh Press, 2011.

Collins, Jim. "Genericity in the 90s: Eclectic Irony and the New Sincerity." In *Film Theory Goes to the Movies,* edited by Jim Collins, Hilary Radner, and Ava Preacher Collins, 242–64. New York: Routledge, 1993.

Corcoran, Michael. "The New Sincerity: Austin in the Eighties." In Corcoran, *All over the Map: True Heroes of Texan Music*, 150–57. Austin: University of Texas Press, 2005.

Couperus, Louis. *Eline Vere*. Amsterdam: Rainbow, 2006.

Dal', Vladimir. *Tolkovyi slovar' zhivogo velikorusskago iazyka*. St. Petersburg: M. O. Vol'f, 1905.

Dalakchieva-Lerinska, Mariia. "Sreshchu vsevlastieto na khorizontalite." *Literaturen forum*, Broi (1) (485) (2002), online at http://www.slovo.bg/old/litforum/201/mlerinska.htm.

Danilkin, Lev. "Serdtse Sorokina." *Afisha*, 29 April 2003, online at http://www.afisha.ru/article/vladimir_sorokin/.

Davie, Donald. "On Sincerity: From Wordsworth to Ginsberg." *Encounter*, October 1968, 61–66.

Davydov, Danila. "Dmitrii Vodennikov, Svetlana Lin: Vkusnyi obed dlia ravnodushnykh koshek." *Kriticheskaia massa* 2 (2005), online at magazines.russ.ru/km/2005/2/dd19-pr.html.

Davydova, Marina. "1960-e: O vechno starcheskom v russkoi kul'ture." *Colta*, 9 June 2014, online at http://bit.ly/1G1q8Ao.

de Castro, Mariana. "Oscar Wilde, Fernando Pessoa, and the Art of Lying." *Portuguese Studies* 22 (2) (2006): 219–49.

de Zengotita, Thomas. *Mediated: How the Media Shapes Your World and the Way You Live in It*. New York: Bloomsbury, 2005.

Degot', Ekaterina. "Kinostsenarii Vladimira Sorokina 'Moskva' v novorusskom i postavangardnom kontekstakh." In *Poetik der Metadiskursivität: Zum postmodernen Prosa-, Film- und Dramenwerk Sorokins*, edited by Dagmar Burkhart, 223–28. Munich: Otto Sagner, 1999.

———. "Die russische Kunst in den 1990er Jahren: vom Neorussischen zum Postkommunistischen." In *Na kurort! Russische Kunst Heute*, edited by Georgij Nikitsch and Matthias Winzen, 38–44. Baden-Baden: Staatliche Kunsthalle, 2004.

Degot', Ekaterina, and Oleg Kulik. "Russkii—eto sotsial'naia kategoriia." *Kriticheskaia massa* 1 (2003), online at http://magazines.russ.ru/km/2003/1/kul.html.

Delaloi, Magali. "Emotsii v mikromire Stalina: Sluchai Nikolaia Bukharina (1937–1938). Tipy bol'shevistskoi muzhestvennosti i praktika emotsii." In *Rossiiskaia imperiia chuvstv: Podkhody k kul'turnoi istorii emotsii*, edited by Jan Plamper, Marc Elie, and Schaha Schammadat, 431–57. Moscow: Novoe literaturnoe obozrenie, 2010.

Deleuze, Gilles. *Logique du sens*. Paris: Minuit, 1969.

den Dulk, Allard. *Love Me Till My Heart Stops: Existentialist Engagement in Contemporary American Literature*. Amsterdam: Free University Amsterdam, 2012.

———. *Over de drempel: Voorbij de postmoderne impasse naar een zelfbewust engagement. De literaire zoektocht van Dave Eggers vergeleken met het denken van Friedrich Nietzsche en Albert Camus*. The Hague: Allard den Dulk, 2004.

————. "Voorbij de doelloze ironie: De romans van Dave Eggers en David Foster Wallace vergeleken met het denken van Søren Kierkegaard." In *Het postmodernisme voorbij?* edited by Loes Derksen, Edwin Koster, and Jan van der Stoep, 83–99. Amsterdam: VU University Press, 2008.

Derrida, Jacques. *De la grammatologie*. Paris: Minuit, 1976.

Digital Icons. Russian Elections and Digital Media. Special issue of *Digital Icons* 7 (2012), online at http://www.digitalicons.org/issue07/.

"Discourse Studies." Centre for Discourse Studies, Aalborg University. Last modified February 19, 2007, online at diskurs.hum.aau.dk/english /discourse.htm.

Dobrenko, Evgeny. "Byl i ostaetsia (vmesto predisloviia)." In *Nekanonicheskii klassik: Dmitrii Aleksandrovich Prigov (1940–2007)*, edited by Evgeny Dobrenko, Ilya Kukulin, Mark Lipovetsky, and Maria Maiofis, 10–13. Moscow: Novoe literaturnoe obozrenie, 2010.

————. "Literary Criticism and the Transformations of the Literary Field during the Cultural Revolution, 1928–1932." In *A History of Russian Literary Theory and Criticism*, edited by Evgeny Dobrenko and Galin Tihanov, 43–64. Pittsburgh: University of Pittsburgh Press, 2011.

————. "Preodolenie ideologii." *Volga* 11 (1990), 183.

Dobrenko, Evgeny, Ilya Kukulin, Mark Lipovetsky, and Maria Maiofis, eds. *Nekanonicheskii klassik: Dmitrii Aleksandrovich Prigov (1940–2007)*. Moscow: Novoe literaturnoe obozrenie, 2010.

Dostoevsky, Fedor. *Sobranie sochinenii v piatnadtsati tomakh*. Leningrad: Nauka, 1995.

Dremliugin, Aleksandr. "Aleksei Beliaev-Gintovt: Veriu v nashu bezogovorochnuiu pobedu!" *Novorossiia*, 27 September 2014, online at http://novorossia .su/ru/node/7186.

Dubin, Boris, and Lev Gudkov, *Literatura kak sotsial'nyi institut*. Moscow: Novoe literaturnoe obozrenie, 1994.

Dudina, Irina, Mikhail Epstein, and Valerii Savchuk, "Svetloi pamiati postmoderna posviashchaetsia." *Khudozhestvennyi zhurnal* 64 (2007), online at xz.gif.ru/numbers/64/epshtein-savchuk/.

Dugin, Aleksandr. "Aleksandr Dugin: Zakoldovannaia sreda novykh imperii." *Khudozhestvennyi zhurnal* 54 (2004), online at http://xz.gif.ru/numbers/54 /dugin/.

————. *Geopolitika postmoderna*. St. Petersburg: Amfora, 2007.

Dukkon, Agnes. "Problema 'literaturnosti' i original'nosti' v proizvedeniiakh Turgeneva 1850-kh gg." In *"Mezhdunarodnaia konferentsiia 'Pushkin i Turgenev,'"* edited by Vladimir Markovich, 41–42. St. Petersburg: Orel, 1998.

Dyer, Richard. *Stars*. London: BFI, 1998.

Eaglestone, Robert. "Postmodernism and Ethics against the Metaphysics of Comprehension." In *The Cambridge Companion to Postmodernism*, edited by Steven Connor, 182–96. Cambridge: Cambridge University Press, 2004.

Eggers, Dave. *A Heartbreaking Work of Staggering Genius*. New York: Simon & Schuster, 2000.

Emerson, Caryl. *The Cambridge Introduction to Russian Literature*. Cambridge: Cambridge University Press, 2012.

Engel, Christine. "Vom Tauwetter zur postsozialistischen Ära (1953–2000)." In *Russische Literaturgeschichte*, edited by Klaus Städtke, 349–406. Stuttgart: Metzler, 2002.

Engels, Frederick, and Karl Marx. *Manifesto of the Communist Party*, 1848, online at http://www.marxists.org/archive/marx/works/download/pdf/Manifesto.pdf.

Epstein, Mikhail N. "After the Future: On the New Consciousness in Literature." *South Atlantic Quarterly* 90 (2) (1991): 409–45.

———. *After the Future: The Paradoxes of Postmodernism and Contemporary Russian Culture*. Amherst: University of Massachusetts Press, 1995.

———. "A Catalog of the New Poetries." In *Re-Entering the Sign: Articulating New Russian Culture*, edited by Ellen Berry and Anesa Miller-Pogacar, 208–12. Ann Arbor: University of Michigan Press, 1995.

———. "Conclusion: On the Place of Postmodernism in Postmodernity." In *Russian Postmodernism: New Perspectives on Post-Soviet Culture*, edited by Mikhail N. Epstein, Alexander A. Genis, and Slobodanka M. Vladiv-Glover, 456–68. New York: Berghahn, 1999.

———. "Katalog novykh poezii." In *Sovremennaia russkaia poeziia posle 1966: Dvuiazychnaia antologiia*, 359–67. Berlin: Oberbaum, 1990.

———. "Nulevoi tsikl stoletiia: Eksploziv—vzryvnoi stil' 2000-kh." *Zvezda* 2 (2006), online at http://magazines.russ.ru/zvezda/2006/2/ep16.html.

———. "O novoi sentimental'nosti." *Strelets* 2 (78) (1996): 223–31.

———. *Postmodern v Rossii*. Moscow: R. Elinina, 2002.

———. "Proto-, ili konets postmodernizma." *Znamia* 3 (1996): 196–209.

Epstein, Mikhail N., Aleksandr A. Genis, and Slobodanka Vladiv-Glover, eds. *Russian Postmodernism: New Perspectives on Post-Soviet Culture*. New York: Berghahn, 1999.

Erofeev, Viktor. "Pamiatnik dlia khrestomatii." *Teatr* (1) (1993): 136–39.

Eshelman, Raoul. "Performatism, or the End of Postmodernism." *Anthropoetics* 6 (2) (2001), online at www.anthropoetics.ucla.edu/apo602/perform.htm.

———. *Performatism, or the End of Postmodernism*. Aurora, Colo.: Davies, 2008.

Etkind, Alexander. "Putin's History Lessons." Project Syndicate, 15 September 2009, online at http://www.project-syndicate.org/commentary/etkind7/English.

———. *Warped Mourning*, Stanford: Stanford University Press, 2013.

Farrell, Frank B. *Subjectivity, Realism, and Postmodernism: The Recovery of the World in Present Philosophy*. Cambridge: Cambridge University Press, 1996.

Febvre, Lucien, and Henri-Jean Martin. *The Coming of the Book*. London: Verso, 1976.

Ferguson, Harvie. "Glamour and the End of Irony." *Hedgehog Review* Fall (1999): 9–16.

Ferrara, Alessandro. *Reflective Authenticity: Rethinking the Project of Modernity.* New York: Routledge, 1998.

Filippo, Maria San. "A Cinema of Recession: Micro-Budgeting, Micro-Drama, and the 'Mumblecore' Movement." *Cineaction* 85 (2011), online at http://nicolekay.com/cine/wp-content/uploads/2014/04/issue85sample.pdf.

Fishzon, Anna. "The Operatics of Everyday Life, or, How Authenticity Was Defined in Late Imperial Russia." *Slavic Review* 70 (4) (2011): 795–818.

Fitzgerald, Jonathan D. *Not Your Mother's Morals: How the New Sincerity Is Changing Pop Culture for the Better.* Colorado Springs: Bondfire Books, 2012.

———. "Sincerity, Not Irony, Is Our Age's New Ethos." *Atlantic*, 20 November 2012, online at http://www.theatlantic.com/entertainment/archive/2012/11/sincerity-not-irony-is-our-ages-ethos/265466/.

Fitzpatrick, Sheila. *Tear off the Masks! Identity and Imposture in Twentieth-Century Russia.* Princeton: Princeton University Press, 2005.

5-TV. "Noch' na piatom: Dmitrii Vodennikov." Television show. 5-TV, directed by Konstantin Shavlovskii, 9 November 2010, online at http://www.5-tv.ru/video/505807/.

Flax, Jane. "Soul Service: Foucault's 'Care of the Self' as Politics and Ethics." In *The Mourning After*, ed. by Josh Toth and Neil Brooks, 79–99. Amsterdam: Rodopi, 2007.

Florida, Richard. *The Rise of the Creative Class: And How It's Transforming Work, Leisure, Community and Everyday Life.* New York: Perseus, 2002.

Fokkema, Douwe. "The Semiotics of Literary Postmodernism." In *International Postmodernism*, edited by Johannes Bertens and Douwe Fokkema, 15–43. Amsterdam: John Benjamins, 1997.

Foster, Hal. *The Return of the Real: The Avant-Garde at the End of the Century.* Cambridge, Mass.: MIT Press, 1996.

Foucault, Michel. *Fearless Speech.* Los Angeles: Semiotext(e), 2001.

Fraser, Nancy. "Transnationalizing the Public Sphere: On the Legitimacy and Efficacy of Public Opinion in a Post-Westphalian World." *Theory, Culture and Society* 24 (4) (2007): 7–30.

Freidin, Gregory. "Transfiguration of Kitsch—Timur Kibirov's *Sentiments*." In *Endquote: Sots-Art Literature and Soviet Grand Style*, edited by Marina Balina, Nancy Condee, and Evgeny Dobrenko, 123–46. Evanston, Ill.: Northwestern University Press, 2000.

Funk, Wolfgang, Florian Gross, and Irmtraud Huber, eds. *The Aesthetics of Authenticity: Medial Constructions of the Real.* Bielefeld: Transcript, 2012.

Gabler, Neil. *Life: the Movie.* New York: Vintage, 1998.

Gabowitsch, Mischa. "Fascism as *Stiob.*" *kultura* 4 (2009): 3–8.

———. *Protest in Putin's Russia.* Cambridge: Polity Press, forthcoming.

———. *Putin Kaputt!? Russlands neue Protestkultur.* Berlin: Suhrkamp, 2013.

Galieva, Zhanna. *Prigov i kontseptualizm: Sbornik statei i materialov.* Moscow: Novoe literaturnoe obozrenie, 2014.

Gandlevsky [Gandlevskii], Sergei. "An Attempt at a Manifesto." In *Third Wave: The New Russian Poetry,* edited by Kent Johnson and Stephen M. Ashby, 117–20. Ann Arbor: University of Michigan Press, 1992.

————. "Razreshenie ot skorbi." In *Lichnoe delo No: Literaturno-khudozhestvennyi al'manakh,* edited by Lev Rubinstein, 226–31. Moscow: V/O Soiuzteatr, 1991.

Gandlevskii, Sergei, and Dmitrii Prigov. "Mezhdu imenem i imidzhem." *Literaturnaia gazeta,* 12 May 1993, 5.

Garlinger, Paul. "All about Agrado, Or the Sincerity of Camp in Almodóvar's Todo Sobre Mi Madre." *Journal of Spanish Cultural Studies* 5 (1) (2004): 117–34.

Gel'fand, Mark. *Protiv burzhuaznogo liberalizma v khudozhestvennoi literature: Diskussiia o "Perevale."* Moscow: Izdatel'stvo Kommunisticheskoi akademii, 1931.

Gibson-Graham, J. K. *A Postcapitalist Politics.* Minneapolis: University of Minnesota Press, 2006.

Gilmore, James H., and B. Joseph Pine II. *Authenticity: What Consumers Really Want.* Boston: Harvard Business School Press, 2007.

Gioia, Ted. *The Imperfect Art: Reflections on Jazz and Modern Culture.* Stanford: Portable Stanford, 1988.

Goffman, Erving. *The Presentation of Self in Everyday Life.* New York: Overlook Press, 1959.

Golynko-Vol'fson, Dmitrii. "Chitaia Prigova: neodnoznachnoe i neochevidnoe." In *Nekanonicheskii klassik: Dmitrii Prigov (1940–2007),* edited by Evgeny Dobrenko, Ilya Kukulin, Mark Lipovetsky, and Maria Maiofis, 145–81. Moscow: Novoe literaturnoe obozrenie, 2010.

————. "'Kopeika' i iznanka ideologii." *Iskusstvo kino* 1 (2003), online at http://kinoart.promodo.ru/2003/n1-article18.html.

————. "SMSte iskrenne: SMS-poeziia v sovremennom medial'nom prostranstve." *Nebosamolet* 4 (2006), online at golynko.narod.ru/critics_lit_sms.htm.

————. "Strategiia i politika vsego novogo: Kak segodnia pisat' kontseptual'nuiu biografiiu Timura Novikova i peterburgskogo iskusstva 90-kh." *Khudozhestvennyi zhurnal* 70 (2008), online at http://xz.gif.ru/numbers/70/golynko-timur/

————. "Totalitarian Laughter as Magic Ritual: The 'Soviet' Poems by D. A. Prigov in the Context of Moscow Conceptualism." Paper presented at conference entitled "Totalitarian Laughter: Cultures of the Comic under Socialism," Princeton University, 15–17 May 2009.

Goscilo, Helena, and Vlad Strukov, eds. *Celebrity and Glamour in Contemporary Russia: Shocking Chic.* Abingdon: Routledge, 2011.

Gountas, Sandra, and Felix Mavondo. "Emotions, Sincerity and Consumer Satisfaction." Paper presented at ANZMAC conference entitled "Services Marketing," 2005, online at smib.vuw.ac.nz:8081/WWW/ANZMAC2005/cd-site/pdfs/16-Services/16-Gountas.pdf.

Gracián, Balthasar. *Oráculo manual y arte de prudencia.* Madrid: Mundo mágico, 2000.

Gray, Christopher. "Something in the Way." *Music,* 9 April 2004, online at http://www.austinchronicle.com/music/2004-04-09/205889/.

Green, Jeremy. *Late Postmodernism: American Fiction at the Millennium.* New York: Palgrave Macmillan, 2005.

Greenblatt, Stephen. *Learning to Curse: Essays in Early Modern Culture.* New York: Routledge, 1990.

———. *Renaissance Self-Fashioning: From More to Shakespeare.* Chicago: University of Chicago Press, 1980.

Greenleaf, Monika, and Stephen Moeller-Sally, eds. *Russian Subjects: Empire, Nation, and the Culture of the Golden Age.* Evanston, Ill.: Northwestern University Press, 1998.

Gribachev, Nikolai. "O samovyrazhenii v lirike." In Gribachev, *Sobranie sochinenii v piati tomakh,* 5: 393–406. Moscow: Khudozhestvennaia literatura, 1971–73.

Gribachev, Nikolai, and Sergei Smirnov, "'Violonchelist' poluchil kanifol'." In Gribachev and Smirnov, *Razgovor pered s"ezdom,* 265–78. Moscow: Sovetskii pisatel', 1954.

Grishkovets, Evgenii. "Evgenii Grishkovets o 'novoi iskrennosti.'" *Time Out* 12 (2009), online at http://www.timeout.ru/journal/feature/3930/.

Gross, Florian. "'Brooklyn Zack Is Real': Irony and Sincere Authenticity in 30 Rock." In *The Aesthetics of Authenticity,* edited by Wolfgang Funk, Florian Gross, and Irmtraud Huber, 237–60. Bielefeld: Transcript, 2012.

Gross, Thomas. "Alter Protest in neuen Klamotten." *Die Zeit* 10 (2003), online at www.zeit.de/2003/10/Alter_Protest_in_neuen_Klamotten.

Groys, Boris. *Die Erfindung Russlands.* Munich: Carl Hanser, 1995.

———. *Gesamtkunstwerk Stalin.* Moscow: Ad Marginem, 2013 (1st publication 1987).

———. "Moskovskii romanticheskii kontseptualizm." *A-Ia* 1 (1979), online at http://plucer.livejournal.com/70772.html and http://plucer.livejournal.com/70956.html.

———. *On the New.* London: Verso, 2014.

———. "The Other Gaze. Russian Unofficial Art's View of the Soviet World." In *Postmodernism and the Postsocialist Condition: Politicized Art under Late Socialism,* edited by Aleš Erjavec, 55–90. Berkeley: University of California Press, 2003.

———. "The Production of Sincerity." In Groys, *Going Public,* 38–49. Berlin: Sternberg Press, 2010.

———. *Unter Verdacht: Eine Phänomenologie der Medien.* Munich: Carl Hanser 2000.

Gubailovskii, Vladimir, and Irina Rodnianskaia. "Knigi neobshchego pol'zovaniia: Opyt dialoga o 'ne takoi' proze." *Zarubezhnye zapiski* 12 (2007), online at magazines.russ.ru/zz/2007/12/ro8.html.

Gudkov, Lev. *Negativnaia identichnost': Stat'i 1997–2002.* Moscow: Novoe literaturnoe obozrenie, 2004.

Guilhamet, Leon. *The Sincere Ideal: Studies in Sincerity in Eighteenth-Century English Literature*. Montreal: McGill-Queens University Press, 1974.

Gusejnov, Gasan. "Berloga vebloga: Vvedenie v erraticheskuiu semantiku." *Govorim po-russki,* March (2005), online at http://speakrus.ru/gg/microprosa _erratica-1.htm.

———. "Instrumenty opisaniia nepolnoi kommunikatsii v blogosfere." In *From Poets to Padonki: Linguistic Authority & Norm Negotiation in Modern Russian Culture,* edited by Ingunn Lunde and Martin Paulsen, 275–88. Bergen: Slavica Bergensia, 2009.

Guy, Josephine M., ed. *The Victorian Age: An Anthology of Sources and Documents*. London: Routledge, 1998.

Guyer, Sara. *Romanticism after Auschwitz*. Stanford: Stanford University Press, 2007.

Habermas, Jürgen. *The Postnational Constellation: Political Essays*. Cambridge, Mass.: MIT Press, 2001.

———. *Vorstudien und Ergänzungen zur Theorie des kommunikativen Handelns*. Frankfurt: Suhrkamp, 1984.

Halfin, Igal. *Terror in My Soul: Communist Autobiographies on Trial*. Cambridge, Mass.: Harvard University Press, 2003.

Halttunen, Karen. *Confidence Men and Painted Women: A Study of Middle-Class Culture in America, 1830–1870*. New Haven: Yale University Press, 1982.

Hamilton, Caroline D. *One Man Zeitgeist: Dave Eggers, Publishing and Publicity*. New York: Continuum, 2010.

Harding, Luke. "Putin's Tears: Why So Sad, Vlad?" *Guardian,* 5 March 2012, online at http://www.theguardian.com/world/2012/mar/05/putin-tears-vlad -election.

Harris, Wendell V., ed. *Beyond Poststructuralism: The Speculations of Theory and the Experience of Reading*. University Park: Penn State University Press, 1996.

Hayles, Katherina, and Todd Gannon. "Mood Swings: The Aesthetics of Ambient Emergence." In *The Mourning After: Attending the Wake of Postmodernism,* edited by Neil Brooks and Josh Todd, 99–143. Amsterdam: Rodopi, 2007.

Hebdige, Dick. *Hiding in the Light: On Images and Things*. London: Routledge, 1988.

Heckel, Theodor. *Werke*. Zurich: Thomas, 1947.

Heisse, David R., and Cassandra Calhan. "Emotion Norms in Interpersonal Events." *Social Psychology Quarterly* 58 (1995): 223–40.

Hellbeck, Jochen. *Revolution on My Mind: Writing a Diary under Stalin*. Cambridge, Mass.: Harvard University Press, 2006.

Hermans, Hubert, and Harry Kempen. *The Dialogical Self: Meaning as Movement*. San Diego: Academic Press, 1993.

Hesmondhalgh, David. "Cultural and Creative Industries." In *Handbook of Cultural Analysis,* edited by Tony Bennett and John Frow, 552–70. Oxford: Blackwell, 2008.

Hoberek, Andrew, ed. *After Postmodernism*. Special issue of *Twentieth-Century Literature* 53 (3) (2007).

Hoerschelmann, Kathrin, and Alison Stenning. "History, Geography and Difference in the Post-Socialist World: Or, Do We Still Need Post-Socialism?" *Antipode* 40 (2) (2008): 312–35.

Holmgren, Beth. "Introduction." In *The Russian Memoir: History and Literature,* edited by Beth Holmgren, ix–xxxix. Evanston, Ill.: Northwestern University Press, 2003.

Hosking, Geoffrey. *Trust: A History*. Oxford: Oxford University Press, 2014.

Hung, Shu, and Joseph Magliaro, eds. *By Hand: The Use of Craft in Contemporary Art*. New York: Princeton Architectural Press, 2007.

Hunt, Lynn. *The Family Romance of the French Revolution*. Berkeley: University of California Press, 1992.

———. *Inventing Human Rights: A History*. New York: Norton, 2007.

Hutcheon, Linda. *Irony's Edge: The Theory and Politics of Irony*. London: Routledge, 1994.

Hutchings, Stephen. "Editorial." *BASEES Newsletter,* February 2011.

Iampol'skii, Mikhail. *Prigov: Ocherki khudozhestvennogo nominalizma*. Moscow: Novoe literaturnoe obozrenie, 2016.

———. "Vysokii parodizm: Filosofiia i poetika romana Dmitriia Aleksandrov-icha Prigova 'Zhivite v Moskve.'" In *Nekanonicheskii klassik: Dmitrii Prigov (1940–2007),* edited by Evgeny Dobrenko, Ilya Kukulin, Mark Lipovetsky, and Maria Maiofis, 181–252. Moscow: Novoe literaturnoe obozrenie, 2010.

Il'in, Ivan. *Poiushchee serdtse*. Moscow: Izdatel'stvo Pravoslavnogo bratstva sviatogo apostola Ioanna Bogoslova, 2009.

———. "Protiv Rossii" (1948), online at http://tonos.ru/articles/greatpredict 7#ilyin.

Ivanova, Ekaterina. "Molodaia poeziia v poiskakh zhivogo slova." *Kontinent* 133 (2007): 419–30.

Ivanova, Nataliia. "Iskusstvo pri svete iskrennosti." *Znamia* 3 (2011), online at http://magazines.russ.ru/znamia/2011/3/iv11.html.

———. *Nostal'iashchee* (1997), online at http://magazines.russ.ru/znamia/dom /ivanova/ivano.html.

Jackson, John. *Real Black: Adventures in Racial Sincerity*. Chicago: University of Chicago Press, 2005.

Jackson, Matthew Jesse. *The Experimental Group: Ilya Kabakov, Moscow Conceptualism, Soviet Avant-Gardes*. Chicago: University of Chicago Press, 2010.

Jameson, Fredric. *Postmodernism: Or, The Cultural Logic of Late Capitalism*. Durham, N.C.: Duke University Press, 1991.

Jeanneney, Jean-Noël. *Google and the Myth of Universal Knowledge: A View from Europe*. Chicago: University of Chicago Press, 2006.

Jenkins, Henry, Katie Clinton, Ravi Purushotma, Alice J. Robison, and Margaret Weigel. "Confronting the Challenges of Participatory Culture: Media

Education for the 21st Century" (2009), online at https://mitpress.mit.edu
/sites/default/files/titles/free_download/9780262513623_Confronting_the
_Challenges.pdf.

Johns, Adrian. *The Nature of Books: Print and Knowledge in the Making.* Chicago:
University of Chicago Press, 1998.

Kabakov, Ilya. "D. A. Prigov i ego 'bezumnaia iskrennost.'" *OpenSpace,* 5 May
2008, online at http://www.openspace.ru/art/events/details/962/.

Kalinin, Ilya. "Dmitri A. Prigov: A Challenge to Cultural Authority." Round-
table contribution presented at the annual meeting of the Association for
Slavic, East European, and Eurasian Studies, Washington, D.C., 17–20
November 2011.

Kanishchev, Pavel. "Beliaev-Gintovt: 'Ia videl absoliutno geroicheskuiu
real'nost'": Interv'iu s khudozhnikom Alekseem Beliaevym-Gintovtom,
vernuvshimsia iz Iuzhnoi Osetii." *Rossiia-3,* undated, online at http://rossia3
.ru/culture/gintovtosetinte.

Kanunova, Faina. "Evoliutsiia sentimentalizma Karamzina ('Moia ispoved')." In
*XVIII vek, sbornik 7: Rol' i znachenie literatury XVIII veka v istorii russkoi
kul'tury: k 70-letiiu so dnia rozhdeniia chlena-korrespondenta AN SSSR P. N.
Berkova,* edited by Dmitrii Likhachev, 286–90. Moscow: Nauka, 1966.

Karamzin, Nikolai. *Sochineniia v dvukh tomakh.* Leningrad: Khudozhestvennaia
literatura, 1984.

Karmodi, Ostap. "Sorokin vyvel sebia v raskhod." *Gazeta.ru,* 29 March 2002,
online at http://www.gazeta.ru/print/2002/03/29/sorokinvyvel.shtml.

Kaspe, Irina. "Govorit tot, kto govorit 'ia': Vmesto epiloga." *Novoe literaturnoe obozrenie* 96 (2009), online at magazines.russ.ru/nlo/2009/96/ka28-pr.html.

———, ed. *Status dokumenta: Okonchatel'naia bumazhka ili otchuzhdennoe
svidetel'stvo?* Moscow: Novoe literaturnoe obozrenie, 2013.

Kaspe, Irina, and Varvara Smurova. "Livejournal.com, russkaia versiia: Poplach'
o nem, poka on zhivoi . . ." *Neprikosnovennyi zapas* 24 (4) (2002), online at
magazines.russ.ru/nz/2002/4/kaspe-pr.html.

Katsov, Gennadii. "V luchshikh svoikh obraztsakh russkaia literatura
70–1990-kh—eto vse-taki ryba bez parashiuta." *Gkatsov.com,* 15 January
1992, online at http://gkatsov.com/russian_literature_70_90.htm.

Katsva, Leonid. *Istoriia Rossii: Sovetskii period (1917–1991).* Moscow: RGU, 2003,
online at http://it-n.ru/communities.aspx?cat_no=2715&lib_no=48533&tmpl
=lib.3.

Kelly, Adam. "David Foster Wallace and the New Sincerity in American Fiction."
In *Consider David Foster Wallace: Critical Essays,* edited by David Hering,
131–47. Los Angeles: Sideshow, 2010.

Kelly, Catriona. "Pravo na emotsii, pravil'nye emotsii: Upravlenie chuvstvami
v Rossii posle epokhi Prosveshcheniia." In *Rossiiskaia imperiia chuvstv:
Podkhody k kul'turnoi istorii emotsii,* edited by Jan Plamper, Marc Elie, and
Schaha Schammadat, 51–78. Moscow: Novoe literaturnoe obozrenie, 2010.

———. *Refining Russia: Advice Literature, Polite Culture, and Gender from Catherine to Yeltsin.* Oxford: Oxford University Press, 2001.

Kessels, Erik. *Amateurism.* Amsterdam: KesselsKramer Publishing, 2008.

Keymolen, Esther. "Esther Keymolen Wondered: Why Is It That We Put So Much Faith in Social Networks and Online Businesses?" Interview Series: Meet Our PhD Candidates. 2016, online at http://www.egs3h.eur.nl /research/meet-our-phd-candidates/esther-keymolen-philosophy/.

———. "Trust on the Line: A Philosophical Exploration of Trust in the Networked Era." Ph.D. diss., Erasmus University Rotterdam, 2016.

Khachaturov, Sergei. "Prisiaga na 'Veriu': Sovremennoe iskusstvo ishchet novuiu iskrennost'." *Vremia novostei,* 5 December 2006, online at http://www.vremya.ru/print/167099.html.

Khersonskii, Mikhail. *Novaia iskrennost': Manifest.* Video. Directed by Mikhail Khersonskii. 2011. YouTube Video, online at http://www.youtube.com/watch ?v=cHO8W5F4ZhA.

Kibirov, Timur. *Kara-baras.* Moscow: Vremia, 2006.

———. "*Kto kuda—a ia v Rossiiu . . .*" Moscow: Vremia, 2001.

Kimerling Wirtschafter, Elise. *Social Identity in Imperial Russia.* DeKalb: Northern Illinois University Press, 1997.

King, Geoff. *Spectacular Narratives: Contemporary Hollywood and Frontier Mythology.* London: Tauris, 2000.

Kirby, Alan. "The Death of Postmodernism and Beyond." *Philosophy Now* 58 (2006), online at https://philosophynow.org/issues/58/The_Death_of _Postmodernism_And_Beyond.

Kirchmaier, Viktor. "Die Verdichtung der Sinne." Exhibition description for *Der Tod,* Tiefbunker am Blochplatz, Berlin, 2001, online at www.mais-de.de /Mais-flash.html.

Kishkovsky, Sophia. "A Cultural Awakening in Russia." *New York Times,* 30 June 2009, online at http://www.nytimes.com/2009/07/01/world/europe/01iht -moscow.html.

Klein, Joachim. "Deržavin: Wahrheit und Aufrichtigkeit im Herrscherlob." *Zeitschrift für Slavische Philologie* 67 (1) (2010): 27–51.

Klosterman, Chuck. "The Carly Simon Principle: Sincerity and Pop Greatness." In *This Is Pop: In Search of the Elusive at Experience Music Project,* edited by Eric Weisbard, 257–65. Cambridge, Mass.: Harvard University Press, 2004.

Kochetkova, Natal'ia. "Dmitrii Prigov: 'Iskrennee vyskazyvanie ushlo v pop-zonu.'" *Izvestiia,* 16 March 2005, online at http://www.izvestia.ru/person /article1394660/.

Koldobskaia, Marina. *Iskusstvo v bol'shom dolgu.* Moscow: Nomi, 2007.

Kolesnikov, Andrei. "O neiskrennosti v literature." *Gazeta.ru,* 12 August 2003, online at http://www.gazeta.ru/column/kolesnikov/171257.shtml.

Komaromi, Ann. "The Material Existence of Soviet Samizdat." *Slavic Review* 63 (3) (2004): 597–618.

Koretskii, Vasilii. "Takaia vot 'novaia iskrennost'": Poludokumental'naia povest' o nastoiashchikh liudiakh iz vnutrennei Mongolii." *Time Out,* 13 November 2007, online at http://www.stengazeta.net/article.html?article=4043.

Korolenko, Psoi. "Put' Bro." *Polit.ru,* 21 September 2004, online at http://www.polit.ru/culture/2004/09/21/sorok.html.

Korsten, Frans-Willem. "The Irreconcilability of Hypocrisy and Sincerity." In *The Rhetoric of Sincerity,* edited by Ernst van Alphen, Mieke Bal, and Carel Smith, 60–77. Stanford: Stanford University Press, 2009.

Korthals Altes, Liesbeth. "Blessedly post-ironic? Enkele tendensen in de hedendaagse literatuur en literatuurwetenschap." Groningen: E. J. Korthals Altes, 2001.

———. "Sincerity, Reliability and Other Ironies—Notes on Dave Eggers' *A Heartbreaking Work of Staggering Genius.*" In *Narrative Unreliability in the Twentieth-Century First-Person Novel,* edited by Elke D'Hoker and Gunther Martens, 107–28. Berlin: Walter de Gruyter, 2008.

Kostiukov, Leonid. "Postoronnie soobrazheniia [review of Dmitrii Bak, ed., *Genius loci*]: Sovremennaia poeziia Moskvy i Peterburga." *Druzhba narodov* 6 (2000): 210–15.

Kostyrko, Sergei. "WWW Obozrenie Sergei Kostyrko." *Novyi mir* 7 (2005), online at magazines.russ.ru/novyi_mi/2005/7/kost18-pr.html.

Kotykhov, Vladimir. "Al'fred Shnittke: Est' nechto bol'shee, chem muzyka i zhizn'." *Moskovskii Komsomolets,* 22 November 1999, online at http://www.mk.ru/old/article/1999/11/22/133579-alfred-shnitke-est-nechto-bolshee-chem-muzyika-i-zhizn.html.

Krijnen, Joost. *Holocaust Impiety in Jewish American Literature: Memory, Identity, (Post-)Postmodernism.* Leiden: Brill, 2016.

———. "Impious Renewal: The Holocaust and Jewish American Fiction after Postmodernism." Ph.D. diss., University of Groningen, 2014.

Kropotkin, Petr. *Memoirs of a Revolutionist.* Boston: Houghton Mifflin, 1899.

———. *Zapiski revolutsionera.* Moscow: Mysl', 1990.

Kruchenykh, Aleksei. "Declaration of Transrational Language." In *Words in Revolution: Russian Futurist Manifestoes 1912–1928,* edited by Anna Lawton and Herbert Eagle, 182–84. Washington: New Academia, 2005.

Kugel', Mariia. "Iskrennost' lzhetsov: Mikhail Lotman—o 'russkom mire' i vnutrennikh varvarakh." *Radio Svoboda,* 1 March 2015, online at http://www.svoboda.org/content/article/26873380.html.

Kukulin, Ilya. "Every Trend Makes a Brand." *Novoe literaturnoe obozrenie* 56 (2002), online at magazines.russ.ru/nlo/2002/56/kuk1.html.

Kukulin, Ilya, and Mark Lipovetsky. "Post-Soviet Literary Criticism." In *A History of Russian Literary Theory and Criticism: The Soviet Age and Beyond,* edited by Evgeny Dobrenko and Galin Tihanov, 287–306. Pittsburgh: University of Pittsburgh Press, 2011.

Kukushkin, Vladimir. "Mudrost' Sorokina." *Novoe literaturnoe obozrenie* 56 (2002), online at http://www.srkn.ru/criticism/kukushkin.shtml.

Kulik, Oleg. "Artist's Favourites." *Spike Art Quarterly* 12 (2007), online at http://www.spikeart.at/en/a/back/back/Artist_s_Favourites_14.

———. "Beseda s Olegom Kulikom." *Zhurnal moskovskogo muzeia sovremennogo iskusstva* 2 (2007): 57–62.

Kulik, Oleg, and Vladimir Sorokin. *V glub' Rossii*. Moscow: Institut Sovremennogo Iskusstva, 1994.

Kulle, Viktor. "'Ia ne veshchaiu, ia boltaiu': Beseda Viktora Kulle s Timurom Kibirovym 21 noiabria 1997 g." *Literaturnoe obozrenie* 1 (1998): 10–16.

———. "'Novaia iskrennost' po-ital'ianski." *Novyi mir,* issue/year not indicated, online at http://magazines.russ.ru:81/novyi_mi/redkol/kulle/dop/article /ono.html.

Kuntsman, Adi. "'With a Shade of Disgust': Affective Politics of Sexuality and Class in Memoirs of the Stalinist Gulag." *Slavic Review* 68 (2) (2009), 308–28.

Küpper, Stephen. "Präprintium: A Berlin Exhibition of Moscow Samizdat Books." *Other Voices* 1 (2) (1998), online at http://www.othervoices.org/1.2 /skuepper/samizdat.html.

Kuritsyn, Viacheslav. *Russkii literaturnyi postmodernizm,* 2000, online at www .guelman.ru/slava/postmod/9.html.

———. "Vremia mnozhit' pristavki: K poniatiiu postpostmodernizma." *Oktiabr'* 7 (1997): 178–83.

Kurliandtseva, Elena. "Absurd spaset mir, schitaet khudozhnik." *Kommersant,* 26 November 1993, online at http://www.kommersant.ru/doc/65723.

Kuz'min, Dmitrii. "Postkontseptualizm: Kak by nabroski k monografii." *Novoe literaturnoe obozrenie* 50 (2001): 459–77.

———. "Russkaia poeziia v nachale XXI veka." *Apollinarii* 1 (2006), online at http://musagetes.com/readText.jsp?tid=677&aid=217&cid=4.

———, ed. *Legko byt' iskrennim: Po sledam IX Moskovskogo Festivalia verlibra.* Moscow: Argo-Risk, 2002.

Laird, Sally. *Voices of Russian Literature: Interviews with Ten Contemporary Writers.* Oxford: Oxford University Press, 1994.

Larrissy, Edward, ed. *Romanticism and Postmodernism.* Cambridge: Cambridge University Press, 2010.

Leiby, Sofia. "I Am Such a Failure: Poetry on, around, and about the Internet." In Jaakko Paallasvuo, *New Sincerity: Exhibition Catalogue.* London: Jaakko Paalasvuo, B.C., Beach London, and Victory Press, 2011, online at http:// pooool.info/i-am-such-a-failure-poetry-on-around-and-about-the-internet/.

Leiderman, Naum. *Postrealizm: Teoreticheskii ocherk.* Ekaterinburg: Slovesnik, 2005.

Leiderman, Naum, and Mark Lipovetsky. "Zhizn' posle smerti, ili novye svedeniia o realizme." *Novyi mir* 7 (1993), online at magazines.russ.ru/novyi _mi/1993/7/litkrit.html.

Lermontov, Mikhail. *A Hero of Our Time.* Translated by Vladimir Nabokov in collaboration with Dmitri Nabokov. Ann Arbor: Ardis, 1998.

————. *Sobranie sochinenii v chetyrekh tomakh*. Moscow/Leningrad: Izdatel'stvo Akademii Nauk SSSR, 1962.

Lipovetsky, Mark. *Paralogii: Transformatsii (post)modernistskogo diskursa v kul'ture 1920–2000-kh godov*. Moscow: Novoe literaturnoe obozrenie, 2008.

————. "Prigov i Batai: Estetika sistemnoi rastraty." In *Nekanonicheskii klassik: Dmitrii Prigov (1940–2007)*, edited by Evgeny Dobrenko, Ilya Kukulin, Mark Lipovetsky, and Maria Maiofis, 328–49. Moscow: Novoe literaturnoe obozrenie, 2010.

————. *Russian Postmodernist Fiction: Dialogue with Chaos*. New York: M. E. Sharpe, 1999.

————. *Russkii postmodernizm: Ocherki istoricheskoi poetiki*. Ekaterinburg: Ural'skii gosudarstvennyi pedagogicheskii universitet, 1997.

Lipsky, David. "The Lost Years & Last Days of David Foster Wallace." *Rolling Stone*, 30 October 2008, 100–111.

Loe, Erlend. *Naiv.Super.* Oslo: Cappelen, 1996.

Lomonosov, Mikhail. *Polnoe sobranie sochinenii*. Moscow: Izdatel'stvo Akademii Nauk SSSSR, 1950–83.

López, José, and Garry Potter, eds. *After Postmodernism: An Introduction to Critical Realism*. New York: Athlone, 2001.

Loshak, Andrei. "Prozhivem bez gosudarstva." *OpenSpace*, 2 November 2010, online at http://os.colta.ru/society/projects/201/details/18512/.

Lotman, Iurii. "Puti razvitiia russkoi prozy 1800–1810-kh godov." *Uchenye zapiski TGU, vypusk 104: Trudy po russkoi i slavianskoi filologii*, 4: 3–57. Tartu: Tartuskii Gosudarstvennyi Universitet, 1961.

————. "Siuzhetnoe prostranstvo v russkom romane XIX stoletiia." In *Izbrannye stat'i v trekh tomakh*, 3: 91–106. Tallin: Aleksandra, 1993.

Luchistyi, Aleksandr. "Slava Zav'ialov, gruppa Kim i Buran." *Be-in journal*, February (2007), online at http://www.be-in.ru/people/399-slava_zavyalov_gruppa_kim_i_bu/.

Lunde, Ingunn, and Martin Paulsen, eds. *From Poets to Padonki: Linguistic Authority & Norm Negotiation in Modern Russian Culture*. Bergen: Slavica Bergensia, 2009.

Lupton, Christina. "Sincere Performances: Franklin, Tillotson, and Steele on the Plain Style." *Eighteenth-Century Studies* 40 (2) (2007): 177–92.

Lutz, Tom. *Crying: A Natural and Cultural History of Tears*. New York: Norton, 2001.

Luzhetskii, Pasha. "Sermiazhnaia pravda russkogo iskusstvo." *Sutki*, 1 October 2008, online at http://www.sutki.net/films/21376-sermyazhnaya_pravda_russkogo_iskusstva.html.

Lyotard, Jean-François. *Le Différend*. Paris: Minuit, 1983.

Lysaker, Paul Henry, and John Timothy Lysaker. "Narrative Structure in Psychosis: Schizophrenia and Disruptions in the Dialogical Self." *Theory and Psychology* 12 (2) (2002): 207–20.

Macdowell, James. "Wes Anderson, Tone, and the Quirky Sensibility." *New Review of Film and Television Studies* 10 (1) (2012): 6–27.

Magill Jr., Jay R. *Sincerity: How a Moral Ideal Born Five Hundred Years Ago Inspired Religious Wars, Modern Art, Hipster Chic, and the Curious Notion That We ALL Have Something to Say (No Matter How Dull).* New York: Norton, 2012.

Maher, Kevin. "If You're Unhappy and You Know It . . ." *Times*, 16 June 2005, online at entertainment.timesonline.co.uk/tol/arts_and_entertainment /film/article533541.ece.

Mail.ru Group. *Sotsial'nye seti v Rossii.* Moscow: Mail.ru Group, 2014, online at https://corp.imgsmail.ru/media/files/issledovanie-auditorij-sotcialnykh -setej.pdf.

Maiofis, Maria. "D. A. Prigov i G. R. Derzhavin." In *Nekanonicheskii klassik: Dmitrii Aleksandrovich Prigov (1940–2007)*, edited by Evgeny Dobrenko, Ilya Kukulin, Mark Lipovetsky, and Maria Maiofis, 281–305. Moscow: Novoe literaturnoe obozrenie, 2010.

Makushinskii, Aleksei. "Otvergnutyi zhenikh, ili Osnovnoi mif russkoi literatury XIX veka." *Voprosy filosofii* 7 (2003): 35–43.

Manjoo, Farhad. *True Enough: Learning to Live in a Post-Fact Society.* Hoboken, N.J.: Wiley, 2008.

Man'kovskaia, Natal'ia. *Estetika postmodernizma.* St. Petersburg: Aleteia, 2000.

———. *Ot modernizma k postpostmodernizmu via postmodernizm.* Moscow: Kollazh, 1998.

Mannisto, Glenn. "The New Sincerity." *Metrotimes*, 5 December 2002, online at http://www.metrotimes.com/editorial/story.asp?id=3261.

Markova, Dar'ia. "Novyi-prenovyi realizm, ili Opiat' dvadtsat' piat'." *Znamia* 6 (2006), online at magazines.russ.ru/znamia/2006/6/ma12.html.

Markovich, Vladimir. " 'Russkii evropeets' v proze Turgeneva 1850-kh godov." In *Ivan S. Turgenev: Leben, Werk und Wirkung. Beiträge der Internationalen Fachkonferenz aus Anlass des 175. Geburtstages an der Otto-Friedrich-Universität Bamberg*, edited by Peter Thiergen, 79–96. Munich: Sagner, 1995.

Markovits, Elizabeth. *The Politics of Sincerity: Plato, Frank, and Democratic Judgment.* University Park: Penn State University Press, 2008.

Marsh, Rosalind. *Literature, History and Identity in Post-Soviet Russia, 1991–2006.* Oxford: Peter Lang, 2007.

Martin, John. "Inventing Sincerity, Refashioning Prudence: The Discovery of the Individual in Renaissance Europe." *American Historical Review* 102 (5) (1997): 1304–42.

Marusenkov, Maksim. *Absurdopediia russkoi zhizni Vladimira Sorokina: Zaum', grotesk i absurd.* St. Petersburg: Aleteia, 2012.

Masing-Delic, Irene. "The Mask Motif in A. Blok's Poetry." *Russian Literature* 2 (3) (1973): 79–101.

Mayer, Tamar, ed. *Gender Ironies of Nationalism: Sexing the Nation*. London: Routledge, 2000.

McCarthy, Brigit. "Soviet Era Dark Humor Makes a Comeback." *PRI*, 29 February 2012, online at http://www.pri.org/stories/2012-02-29/soviet-era-dark -humor-makes-comeback.

Medvedev, Kirill. *Reaktsiia voobshche*. Moscow: Svobodnoe marksistskoe izdatel'stvo, 2007.

———. "The Writer in Russia: Individualism and the 'New Emotionalism.'" *Dissent* 55 (4) (2008): 13–22.

Meindl, Matthias, and Georg Witte. "Die neue Aufrichtigkeit: Kirill Medvedevs politische Sprache." *Schreibheft: Zeitschrift für Literatur* 76 (2011): 176–81.

Menzel, Birgit. *Bürgerkrieg um Worte: Die russische Literaturkritik der Perestrojka*. Cologne: Böhlau, 2001.

Menzel, Birgit, and Ulrich Schmid, eds. *Der Osten im Westen: Importe der Populärkultur*. Special issue of *Osteuropa* (5) (2007).

Metelitsa, Katia. "Igra v otkrovenie: Starye babki i 'novaia iskrennost'." *Nezavisi-maia gazeta*, 16 December 2004, online at http://www.ng.ru/style/2004-12 -16/8_game.html.

Metzinger, Thomas. *Being No One: The Self-Model Theory of Subjectivity*. Cambridge, Mass.: MIT Press, 2003.

Mezhieva, Marina, and Natal'ia Konradova. *Okno v mir: Sovremennaia russkaia literatura*. Moscow: Russkii iazyk, 2006.

Mikhailovskaia, Ekaterina. "Politicheskie slova kak veshchi, ili Opyt chteniia odnoi stenogrammy." *Novoe literaturnoe obozrenie* 83 (1) (2007): 165–89.

Mikhailovskaia, Ol'ga. "'Novaia iskrennost': V Barvikhe otkrylsia butik Marni." *Kommersant*, 2 March 2007, online at http://www.kommersant.ru/Doc /746373/Print.

Milnes, Timothy, and Kerry Sinanan, eds. *Romanticism, Sincerity, and Authenticity*. Basingstoke: Palgrave Macmillan, 2010.

Misiano, Viktor. "Dubossarsky and Vinogradov's 'New Sincerity.'" Exhibition description for *On the Block*, Charlotte Moser Gallery, Geneva, 2010, online at www.dubossarskyvinogradov.com/exhibitions/on_the_block/new _sincerity.

Mitrenina, Marina. "Netneizm i traditsionnaia kul'tura." *Russkii zhurnal*, 24 March 2003, online at http://old.russ.ru/netcult/20030324_mitrenina -pr.html.

Mombert, Jason. "The New Sincerity." Installation description for *The New Sincerity*, undated, online at http://www.betaart.com/mombert/the_new _sincerity_statement.html.

Morris, Jason. "The Time between Time: Messianism & The Promise of a 'New Sincerity.'" *Jacket* 35 (2008), online at http://jacketmagazine.com/35/morris -sincerity.shtml.

Mosse, George. *Nationalism and Sexuality: Respectability and Abnormal Sexuality in Modern Europe*. New York: Howard Fertig, 1985.

Most, Glenn W. *Doubting Thomas.* Cambridge, Mass.: Harvard University Press, 2005.

Mukhomor. *Zolotoi disk.* © 1982. Compact disc.

Murray, James. "Fuck You Damien Hirst!" *James Austin Murray,* 11 January 2012, online at http://jamesaustinmurray.com/?p=1073.

Myers, Greg. "Entitlement and Sincerity in Broadcast Interviews about Princess Diana." *Media, Culture and Society* 22 (2) (2000): 167–85.

Nadkarni, Maya, and Olga Shevchenko. "The Politics of Nostalgia: A Case for Comparative Analysis of Postsocialist Practices." *Ab Imperio* 2 (2004): 487–519.

Natarov, Evgenii. "Timur Kibirov: Obzor kritiki." *Literaturnoe obozrenie* 1 (1998): 38–40.

Neef, Sonja, Jose van Dijck, Eric Ketelaar, eds. *Sign Here! Handwriting in the Age of New Media.* Amsterdam: University of Amsterdam Press, 2006.

Nemoianu, Virgil. *Imperfection and Defeat: The Role of Aesthetic Imagination in Society.* Budapest: Central European University Press, 2006.

Newman, Gerald. *The Rise of English Nationalism: A Cultural History, 1740–1830.* London: Macmillan, 1997.

Nietzsche, Friedrich. *Beyond Good and Evil.* Translated by Walter Kaufmann. New York: Random House, 1966.

Noordenbos, Boris. *Post-Soviet Literature and the Search for a Russian Identity.* Basingstoke: Palgrave, 2016.

Nord, Philip. *The Republican Moment: Struggles for Democracy in Nineteenth-Century France.* Cambridge, Mass.: Harvard University Press, 1995.

Nowak, Andrzej. *History and Geopolitics: A Contest for Eastern Europe.* Warsaw: Polish Institute of International Affairs, 2008.

Oates, Sarah. "The Neo-Soviet Model of the Media." *Europe-Asia Studies* 59 (8) (2007): 1279–97.

Obermayr, Brigitte. "Semantic Poetry and Sincerity Revisited." Paper presented at the annual meeting of the Association for Slavic, East European, and Eurasian Studies Conference, Boston, 12–15 November 2009.

Ognyanova, Katherine. "Careful What You Say: Media Control In Putin's Russia—Implications for Online Content." *International Journal of E-Politics* 1 (2) (2010), online at http://bit.ly/1RHPQOj.

Oleg Kulik: Vyzov i provokatsiia. DVD. Directed by Evgeniia Mitta and Aleksandr Shein. Moscow: 2Plan2, 2008.

Olsen, Mark. "If I Can Dream: The Everlasting Boyhoods of Wes Anderson." *Film Comment* 35 (1) (1999): 12–14.

Osaulenko, Irina. "LOMOgrafiia. Snimki s bedra." *Flashartstudio,* 28 March 2011, online at http://flashartstudio.uol.ua/blog/tags/10572/lomografiya/.

Oushakine, Serguei. " 'We're Nostalgic but We're Not Crazy': Retrofitting the Past in Russia." *Russian Review* 66 (3) (2007): 451–82.

Paperno, Irina. *Chernyshevsky and the Age of Realism: A Study in the Semiotics of Behavior.* Stanford: Stanford University Press, 1988.

———. *Stories of the Soviet Experience: Memoirs, Diaries, Dreams*. Ithaca, N.Y.: Cornell University Press, 2009.

Pariser, Eli. *The Filter Bubble: What the Internet Is Hiding from You*. London: Penguin, 2011.

Pavlova, Vera. *Pis'ma v sosedniuiu komnatu: Tysiacha i odno obiasnenii v liubi*. Moscow: AST, 2006.

Peck, Jamie. "Struggling with the Creative Class." *International Journal of Urban and Regional Research* 29 (4) (2005): 740–70.

Pelevin, Viktor. *S.N.U.F.F.* Moscow: Eksmo, 2011.

Perkins, David. *Wordsworth and the Poetry of Sincerity*. Cambridge, Mass.: Belknap Press of Harvard University Press, 1964.

Pertsev, Andrei. "Novaia iskrennost': Kogda propagandist ne vret." *Slon.ru*, 10 March 2014, online at http://slon.ru/russia/novaya_iskrennost_kogda _propagandist_ne_vret-1166698.xhtml.

Pessoa, Fernando. *A Little Larger Than the Entire Universe*, edited and translated by Richard Zenith. London: Penguin, 2006.

Peters, Arjan. "Een rebelse mandarijn." *Volkskrant*, 17 April 2009, 33.

Petrovskaia, Elena. "Dusha Pautiny: Masiania i 'novaia' iskrennost'." *Iskusstvo kino* 9 (2002), online at http://kinoart.ru/2002/n9-article17.html.

Petrushanskaia, Olga. "Mikhail Ugarov: 'Nuzhno otrazhat' zhizn' takoi, kakaia ona est!'" *Sovremennaia dramaturgiia* 2 (2005): 185–87.

Peyre, Henri. *Literature and Sincerity*. New Haven: Yale University Press, 1963.

Piccalo, Gina. "Looking for 'Real.'" *Los Angeles Times*, 6 December 2003, online at http://articles.latimes.com/2003/dec/06/entertainment/et -piccalo6.

Pivinskii, Aleksandr. "Coquetting with Cuff Links" ("Koketnichaia zaponkami"), a poem posted in 2012 (http://users.livejournal.com/_a_moi_5_kopeek /547631.html, accessed 5 January 2015).

Plamper, Jan. "Emotional Turn? Feelings in Russian History and Culture: Introduction." *Slavic Review* 68 (2) (2009): 229–38.

———. "Vvedenie I: Emotsii v russkoi istorii." In *Rossiiskaia imperiia chuvstv: Podkhody k kul'turnoi istorii emotsii*, edited by Jan Plamper, Marc Elie, and Schamma Schahadat, 11–37. Moscow: Novoe literaturnoe obozrenie, 2010.

Plamper, Jan, Marc Elie, and Schamma Schahadat, eds. *Rossiiskaia imperiia chuvstv: Podkhody k kul'turnoi istorii emotsii*. Moscow: Novoe literaturnoe obozrenie, 2010.

Plato, *Phaedrus*. Oxford: Oxford University Press, 2002.

Platt, Kevin. "The Post-Soviet Is Over: On Reading the Ruins." *Republics of Letters: A Journal for the Study of Knowledge, Politics, and the Arts* 1 (1) (2009), online at http://rofl.stanford.edu/node/41.

Pogrebizhskaia, Elena. "Elena Pogrebizhskaia o lichnom balanse mezhdu pravdoi i professiei." *Sinefantom* 13 (198) (2009): 4–5.

Polanyi, Michael, and Richard Rorty. "Postmodern Ethics." *Southern Humanities Review* 29 (1) (1995): 15–34.

Polit.ru. "V gostiakh u tsiklopov." *Polit.ru*, 17 April 2005, online at http://www
.polit.ru/culture/2005/04/17/ciklopy.html.

Pomerantsev, Peter. *Nothing Is True and Everything Is Possible: The Surreal Heart
of the New Russia*. Philadelphia: Public Affairs, 2014.

Pomerantsev, Vladimir. "Ob iskrennosti v literature." *Novyi mir* 12 (1953), online
at http://vivovoco.rsl.ru/VV/PAPERS/LITRA/MEMO/POMER.HTM.

Ponomareva, Ol'ga. "Neonorma." *OM* 12 (2005): 66–71.

Popov, Evgenii. "Priznaius' . . ." *Oktiabr* 12 (2009), online at http://magazines
.russ.ru/october/2009/12/le2.html.

Pospelov, Petr. "Novaia iskrennost' na chetverykh: Kvartet Tomasa Tseetmaira v
Bol'shom teatre." *Vedomosti*, 26 May 2003, online at http://www.vedomosti
.ru/newspaper/article.shtml?2003/03/26/59622.

Potter, Andrew. *The Authenticity Hoax: Why the "Real" Things We Seek Don't
Make Us Happy*. New York: Harper, 2010.

Powhida, William. "Outpost." *Brooklyn Rail*, 21 January 2009, online at http://
www.brooklynrail.org/2003/08/artseen/outpost.

Prigov, Dmitrii. "Iskrennost'—vot shto nam vsego dorozhe." *Polit.ru*, 27 August
2005, online at http://polit.ru/article/2005/08/27/prigov12082005/.

———. *Novaia iskrennost'*. Moscow: samizdat (unpublished), 1986.

———. "Pirogovskii narkoz." *Polit.ru*, 27 April 2005, online at http://polit.ru
/article/2005/04/27/pirogov/.

———. *Sbornik preduvedomlenii k raznoobraznym veshcham*. Moscow: Ad
Marginem, 1996.

———. *Sobranie stikhov*, edited by Brigitte Obermayr. Vienna: Gesellschaft zur
Förderung slawistischer Studien, 1996–.

———. *Sovetskie teksty 1979–1984*. St. Petersburg: Ivan Limbakha, 1997.

———. "What More Is There to Say?" In *Third Wave: The New Russian Poetry*,
edited by Kent Johnson and Stephen M. Ashby, 101–4. Ann Arbor: Michigan
University Press, 1992.

Prigov, Dmitrii, and Mikhail Epstein. "Popytka ne byt' identifitsiirovannym." In
Nekanonicheskii klassik: Dmitrii Aleksandrovich Prigov (1940–2007), edited
by Evgeny Dobrenko, Ilya Kukulin, Mark Lipovetsky, and Maria Maiofis,
52–72. Moscow: Novoe literaturnoe obozrenie, 2010.

Prigov, Dmitrii, and Sergei Shapoval. *Portretnaia galereia D.A.P.* Moscow: Novoe
literaturnoe obozrenie, 2003.

Prokhorov, Aleksandr. "Inherited Discourse: Stalinist Tropes in Thaw Culture."
Ph.D. diss., University of Pittsburgh, 2002, online at http://d-scholarship
.pitt.edu/8550/1/prokhorov2002.pdf.

———. "The Unknown New Wave: Soviet Cinema of the 1960s." In *Springtime
for Soviet Cinema: Re/Viewing the 1960s*, edited by Aleksandr Prokhorov,
2001, online at http://www.rusfilm.pitt.edu/.

Prokhorova, Irina. "Nedavnee proshloe kak vyzov istoriku (na pravakh
vstupitel'noi zametki." *Novoe literaturnoe obozrenie* 83 (2007), online at
http://magazines.russ.ru/nlo/2007/83/pr1.html.

Purdy, Jedediah. *For Common Things: Irony, Trust and Commitment*. New York: Knopf, 1999.

———. "The State of Irony." *Slate*, 23 September 1999, online at http://www .slate.com/id/35152/.

Radishchev, Aleksandr. *Puteshestvie iz Peterburga v Moskvu: Vol'nost'*. St. Petersburg: Nauka, 1992.

Radzievskii, Aleksandr. "Moskou: nieuwe oprechte kunst." *Gonzo Circus* 71 (2005): 54–57.

Ramakers, Renny. *Less+More: Droog Design in Context*. Rotterdam: 010 Publishers, 2002.

Ramos, Telly. *New Sincerity*. Short film. Directed by Telly Ramos. 2009. Studio 22 Productions, 2009.

Ratcliff, Carter. *Komar & Melamid*. New York: Abbeville, 1988.

Read, Herbert. *The Cult of Sincerity*. London: Faber & Faber, 1968.

Ready, Oliver. "Aleksei Slapovskii and the Art of Adapting." *Modern Language Review* 105 (4) (2010): 1105–29.

———. "Saplings in the Jungle: The Vitality of the Russian Literary Scene—and Why It Is a Problem." *Times Literary Supplement* 5640, 6 May 2011, 14–15.

Rebein, Robert. *Hicks, Tribes, and Dirty Realists: American Fiction after Postmodernism*. Lexington: University Press of Kentucky, 2001.

Reddy, William M. *The Navigation of Feeling: A Framework for the History of Emotions*. Cambridge: Cambridge University Press, 2001.

Reid, Calvin. "Art Spiegelman and Françoise Mouly: The Literature of Comics." *Publishers Weekly*, 16 October 2000, online at http://www.publishersweekly .com/pw/by-topic/authors/interviews/article/18809-art-spiegelman-and -fran-oise-mouly-the-literature-of-comics.html.

Rettberg, Jill Walker. *Blogging*. Cambridge: Polity Press, 2008.

Reynolds, Roo. "Welcome to the New Sincerity." *rooreynolds.com*, 28 May 2008, online at http://rooreynolds.com/2008/05/28/welcome-to-the-new-sincerity/.

Riasanovsky, Nicholas. *A Parting of Ways: Government and Educated Public in Russia 1801–55*. Oxford: Clarendon Press, 1976.

Robinson, Anthony. "A Few Notes from a New Sincerist." *Geneva Convention Archives*, 22 July 2005, online at http://luckyerror.blogspot.nl/2005/07/few -notes-from-new-sincerist.html.

Rogers, Douglas. "Postsocialisms Unbound: Connections, Critiques, Comparisons." *Slavic Review* 69 (1) (2010): 1–16.

Rogers, Richard. *The End of the Virtual: Digital Methods*. Amsterdam: Vossiuspers UvA/Amsterdam University Press, 2009.

Rombes, Nicholas. *Cinema in the Digital Age*. London: Wallflower, 2008.

———. "The Razor's Edge of American Cinema: The New Sincerity of Post-Ironic Films," undated, online at http://www.webdelsol.com/SolPix/sp-nicknew2.htm.

———. "The Rebirth of the Author." In *1000 Days of Theory*, edited by Arthur Kroker and Marilouise Kroker, 2005, online at http://www.ctheory.net /articles.aspx?id=480.

Rosenbaum, Susan. *Professing Sincerity: Modern Lyric Poetry, Commercial Culture, and the Crisis in Reading.* Charlottesville: University of Virginia Press, 2007.

Rosenblatt, Roger. "The Age of Irony Comes to an End: No Longer Will We Fail to Take Things Seriously." *Time* magazine, 24 September 2001, online at http://www.time.com/time/magazine/article/0,9171,10000893,00.html.

Rosenwein, Barbara. *Emotional Communities in the Early Middle Ages.* Ithaca, N.Y.: Cornell University Press, 2006.

———. "Worrying about Emotions in History." *American Historical Review* 107 (3) (2002): 821–45.

Roth-Ey, Kristin. *Moscow Prime Time: How the Soviet Union Built the Media Empire That Lost the Cultural Cold War.* Ithaca, N.Y.: Cornell University Press, 2011.

Rothstein, Edward. "Attacks on U.S. Challenge Postmodern True Believers." *New York Times,* 22 September 2001, online at http://www.nytimes.com/2001/09/22/arts/22CONN.html?pagewanted=all.

Rugoff, Ralph. "Other Experts." In *Amateurs,* edited by Grace Kook-Anderson and Claire Fitzsimmons, 9–15. San Francisco: California College of the Arts, 2008.

Ruskin, John. *The Laws of Fésole: Principles of Drawing & Painting from the Tuscan Masters.* New York: Allworth, 1996.

Russia Today. "Russia Shocked as Volunteers Report Grim Facts about Nursing Home." *Russia Today,* 28 October 2009, online at http://rt.com/news/volunteers-nursing-house-outrage/.

Rutten, Ellen. "Deliberate Incompletion." *Mark Magazine* 23 (2009): 102–14.

———. "Flirten met Stalin: Onrust in de Russische kunstwereld." *Groene Amsterdammer* 9 (2009): 32–34.

———. "Judge a Book by Its Cover . . . Timur Kibirov. *Stichi o ljubvi. Al'bom-portret.*" In *Literature and Beyond: Festschrift for Willem G. Weststeijn.* Volume 2, edited by Eric de Haard, Wim Honselaar, and Jenny Stelleman, 689–701. Amsterdam: Pegasus, 2008.

———. "New-Media Language: Towards a Transcultural Approach." Paper presented at the conference entitled "Runet in a Global Context," University of Passau, 3–6 February 2011.

———. "(Russian) Writer-Bloggers: Digital Perfection and the Aesthetics of Imperfection." *Journal of Computer-Mediated Communication* 19 (4) (2014): 744–62.

———. "Sincere e-Self-Fashioning: Dmitrii Vodennikov (1968)." In *Idolizing Authorship: Literary Celebrity and the Construction of Identity,* edited by Gaston Franssen and Rick Honings. Amsterdam: Amsterdam University Press, forthcoming.

———. "Strategic Sentiments: Pleas for a New Sincerity in Contemporary Russian Literature." In *Dutch Contributions to the Fourteenth International Congress of Slavists,* edited by Sander Brouwer, 201–17. Amsterdam: Rodopi, 2008.

————. *Unattainable Bride Russia: Engendering Nation, State, and Intelligentsia in Russian Intellectual Culture.* Evanston, Ill.: Northwestern University Press, 2010.

————. "Vintage_Russia: Wat imperfectie sexy maakt." Inaugural address presented at the University of Amsterdam, 13 June 2013, online at http://www.oratiereeks.nl/upload/pdf/PDF-5229Weboratie_Rutten.pdf.

————. "Where Postmodern Provocation Meets Social Strategy: Deep into Russia." In *Provocation and Extravagance in Modern Russian Literature and Culture,* edited by Ben Dhooge, Thomas Langerak, and Eric Metz, 163–79. Amsterdam: Pegasus, 2008.

Ryklin, Mikhail. "Proekt dlinoi v zhizni." In *Nekanonicheskii klassik: Dmitrii Aleksandrovich Prigov (1940–2007),* edited by Evgeny Dobrenko, Ilya Kukulin, Mark Lipovetsky, and Maria Maiofis, 81–96. Moscow: Novoe literaturnoe obozrenie, 2010.

————. *Vremia diagnoza.* Moscow: Logos, 2003.

Safronova, Iuliia. "Smert' gosudaria." In *Rossiiskaia imperiia chuvstv: Podkhody k kul'turnoi istorii emotsii,* edited by Jan Plamper, Marc Elie, and Schaha Schammadat, 166–84. Moscow: Novoe literaturnoe obozrenie, 2010.

Saltz, Jerry. "Sincerity and Irony Hug It Out." *New Yorker,* 27 May 2010, online at http://nymag.com/arts/art/reviews/66277/.

Sal'nikov, Vladimir. "Authorship and the Artwork in the Age of Transgression." *Khudozhestvennyi zhurnal* 1993/2005 (English digest), online at http://xz.gif.ru/numbers/moscow-art-magazine/authorship/.

Sancho-Rodriguez', Eva. "The Merit of Genre Versus Cinematic Tone and Mood: Does Analysis Through Genre Open Up 'Better' Kinds of Questions?" Paper presented at the worshop entitled "Thinking Through Genre: The Second Cinematic Thinking," Pratt Institute, 2 November 2013.

Sanneh, Kelefa. "Mr. Sincerity Tries a New Trick." *New York Times,* 16 January 2005, online at http://www.nytimes.com/2005/01/16/arts/music/16sann.html.

Sapiro, Gisèle. *La guerre des écrivains, 1940–1953.* Paris: Fayard, 1999.

Sarjono, Agus R. "Poetry and Sincerity." In *Poetry and Sincerity: International Poetry Festival Indonesia 2006,* edited by Agus R. Sarjono and Martin Mooij, 8–11. Jakarta: Cipta, 2006.

Sartre, Jean-Paul. *Being and Nothingness.* Translated by Hazel E. Barnes. New York: Washington Square Press, 1992.

————. *L'Être et le néant.* Paris: Galimard, 1943.

Savchuk, Valerii. "Ideologiia postinformatsionnoi iskrennosti." *Khudozhestvennyi zhurnal* 30–31 (1999), online at http://anthropology.ru/ru/texts/savchuk/artconv_01.html#p5.

Scharg, Calvin O. *The Self after Postmodernity.* New Haven: Yale University Press, 1997.

Scherrer, Jutta. "Anciens/Nouveaux lieux de mémoire en Russie." *Outre-terre* 19 (2007): 187–94.

Schmid, Ulrich. *Ichentwürfe: Russische Autobiographien zwischen Avvakum und Gercen*. Zürich: Pano, 2003.

———, ed. *Russische Medientheorien*. Bern: Haupt, 2005.

Schmidt, Henrike. *Russische Literatur im Internet: Zwischen digitaler Folklore und politischer Propaganda*. Bielefeld: Transcript, 2011.

Schönle, Andreas. "The Scare of the Self: Sentimentalism, Privacy, and Private Life in Russian Culture, 1780–1820." *Slavic Review* 57 (4) (1998): 723–46.

Schouwenberg, Louise. *Hella Jongerius: Misfit*. London: Phaidon, 2011.

Seligman, Adam B., Robert P. Weller, Michael J. Puett, and Bennett Simon. *Ritual and Its Consequences: An Essay on the Limits of Sincerity*. Oxford: Oxford University Press, 2008.

Sella, Marshall. "Against Irony." *New York Times Magazine*, 5 September 1999, online at http://www.nytimes.com/1999/09/05/magazine/against-irony.html?pagewanted=all.

Sel'vinskii, Il'ia. "Nabolevshii vopros." *Literaturnaia gazeta*, 19 October 1954.

Semionov, Sergei. "Novaia iskrennost'." *Ekspert* 4 (55) (2006), online at http://www.expert.ua/articles/10/0/1466/.

Setevaia poeziia. Pravda i iskrennost' v iskusstve. Special issue of *Setevaia poeziia* 4 (2004).

Shaikevich, Anatolii, Vladislav Andriushchenko, and Natalia Rebetskaia, eds. *Statisticheskii slovar' iazyka Dostoevskogo*. Moscow: Iazyki slavianskoi kul'tury, 2003.

Shank, Barry. *Dissonant Identities: The Rock'n'Roll Scene in Austin, Texas*. Hanover, N.H.: University Press of New England, 1994.

Shevelev, Igor'. "Slediashchie za slediashchim: ZhZh kak luchshee sredstvo protiv okhranki i moli." *Nezavisimaia gazeta*, 14 February 2008, online at http://exlibris.ng.ru/printed/206297.

Shevtsov, Vasilii. "Put' moralista." *Topos*, 29 September 2004, online at http://www.topos.ru/article/2810.

Shneidman, Norman N. *Russian Literature 1988–1994: The End of an Era*. Toronto: University of Toronto Press, 1995.

Siegel, Lee. "As You Were: Culture after 9/11." *The Economist/Intelligent Life*, September (2011), online at http://moreintelligentlife.com/content/ideas/lee-siegel/title-here.

Sigutina, Mariia. "Berlinskaia koloniale." *OpenSpace*, 1 February 2008, online at http://www.openspace.ru/art/projects/121/details/994/.

Sim, Luke, and James T. Bretzke. "The Notion of Sincerity (*Ch'eng*) in the Confucian Classics." *Journal of Chinese Philosophy* 21 (1994): 179–212.

Skorino, Liudmila. "Razgovor nachistotu (po povodu stat'i V. Pomerantseva)." *Znamia* 2 (1954).

Skoropanova, Irina. *Russkaia postmodernistskaia literatura*. Moscow: Flint/Nauka, 1999.

Smail, Daniel Lord. *On Deep History and the Brain*. Berkeley: University of California Press, 2008.

Smirnov, Igor'. *Filosofiia na kazhdyi den'*. Moscow: FNI Pragmatika kul'tury, 2003.

———. "Vladimir Sorokin: Put' Bro," *Kriticheskaia Massa* 4 (2004), online at http://srkn.ru/criticism/smirnov3.shtml.

Smith, Kathleen. *Mythmaking in the New Russia: Politics and Memory in the Yeltsin Era*. Ithaca, N.Y.: Cornell University Press, 2002.

Smith, Terry, Okwui Enwezor, and Nancy Condee, eds. *Antinomies of Art and Culture: Modernity, Postmodernity, Contemporaneity*. Durham, N.C.: Duke University Press, 2009.

Sofronov, Vladislav. "Shto-to proiskhodit." *Khudozhestvennyi zhurnal* 14 (1996), on xz.gif.ru/numbers/14/chto-to-proiskhodit.

Sokolov, Boris. *Moia kniga o Vladimire Sorokine*. Moscow: AIRO-XXI, 2005.

Solomon, Andrew. *The Irony Tower: Soviet Artists in a Time of Glasnost*. New York: Alfred A. Knopf, 1991.

Sorokin, Vladimir. "'Ia v sovok opiat' ne khochu: I v andegraund—tozhe. Interview with Nataliia Kochetkova." *Izvestiia*, 5 August 2005, online at http://www.izvestia.ru/culture/article2460478/.

———. "Idushchie vmeste' protiv 'Deti Rozentalia'." *Radio sovoboda*, 22 March 2005, online at http://www.svoboda.org/ll/grani/0305/ll.032205-1.asp.

———. "Interview with Author Vladimir Sorokin: 'Russia Is Slipping Back into an Authoritarian Empire.'" *Spiegel Online*, 2 February 2007, online at http://www.spiegel.de/international/spiegel/spiegel-interview-with-author-vladimir-sorokin-russia-is-slipping-back-into-an-authoritarian-empire-a-463860.html.

———. "Kogda nachinaet ottepel', obnazhaiutsia gnilye mesta." *Snob*, 6 May 2009, online at http://snob.ru/selected/entry/2969#comment_6486.

———. "Mea Culpa?" *Nezavisimaia gazeta*, 14 April 2005, online at http://www.ng.ru/ng_exlibris/2005–04–14/5_culpa.html.

———. *Mesiats v Dakhau*. Cologne: MA, 1992.

———. *Moskva*. Moscow: Ad Marginem, 2001.

———. "Po Bol'shomu: Interview with Elena Sizenko." *Itogi*, 10 March 2005, online at http://www.itogi.ru/archive/2005/10/60061.html.

———. "Pravila zhizni: Vladimir Sorokin." *Esquire* 13 (2006), online at http://esquire.ru/wil/vladimir-sorokin.

———. *Sobranie sochinenii*. Moscow: Ad Marginem, 2002.

———. "Tekst kak narkotik: Interview with Tat'iana Rasskazova." In *Sbornik rasskazov*, 119–26. Moscow: Russlit, 1992.

———. *Trilogiia*. Moscow: Zakharov, 2006.

———. "Vladimir Sorokin: Rossiia ostaetsia liubovnitsei totalitarizma. Interview with Boris Sokolov." *Grani*, 23 May 2005, online at http://www.grani.ru/Culture/Music/m.86612.html.

———. "Vladimir Sorokin ne khochet byt' prorokom kak Lev Tolstoi." *Nezavisimaia gazeta*, 2 July 2003.

————. "Vladimir Sorokin v proekte 'Velikany.'" *OpenSpace,* 24 December 2008, online at http://os.colta.ru/mediathek/details/6949/.

Sorokin, Wladimir, and Alina Wituchnowskaja. "Nichts leichter, als ein Held zu sein: Wladimir Sorokin und Alina Wituchnowskaja im Gespräch." *Die Zeit,* 9 November 2000, 67–68.

Spiering, Hendrik. "In de vroege Middeleeuwen was kritiek nog welkom." *NRC Handelsblad,* 2 October 2014, 10.

Sreznevskii, Izmail, ed. *Materialy dlia slovaria drevnerusskogo iazyka.* Moscow: Gosudarstvennoe izdanie inostrannykh i national'nykh slovarei, 1958.

Steinberg, Mark D., and Valeria Sobol, eds. *Interpreting Emotions in Russia and Eastern Europe.* De Kalb: Northern Illinois University Press, 2011.

Stierstorfer, Klaus, ed. *Beyond Postmodernism: Reassessments in Literature, Theory, and Culture.* Berlin: De Gruyter, 2003.

Stöckmann, Ingo. "Bismarcks Antlitz. Über den lyrischen Gebrauchssinn deutscher Aufrichtigkeit." *Text und Kritik* 173 (2007): 14–29.

————. "Deutsche Aufrichtigkeit: Rhetorik, Nation und politische Inkluzion im 17. Jahrhundert." *Deutsche Vierteljahrsschrift* 78 (3) (2004): 373–97.

Stodolsky, Ivor. "A Multi-Lectic Anatomy of Stiob and Poshlost': Case Studies in the Oeuvre of Timur Novikov." *Laboratorium* 3 (1) (2011): 24–50.

Straub, Julia, ed. *Paradoxes of Authenticity: Studies on a Critical Concept.* Bielefeld: Transcript, 2012.

Strauss, William, and Neil Howe. *Generations: The History of America's Future, 1584 to 2069.* New York: Morrow, 1991.

Svirskii, Grigorii. *A History of Post-War Soviet Writing: The Literature of Moral Opposition.* Ann Arbor: Ardis, 1981.

————. *Na lobnom meste: Literatura nravstvennogo soprotivleniia 1946–1976.* London: Novaia literaturnaia biblioteka, 1979.

Taft, Michail. "An Interview with Thomas Metzinger: What Is the Self?" *Being Human,* 28 September 2012, online at http://www.beinghuman.org/article/interview-thomas-metzinger-what-self.

Tamir, Diana I., and Jason P. Mitchell. "Disclosing Information about the Self Is Intrinsically Rewarding." *Proceedings of the National Academy of Sciences,* Early Edition (2012), online at http://wjh.harvard.edu/~dtamir/Tamir-PNAS-2012.pdf.

Tarasov, P. "Ob oshibkakh zhurnala 'Novyi mir': Rezoliutsiia prezidium pravleniia Soiuza sovetskikh pisatelei." *Literaturnaia gazeta* 98 (1954).

Thacker, Justin. *Postmodernism and the Ethics of Theological Knowledge.* Aldershot: Ashgate, 2007.

Thorn, Jesse. "A Manifesto for the New Sincerity" (2006), online at http://www.maximumfun.org/blog/2006/02/manifesto-for-new-sincerity.html.

Thumfart, Johannes. "Das Kulturphänomen 'New Sincerity': Und jetzt mal ehrlich." *TAZ,* 27 April 2013, online at http://www.taz.de/!115184/.

Thurber Stone, Emma. "Summer Musings: 'Bach' to the Basics." *Chicago Maroon,* 30 August 2013.

Tikhomirov, Alexey. "The Regime of Forced Trust: Making and Breaking Emotional Bonds between People and State in Soviet Russia, 1917–1941." *Slavic and East European Review* 91 (1) (2013): 78–118.

Timmer, Nicoline. *Do You Feel It Too? The Post-Postmodern Syndrome in American Fiction at the Turn of the Millennium.* Amsterdam: Rodopi, 2010.

Tiutchev, Fedor. *Lirika v dvukh tomakh.* Moscow: Nauka, 1966.

Todorova, Maria. "Introduction: From Utopia to Propaganda and Back." In *Post-Communist Nostalgia,* edited by Maria Todorova and Zsuzsa Gille, 1–14. New York: Berghahn, 2010.

Tolstoy, Lev. *Sobranie sochinenii v 22 tomakh.* Moscow: Khudozhestvennaia literatura, 1978–85.

Trepper, Hartmute. "Die Auseinandersetzung um die Zeitschrift 'Novyj mir' und ihren Chefredakteur A. Tvardovskij." *Arbeitspapiere & Materialien der Forschungsstelle Osteuropa* 1 (1991): 24–46.

Trilling, Lionel. *Sincerity and Authenticity.* Cambridge, Mass.: Harvard University Press, 1971.

Trubina, Elena. "Tramvai, polnyi Wi-Fi: O retseptsii idei Richarda Floridy v Rossii." *Neprikosnovennyi zapas* 6 (92) (2013), online at http://magazines.russ.ru/nz/2013/6/13t.html.

Tseëlon, Efrat. "Is the Present Self Sincere? Goffman, Impression Management and the Postmodern Self." *Theory, Culture and Society* 9 (2) (1992): 115–28.

Tsvetkov, Aleksei. "Kirill Medvedev: 'Intellektual—ne privilegiia!'" *Rabkoru.ru,* 31 July 2009, online at http://commons.com.ua/kirill-medvedev-intellektual-ne-p/.

Turgenev, Ivan. *Polnoe sobranie sochinenii i pisem v dvadtsati vos'mi tomakh.* Moscow: Nauka, 1960–68.

Turner, Tom. *City as Landscape: A Post-Postmodern View of Design and Planning.* London: Taylor & Francis, 1995.

Uffelmann, Dirk. "'Led Tronulsia': The Overlapping Periods in Vladimir Sorokin's Work from the Materialization of Metaphors to Fantastic Substantialism." In *Landslide of the Norm: Language Culture in Post-Soviet Russia,* edited by Ingunn Lunde and Tine Roesen, 100–125. Bergen: Slavica Bergensia, 2006.

Ulanov, Aleksandr. "Sny o chem-to bol'shom." *Druzhba narodov* 2 (2002), online at magazines.russ.ru/druzhba/2002/2/ulan.html.

Ushkov, Nikolai. "Fishka 'dukhovnost'." *Muzhkoi zhurnal* 6 (2009), online at http://www.gq.ru/magazine/?year=2009&issue=6 (accessed 4 September 2009; no longer available).

Vaessens, Thomas. *De revanche van de roman: Literatuur, autoriteit en engagement.* Nijmegen: Van Tilt, 2009.

———. "'Ik ga met je mee ik durf het': Ilja Leonard Pfeijffers De man van vele manieren (2008) als keerpunt." In *"Ergens beginnen": Bijdragen over Nederlandse poëzie (1967–2009) voor Hugo Brems bij zijn emeritaat,* edited by Dirk de Geest, Marc van Vaeck, and Piet Couttenier. Leuven: Peeters, 2009, online at http://bit.ly/1Jd8oEG.

Vaessens, Thomas, and Yra van Dijk. "Introduction." In *Reconsidering the Postmodern: European Literature Beyond Relativism,* edited by Thomas Vaessens and Yra van Dijk, 7–23. Amsterdam: Amsterdam University Press, 2011.

———. eds. *Reconsidering the Postmodern: European Literature beyond Relativism.* Amsterdam: Amsterdam University Press, 2011.

Vail', Petr, and Aleksander Genis. *60-e: Mir sovetskogo cheloveka.* Moscow: Novoe literaturnoe obozrenie, 1998.

van Alphen, Ernst, and Mieke Bal. "Introduction." In *The Rhetoric of Sincerity,* edited by Ernst van Alphen, Mieke Bal, and Carel Smith, 1–16. Stanford: Stanford University Press, 2009.

van Alphen, Ernst, Mieke Bal, and Carel Smith, eds. *The Rhetoric of Sincerity.* Stanford: Stanford University Press, 2009.

van Renswoude, Irene. "Licence to Speak: The Rhetoric of Free Speech in Late Antiquity and the Early Middle Ages." Ph.D. diss., Utrecht University, 2011.

———. "Licence to Speak: The Rhetoric of Free Speech in Late Antiquity and the Early Middle Ages." Acceptance speech, Praemium Erasmianum Research Prize. In *The Cultural Significance of the Natural Sciences: Praemium Erasmianum Yearbook 2012,* 49–50. Amsterdam: Praemium Erasmianum Foundation, 2013.

Vasilevskii, V. "S nevernykh pozitsii." *Literaturnaia gazeta* 13 (1954).

Vasmer, Max. *Etimologicheskii slovar' russkogo iazyka.* Moscow: Progress, 1986.

———. *Russisches etymologisches Wörterbuch.* Heidelberg: Carl Winter, 1953.

Veriu. Special issue of *Zhurnal moskovskogo muzeia sovremennogo iskusstva* 2 (2007).

Vezhlian, Evgeniia. "Pamiat' momentam." *Novyi mir* 7 (2009), online at magazines.russ.ru/novyi_mir/2009/7/ve16.html.

Vinogradov, Viktor, ed., *Slovar' iazyka Pushkina v chetyrekh tomakh.* Moscow: Azbukovnik, 2000.

Vodennikov, Dmitrii. "Iz knigi 'Chernovik.'" *Novyi mir* 8 (2006), online at http://magazines.russ.ru/novyi_mi/2006/8/vo9.html.

von den Brincken, Bernd. "Medical Hermeneutics" (1997), online interview on http://www.kanka.de/aurora/pp_b1.htm.

Wachtel, Andrew Baruch. *Remaining Relevant after Communism: The Role of the Writer in Eastern Europe.* Chicago: University of Chicago Press, 2006.

Wallace, David Foster. "E Unibus Pluram: Television and U.S. Fiction." *Review of Contemporary Fiction* 31 (2) (1993): 151–95.

Wampole, Christy. "How to Live without Irony." *New York Times,* 17 November 2012, online at http://opinionator.blogs.nytimes.com/2012/11/17/how-to-live-without-irony/.

Warhol, Andy. *The Philosophy of Andy Warhol (From A to B and Back Again).* New York: Harvest Books, 1977.

Watercutter, Angela. "My Little Pony Corrals Unlikely Fanboys Known as 'Bronies.'" *Wired,* 6 September 2011, online at http://www.wired.com/2011/06/bronies-my-little-ponys/.

————. "Sincerely Ours: *Glee*'s Success Cements Age of Geeky 'New Sincerity.'"
    Wired, 21 September 2010, online at http://www.wired.com/underwire/2010
    /09/new-sincerity/.

West, Sally. *I Shop in Moscow: Advertising and the Creation of Consumer Culture in
    Late Tsarist Russia*. DeKalb: Northern Illinois University Press, 2011.

Weststeijn, Willem. "After Postmodernism." In *Dutch Contributions to the
    Twelfth International Congress of Slavists*, edited by Willem Weststeijn,
    211–24. Amsterdam: Rodopi, 1999.

Wierzbicka, Anna. "Russkie kul'turnye skripty i ikh otrazhenie v iazyke." *Russkii
    iazyk v nauchnom osveshchenii* 4 (2002): 6–34.

Wikander, Matthew. *Fangs of Malice: Hypocrisy, Sincerity, and Acting*. Iowa City:
    Iowa University Press, 2002.

Wilde, Oscar. *Intentions* (1891), online at http://www.gutenberg.org/dirs/etext97
    /ntntn1oh.htm.

————. *The Picture of Dorian Gray* (1890), online at http://www.gutenberg.org
    /files/174/174-h/174-h.htm#chap11.

————. "The Truth of Masks" (1891), online at http://www.wilde-online.info/the
    -truth-of-masks.html.

Williams, Robert C. "The Russian Soul: A Study in European Thought and
    Non-European Nationalism." *Journal of the History of Ideas* 31 (4) (1970): 573–88.

Williams, Simon. *Emotion and Social Theory*. London: Sage, 2001.

Williams, Zoe. "The Final Irony." *Guardian*, 28 June 2003, online at http://www
    .guardian.co.uk/weekend/story/0,3605,985375,00.html.

Witte, Georg, and Sabine Hänsgen. "O nemetskoi poeticheskoi knige Dmitriia
    Aleksandrovicha Prigova 'Der Milizionär und die Anderen.'" *NLO* 87
    (2007), online at http://magazines.russ.ru/nlo/2007/87/vi22.html.

Wu, Zhaohua, Norden E. Huang, Steven R. Long, and Chung-Kang Peng. "On
    the Trend, Detrending, and Variability of Nonlinear and Nonstationary
    Time Series." *Proceedings of the National Academy of Sciences of the United
    States of America* 104 (2007), online at http://www.pnas.org/content/104/38
    /14889.full.

Yurchak, Alexei. *Everything Was Forever Until It Was No More: The Last Soviet
    Generation*. Princeton: Princeton University Press, 2006.

————. "Post-Post-Communist Sincerity: Pioneers, Cosmonauts, and Other
    Soviet Heroes Born Today." In *What Is Soviet Now? Identities, Legacies,
    Memories*, edited by Thomas Lahusen and Peter Solomon Jr., 257–77.
    Berlin: LIT, 2008.

Yuval-Davis, Nira. *Gender and Nation*. London: Sage, 1997.

Zakharov, Vadim. "Dumaia o nastoiashchem." In *Nekanonicheskii klassik:
    Dmitrii Aleksandrovich Prigov (1940–2007)*, edited by Evgeny Dobrenko, Ilya
    Kukulin, Mark Lipovetsky, and Maria Maiofis, 702–9. Moscow: Novoe
    literaturnoe obozrenie, 2010.

Zapiska, "Zapiska Otdela nauki i kul'tury TsK KPSS o 'nezdorovykh' nastroeni-
    iakh sredi khudozhestvennoi intelligentsii, 8 fevralia 1954 g. Sekretariu TsK

KPSS, tov. Pospelovu P.N.," online at http://www.hrono.info/dokum/195
_dok/19540208intel.html.

Zalizniak, Anna, Irina Levontina, and Aleksei Shmelev, eds. *Kliuchevye idei russkoi iazykovoi kartiny mira.* Moscow: Iazyki slavianskoi kul'tury, 2005.

Zavialov, Sergei. "Kto eti liudi v chernykh plashchakh? Russkaia poeziia v nachale XXI veka." *Toronto Slavic Quarterly* 8 (2004), online at http://www.utoronto.ca/tsq/08/zaviyalov08.shtml.

Zharikov, Sergei. "Terra Inc. Obzor nezasluzhenno zabytykh muzykal'nykh proektov." *Ozon,* November (2001), online at http://dk.lenin.ru/misc4.html.

Ziegler, Heide, ed. *The End of Postmodernism: New Directions. Proceedings of the First Stuttgart Seminar in Cultural Studies, 04.08–18.08.1991.* Stuttgart: M & P, 1993.

Zintsov, Oleg. "Chitai serdtsem: Novaia iskrennost' v spektakliakh Alvisa Khermanisa." *Vedomosti,* 4 May (79), 2006.

Zimmer, Benjamin. "Truthiness or Trustiness?" *Language Log,* 26 October 2005, online at http://itre.cis.upenn.edu/~myl/languagelog/archives/002586.html.

Zorin, Andrei. "'Al'manakh'—vzgliad iz zala." In *Lichnoe delo No . . . ,* edited by Lev Rubinstein, 246–72. Moscow: V/O Soiuzteatr, 1991.

———. "Dmitrii Aleksandrovich Prigov (1940–2007)." *Slavonica* 14 (1) (2008): 78–83.

———. "Import chuvstv: K istorii emotsional'noi evropeizatsii russkogo dvorianstva." In *Rossiiskaia imperiia chuvstv: Podkhody k kul'turnoi istorii emotsii,* edited by Jan Plamper, Marc Elie, and Schamma Schahadat, 117–31. Moscow: Novoe literaturnoe obozrenie, 2010.

———. "Slushaia Prigova (zapisannoe za chetvert' veka)." In *Nekanonicheskii klassik: Dmitrii Aleksandrovich Prigov (1940–2007),* edited by Evgeny Dobrenko, Ilya Kukulin, Mark Lipovetsky, and Maria Maiofis, 430–51. Moscow: Novoe literaturnoe obozrenie, 2010.

Zorin, Andrei, and Dmitrii Prigov. "Prigov kak Pushkin." *Teatr* 1 (1993): 116–30.

Zubok, Vladislav. *Zhivago's Children: The Last Russian Intelligentsia.* Cambridge, Mass.: Harvard University Press, 2009.

Zvereva, Vera. "'Iazyk padonkaf': Diskussii pol'zovatelei Runeta." In *From Poets to Padonki: Linguistic Authority & Norm Negotiation in Modern Russian Culture,* edited by Ingunn Lunde and Martin Paulsen, 49–79. Bergen: Slavica Bergensia, 2009.

INDEX

Page numbers in *italic* type indicate illustrations.

AAASS conferences (2008, 2009), 26
Adorno, Theodor, 61, 70
aesthetic imperfection. *See* imperfection (aesthetics of)
Ahmed, Sara, 26–27
A-Ia (journal), 94
Aizenberg, Mikhail, 28, 103, 125
Alexander II, Tsar, 55
Alexievich, Svetlana, 99
Algerian War, 90
amateurism, 23, 70, 87, 160, 182–84, 189–90, 193; imitations and, 60, *61*, *62*, 74, 79. *See also* handcrafted
An, Yanming, 25
ancient cultures, 24, 37–38, 40, 42
Anderson, Amanda, 25, 72
Anderson, Wes, 164
Anglophone. *See* English language
animation, 119, 123, 171
anticapitalist new sincerity, 149–51
Apexart Gallery (N.Y.C.), 107
appearance: inner feelings vs., 57; reality and, 69, 138–39
architecture, 14, 59, 112, 161, 189

Aristotle, 24, 34; *Rhetorics,* 38
art, 6, 11, 14, 119, 135; amateurism and, 70; curative property of, 90; individual expression and, 62; New Artists and, 85; new sincerity and, 2, *3*, 30, 72, 73, 83, 109, 123; postcapitalist sincerity and, 150–51; postmodernism and, 7, 29, 90–91, 188–89; post-post-Communist nostalgia and, 30, 109, *110*; post-postmodernism and Russian, 28. *See also* design; Moscow Conceptualism
"Art Instead of Art exhibition" (1989, Moscow), 88–89
artist as therapist, 105, 107
artistic integrity, 49, 58, 139, 177
artistic pragmatism, 55–56, 72, 117, *118*. *See also* commodification
artistic sincerity, 9, 31, 55, 81–84, 89–90; Russian emphasis on, 2, 30, 52, 53, 59, 72, 73, 75, 83, 123
ArtPlay, 200
Ash (web user), 1, 33, 34, 168

Ashton, Jennifer, 25
Assmann, Aleida, 25
atomic bomb, 90
Augustine, Saint, 38, 95
Auschwitz, 197
authenticity, 4, 10, 22–24, 38, 59, 94, 151, 159, 165, 190–94; creative imperfection and, 182–88; fake vs., 86, 141, 155; inward direction of, 51, 188; Russian equivalent of, 51–52; sincerity vs., 19, 51, 52, 192, 194; technology vs., 24, 47, 79, 161, 174, 182–83, 184, 187–88
autobiography, 43, 72, 88, 219n155; blogs and, 170; Soviet era and, 66, 108
automatization, 22, 36–37, 187, 192
avant-garde, 50, 59–60, 79, 85
Avvakum (archpriest), 34, 43, 47, 88; *Life*, 43

Babitskaia, Varvara, 164–65
Backstein, Joseph, 151
Bal, Mieke, 17, 27, 39, 119, 162, 197; *The Rhetoric of Sincerity*, 25, 162
Barash, Aleksandr, 104
Baretskii, Stas, 190
Barrett, Claire, 184
Barthes, Roland, 69
Bates, Tomas, 183
Baudelaire, Charles, 53
Baudrillard, Jean, 161
Bavil'skii, Dmitrii, 123–24, 127, 140, 146; "On Sincerity in Art," 123–24
Baym, Nancy, 179, 186–87, 194
Beeman, William, 25
Belarus, 5, 16, 115–16
Beliaev-Gintovt, Aleksei, 111–12, 113, 114
Beliak, Sergei, 189–90
Benjamin, Walter, 183; "The Work of Art in the Age of Mechanical Reproduction," 59
Benthien, Claudia, 25
Berdiaev, Nikolai, *Self-Knowledge*, 64
Berg, Mikhail, 21, 154, 156
Berry, David, 22
Beslan school siege (2004), 93

Beumers, Birgit, 36, 165–66
Blagg, Alex, 72, 171, 172
blogs, 74, 116, 118, 123, 160, 175–80, 191, 196–97, 337n65; new sincerity and, 1, 2, 5, 7, 11–16, 22, 27, 32, 72–73, 160, 168–72; political activism and, 181; by Russian literary authors, 126, 136–37
Blok, Aleksandr, 63, 64
Bogdanova, Ol'ga, 225n83
Boiarinov, Denis, 190
Bolsheviks, 65
Bondarenko, Mariia, 140
books: distrust of printing and, 22, 23, 39–40, 48, 162, 182; quasi-amateur design of, 60, *61*, *62*, 190; quasi-handwritten fonts and, 49, 79
bordzhia (web user), 1, 33, 34, 168
Borisovich, Boris, 151
Bourdieu, Pierre, 21, 70, 72, 154, 156
Bourova, Nadezhda, 100
Boym, Svetlana, 2, 30, 41–42, 51, 90
Brener, Aleksandr, 28, 132
Bright Eyes (indie band), 11, *12*, 32
Brinton, Jessica, "Who Needs Money?," 150
Brodsky, Sasha, 189
"Bronies" (male fans), 171
Brothers of Light sect (fictional), 127–28
Bruns, Axel, 23, 160; "produsers (term)," 23, 160, 179
Bruskin, Grisha, 108
Bulgaria, 5, 27
"business-artist." *See* commodification
Butler, Judith, 69

Café Pushkin (Moscow), 137
Calvinism, 39, 40, 96
camp, 70, 156
capitalism, 4, 22, 73, 143, 149–52, 157
Carraway, Kate, 167
Catholicism, 39, 40
celebrity culture, 16, 49, 59, 67, 68, 123, 124, 149, 151, 153, 155, 190; Sorokin self-fashioning and, 136–39

Cervantes, Lorna Dee, "Ten Top Trivia
    Tips about The New Sincerity!,"
    171–72
Chabon, Michael, 92
chat rooms, 12, 33, 34, 168
Chechnya, 92
Chen, Andrew, 25, 170–71
cheng (truthfulness to oneself), 24, 38
Chernyshevskii, Nikolai, 132
China, 2, 24, 27, 38, 41
Chung, Yupin, 25
Chuprinin, Sergei, 30, 84
chuvstvitel'nost' (ability to be emotionally
    moved), 46
Cicero, 38
cinema. *See* films
city life. *See* urbanization
Clinton, Bill, 164
Cobain, Kurt, 73
Colbert, Stephen, 23, 161–62; "truthiness
    (term)," 23, 162
collective memory. *See* cultural memory
Collins, Jim, 25, 162–63, 184, 186, 187
commodification, 4, 15, 33, 67, 118, 200;
    literary, 19–20, 49, 56, 70–71,
    144–49, 153, 157–58; new sincerity
    and, 73, 74, 79, 116–17, 145–51, 173,
    197; origination of, 152; selling out
    and, 49, 50, 56, 144, 146, 148, 155;
    sincerity interplay with, 19–24, 36,
    55–56, 58, 59, 68, 144–46, 151–58,
    180, 198. *See also* consumerism
common people, 45, 47, 50, 53, 55, 65,
    67, 83, 96, 216n92
Communist experience. *See* Soviet
    Russia; Soviet trauma
Conceptualists. *See* Moscow
    Conceptualism
confessional genres, 38, 77, 219n155
Confucius, 24, 34, 38
consumerism, 123, 139, 156, 160, 166, 174;
    authenticity and, 187; authenticity
    vs. sincerity and, 194, 199; DIY ("do
    it yourself") vs., 150
Corcoran, Michael, 25
Correll Correll, *186*

country people. *See* common people
Couperus, Louis, *Eline Vere,* 65
court life, 55–56, 96
craft. *See* handcrafted
creative imperfections, 182–92, 199
creative professionals, definition of, 5
critical sentimentalism, 83, 84, 89, 105,
    113–14, 124–27
*Critical Sentimentalism, Sentimental
    Criticism* exhibition (1992,
    St. Petersburg), 84
"Crying Artists" (2005 art project), 117
cultural commentators, 2, 5, 16–17, 70,
    72, 73–74, 91, 166, 200–201
cultural laborers, 5
cultural memory, 9, 15, 75, 88, 90,
    91–93, 101, 111, 142–43, 197;
    Cambridge workshop on, 206n46;
    forgetting and, 17–18; sincerity
    revival and, 105–6, 107, 115, 118; soft
    vs. hard memory and, 119; "soft-
    ware" of, 18. *See also* curative
    sincerity
cultural transfer, 31–32, 169
cultural trauma. *See* cultural memory
cultural workers, definition of, 5
curative sincerity, 18, 89–93, 97, 100,
    105, 107–15, 120–21, 151, 159, 197–98
cynicism, 69, 71, 112, 113, 157, 181
cyrill–lipatov (blogger), 180, 194

Danilkin, Lev, 140
Danilov, Dmitrii, 127
Danish cinema, 166
DAP (Prigov project), 93–94, 98–99,
    103, 104, 118
Davydov, Danila, 126, 146
Davydova, Marina, 227n29
deconstruction, 19, 69, 70, 79, 81, 102,
    104, 120–121, 129, 130
Degot', Ekaterina, 30, 91, 135, 146–47,
    148, 165, 166
Deleuze, Gilles, *Logique du sens,* 90
deliberate imperfection. *See* imperfec-
    tion (aesthetics of)
Del Rey, Lana, 180

den Dulk, Allard, 25
Derrida, Jacques, 69, 128, 130
Derzhavin, Gavriil, 55–56, 145, 152–53, 156
derznovenie (boldness/impudence), 42
Desiatnikov, Leonid, *Rosenthal's Children* (opera), 133
design, 14, 59–62, *61*, *62*, 123, *173*, 184, 189
de Zengotita, Thomas, 23, 161
Dieter, Michael, 22
digital photography
digitization, 22–23; creative imperfections as response to, 182–92; sincere expression and, 60, 74, 118, 159–61, 165, 174, 175, 182. *See also* new media; postdigital age
direct expression, 79, 115, 134, 135
dissent, 76, 83, 103, 113, 133, 176
distrust, 37–39, 56, 65, 66, 68, 88, 110, 181
DIY ("do it yourself") ethos, 150
Dobrenko, Evgeny, 91, 104
Dogme movement (Danish cinema), 164, 166
Donetsk (Ukraine), 166
Dostoevsky, Fedor, 58, 96, 132, 217n114; *Demons*, 58, 59; *Notes from Underground*, 50
drama. *See* theater
Drawn2Design (blogger), *173*
Droog (Dutch design company), 184
Dubossarsky, Vladimir, 122
Dugin, Aleksandr, 114
Dunham, Lena, 233–34n16
Dutch literature, 92, 164

early Christianity, 38
early modernity, 22, 24, 39–41, 48, 79, 162, 179. *See also* Renaissance
early twentieth century, 59–67, 162
economic transition. *See* socioeconomic change
Eggers, Dave, 31–32, 164, 211n103
eighteenth century, 43–46, 52, 55, 56; literary commodification and,

152–53; revolutionary events of, 44, 45, 46, 48, 66, 90, 96–97
Elizarov, Mikhail, 142
Emerson, Caryl, 138
emotions, 21–22, 57, 142, 198; duplicity and, 66–67; French vocabulary of, 43–44; Russian equal rights of, 47; unmediated, 135
Engels, Friedrich, 51
English Calvinism, 39, 40, 96
English language, 6, 23; digital authenticity and, 188; online new sincerity and, 11–12, 32, 72–73, 169–72, 180; post-postmodernism and, 32; sincerity studies and, 21, 152, 155, 201; word "sincerity" entrance into, 39
English nationalism, 44–45, 50, 52, 55
Enlightenment, 55–56, 90
Eno, Brian, 80
Epstein, Mikhail, 13, 28, 29, 30, 32, 77, 92–93, 109–10, 125; "hangover poetics" and, 106, 114; new sincerity and, 2, 6, 9–11, 169, 171, 196; on Prigov, 102–3, 104, 106
Erofeev, Andrei, 112
Erofeev, Victor, 101–2
Erotic Hallucinations of a Russian Lawyer (album), 190
Esipovich, Alla, 2; *Untitled*, *3*
ethics, 10, 24, 57, 103
ethos, 38
Etkind, Alexander, 17–18, 119
European Union, 116
Expressionism, 164

Facebook, 160, 167, 175, 177
fake vs. real, 86, 141, 155
fascism, 226n129
fashion, 14, 123, 186, *186*
feeling. *See* emotions
feminine embodiments of ideals, 53–54, 216n92
Ferguson, Harvie, 138–39
films, 18, 29, 59, 75, 119, 166; conscious technical flaws and, 184, 187, 199;

new sincerity and, 14, 72, 73, 85, 123, 162–63, 164, 174, 184, 233–34n16

fin de siècle culture, 62–65

first-person writing, 136–37. *See also* autobiography; confessional genres

Fishzon, Anna, 59, 60, 61

Fitzgerald, Jonathan D., 25

Fitzpatrick, Sheila, 65, 66

Flarf (collaborative poetry movement), 170

Flax, Jane, 90

flippi754 (Russian blogger), 32

Foer, Jonathan Safran, 92

Fokkema, Douwe, 29

forgetting, 17–18

Foster, Hal, "Return of the Real," 131–32

Foucault, Michel, 69, 128

France, 2, 49–50, 51, 52, 55; sincerity rhetoric and, 39, 41, 43–44; revolutionaries, 44, 45, 46, 48, 66, 96–97, 99

Frank, Ze, 170

Franzen, Jonathan, 164

free expression, 23

free market. *See* capitalism

Freemasons, 46

free speech, 38, 40, 143, 175

Freidin, Gregory, 223n40

Freud, Sigmund, *Civilization and Its Discontents*, 62–63

Fursey, Dasha, "Pioneer Girls" series, 109, *110*

Futurists, 60–62, *61*, *62*

Gabler, Neil, 161

Gabowitsch, Mischa, 112, 175–76, 226n129

Gagarin, Yuri, 109

Gandlevskii, Sergei, 83, 84, 85, 89, 95, 105, 110, 113–14, 125, 127, 207n65; "critical sentimentalism," 83, 84, 89, 105, 113

Gannon, Todd, 161

Garlinger, Patrick, 25

generation, 8, 18, 22, 57, 74, 82, 173–74, 189, 207n65, 235n44

Genis, Aleksandr, 76, 77, 114

genuine, 37, 59, 188

German, Aleksei, *My Friend Ivan Lapshin* (film), 89

Germany, 2, 40, 50–51

Gilmore, James, 187–88, 194

Girls (TV series), 164, 235n16

glasnost rhetoric, 83

Glee (TV series), 123, 163

Goffman, Erving, 69

Gogol, Nikolai, 132

Golynko-Vol'fson, Dmitrii, 86, 87, 88, 114, 145, 147, 176

Goncharova, Nataliia, 60, 61, 62

Gondry, Michel, 164

Google (search engine), 11, 168, 172

Gorbachev, Mikhail, 83, 143

Goscilo, Helena, 139

Gountas, Sandra, 25

Gracián, 55–56

Gray, Christopher, 73

Greek philosophy, 38

Greenblatt, Stephen, 39

Grigoriev, Apollon, "On Truth and Sincerity in Art," 57–58

Grishkovets, Evgenii, 124, 127

Gross, Florian, 25

Groys, Boris, 6, 25, 59–60, 71, 135, 139, 156, 162, 168; "Moscow Romantic Conceptualism," 103

gulag, 90, 197

Gundlakh, Sven, 80, 83, 85, 88–89, 105

Guyer, Sara, *Romanticism after Auschwitz*, 4

Habermas, Jürgen, 69

Halfin, Igal, 66

Halttunen, Karen, 49

handcrafted, 23, 39, 40, 70, 74, 87, 92, 150, 160, 182–86, *185*, *186*, 189, 193, 199

handwritten texts, 39, 40, 48, 190; font imitations, 49, 60, 79

Hänsgen, Sabine, 104

hard memory, definition of, 18, 119

hashtag #newsincerity, 167

Hayles, Katherine, 161
healing sincerity. *See* curative sincerity
Hebdige, Dick, 8–9
Henriksen, Katy, 25
Hesmondhalgh, David, 5
Hipstamatic, 183
hipster culture, 14, 33
Hirst, Damien, 71; *For the Love of God,* 71
historical trauma. *See* curative sincerity;
    Holocaust; 9/11 attacks (2001);
    Soviet trauma
Hoffmann, E. T. A., *Sandman,* 48
Holmgren, Beth, 76
Holocaust, 4, 78, 90, 92, 107, 197
homemade. *See* handcrafted
homophobic imagery, 156
Honest tea bottles, 171, *173*
honesty, 4, 23, 56, 105, 143, 162; bloggers
    and, 175, 177; toward external
    audience, 38; public testimony of,
    114; technical imperfection as, 190.
    See also self-revelation; truthfulness
Hosking, Geoffrey, *Truth: A History,* 70
Hughes, Ted, 13
humanist criticism, 168
human rights, 45
Hunt, Lynn, 44
Hutcheon, Linda, 135
hypocrisy, 40, 41, 43, 45, 49, 52, 53, 55,
    64, 65, 77; Putin's Russia and, 113,
    157, 181; Soviet society and, 83, 96,
    97, 98

Iampol'skii, Mikhail, 104
identity, 4, 9, 65–66, 138–39, 161;
    national, 52; online, 9, 180
Il'in, Ivan: "Against Russia," 65; "On
    Sincerity," 64
imperfection (aesthetics of), 60, 61–62,
    71, *186*; authenticity and, 182–88;
    online writing and, 47, 191–92; Rus-
    sian discourse of, 188–92, 193, 199;
    as sincerity hallmark, 39–40, 62,
    67, 70, 79–80, 182–84, 192–93.
    See also amateurism; handcrafted
imperial stiob (term), 113

Indonesian Poetry and Sincerity Festival
    (2006), 27, 167
industrialization, 48–49, 179, 182
"Innovative Marketing Communication"
    (forum), 174
insincerity, 38, 45, 66, 75
Instagram, 160, 167, 183, 184
integrity. *See* artistic integrity
interactivity, 170, 174
intercultural conflict, 17, 119, 120, 197
intimacy, 42, 46, 57, 159
intracultural conflict, 17, 120, 197
irony, 10, 18, 31, 33–35, 134, 163; appear-
    ance and, 138; nostalgia and, 91, 114;
    pathos and, 135; performativity and,
    35, 82; postmodernism and, 104,
    224n63; post-Stalinist culture and,
    135; seriousness and, 81, 85–86;
    sincerity and, 36, 50, 68, 73, 77, 82,
    84, 95, 98, 100, 107. *See also*
    post-ironic sincerity
iskrennii (sincere), 41
iskrennost' (sincerity), 52, 56–57, 58, 64,
    65, 74–77, 217n108; as everyday
    term, 75; historical significance of,
    192; meanings of, 41–42, 46–48;
    politicization of, 76–77; reconcep-
    tion of, 47
Iskusstvo (journal), 94
It's Easy to Be Sincere (anthology), 127
Ivanova, Nataliia, 28, 106–7, 109–10, 125;
    "Art in the Light of Sincerity," 106;
    The Nostalgic Present, 106

Jackson, John, 25
Jacobi, Thomas, 25
Jameson, Fredric, 150
jazz, 61–62
Jenkins, Henry, 175
Jimmy (Uzbek singer), 14
Jongerius, Hella, 184, *185*
journalism, 33, 59, 123

Kabakov, Emilia, 107, 109–10
Kabakov, Ilya, 103, 107, 109–10; *Red
    Wagon* (installation), 81

Kalinin, Ilya, 105
Kamenskii, Aleksei, 80
Kandinsky Prize, 112
Karamzin, Nikolai, 47, 48, 99; *My Confession*, 47; "Poor Liza," 47
Karmodi, Ostap, 140
Kaspe, Irina, 127, 176
Kelly, Adam, 25, 163, 225n99
Kelly, Catriona, 42, 47, 52, 132–33
Kessels, Erik, 187
Ketro, Marta, 127
Keymolen, Esther, 179
KGB, 98
Khachaturov, Sergei, 151
Khlebnikov, Velimir, 60, *61, 62*
Khrushchev, Nikita, 128
Kibirov, Timur, 20, 83, 89, 144, 148, 177, 207n65; *Poems on Love*, 87
Kierkegaard, Søren, 49
Kim and Buran (retro-Soviet band), 109
Kirby, Alan, 161
Kishkovsky, Sophia, 199, 200
kitsch, 148
Klein, Joachim, 55, 56, 156
Klosterman, Chuck, 25
Koldobskaia, Marina, 30, 188
Komar, Aleksandr, 91
Korolenko, Psoi, 140
Korthals Altes, Liesbeth, 25, 38
Kostikov, Leonid, 126–27
Kostyrko, Sergei, 176, 177
Kremlin, 92, 161, 166
Krijnen, Joost, 78, 92
Kropotkin, Petr, 53
Kruchenykh, Aleksei, 60, *61, 62*
Kucherskaia, Maia, 140
Kukulin, Ilya, 7, 125–26, 145, 157–58
Kukushkin, Vladimir, 140
Kulik, Oleg, 2, 148–49, 150–51; *Deep into Russia* (album), 87; nude performances and, 150
Kuntsman, Adi, 156
Kuritsyn, Viacheslav, 28, 125, 188–89
Kuryokhin, Sergei, 80, 81, 85, 86
Kuz'min, Dmitrii, 125, 127, 136, 174

Kuznetsov, Sergey, 178, 179, 207n65
kvartirniki (apartment concerts), 199

Lady Gaga, 123, 163
Laird, Sally, 135
language, 4, 15, 59, 101, 132; invented, 60; metadiscursivity and, 132, 139–40, 230n41; online, 191. *See also* English language; Russian language
Larionov, Mikhail, *62*
La Rochefoucauld, François de, 35
late postmodernism, 24, 29, 72, 79, 92, 107, 150, 164, 206–7n53, 209n79, 231n76
Leavis, F. R., 219n155
Le Corbusier, 59
Legouvé, Ernest, 51
Leiby, Sofia, 22
Lenin, Vladimir, 85
Lermontov, Mikhail, 145; *Hero of Our Time*, 57
Lipovetsky, Mark, 2, 6, 28, 30, 36, 91, 104, 125; curative sincerity concept and, 107–8, 109–10; new Russian drama and, 165–66; *Paralogues*, 29, 30, 107–8; "Post-Sots" (term), 112; on Sorokin's works, 129–30, 141, 229nn21,23, 231n76
literary celebrities. *See* celebrity culture
literary marketplace. *See* commodification
literary sociology, 21, 154–56, 198
literature. *See* poetry; Russian literature; *specific writers*
Litvinova, Renata, 124
Loe, Erlend, 31–32, 211n103
logos, 38
Lomography, 183, 189
Lomonosov, Mikhail, 46, 48
London Book Fair (2011), 142
Loshak, Andrei, 176
Lotman, Mikhail, 99
low-fi, 49, 70, 164, 182
Luchador (Nike sneaker), 171
Lukashenko, Alexander, 16, 115–16
Lutz, Tom, 117

Lyotard, Jean-François, 103
lyricism, 11, 20, 102, 103, 117, 120

Magill, R. Jay, Jr., 196, 197; *Sincerity*, 25
Maiofis, Maria, 104
Makushinskii, Aleksei, 53–54, 133
Malevich, Kazimir, *Black Square*, 59
Manjoo, Fathad, 161
Man'kovskaia, Nadezhda, 29–30
Mannisto, Glenn, "The New
    Sincerity," 163
market economy. *See* capitalism
marketing. *See* commodification
Markovits, Elizabeth, 25
Marsh, Rosalind, 6, 119, 173–74
Martin, John, 40
Martus, Steffen, 25
Marusenkov, Maksim, 141
Marx, Karl, 51
masculine-feminine dichotomies, 53–54
Masing-Delic, Irene, 63
masks, 63–64, 218n130. *See also* veils
mass media: irony and, 73; literary
    celebrity and, 136–38, 147, 153;
    manipulation by, 59; new sincerity
    and, 9, 11–12, 72, 156, 162–66;
    post-postmodernism and, 161;
    Putin's restrictions on, 165, 175, 199;
    Soviet propaganda and, 23, 161. *See
    also* new media; *specific types*
Mavondo, Felix, 25
media. *See* mass media; new media
Medical Hermeneutics (art group), 91
Medvedev, Kirill, 16, 181, 207n65; "The
    Writer in Russia," 115, 116
Melamid, Aleksandr, 107
Melamid, Vitalii, 91
memoir, 53, 72, 108
memory, 18, 22, 33, 102, 200; hard vs.
    soft, 17–18, 119, 120; Putin's Russia
    and, 111, 113–14, 116, 119; sincerity
    and, 16–19, 36, 58, 105, 106, 108,
    109, 115, 118, 119, 180, 198. *See also*
    cultural memory
Menzel, Birgit, 21, 156
metadiscursivity, 132, 139–40, 230n41

Metelitsa, Katia, 175
Middle Ages, 38
Mikhailov, Boris, 88; *Unfinished
    Dissertation*, 87, 88
Milnes, Timothy, *Romanticism, Sincerity,
    and Authenticity*, 25
Mironenko, Vladimir and Sergei, 80
"Misfit" exhibition (2010, Rotterdam), 184
Misiano, Viktor, 122
Mitrenina, Marina, 191–92, 194
Mitrofanova, Alla, 201
modernism, 10, 59–60, 65, 96, 109,
    229n23. *See also* early modernity;
    postmodernism
Mombert, Jason, *The New Sincerity*
    (video), 149, *149*
Mondrian, Piet, lozenge paintings, 59
Montaigne, Michel de, 35
Moral Code of the Builder of Commu-
    nism (1961), 76–77
Morev, Gleb, 145
Morris, Jason, 163–64
Moscow (film), 129
Moscow Biennale "I Believe" (2005,
    Moscow), 151, 166
Moscow Conceptualism, 6–7, 11, 28, 81,
    85, 86, 91, 94, 102, 104, 107, 130,
    133, 136
Moscow galleries, 125, 126, 200
Moscow theater collective, 165–66
Most, Glenn, 14
Mukhomor (rock band), 80, 81–82,
    83, 104
multiculturalism, 73
mumblecore films, 164, 233n15
music: imperfection aesthetic and,
    61–62, 189–90; new sincerity and,
    2, 14, 72–74, 79–82, 85, 91, 109, 118,
    123; soft memory and, 18; technology
    and, 30, 59, 60, 62. *See also* rock
    bands
Myers, Greg, 25
My Little Pony (TV series), 171, 180

nakedness, 150
narod (common people), 55, 216n92

Natarov, Evgenii, 222n16
nationalism, 44–45, 50–55, 65, 80, 114;
    feminine embodiment of, 53–54,
    216n92
Navalny, Aleksei, 181
Nazis, 106, 116, 118
Neoacademism, 85
neoconservatism, 73, 114, 115, 142, 147
neosentimentalism. *See* new
    sentimentality
neo-sincerity. *See* new sincerity
Neo Sincerity exhibition (2006, New
    York), 107
neotraditionalism, post-Soviet,
    113, 142
new authenticity, 10, 11, 12, 205n32,
    205–6n35
New Collectives and Institutions
    (Novikov initiatives), 85
New Historicist scholars, 14–15
Newman, Gerald, 44
new media, 19–25, 30, 36–37, 39–40,
    79–80, 158–92; authenticity and,
    161, 182–88, 193–94; disclosure of
    personal information and, 179;
    humanness and, 183, 193, 199; new
    sincerity and, 9, 11–12, 19–22, 23,
    32, 40, 72–73, 74, 118, 123, 159,
    169–94; post-postmodern social
    engagement and, 118; in Russia, 5,
    165–66, 172–79, 180, 192–92, 199;
    tools for perfection and, 182; user
    characteristics, 160, 161, 168. *See
    also* blogs; digitization; postdigital
    age; social media; web users
new narrativity, 10
new realism, 11, 12, 24, 205n32,
    205–6n35
new sentimentality, 84, 86, 106, 123–24,
    141, 174
new seriousness, 11, 86, 114, 115
new sincerity: as anticapitalist, 149–51; as
    catchword of mainstream culture,
    13, 33–34; commercial concerns
    about (*see* commodification);
    concept of, 1–3; controversies and,

33–34; cultural transfer and, 31–32,
    169; current components of, 72–73;
    definitions of, 3, 7–13, 126–27, 201;
    DIY ("do it yourself") and, 150;
    emergence of, 14, 27, 78, 79–88,
    162; founders of, 163, 169, 171, 196;
    international scope of, 27–28, 92,
    108; Medvedev's definition of,
    115–16, 118; new trends and, 10–11,
    27–31; 1980s and, 79–88, 114; in
    package design, *173*; as post-ironic
    (*see* post-ironic sincerity); post-post-
    Communist, 2, 11, 30, 108–9, *110*,
    111, 113; posttraumatic function of,
    122; Prigov projects and (*see under*
    Prigov, Dmitrii); satirical/deroga-
    tory takes on, 33, 182; scholarship
    on, 26–27, 29–30; social media
    identity and, 159–60; wide-ranging
    contexts for, 72; Wikipedia entry
    for, 11, 32, 167. *See also* sincere
    expression; *under specific subjects*
New Sincerity: A Manifesto (film), 174
New Wave music, 79, 80
Nietzsche, Friedrich, 50–51
nihilists, 53, 57, 58, 80
Nike sneaker, 171
Nikon (patriarch), 43
9/11 attacks (2001), 16–17, 73, 74, 79,
    91–92
1980s. *See* perestroika era (1980s)
nineteenth century, 48–58, 96, 131–33;
    fin de siècle, 62–65. *See also*
    Romanticism
nonconformist culture, 38, 77, 81, 85, 87,
    93–104, 108, 165
Noordenbos, Boris, 113, 142; "imperial
    stiob" (term), 113
Norton (publisher), 196
Norway, 31
nostalgia, 2, 30, 91, 108–10, 114,
    223nn40, 44; restorationist vs.
    curative, 90
novaia iskrennost' (new sincerity), 2
Novikov, Timur, 85, 86, 88, 104, 114
nudity, 150

Obama, Barack, 123, 163, 183
Obermayr, Brigitte, 103–4
Oberst, Conor, 12
objective truth, 219n155
OpenSpace (online portal), 137, 151, 176
Osaulenko, Irina, 189
Osmolovskii, Anatolii, 28; "After
    Postmodernism, All One Can Do Is
    Scream" (photo installation), 29
Ostengruppe (design lab), 189
Oushakine, Serguei, 108–9

padonki (online language), 191
Palmer, Barton, 25
Paperno, Irina, 66–67, 101
parody, 50, 52, 85, 102, 171–72
parrhesia (duty to speak openly), 38, 40,
    42, 69, 213n22
pastoral ideal, 53, 65, 137–38
pathos, 38, 135
Paul, Saint, 38
Pavlova, Vera, 127, 190; *Letters to the
    Neighboring Room*, 190
Pavolga, Ol'ga, 147
Pepperstein, Pavel, 91
perestroika era (1980s), 2, 6, 16, 18, 20,
    22, 33, 75, 76, 77, 78–121, 197;
    artistic sincerity and, 85, 143;
    characterization of, 82–83;
    cultivation of amateurism and, 193;
    literary freedom and, 143; new
    sincerity and, 27, 78, 80–88;
    revived sentimentalism and, 83–84,
    89, 105; sincerity rhetoric and,
    84–85, 120, 189, 192, 197–98, 200,
    201; "social amnesia" and, 87; stiob
    and, 85–86
performance: irony and, 35, 82, 94;
    sincere and false, 37, 65, 67, 69,
    139; unprofessional, 70, 79. *See also*
    self-revelation
Pertsev, Andrei, 166
Pessoa, Fernando, 63
Peter the Great, Tsar, 46
Petrov, Avvakum. *See* Avvakum
    (archpriest)

Pett, Michael, 25
Peyre, Henri, 24, 44, 68, 74, 196;
    Literature and Sincerity, 35, 36, 68
philosophy, 1, 10, 25, 38, 43, 50, 167
photography, 59, 183, 184, 189; digital vs.
    analog, 183
Photoshop, 182
Picasso, Pablo, 130
Piccalo, Gina, 182
Pine, Joseph, 187–88, 194, 199
Pivinskii, Aleksandr, "Coquetting with
    Cuff Links," 195, 197, 199
plastic, 70, 71
Plath, Sylvia, 153
Platonic distinction, 38, 63–64
podlinnost' (authenticity), 51
Poetics of Metadiscursivity (edited
    volume), 139–40
poetry, 17, 72, 76, 95, 160; commodifica-
    tion and, 55–56; digitization and,
    170, 171; new sincerity and, 13–14,
    20, 81–82, 83, 165; postconceptual-
    ism and, 125, 127, 136; self-
    fashioning and, 145–46; Symbolists
    and, 63–64; university as patron
    of, 68
Pogrebizhskaia, Elena, 176, 179
politeness, Russian sincerity vs., 52
politics, 2, 16, 17, 119; Kremlin propa-
    ganda and, 161, 166; online
    platforms and, 181; postmodern
    rhetoric and, 111; Putin's Russia and
    reactionary, 111–15, 139, 180–81;
    sincerity and, 37, 40–42, 45–48,
    76–77, 78, 83, 96–97, 114, 193, 198;
    Soviet thaw era and, 76–77
Polit.ru (portal), 99
Pomerantsev, Peter, 113
Pomerantsev, Vladimir, 97, 98, 100,
    181; "On Sincerity in Literature,"
    75, 76
pop art, 7, 70
pop culture. *See* popular culture
pop music, 80, 85, 189. *See also* rock
    bands
Popov, Evgenii, 126

popular culture, 13, 25, 124, 168, 171, 180, 196

populism, 50, 51

pornography, 128, 229n21

postcapitalism, 150, 151, 232n97

post-Communism. *See* post-Soviet society; socioeconomic change

postconceptualism, 11, 13, 125, 127, 136, 147, 174

postdigital age, 4, 22–23,159; sublime imperfections and, 182–94, 199

post-ironic sincerity, 10, 17, 31, 79, 80, 91–92, 95, 187; emblems of, 123, 163

postmodernism, 6, 7, 8, 13, 18–19, 25, 69–71, 78, 88–95, 116, 125, 130, 132, 134, 154, 188–89, 198, 200–201; capitalism and, 150; collective memory and, 91–92; "death" of notion of, 28–30; economic transition and, 150; irony and, 104, 135, 224n63; Moscow Conceptualism as, 28; new cultural trends replacing, 10, 19; Popov attack on, 126; post-Soviet society and, 28, 104–5, 111, 135; problem of sincerity and, 18–19, 104, 120–21, 123; relativism and, 10, 73, 83, 93, 101, 104, 121, 126; Romanticism and, 103, 120; selfhood and, 69–70; sentimentalism revival and, 83–84, 89, 105

post-postmodernism, 11, 13, 78; academic studies of, 6, 24, 30, 32, 200–201; as cultural trauma coping vehicle, 16–17, 79, 91–92, 231n76; discussion catchwords and, 10; DIY ("do it yourself") ethos and, 150; mass media and, 161; post-Soviet Russia and, 28–31, 115, 118, 120, 123–27, 130–31; sincere expression and, 79, 115, 96–97. *See also* new sincerity

post-quotational art, 11

postrealism. *See* new realism

Post-Sots (term), 112

post-Soviet society, 4–5, 20, 27–31, 116, 118–21, 122–58, 197, 201; art and, 2,

3, 112, 135; collective forgetting and, 17–18; commodification-sincerity interplay and, 146–51, 153–58; cultural memory and, 17–18, 105, 119–20; imperfection aesthetics and, 188–92, 193; literary life and (*see under* Russian literature); new sincerity and, 11–27, 29–30, 78, 128–36; nostalgia and, 90, 108, 109–10, *110*, 223n40; postmodernism and, 28, 104–5; post-post modernism and, 28–34, 115, 118, 120, 124–27, 130–31; public sphere and, 6, 15–16; self-expression and, 109–10; Soviet aesthetics and, 108–9; stiob and, 112–13. *See also* Putin-era Russia; socioeconomic change

pottery, imperfect, 184, *185*

Powhida, William, *149*

pragmatism. *See* artistic pragmatism

Prigov, Andrei (son), 117

Prigov, Dmitrii, 13–14, 17, 31, 81–87, 93–105, 121, 133–36, 145, 160, 207n65; arrest and imprisonment of, 98; artistic achievements of, 93–94; commodification concerns and, 116–18; critical reception of, 101–5; "Crying Artists," 117, 118; cultural memory and, 96–100, 102, 114, 118, 119; curative sincerity and, 105, 107–8, 110, 197–98; "DAP" behavioral project, 93–94, 98–99, 103, 104, 118; death (2007) of, 103; global celebrity of, 93; *New Sincerity*, 14, 82; New Sincerity and, 14, 17, 78, 81–82, 83, 86, 94, 97–98, 102, 111, 125, 126, 133–34, 177, 180, 196–97; online projects of, 117–18; posthumous reviews of, 103–4; "shimmering" author-text relationship and, 94; "Sincerity: That Is What We Cherish Most of All," 99, 100; *Sincerity on Negotiated Terms or Tears of a Heraldic Soul*, 97; Soviet trauma and, 96–100, 102; "Stories about Stalin," 93; website of, 117, 118

Prigov, Georgii (grandson), 100–101
printing techniques, 22, 23, 39–40, 48, 162, 182; "sincere" effects, 49, 60–61, 71
privacy, protection of, 179
produsers (term), 23, 160, 179
professionalism, 55, 70, 106, 187
Prokhorov, Aleksandr, 83
Prokhorova, Irina, 87
propaganda, 4, 23, 161, 165, 198–99
protests. *See* dissent
Proust, Marcel, 65
psychoanalysis, 25, 219n155
public self, 55–56, 131–32; private self vs., 69. *See also* self-revelation
public sincerity, 51, 139, 145–46, 172–79, 175, 179
public sphere, 6, 15, 40, 43
publishers, 39, 60, 68, 79
Puett, Michael, 72
punk-rock bands, 73, 79, 199
Purdy, Jedediah, *For Common Things*, 73
Pushkin, Alexander, 57, 58, 145; *Eugene Onegin*, 54, 84, 217n108
Pussy Riot (punk-rock group), 199
Putin, Vladimir, 2, 16, 111, 115, 116, 181, 199; public tears of, 117, 227n151
Putin-era Russia, 100, 110–16, 159–201; blog popularity in, 3, 16, 22, 47, 172–79, 191; critics of, 115–16; "culture of cynicism" and, 157, 181; glamour and celebrity focus of, 139, 155; media restrictions and, 2, 161, 165, 175, 199; new sincerity and, 147, 164–65, 172–79, 199–200; official idealization of past and, 111, 113–14; protest cultures and, 113, 115; social media users and, 180–82

Radischchev, Alexander, 76, 181; *Journey from St. Petersburg to Moscow*, 47–48
Ramakers, Renny, 184
Read, Herbert, 219n155
Ready, Oliver, 84, 142
reality, 12, 23, 24; appearance and, 69, 138–39

recording industry, 60, 61
Reddy, William, 45
refinement, Russian sincerity vs., 46, 52
relativism, 10, 73, 79, 83, 101, 104, 121, 126
Renaissance, 24, 39, 40, 48, 79, 179
Repin, Ilya, 138
reproduction techniques, 59, 162, 182
Rettberg, Jill Walker, 170
revolutionaries, 44, 45–46, 48, 66, 90, 96–97
Reynolds, Roo, 170, 171
Riefenstahl, Leni, 112
Robespierre, Maximilien, 96–97
rock bands, 73, 93, 149, 199; new sincerity and, 11–12, *12*, 31, 79–82
Romanticism, 7, 10, 25, 48, 57, 90, 102, 146, 153, 155, 179; French *sincerité* and, 44; irony and, 50; postmodernism and, 103, 120; renewed interest in, 68, 175; sincerity and, 50, 53, 55, 57; stock motifs of, 53–54
Rombes, Nicholas, 183, 187
Rorty, Richard, 35
Rosenbaum, Susan, 20, 21, 25, 39, 68, 151, 152, 153, 155
Roth-Ey, Kristin, 23
Rothstein, Edward, 91–92
Roundhouse Kicks (blogger), 171
Rousseau, Jean-Jacques, 44, 46, 47, 64, 95
Rubinstein, Lev, 86–87, 104, 108, 125, 127, 136, 176–77, 207n65
Rudin, Dmitrii (fictional), 54
rural life. *See* common people; pastoral ideal
Ruskin, John, 48–49, 183, 184
Russia (pre-Communist), 34, 41–43, 46–47; commodification concerns and, 59, 60; eighteenth-century sentimentalism and, 46–48, 191; long nineteenth century and, 51–58, 132–33; nostalgia for, 114; sincerity connotations and, 51–53, 61, 63–64, 65; Symbolism and, 63–64

Russia (1922–91). *See* Soviet Russia; Soviet trauma; Thaw era (1950s–early 1960s)

Russia (1991–21st century). *See* post-Soviet society; Putin-era Russia

Russian Association of Proletarian Writers, 66

Russian language, 12–13, 51; new media and, 172–79, 191; status of word *iskrennost'* in, 41–42

Russian literature: career success stories and, 19–20; commodification and, 19–20, 49, 56, 70–71, 148, 153, 157–58; cultivated imperfections and, 190–92; early milestone of, 43; heroine portrayals and, 54; moral searching (1950s–80s) and, 77; neosentimentalism and, 174; new sincerity and, 14, 19–20, 27, 30, 72, 106, 123, 124–46; nineteenth-century classics of, 53–54, 96, 132–33; notions of self and, 43, 50, 64; popular late-Soviet genres and, 77; post-Soviet writers and, 17, 18–19, 21, 106, 113, 119–20, 199; Prigov's status in, 93; professionalization and, 55; psychological realism and, 58; Romanticism and, 50, 53–54, 57; sincere confession and, 75; sincerity/irony dichotomy and, 36, 53; Sorokin's status in, 144; Soviet genres and, 77; Symbolists and, 63–64; unpolished writing style and, 47, 190–92. *See also* poetry

Russian national character ("Russian soul"), 42

Russian Orthodox Church, 34, 43, 103

Russo-Georgian war (2008), 112

Ryklin, Mikhail, 144

Saatchi Gallery (London), 109

Safronova, Iuliia, 54–55

St. Petersburg, 86, 113, 164, 200; nonconformist artists, 85, 165–66

Sal'nikov, Vladimir, 140

samizdat (Soviet-era self-publishing), 13–14, 81, 82, 87–88, 222n9

Samokhvalov, Pavel, 231n58

Sanneh, Kelefa, 74, 149

Sapiro, Gisèle, 21

Savchuk, Valerii, 30, 165, 166

Schmid, Ulrich, 43

Schmidt, Henrike, 178–79, 190–91

Schnittke, Alfred, 77

self, 34, 58, 62, 64, 199; autonomous, 42, 69; "disintegration" of, 59; honesty with, 38, 40; inner life and, 9; media representation of, 137; new conceptualizations of, 26–27, 39, 43; non-binary views on outer/inner, 26–27; outer and inner, 40, 50 (*see also* true self); postmodernism and, 69–70; preoccupations with, 59; return of, 10; true to, 50, 66–67, 99, 129, 174

self-disclosure. *See* self-revelation

self-expression, 75, 95, 175–80; authenticity and, 51. *See also* sincere expression

self-fashioning, 19–20, 67, 130–32, 136–38, 139, 143–46

selfhood. *See* self

self-revelation, 13, 38, 63–64, 70, 155, 159; authenticity of, 59, 84, 136; blogging and, 175–78, 179; honesty and, 9, 56, 105, 163; irony and, 135; mass media and, 165, 166; self-profit and, 153–54, 198. *See also* public self

Seligman, Adam, 25, 72

Sella, Marshall, 73

selling out, 49, 50, 56, 144, 146, 148, 155

sentimentalism, 10, 45–46, 47, 68, 163; as conscious career strategy, 148; Kibirov's defense of, 89; neosentimentalism and, 84, 106, 141, 174; revival of, 83–84, 89, 105; as top-down instrument, 114; unpolished writing and, 191. *See also* critical sentimentalism

September 11 attacks. *See* 9/11 attacks (2001)

seriousness, 81, 85–86, 114

seventeenth century, 34, 40, 43, 44

Shank, Barry, 79

Shavlovskii, Konstantin, 146

Shelley, Mary Wollstonecraft, *Franken-stein*, 48

Shevelev, Igor', 175

Shevtsov, Vasilii, 140

Siegel, Lee, 79

Simon, Bennett, 25, 72

Sinanan, Kerry, *Romanticism, Sincerity, and Authenticity*, 25

sincere expression, 54, 56, 58, 69, 84, 86, 109–10, 134–35, 177; commercial interests and, 144, 148, 149, 157–58; digitization and, 60, 74, 118, 159, 160, 161, 165, 174, 175, 182; healing potential of, 198; mask motif and, 63; modernist writers and, 65; padonki (online language) and, 191; post-postmodernism and, 79, 115, 196–97; socioeconomic change and, 20, 68, 122–23, 151–54. *See also* Prigov, Dmitrii; Sorokin, Vladimir

"sinceriod" (new punctuation mark), 171, 172

sincerity: academic studies of, 24–30, 35–77, 152; anxieties about, 39, 41, 62–63, 101, 152; birth of term, 40; connotations of, 37–39, 51; critical thinking on, 24–34, 68–69; cult of, 41, 49, 68–69, 72–73; as cultural construct, 69, 95; definitions of, 26–27, 219n155; dichotomous readings of, 153–54; distrust and doubt of, 36, 68–69, 157; doing (as opposed to being sincere), 27; as externally oriented, 51, 188; as healing tool (*see* curative sincerity); historical problematizing of, 56–57, 68; history of concept, 24–27, 35–77, 152–55; public vs. private aspects of, 39, 40, 51, 139; Russia as ultimate locus of, 41–42, 53, 132,

148–49, 192; Russian term for (see *iskrennost'* [sincerity]); Russian vs. Western codes of, 42, 53; "selling-out" concerns and, 49, 50, 56, 144, 146, 148, 155; semantic history of, 13, 39, 40, 46–47; skeptical readings of, 68–72. *See also* artistic sincerity; authenticity; honesty; imperfection; new sincerity; *under specific subjects*

skepticism, 37, 69, 72, 120

Slapovskii, Aleksei, "The Sincere Artist," 84–85

Slavic Forum (2001), 26

Slavophile movement, 52

Smirnov, Igor', 140, 145, 154

Smith, Carel, *The Rhetoric of Sincerity*, 25

Smurova, Varvara, 176

Snob (social media project), 136–37

Sobchak, Ksenia, 182

social class, 16, 41, 45, 47, 50, 51, 53, 65, 67, 83, 96, 168

socialist realism, 6–7, 66, 67, 81, 100, 111; "insincerity" critique of, 75, 181, 192

social media, 14, 27, 22, 33, 36, 117, 123, 136–37, 159–60, 164, 168, 174, 177, 179, 180; explanation for popularity of, 179; thematic heterogeneity new sincerity rhetoric and, 14, 123, 159–60, 171–72, 181–82; users/producers of, 23, 160. *See also* blogs

social mobility, 39, 49, 179

society, concept of, 40, 58

socioeconomic change, 4, 19, 21, 22, 128, 143; artistic sincerity anxieties and, 122–23, 151, 155–58; postmodern logic and, 150

Sofronov, Vladislav, 30

soft memory, definition of, 18, 119, 120

Sorokin, Vladimir, 81–82, 97–98, 127–45, 155, 160; *Blue Lard*, 129, 229n23; *Bro's Way*, 127, 141, 145; commercial success of, 56, 144–45, 198; controversy and, 20, 198; copulating dogs image and, 137, 231n58; cultural memory and,

142–43; deconstruction and, 122–23, 129, 130; *Deep into Russia* (photo-prose album), 87; emotive personal shift of, 134–35, 136–38; *Ice*, 127, 140, 144, 145, 154, 155; literary critiques of, 139–42, 144–46; literary transformation of, 129–37, 144; *Moscow* (film), 129, 229n23; pornography charges and, 128, 229n21; postmodernism and, 104, 128, 129, 130, 132, 134, 141; public self-styling of, 19–20, 130–32, 136–38, 139, 143–45; *Rosenthal's Children* (opera libretto), 133; Russian mainstream literary success of, 144; sincere expression concern of, 19–20, 130, 135–38, 140, 141, 142, 144, 155, 196–97, 198; Tolstoy affinity of, 131, 137, 138; *Trilogy*, 127–30, 132, 134, 140–45, 151, 154, 156, 157, 158, 198; *23,000*, 127; website of, 137

Sotheby's, 71

Sots Art, 81, 85, 91, 107, 135

Soviet Russia, 5, 6–7, 17, 33, 106, 111–12, 143, 157; aesthetics of, 108–9, 111; amateurism and, 193; cultural icons and, 109, *110;* economic doctrine and, 157; as failed experiment, 151; hidden "true self" and, 65–67, 99; hypocrisy and, 83, 96, 97, 98; literary genres and, 77; Moral Code (1961) and, 76–77; nonconformist culture and, 81, 93–104; nostalgia for, 2, 90, 91, 108–9, 223n44; parodies of ideology of, 103; postmodern thought and, 28, 91, 94, 105, 107–8, 111; propaganda and, 161, 165, 198–99; retrospective criticism of, 88–89; sincerity and, 2, 36, 65, 66–67, 69, 74–80, 173, 197; underground culture of, 199, 226–27n129 (see also *samizdat* [Soviet-era self-publishing]). *See also* perestroika era (1980s); post-Soviet society; Soviet trauma; Thaw era (1950s–early 1960s)

Soviet trauma: curative sincerity and, 18–19, 90, 93, 110, 116, 120–21, 142; sincerity as coping tool and, 4, 16, 17–18, 22–23, 89–92, 96–100, 105–6, 107–9, 115, 119, 122, 142–43, 151, 197, 200

speech act theory, 38, 68–69

Spiegelman, Art, 107

Stalin, Joseph, 106, 107, 125–26, 128, 142; portraits of, 91; Putin-era Russia and, 100, 111, 112, 113, 114, 120; traumatic legacy of, 74–76

Starbucks, cute girls at (blog posts), 14, 32, 160

Stavrogin, Nikolai (fictional), 58

stiob aesthetic, 77, 98, 100, 106, 108, 135, 226n129; concept of, 85–86; Putin's Russia and, 111, 112–13

Stöckmann, Ingo, 40

Stodolsky, Ivor, 86, 113, 114

Strukov, Vlad, 139

subjectivity, 35, 39, 69, 138

Sublett, Jesse, 79, 80, 81

sublime imperfections, 182–92, 199

Svirskii, Grigorii, 75

Symbolists, 63–64

tears, 13, 117–18, 131, 222n152, 227n151

Teatr.doc (Moscow), 165–66

technological advancement: amateurism vs., 189–91; human self-revelation and, 166, 199; projection of sincerity and, 40, 49, 51, 58, 60, 61, 62, 67, 79, 199; Romantic age aversion to, 48–49; suspicions about, 39–40, 48, 60, 65. *See also* digitization; postdigital age

television, 14, 123, 163, 164, 166

Texan "New Sincere" bands, 31, 79, 81, 82

Thaw era (1950s–early 1960s), 9, 16–17, 52, 134, 192, 221n201, 222n12; Communist party ideology and, 65; sincerity and, 27, 75–77, 82–83, 114

theater, 25, 39, 41, 85, 93, 119; new Russian drama and, 165–66; new sincerity and, 123 therapeutic sincerity. *See* curative sincerity

Thorn, Jesse, 169, 171; "Manifesto on the New Sincerity," 169

Tikhomirov, Alexey, 65–66

Tiutchev, Fedor, 56, 57, 58, 217n108; "Silentium!" 56

Todorova, Maria, 90

Tolstoy, Leo, 58, 131–33, 153; Sorokin identification with, 131, 137, 138; "What Is Art?" 53, 56, 133

traumatic past. *See* cultural memory; Soviet trauma

Trilling, Lionel, 24, 59, 68, 71, 196, 213n22; *Sincerity and Authenticity*, 35, 36, 188; on sincerity vs. authenticity, 51, 52, 192

true self, 50, 66–67, 99, 174

trust, 38, 65–66, 70, 162, 179. *See also* distrust

truthfulness, 34, 37, 39, 42, 58, 64, 69, 142, 151; media and, 161, 162; objective, 219n155. *See also* honesty

truthiness (term), 161–62; definition of, 23, 162

Tseëlon, Efrat, 25, 69

Turgenev, Ivan, 58; works: *Asia*, 54; *Fathers and Sons*, 54; "Faust," 54; *Rudin*, 54

TV. *See* television

Tvardovskii, Aleksandr, 76, 98

twentieth century. *See* early twentieth century; Soviet Russia; Soviet trauma

Twitter, 33, 160, 167, 175, 180

Uffelmann, Dirk, 129, 141, 155

Ugarov, Mikhail, 165–66

Uhrwerk (Berlin gallery), 151

Ukraine, 2, 5, 111, 166

United States, 6, 16–17, 41, 180; authenticity and, 182–87, 192; mid-nineteenth-century cult of sincerity and, 49; mid-twentieth-century cult of sincerity and, 68–74; new sincerity and, 2, 27, 31, 73, 78, 79, 81, 82, 91–92, 149, 163–64; 9/11 attacks and, 17, 73, 74, 79, 91, 92

University of Amsterdam, 10, 209n78

University of Cambridge, 17, 206n46, 209n78

urbanization, 39, 48, 49, 54, 58, 179; new sincerity and, 11, 14, 168; upper class and, 65, 96

Ushkov, Nikolai, 182

Vaessens, Thomas, 92, 164, 224n62

Vail', Petr, 76, 77, 114

van Alphen Ernst, 24–25, 27, 39, 119, 162, 197; *The Rhetoric of Sincerity*, 25, 162

van Renswoude, Irene, 38

veils, 64, 65. *See also* masks

Verkhovenskii, Petr (fictional), 58, 59, 96

Verlaine, Paul, 49–50, 53, 71, 145, 148

videos, 8, 94, 137–38, 170; amateur, 184; Mombert performance, 149, 149

Vinogradov, Alexander, 122

Vinzavod (Moscow gallery), 125, 126, 200

virtuality, 174

Vodennikov, Dmitrii, 127, 160, 207n65; blogging and, 191; dramatic self-portraits of, 147, 177; "Men Can Also Fake an Orgasm," 146; questioned genuine new sincerity of, 145–46, 177–78

von Trier, Lars, 164

Wachtel, Andrew, 6, 21, 143, 145–46, 156

Wallace, David Foster, 25, 71, 163, 225n99

Wampole, Christy, 25; "How to Live without Irony," 33–34, 73

Warhol, Andy, 70, 71, 148

Watercutter, Angela, 123, 163

web users, 160, 161; characteristics of, 168. *See also* blogs; social media

Weller, Robert, 25, 72

Western Europe, 16–17, 39–41, 48–52; audience for sentimentality in, 148, 150; authenticity and, 187–88, 192;

early modernity and, 22, 24, 39–41, 48, 79, 162, 179; early twentieth century and, 59–71; newly defined sincerity in, 27, 31, 49–50; new sincerity and, 164, 196; post-postmodernism studies and, 6, 31, 200–201; post–World War II sincerity and, 67–74; as Russian art market, 150, 151; Russian otherness toward, 52, 192; Russian Romanticism and, 52, 53, 55; Sorokin view of, 132
Wierzbicka, Anna, 41
Wikander, Matthew, 25
Wikipedia, "New Sincerity" entry, 11, 32, 167
Wilde, Oscar, 63, 67, 71; "The Truth of the Mask," 63
Wilders, Geert, 38
Winfrey, Oprah, 164
Wired (online journal), 123, 163, 171

Witte, Georg, 104
Woolf, Virginia, 65
World Trade Center attack. *See* 9/11 attacks (2001)
World War II, 67–71, 111
World Wide Web. *See* web users

Yandex (search engine), 11, 12, 168
Yeltsin, Boris, 143
Yurchak, Alexei, 2, 30, 85, 98, 108–11, 113, 196

Zakharov (publisher), 144
Zalizniak, Anna, 41
zaum (invented language), 60
Zemfira (singer-songwriter), 124
Zharikov, Sergei, 80, 189–90
Zintsov, Oleg, 145
Zorin, Andrei, 102, 103
Zubok, Vladislav, 74
Zvezdochotov, Konstantin, 80